The Complete Idiot's Reference Card

The Leader's Ten Keys to Motivating Team Members

1. Know each team member's abilities and give them assignments based on these abilities.
2. Give clear directions that are understood and accepted.
3. Allow team members to make decisions related to their jobs.
4. Be accessible. Listen actively and empathetically.
5. Give credit and praise for jobs well done.
6. Treat team members fairly, and with respect and consideration.
7. Show interest and concern for each person as an individual.
8. Make each person an integral member of the team.
9. Keep team members challenged and excited by their work.
10. Support team members in their efforts to perform superbly.

The 4 C's of Team Success

➤ **Collegiality:** Members of successful teams work as colleagues. Each respects the intelligence and capabilities of the other members.

➤ **Collaboration:** Once team members are melded into a team of colleagues, they are prepared to collaborate in working toward the achievement of the team's goals.

➤ **Coordination:** In a well-coordinated team, members can anticipate every action teammates will take and be prepared to react to it.

➤ **Coaching:** The team leader is the team's coach, who guides the team in setting goals, trains the team in the skills needed to achieve those goals, works with the team to coordinate the members' actions, and motivates the team to work creatively toward its goals.

Ten Tips for Improving Mentoring

1. Know the work. Review the basics. Be prepared to answer questions about every aspect of the job.
2. Know your company. Help the trainee overcome the hurdles of unfamiliar company policies and practices.
3. Get to know your protégé. Learn as much as you can about the person you are mentoring.
4. Learn to teach. If you have minimal experience in teaching, pick up pointers on teaching methods from the best trainers you know.
5. Learn to learn. Never stop learning—not only the latest techniques in your own field, but developments in your industry, in the business, and in the overall field of management.
6. Be patient. Patience is key to success in mentoring.
7. Be tactful. Be kind. Be courteous. Be gentle—but be firm, and let the trainee know you expect the best.
8. Don't be afraid to take risks. Give your protégé assignments that will challenge his or her capabilities. Failures may occur, but we learn from our failures.
9. Celebrate successes. Let trainees know you are proud of their accomplishments and progress made.
10. Encourage your protégé to become a mentor.

alpha books

Six Ways to Make Praise More Meaningful

1. **Don't overdo it.** Too much praise reduces its value.

2. **Be sincere.** You can't fake sincerity. You must truly believe that what you're praising your associate for is actually commendable.

3. **Be specific about the reason for your praise.** Rather than say, "Great job!," specify the accomplishment you are praising someone for.

4. **Ask for your team members' advice.** Nothing is more flattering than to be asked for advice about how to handle a situation.

5. **Publicize praise.** If other team members are aware of the praise you give a colleague, it acts as a spur to them to work for similar recognition.

6. **Give them something they can keep.** Telling people that you appreciate what they've done is a great idea, but writing it is even more effective.

Five Ways to Effective Team Leadership

1. **Know each associate as a human being.** Know about family, hobbies, interests, philosophy of life.

2. **Develop team goals collaboratively with your members.** This will ensure their commitment to them.

3. **Remember that communication is two-way.** Ensure that members understand what you convey to them and that you understand what they convey to you.

4. **MBWA: Manage by walking around.** Get out of your office and into the area where your team works.

5. **Don't dominate the team.** Encourage team members to share ideas with you and the other associates.

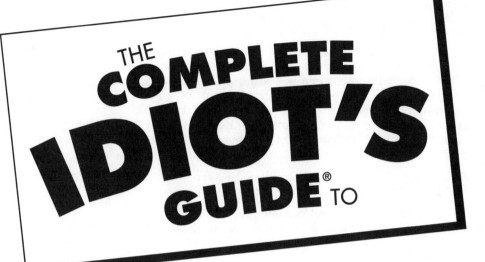

THE COMPLETE IDIOT'S GUIDE® TO

Team Building

by Arthur R. Pell, Ph.D.

alpha books

Macmillan USA, Inc.
201 West 103rd Street
Indianapolis, IN 46290

A Pearson Education Company

Dedicated to my grandsons, Benji and Caellan.

Copyright © 1999 by Arthur R. Pell, Ph.D.

International Standard Book Number: 0-02-863656-2
Library of Congress Catalog Card Number: Available on request.

02   01   00   8   7   6   5   4   3   2   1

Interpretation of the printing code: The rightmost number of the first series of numbers is the year of the book's printing; the rightmost number of the second series of numbers is the number of the book's printing. For example, a printing code of 00-1 shows that the first printing occurred in 2000.

Printed in the United States of America

Publisher
Marie Butler-Knight

Editorial Director
Gary M. Krebs

Product Manager
Phil Kitchel

Associate Managing Editor
Cari Shaw Fischer

Acquisitions Editor
Gary M. Krebs

Development Editor
Doris Cross

Production Editor
JoAnna Kremer

Copy Editor
Faren Bachelis

Technical Editor
Scott W. Ventrella

Illustrator
Jody P. Schaeffer

Cover Designers
Mike Freeland
Kevin Spear

Book Designers
Scott Cook and Amy Adams of DesignLab

Indexer
Riofrancos and Company Indexes

Layout/Proofreading
Terri Edwards
Diana Moore
Mike Poor
Gloria Schurick

Contents at a Glance

Contents

ix

19 When the Team Is Brand-New   269

20 Recruiting Candidates from Outside the Company   285

21 Separating the Wheat from the Chaff   301

22 Making the Hiring Decision   317

Foreword

The world of work has changed more radically during the past decade than at any time since the Industrial Revolution, and things are likely to change even more dramatically as we enter the 21st century. New concepts of people management have come into being that have increased productivity, enriched the workplace, and stimulated creativity and innovation. More and more companies are replacing the traditional hierarchical "boss-subordinate" structure with empowered teams. The key to the success of the team format rests with the former "supervisor"—now "team leader"—who often must change his or her management style to fit the new concept.

Change is not easy for most people, and is particularly difficult for managers, who for years made the decisions, gave the orders, and *commanded* and *controlled* their staffs. Shifting from supervising a traditional work group to leading a collaborative team is hard work. Team leaders—whether experienced, old-time supervisors, or newly appointed managers—must learn and apply a new set of tools and techniques if their team is to function successfully.

This need is met in *The Complete Idiot's Guide to Team Building*. Dr. Pell has written a delightfully entertaining "how-to" manual that is not only a prime training tool for new team leaders, but also a reference guide for all managers, regardless of their level of proficiency and experience.

This is a no-nonsense book, chock-full of pragmatic suggestions on dealing with everyday leadership issues. It covers every aspect of building a team—from selecting and training new members to dealing with terminations and downsizings—and all the steps in between.

Leaders will learn how to develop critical upward and downward communications with their teams, how to run meaningful and productive meetings, and how to make every team member an active participant in decision-making and implementation. I was particularly impressed by Dr. Pell's insight into motivating team members, coaching and mentoring, and such sensitive issues as maintaining team harmony and resolving conflicts among members.

It takes more than a dynamic team leader to make a team successful. Equally important are the team members, who must leave behind any tendency to think of themselves as order-followers, and transform themselves to collaborative, active participants in the team's activities. Throughout the book, team members are counseled on how they can become better collaborators. This will become even more significant as self-directed teams—teams without permanent leaders—proliferate.

This is an easy-to-read book augmented by specific examples drawn from Dr. Pell's extensive experience in dealing with organizational development and human resource management. If you're among the many struggling with the demands of doing more with less, and needing to get better results through team building, this book is a must-read.

—Franklin C. Ashby, Ph.D.

Dr. Franklin C. Ashby is the president of Manchester Training. Recognized as a leading authority on organizational effectiveness and improvement strategies, he was formerly the vice president and chief educational officer of Dale Carnegie & Associates, Inc., responsible for matters pertaining to the design, delivery, and administration of all products and services in 77 countries. Dr. Ashby is the author of *Revitalize Your Corporate Culture* (Gulf, 1999) and *Effective Leadership Programs* (ASTD, 1999). He lives with his wife, Rita, and their son, Danny, on Long Island, New York.

Introduction

The trend toward team development in organizations in every industry and in most developed countries has proliferated over the past decade. Research at the Center for the Study of Work Teams at the University of North Texas indicates that as we enter the twenty-first century, 80 percent of Fortune 500 companies will have half their employees on teams.

Many of the people who lead these teams will have previously been supervisors of traditional work groups. To succeed in their new roles as team leaders, they will have to rethink their concepts of leadership and often make major changes in their behavior.

Other team leaders will be promoted from the ranks with the opportunity to start their new careers without carrying the baggage of obsolete leadership techniques.

Although some organizations provide special training in team leadership to all team leaders, in most cases the burden of learning how to lead a team is left primarily to the team leader.

How to Use This Book

Reading a book like this one can be interesting, enlightening, and amusing. I hope that this book will be all these things to you. More important, it should provide you with ideas you can use on the job. You'll find lots of these ideas in the following pages.

But it will all be a waste of your money, time, and energy if you don't take what you read and put it into effect in the way you perform your day-to-day managerial functions.

Following these five steps should ensure that this book isn't just a reading exercise but also a plan of action for you:

1. After you read each chapter, create an action plan to implement what you've learned. Indicate what action you will take, with whom you will take the action, and when you will begin.

2. Share your plan of action with your associates. Get them involved.

3. Set a follow-up date to check whether you did what you planned to do.

4. If not, reread the chapter, rethink what you did or didn't do, and make a new plan of action.

5. Review what you have done periodically. Renew your commitment.

This book will provide current and potential team leaders with the tools and techniques of successful team leadership. Here's a quick overview of what you will learn:

Part 1: Teams: Gimmicks, Fads, or the Real Stuff?

This part explores the entire concept of team development. It provides team leaders with a chance to rethink their leadership styles, and it shows team members how teams can make their jobs more rewarding. It also warns the reader about some of the barriers to team success and what to do to overcome them.

Part 2: Molding a Group Into a Working Team

Part 2 covers some of the basic tools of team leadership. You'll learn how to communicate effectively both orally and in writing, make meetings meaningful, and delegate work and ensure that it's done properly without micromanaging. Team leaders will learn to become team coaches, and team members will learn how to become mentors to associates who need help.

Part 3: Can't We All Just Get Along?

In these chapters, the critical problem of how to deal with troublemakers and maintain team harmony will be explored. Also covered are setting standards and measuring performance, handling discipline and termination of team members, and dealing with voluntary quits and downsizing.

Part 4: T-E-A-M—Yay TEAM!

In Part 4 you'll learn what empowerment really means, how to motivate members who have varying agendas, and the value (or lack of value) of money as a motivator.

Part 5: Staffing the Team—And Getting It Going

This part concentrates on forming the teams, whether the members are drawn from within the company or recruited from outside. You'll learn how to screen applicants, interview prospects, check references, and make sound hiring decisions. In this part you'll pick up techniques for orienting and training new members.

Part 6: Special Teams for Special Purposes

These chapters will teach you about self-directed teams—teams that have no permanent leader. Also discussed are cross-functional teams, in which members are drawn from different departments or disciplines, and the complexities of working with teams whose members are located in remote locations.

Extras

To add to the material in the main text, a series of shaded boxes throughout the book highlight specific items that can help you understand and implement the material in each chapter:

Team Terms

You may have an idea of what most of these expressions mean, but you don't have to guess about their meanings and implications. These definitions will put you in the know so when your boss throws these terms at you, you won't have to bluff your way through.

Team Builder

Tips and techniques to help you implement some of the ideas you pick up in this book. Some come from the writings of management gurus, and others come from the experience of team leaders like you, who are happy to share them.

Heads Up!

Warnings about common mistakes made by team leaders that could cost you time, money, energy, and embarrassment.

FYI

For your information: Tidbits that may add to your knowledge, or just amuse you.

Acknowledgments

Special thanks to B. K. Nelson, my agent, for introducing me to the editors of "The Complete Idiot's" series; Dr. Afife Sayin, for her assistance in the research for this book; Dr. Frank Ashby for writing the foreword; Doris Cross, my editor, for her ideas, suggestions, and encouragement; and to my wife, Erica, for many years of peace, support and love.

Special Thanks to the Technical Reviewer

For his painstaking technical review of the manuscript, I am deeply grateful to Scott W. Ventrella, Principal of Positive Dynamics, who brought over 15 years of organizational development experience and his unique blend of solid, real-world application and academic credentials to the task.

Trademarks

All terms mentioned in this book that are known to be or are suspected of being trademarks or service marks have been appropriately capitalized. Alpha Books and Macmillan USA, Inc., cannot attest to the accuracy of this information. Use of a term in this book should not be regarded as affecting the validity of any trademark or service mark.

Part 1

Teams: Gimmicks, Fads, or the Real Stuff?

The history of management is loaded with fads. They come and go. Some are wild ideas—gimmicks, advocated by some charismatic guru. They have a brief moment in the sun and fade away as fast as they began.

Others, like Sensitivity Training, Management by Objectives, Reengineering, and Total Quality Management, have a longer life. They're tried by many companies, are often successful, but sooner or later, the enthusiasm for them is lost.

Are teams a current fad or is the concept truly a sea change in the way organizations will be run as we enter the twenty-first century?

Only time will tell, but many organizations that have been using teams over the past several years have praised their value as a means of solving problems, improving processes, and promoting innovation.

Sure, some team efforts have failed. That's to be expected with any human endeavor. Perhaps all that is needed to avoid failure and ensure success lies in the way the teams are organized, built, and operated.

Let's take a look at what's new about teams, why teams sometimes fail, and what can be done to get teams off the ground with a good chance of success.

Chapter 1

What's So New About Teams?

> ## In This Chapter
>
> ➤ Let's talk about teams
>
> ➤ Choosing between teams and work groups
>
> ➤ What teams can and cannot do
>
> ➤ The role of the team leader
>
> ➤ Becoming an effective team member

The world of work has changed radically during the past decade, and it continues to change more rapidly than at any time since the Industrial Revolution. Things are likely to change even more dramatically as we enter the twenty-first century.

We have already seen how computers give managers immediate and continuous access to new information, but that is only one aspect of change. Changes in management structure have made the way we work quite different from that of previous generations.

In this chapter we'll explore these changes and see how they affect the way supervisors will function in their new role as team leaders.

Why Teams?

It used to be that top management made all the decisions and filtered them down through a series of layers to the rank-and-file workers. We have seen and continue to

Team Terms

A **team** is a group of people who collaborate and interact to reach a common goal. The team is made up of a **team leader** who coordinates the work of team members, often referred to as **associates**.

see this being replaced by a more collaborative organization in which people at all levels are expected to contribute to every aspect of their organization's activities.

Getting things done is now assumed by teams—groups of people, usually headed by a team leader, who together as a team plan, implement, and control the work.

What to Expect from a Team

The essence of a team is common commitment. Without it, the members of the group perform as individuals; with it they become a powerful unit of collective performance.

In the ideal team, each associate performs his or her function in such a way that it dovetails with that of other team members to enable the team to achieve its goals. By this collaboration, the whole becomes greater than the sum of its parts.

FYI

According to a study made by the University of North Texas, by the year 2000, 80 percent of Fortune 500 organizations will have half of their employees on teams.

An excellent example of this is a surgical team. Every member of the team—the surgeons, the anesthesiologist, the nurses, and the other technicians—carries out his or her individual functions expertly. But when they work as a team, interactions flow seamlessly among them. All are committed to one goal—the well-being of the patient.

There are examples of successful teams in every endeavor: championship sports teams, disease-curing research teams, fire-fighting rescue teams, and in every aspect of business.

Teams or Work Groups—What's the Big Difference?

Not all groups are teams. The traditional working group is made up of individuals whose work is directed by a supervisor. The members do whatever they are assigned to do, and are measured by their individual performances. In a team, the team leader guides and facilitates the work of the members, who share the responsibility of getting the work done.

Teams differ fundamentally from work groups in that they require both individual and mutual accountability. This makes possible performance levels greater than the individuals could achieve themselves even when performing at optimal levels.

Although the team option promises greater performance, it also brings more risks. Working groups need little time to plan the work because the planning has been already done by the supervisor. Decisions are implemented through specific individual assignments. If performance expectations can be met in this manner, using traditional work groups is more comfortable, less risky, less time consuming, and less disruptive than using teams.

However, if the organization seeks creative approaches, performance that is more than just satisfactory, and the opportunity to develop employees' capabilities, it should use the team approach.

FYI

The team is a collaborative group, not just people taking orders and carrying them out. When team members participate in setting a goal, they are more committed to its accomplishment. As Joe Paterno, Penn State's football coach, pointed out: "When a team outgrows individual performance and learns team confidence, excellence becomes a reality."

The following chart differentiates between groups and teams:

Traditional Work Groups	Teams
Leader dominates and controls the team	The leader is facilitator and coach
Goals set by organization	Goals set by team members
Leader conducts meetings	Meetings are participative discussions
Leader assigns work	Team plans work assignments

continues

5

continued

Traditional Work Groups	Teams
Emphasis on individual performances	Emphasis on team performance
Workers compete against each other	Team members work as cooperative unit
Communication flows down from leader	Communication flows upward and downward (to and from leader)
Information is often hoarded by workers	Information is shared
Decisions made by leader	Decisions made by entire team

Convert to Teams?—Yes or No?

Don't look at teams as a panacea for all your company's ills. There are many departments where strong leaders are needed, where the employees are not qualified or not ready to be participative team members. Changing abruptly to teams will confuse and confound the workers and be counterproductive.

Teams are feasible when

➤ A fresh approach to accomplishing the goals of the group is desirable.

➤ There is a breakdown in communication within the group.

➤ A project requires a staff of people with diversified backgrounds.

➤ The culture of the organization is becoming more participative.

➤ Senior managers are committed to the creation and implementation of the team concept.

Here are some situations where using teams is not desirable:

Team Builder

In organizations where teams have been successful, they have had the full support of top management. In organizations where teams did not live up to expectations, management had never been enthusiastic about the concept. To build a successful team, first get the full support of top management.

➤ When there is a heavy turnover in the department. Teams require a group of stable members who are likely to work together for a long time. It takes quite a while to develop the working relationships within a team. Members must win the trust and confidence of all their teammates. They must learn to coordinate their efforts. Only over time does the team build a relationship in which members can anticipate another member's actions, and be ready to react instantly.

➤ When the company has a small cadre of key personnel and uses temps or outsourcing to do most of the work.

➤ When the work of the group is routine and is unlikely to change in the near future.

➤ When the group leader is strongly opposed to teams. He or she will sabotage the effort. If for other reasons, shifting to teams is advantageous, the group leader must be replaced.

Heads Up!

You can't force reluctant managers to accept the team concept. You have to sell them on accepting the idea and implementing it in their work groups.

In most organizations there's a mixture of traditional work groups and teams. As new processes and projects are instituted, the groups assigned to them are more likely to be constituted as teams.

Types of Teams

Teams can be used for a variety of purposes. Let's look at some of the types of teams:

➤ **Working teams:** Teams that make or do things. These teams do the frontline work of every organization. They manufacture goods, conduct research, design systems, sell merchandise, keep the records. They perform the tasks that are basic to the operation of the organization. Members are assigned to the teams on a permanent basis. Although there may be deadlines established for some parts of the work, most of the work is ongoing.

➤ **Special purpose or project teams:** Teams that are formed to deal with specific situations such as improving quality or cutting costs. They may be created to plan a new company activity, such as introducing a new product or service. They may be appointed to investigate and report on changes in systems or complying with a new government regulation. These teams are sometimes called task forces or project groups. Members may all come from the same department or may be chosen from several departments in the organization. They may be detached from their usual work for the duration of the project, or they may continue their regular work and function as a special purpose team on a time limit to complete the assignment.

➤ **Multifunctional teams:** Teams that are drawn from several different disciplines. They may function on a permanent or temporary basis. How these teams operate is discussed in Chapter 25.

➤ **Self-directed teams:** Teams that do not have a permanent team leader. All members share leadership. Self-directed teams have often been compared to jazz combos or string quartets, musical groups that perform without a conductor. How these teams operate is discussed in Chapter 24.

➤ **Management teams:** Teams that make management decisions. In some companies, the job of the president has been replaced by a management team, sometimes called "the office of the president." In others, the chief executive officer (CEO) uses a management team to act as a "cabinet" that discusses and reaches consensus on major decisions.

Team Terms

Top management teams are sometimes referred to as C-Teams because they are composed of the CEO (chief executive officer), COO (chief operating officer), CFO (chief financial officer), CIO (chief information officer), CMO (chief marketing officer), and others whose acronymic titles begin with C.

Team Leaders: Rethink Your Roles

If your philosophy of managing people is: "Do it my way or you're on the highway," you'd better prepare to make an about-face. The team leader does not function like that old-school tyrant. He or she is a facilitator who develops and coordinates an intelligent, motivated team to get things done. The emphasis is on developing the skills and coordinating the efforts of a team of intelligent, motivated associates.

Don't Boss—Lead

You have to stop thinking like a "boss." Bosses make decisions and give orders. Team leaders coordinate groups of thinking adults who together face and work out the problems that face them. Successful team leaders provide a climate in which their team members are encouraged to make their own analyses of problems, suggest solutions, and participate in decisions.

Let's look at some of the ways team leaders do this:

➤ They make sure the team members know the company's and the team's vision and mission and keep them focused on achieving them.

➤ They're expert communicators. They recognize that communication is a two-way street. It is important for them to convey their instructions and concepts to team members, but it is equally important for them to open their ears to the ideas and suggestions of team members.

➤ Their mission is to develop the skills and capabilities of their team members. They take the time to identify each team member's strengths and weaknesses and work with each to improve his or her performance. They encourage team members to commit to lifelong learning and recommend sources, both within and outside the organization, that can help them grow as individuals and as team contributors.

➤ They work with members to set performance standards that are clear, attainable, and measurable, and establish a means to let members know how they are doing.

➤ They motivate and inspire individual members by recognition, praise, and reward. They motivate and inspire the team with pep talks and team recognition, and by creating a climate of enthusiasm.

Heads Up!

When you know that your way to do a job works, it seems sensible to insist team members do it your way. Don't! Get some of their ideas. Could be they may come up with a better way.

In later chapters you can learn how to apply these and other team-building concepts to the way you lead your team.

How do you think you shape up as a team leader? Find out by taking the following inventory.

Read each statement, decide whether you agree or disagree with it, and circle the appropriate answer. Then compare your responses to the answers that follow.

Agree   Disagree   1. It isn't necessary for a manager to discuss long-range goals with team members. As long as they are aware of the immediate objective, they can do their work effectively.

Agree   Disagree   2. The best way to make a reprimand effective is to admonish an offender in front of coworkers.

Agree   Disagree   3. Team leaders appear ignorant and risk loss of face if they answer a question with, "I don't know, but I'll find out and let you know."

Agree   Disagree   4. It pays for a team leader to spend a great deal of time with a new team member to ensure that training has been effective.

Agree   Disagree   5. Team leaders should encourage their associates to share their ideas about work methods.

Agree   Disagree   6. When disciplining is required, team leaders should be careful to avoid saying or doing anything that may cause resentment.

Agree   Disagree   7. People will work best for tough leaders.

Agree   Disagree   8. It's more important for a team to be composed of members who like their jobs than of people who do their jobs well.

Agree   Disagree   9. Work gets done most efficiently if the team leader lays out plans in great detail.

Agree   Disagree   10. To lead an effective team, leaders should keep in mind the feelings, attitudes, and ideas of the team's members.

Okay, you've answered all the questions. Now look at the responses based on the advice of successful team leaders.

1. **Disagree.** People who know where they're going—who can see the big picture—are more committed and will work harder to reaching those objectives than people who are aware only of immediate goals.

2. **Disagree.** Admonishing a person doesn't solve the problem; it only makes the person feel small in front of coworkers. A constructive critique, in private, corrects a problem without humiliating the person.

3. **Disagree.** It's better to admit ignorance of a matter than to try to bluff. People respect leaders who accept that they don't know everything.

4. **Agree.** The most important step in developing the full capabilities of associates is good training. Team leaders who invest the time to lay a solid foundation in the beginning will reap huge returns.

5. **Agree.** People directly involved with the job can often contribute good ideas toward the solution of problems related to their work.

6. **Agree.** Resentment creates low morale and often leads to conscious or subconscious sabotage.

7. **Disagree.** Toughness is not as important as fairness and an inspiring attitude.

Team Builder

If a critical problem arises and requires immediate and concentrated attention, appoint a **task force** or **special project team** to deal with it.

8. **Disagree.** The happiness and satisfaction of team members on the job are important, but they are secondary to getting the job done. Work with members to find ways to combine performance with job satisfaction.

9. **Disagree.** Some people work better when they are given broad project guidelines and can work out the details themselves. Others work better when tasks are given to them in detail. A good leader recognizes the styles in which people work and then adapts to them.

10. **Agree.** Communication is a two-way street. To manage effectively, it's important to know what team members are thinking and how they feel about their jobs.

There's no passing or failing score for this inventory. Its purpose is to make you think about how you lead people. You may not agree with all the experts' answers, but do pay them some heed. Most of what you find here will be discussed in detail later in this book.

Team Members: Rethink Your Roles

If you've been working in a traditional work group for some time, you probably have been conditioned to take orders and carry them out whether you agreed with them or not. Your boss had the authority, and you were paid to do what you were told.

FYI

Charles Darwin said, "It's not the strongest species that survives, nor the most intelligent, but rather the one that is most adaptable to change."

This changes when the group becomes a team. You are expected to help plan the work and determine how it will be carried out.

Why Change?

Changing the way you work is often not easy. It requires a radical change in the way you look at your job—and at yourself. Nobody really likes to change the way he or she does things. You're accustomed to doing your job in a certain way. It's comfortable to keep doing it that way. To change takes you out of this comfort zone. But progress can't be made unless you become uncomfortable.

Even though the changes your discomfort engenders may lead to progress for the company, you may ask what's in it for you.

Some of the benefits you gain are

1. **Your job.** It's as simple as that. If the company goes down the drain, you have no job. If the company prospers, not only do you have a job, but the opportunities within the firm expand. In today's highly competitive world, if a company is to thrive—even survive—it must change. But no company can change unless all of its members contribute to that change. By accepting change, you are doing a small part in keeping your company viable. By enthusiastically supporting change, you are increasing your company's capability to meet the competition.

2. **Your personal growth.** The team environment challenges its members to use their intelligence, their creativity, and their skills in working on team problems. Now, often for the first time, you can express your ideas and contribute to the way a job is done. This stimulates your mind and encourages you to build up your knowledge. With each success, your self-confidence increases. It also helps when there are setbacks—and there will be. They develop the inner resilience you need to accept and learn from them.

3. **Your career.** If your goal is to move up the organizational ladder, active participation in team activities gives you experience in leadership. You'll take part in running meetings, leading projects, and training and mentoring associates. You'll catch the eye of higher level managers as your contributions are recognized. When new teams are formed, you will be prepared to be moved into team leadership.

What It Takes to Be a Great Team Member

It starts with performing your job superbly. All team members are depended upon to be good performers. But top performance by itself is not enough. There's much more to becoming a great team member.

➤ Participate fully in team discussions. Listen actively. Contribute to every discussion. Even if you have no original ideas to present, comment on other members' suggestions. Ask good questions. Offer your support. Volunteer to serve on subcommittees and take on extra assignments.

➤ Motivate yourself. Set personal goals that are in line with the team's mission. Participate in establishing team goals. You are going to have to work to meet them, so you should have a say in determining them.

Team Builder

One way to build team spirit in your team members is to show them how what they accomplish contributes to the bottom line.

➤ Try new things. Don't be afraid to take risks. This is the way to get ahead. Remember the turtle. It's perfectly secure if it stays inside the shell, but if it wants to move ahead, it has to stick out its neck.

➤ Look beyond your team. Study the culture of your company. Know and understand the company's mission statement. Measure how closely your team complies with company and departmental goals. Think about how your work fits into the larger picture.

➤ Be sensitive to other points of view. Listen to the opinions of other team members. Don't be afraid to express your view even if it is different or even opposite of everybody else's. Stand up for what you believe, but don't be stubborn about it. Be willing to compromise to achieve consensus.

➤ Be a team player. Cooperate. Don't compete. Support your teammates. Help them grow by sharing information, taking tough assignments, and training and mentoring new members. Praise associates who have done well. Show appreciation to members who have been especially helpful to you or the team.

➤ Know your teammates. Know their strengths and limitations. Know their personal goals and ambitions. Know their idiosyncrasies and pet peeves. This will make working with them easier and more pleasant.

➤ Build up your own self-confidence. Read self-improvement books and articles. Study yourself. Be aware of areas where you need improvement. For example, if you are shy, take assertive training; if you are a poor speaker or writer, take courses to correct it.

➤ If you and a teammate have a disagreement or more serious conflict, resolve it as rapidly as possible. Don't let it fester. Once it is resolved, forget about it. Don't bear a grudge: "Let the dead past bury its dead."

➤ Learn other jobs within the team. Train to do the work of other team members. In this way you expand your value to the team as you can take over in case of absence, heavy work loads, or other contingencies.

➤ Keep tabs on your progress. Periodically review your personal and team goals. Measure how close you are to reaching them. Be prepared to take steps to correct problems that are impeding your progress.

➤ Celebrate successes. When the team completes a project or makes a significant achievement, share the joy of success by going out to lunch or dinner together.

As a full participant in team activities, you will not only enjoy your work more, and make more effective contributions to the team's success, you'll enhance your personal growth and prepare for moving ahead in your career.

> **CAUTION**
>
> **Heads Up!**
>
> Team members: Improve your skills. Don't be complacent. Don't be content with "satisfactory" work. If you need added training or coaching, ask for it. Take training seriously and apply what you learn.

FYI

There is no *I* in *TEAM*. Teams are made up of people, each with his or her individuality, but for that team to succeed, individual agendas must take second place to that of the team. Each member is expected to do his or her best, but successful teams have no "stars" or "rugged individualists." The ego, the "I," is replaced by the team, the "we."

The Least You Need to Know

➤ A team is a group of people who collaborate and interact to reach a common goal.

➤ Teams differ fundamentally from work groups in that teams require both individual and mutual accountability. Team members can achieve higher individual performance levels than they would when working without a team.

➤ Teams require a group of stable members who are likely to work together for a long time.

➤ The team leader is a facilitator who develops and coordinates an intelligent, motivated team to get things done.

➤ Changing the way you work is often not easy. To change takes you out of the comfort zone, but progress can't be made unless you become uncomfortable.

➤ To succeed as a team member, don't be satisfied if your work is "satisfactory." Strive to do superb work. If you need added training or coaching, ask for it.

➤ Participation is the key to team success. Team leaders should establish a climate in which participation is a "way of life."

Chapter 2

The Barriers to Team Success

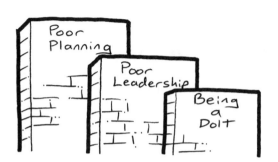

In This Chapter

➤ When plans are inadequate

➤ Leaders without leadership skills

➤ When members have poor attitudes

➤ Training that doesn't train

➤ Communications breakdowns

➤ Team members don't get along

➤ Rewards and recognition programs that don't work

The team can be a great boon to an organization. It can revitalize organizations that are going downhill; it can stimulate employees to become more creative and more productive. It can develop leaders for the future. But teams don't always work. Although most companies report success in using them, there are a good many organizations in which shifting to teams has been disappointing.

Why should this happen? In this chapter we'll look at the many barriers that impede team success. The balance of the book will address these problems and discuss how they can be overcome. Understanding the reasons for failures and learning how to avoid them will keep you from repeating the mistakes others have made.

Poor Planning

You just don't shift from work groups to teams by an edict from top management: "Effective this date you are a team."

You have to take the time to plan exactly what you want to do and how you intend to do it.

Team Terms

Goals and **objectives** are interchangeable terms that describe the purpose, or long-term results, toward which an organization's or individual's endeavors are directed.

Planting Your Goalposts

Unless you know what exactly you want to achieve, there's no way to measure how close you are to achieving it. Specific goals give you a standard against which to measure your progress.

The goals you set for accomplishing your team's mission must be in line with the larger goals your company sets for you to accomplish. If the objectives you plan to achieve for your job, department, or team aren't coordinated with the objectives of your organization, you'll waste your time and energy.

In most organizations, overall goals are established by top management and filtered down to departments or teams to use as guides in establishing their own goals.

The process of setting goals takes time, energy, and effort. Goals aren't something you scribble on a napkin during a coffee break; you must plan what you truly want to accomplish, establish timetables, determine who will be responsible for each aspect of the job, and then anticipate and plan resolutions for any obstacles that may threaten to thwart the achievement of your goals.

Not "Sounding the Depths"

Before you can set goals for your team, you have to diagnose the "as-is situation." Too often, managers deceive themselves about the true condition of their organization. Of course, they know the figures: sales volume, market share, production, payroll, and all the tangible statistics. But they delude themselves on such vital information as employee attitudes and morale, the currency of the skills of their people, the willingness of their people to cooperate and extend themselves, and the commitment of staff at all levels to company goals.

Each of us tends to accept as truthful information that which is compatible with our own perceptions. To us it is reality. However, in the minds of others, be they superiors, peers, or subordinates, the same information may be perceived totally differently.

Just as in our bodies, many critical problems may not show up in routine tests; subtle and incipient conditions exist in an organization that may not be uncovered by traditional business analyses.

You must go deeper. To do this you must get to know the people with whom you interrelate: members of the team, other team leaders and managers, and others within and outside the firm. You must learn their strengths and weaknesses, attitudes toward the job, the company, and the leaders. Some companies accomplish this by employee attitude surveys, focus groups, or using a special consultant to interview the staff.

FYI

"The manager who comes up with the right solution to the wrong problem is more dangerous than the manager who comes up with the wrong solution to the right problem."

—Peter Drucker

Flying by the Seat of the Pants

Some leaders run their department without real planning. Like the pioneer aviators, they fly by the seat of their pants. They make decisions based on their experience and intuition, and often they are right on the money.

But as airplanes became more sophisticated, pilots could no longer depend on their intuition. They had to learn to fly by instruments.

This is true of the supervisors and leaders in today's world of business. The technology and complexities of running a team, a department, and entire enterprise have made "seat of the pants" management obsolete.

Like the old aviators, the supervisor, now a team leader, has to use all available instruments and tools to make planning the work a collaborative effort.

Poorly Conceived Organization

To make teams work, the traditional hierarchical organizational structure has to be modified. I bet your company has an organizational chart showing where each department fits in the company. It looks like a pyramid, and somewhere near the bottom you'll find your team.

Team Builder

Flexibility is a key factor when organizing a team. Unless members have highly specialized skills that are unique to them, avoid giving each member a permanent function. Every member should be able and willing to perform every job activity.

The function of the organizational chart is to show employees which activities they are responsible for, to whom they report, and who reports to them. In addition it enables anyone to view the entire corporate structure.

However, rigid adherence to this structure can impede the work of teams. Teams often cross structural lines. They don't fit neatly into a box. For example, a product development team may engage in functions that fall under Engineering, R & D, Marketing, and Finance. Artificially placing it under just one of those departments would complicate its work.

Better ways to organize teams of this sort are discussed in Chapter 25.

Poor Leadership

Blame it on the boss! And often the boss is to blame. The team leader has the responsibility to make that team succeed. No matter how competent the team members may be, unless they are guided by a knowledgeable, dedicated, inspiring leader, it will be tough for them to achieve their goals.

The role of the leader was discussed in the first chapter. Now let's look at how poor leadership can impede the team's success.

Confusion in the Ranks

If the leader doesn't lead, the team can't follow. Worse, if the leader leads badly, the team will perform badly.

Let's look at how one team leader abdicated his leadership role. When Rick D. was appointed leader of a marketing development team, he studied books on team leadership, attended seminars, and asked advice of other leaders. He was convinced that his team would be participative, that he would give his members enough autonomy so they could use their talents and grow by making decisions on their own.

When the team was assembled, Rick presented a broad outline of the team's purpose and asked them to determine what should be done and who would do it. When a member had questions about his role, Rick responded, "That's for you to determine."

Theoretically, that's how a participative team works. But what happened? Some members selected aspects of the project that they felt competent to do and began to work on it. Others spent weeks figuring out their roles; still others began working on part of the project only to find that somebody else was doing the same thing.

Without leadership, there was total confusion. It didn't take long for Rick's boss to note the lack of progress. When questioned about this, Rick responded that he was taught that giving team members autonomy would result in long-term benefit to all. What he failed to understand was that a project has to be completed in a timely manner. If a team has never done a project of this type before, it needs strong guidance from the leader, frequent feedback on progress, and active steps to keep the team moving on track. All this could be accomplished within the parameters of participative team leadership.

FYI

The hierarchical organizational structure is a carryover from the time when businesses used the military as the example of the ideal organization. But today, even military units have modified, and in some cases eliminated, this rigid organization.

Poor Training

A team is like a rocket. The rocket is made up of a series of components. If that rocket is to be successfully launched, each component must be in tiptop condition. Only then can the components be integrated to work together to get that rocket off the ground. Each team member is a component of the team. Unless all are able to perform their functions excellently, the team will never be able to move ahead. So the first training objective is to perfect skills. But that is not enough. In order for the team members to work as an integrated unit, they must also be trained in working together as a team.

You'll find advice on making training more effective in Chapters 8 and 23.

Poor Attitude

Another barrier to team success is the poor attitude that many team members have about the team process, the team leader, and often their teammates.

Heads Up!

Don't let a team member feel like an "outsider." Often new team members stick to themselves and don't easily integrate into the team. Draw the member out by soliciting his or her opinions. Suggest that one of the established team members mentor the newcomer.

"It's not my job."

In the traditional work group, the duties and responsibilities of a job are specified in a formal job description. Job descriptions have their place in the team setup, too. They give the members a guide to the work they are expected to perform, but all members are expected to do any work that will propel the team toward its goals.

Yet, there are still members who look upon their jobs as being limited to the job description. When asked to help other members or to take on any assignment not specifically listed in the job description, they complain, "It's not my job."

The concept of the team is based on the principle that its members all work together to achieve the desired results. This means that all team members do whatever has to be done to accomplish the job. This includes doing work you don't enjoy, helping slower members catch up, and putting aside pet projects to keep the team on target for higher priority assignments.

Members find all kinds of excuses to avoid doing work that they don't like. They'll say

"Let Bill do it; he can do it better and faster."

"I did it last time. Let someone else do it now."

"Last time I did that, I botched it up."

"I've more important things to do."

How to deal with assigning unpleasant tasks in a manner that is fair to the entire team is discussed in Chapter 7.

Lack of Trust

The basis for any relationship, on or off the job, is trust. When team members do not trust their leader or one or more of their teammates, the team will never get off the ground.

The success or failure of a team leader depends on the trust of his or her team. If people trust you, anything you say can be heard. If people don't trust you, then most of what you say will be ignored.

It doesn't take much for a person to lose trust in another. The team leader makes a promise and then fails to live up to it. Trust is lost. A member withholds needed information from other members; nobody trusts him or her again.

Rebuilding trust is not easy. If the lack of trust is among team members, the team leader can step in to alleviate the problem. However, if the team leader has lost the trust of the team members, it will take extraordinary effort to reestablish a trusting relationship.

Some suggestions on dealing with this problem will be found in Chapters 10 and 11.

"My teammates don't pull their loads."

Sandra was mad. Once again the team was behind schedule and that meant she would have to work overtime. And whose fault was that? Not hers. She knocked herself out to get work done on time, but some of her teammates, like Carl and Tricia, just plodded along. When she complained to Rita, the team leader, she was told that they were doing the best they could.

This is not an unusual situation. True, some people work faster than others, some are more thorough than others, some are more creative than others. It's human nature for the Sandras of this world to resent the Carls and Tricias who, in their opinions, are not contributing as much to the team effort as they are. This is exacerbated when the Sandras have to make up for these deficiencies by doing extra work.

No team can succeed unless every member does his or her share. The team leader cannot accept the excuse that Carl and Tricia are doing their best. She has to identify the reasons for their poorer performance and take steps to correct it. Perhaps they need additional training; perhaps they have personal problems that are impeding their performance. How to get the entire team working at optimum capacity is discussed in Chapters 8, 12, and 13.

"I'm not paid to make decisions."

Employees who have been accustomed to working in traditional settings have been conditioned to taking orders. For years, they were excluded from the decision-making process. As team members they feel uncomfortable when asked to participate in decision making.

Often they'd been told that one reason supervisors and managers were paid more than rank-and-file workers was they had the responsibility of making decisions. Now, they as team members—not paid any more than before—are given this responsibility. It's logical for them to feel that making decisions is not their job.

Team Builder

If you are the team member who is not pulling your load, determine the reason. If you need to improve your skills, seek help from the leader or your teammates. If you lack self-confidence, seek out a program that can help you.

Team Terms

Under both federal and state wage and hour laws, an **exempt** employee is one who is engaged in management, administration, professional work, or other work that requires "independent judgment." All others are **nonexempt**. Nonexempt employees must be paid at the rate of time and a half for all work done in excess of 40 hours in a week. **Exempt** employees can be required to work overtime at no extra compensation.

In most companies, team leaders do get higher base pay than team members, but as you'll note in Chapter 17, the compensation system is changing to overcome this. There is a trend to create greater parity between leaders and members. This should result in members being less reluctant to participate in decision making.

Team leaders and their bosses have to build time for training into the regular work schedules. One way is to schedule the training to be done after regular work hours. This is often resisted by companies because it is costly when training nonexempt workers who must be paid overtime. Many people, whether they do or do not receive overtime pay, resent being asked to give up personal time for training that many feel they will rarely use.

Poor Communications

You've heard it over and over again. The reason (or maybe an excuse for a failure) is a breakdown in communications. You say one thing and your associate hears something quite different. Why? It could be how you said it, or how the associate received it. Trite as it may sound, poor communications is a major barrier to the success of team efforts.

"What did he say?"

You thought your instructions were clearly stated. But the minute you leave the room, your associate turns to another team member for clarification. You didn't get through.

Why? Maybe it was your fault. Perhaps you spoke indistinctly. Perhaps you used language that was not familiar to the listener. Perhaps your body language sent a different message from your words. Maybe the problem emanated from the associate. He didn't fully listen. She didn't take you seriously.

Whether you are the team leader or a team member expressing your views, you have to be alert to how you come across to others. Get feedback from your associates. Ask them for critiques on your presentations at meetings or just in team discussions. If you are making a planned presentation, rehearse it in front of a mirror or videotape it. You can find many more ideas on improving communication skills in Chapter 4.

The Leader Who Doesn't Listen

Successful team leaders make it a point to listen to their members. Unless you keep your ears and your mind open, not only will you not benefit from the many ideas your team members can contribute, you will miss cues of team discontent or impending problems.

You can learn to overcome this. It takes commitment and effort to achieve it. You'll learn how to become an active listener when you read Chapter 4.

Heads Up!

When you speak never put your hands in front of your face, or play with your hair or your glasses. People who do this appear wishy-washy, and listeners may feel you are not sure of yourself.

Meetings That Waste Time

Got a problem? Call a meeting. One of the big complaints about teams is that too much time is wasted in meetings.

There are three major reasons meetings are time wasters.

1. There was no need for the meeting.
2. The meeting got out of control: The main objective of the meeting was lost in digressions, pointless arguments, extended discussions, and grandstanding by some participants.
3. The meeting was poorly planned or not planned at all.

If you are concerned about whether or not to call meetings and want to make the most of the meetings you conduct, you'll find suggestions in Chapter 6.

Poor Rapport Among Team Members

The essence of team success is a close, comfortable, coordinated, collaborative group of team members. If the members don't get along, the team dissolves into chaos. Instead of working out problems, members bicker among themselves. Instead of following the motto "One for all and all for one," it becomes "Every man for himself." Let's look at some of the causes of conflict among team members. The solutions will be found in Part 3 of this book.

Team Builder

A meeting of the entire team is not warranted if only two or three members are involved in a project. The team leader should hold a miniconference with that group. If new ideas or objective analyses by others not in the group are desired, discuss it at a meeting of the full team.

Conflicting Agendas

The purpose of a team is to work in a coordinated fashion to accomplish the team's objectives. When different team members push their own agendas ahead of the team's, there's no way the team's goals will be achieved.

I recently observed a good example of how conflicting agendas destroyed a team project. The company, a small but growing fast food retailer in the New England states, set up a task force to plan how to expand its product line. One of the members, Margo L., had made up her mind that the best approach would be to introduce a breakfast menu. In addition to the operational problems and a major marketing program to attract breakfast customers, this would involve opening the stores at 6 A.M. instead of the current 10 A.M. It would require a major recruiting campaign to get additional help, and store managers would have to put in many more hours.

Margo was so sure she was right that she refused to listen to objections and the alternative solutions offered by other members. She pressed so hard for her agenda that the meetings became exercises in futility. After several months of bickering and recriminations, the task force gave up and made no recommendations.

Jealousies and Rivalries

Starting with Cain and Abel, jealousies and rivalries have been part of the human experience. Of course, you'll find them in your company and in your team.

People envy those who are smarter, who are more attractive, who have more money, who they believe have been given better breaks than they have. There's no way a team leader can eliminate this, but an astute team leader can keep it from interfering with the team. It requires a keen understanding of each team member's personality and attitudes, diplomacy in dealing with rivals, and establishing a program to resolve conflicts.

Heads Up!

Trust is built when team members feel that they have everything to gain and really nothing to lose by building an appropriate and effective level of trust. If they don't get to know each other, and themselves, better, and don't have the kind of leader who inspires them to follow through, they won't have an effective team.

Personality Conflicts

When people work together, another common problem is personality conflicts. You've probably met people with whom you just couldn't get along. You may disagree about how to do a job. You may have conflicting ideas on goals. You may just not like each other. What can a team leader do when he or she doesn't relate well to a team member? What can a team leader do when members of the team can't work together? In Chapter 11 you'll find some interesting approaches to this delicate subject.

Carrying Poor Performers

One of the most common complaints team members make about associates is that they don't do their share of the work. Their poor performance may be caused by technical incompetence or perhaps a lack of motivation. Whatever the reason, the better workers have to make up the work.

As noted earlier in this chapter, the team leader has to identify the cause and take steps to correct it. But often this does not work. The member just isn't going to make it.

Many leaders are reluctant to remove a poor employee. It's often difficult, if not impossible, to find another spot in the organization for which they are better suited. The alternative, termination, is not an easy decision to make, either.

As a team leader, your responsibility is to develop and maintain a successful group of team members. If a member is not productive and you have exhausted all your options to make that person succeed, you have no choice but to remove him or her from the team.

How to deal with poor performance and how to terminate a member legally and tactfully are discussed in Chapters 13 and 14.

Poor Recognition and Rewards Programs

People expect that when they perform well they will be rewarded. It may be in the form of financial reward, such as bonuses or raises, but it is not limited to money. Such tangible recognition is a great way of rewarding high performance, but it is not the only way—and maybe not the best. There are many ways of letting people know you appreciate their work. It can be as simple as a pat on the back or as formal as an awards ceremony.

Individual Accomplishments

For years companies have based their recognition programs on individual accomplishments. Employees who stood out from the others by high production, creative ideas, or outstanding accomplishments were rewarded.

It is still important that superior performance be rewarded, but with the increased emphasis on team building, awards for individual accomplishment have been supplemented, and sometimes replaced, by rewards for team achievement.

Good idea? Not necessarily. Some high-achieving members want to be rewarded for their performance and resent sharing rewards with less productive team members.

There are ways to reward both the individual and the team equitably. You can learn how in Part 4.

FYI

Rather than have an annual appreciation day at which awards are presented to outstanding achievers, some organizations hold recognition celebrations throughout the year. They find that timely recognition serves as a continuing motivator.

Team Achievements

Programs to recognize entire reams are relatively new. Much has still to be learned from the experience of companies that are experimenting with this.

In Chapter 18 I look at some approaches and suggest some ideas that may be appropriate for your team.

Do barriers exist that may impede your team's success? This quiz will help you identify some of them. Circle the answers that apply to your team:

Yes	No	1.	Members complain that they're not getting information they need when they need it.
Yes	No	2.	Team meetings bog down in interminable discussions and arguments over petty matters.
Yes	No	3.	Some members tend to dominate the team.
Yes	No	4.	Team members don't listen to one another.
Yes	No	5.	Some members never participate in discussions about team projects.
Yes	No	6.	Poor performance of some team members slows down the work of the entire team.
Yes	No	7.	The amount of training in the soft skills is negligible.
Yes	No	8.	The team leader micromanages most of the team's work.
Yes	No	9.	Team goals are not clearly understood or accepted by some team members.
Yes	No	10.	Individual achievement rather than team accomplishment is the basis of the company's reward and recognition program.

A "yes" answer to any of these questions is an indicator of a barrier your team must overcome if the team is to succeed.

The Least You Need to Know

➤ You don't shift from work groups to teams by an edict from top management.

➤ Take "soundings" of your team to uncover hidden problems.

➤ If the leader doesn't lead, the team can't follow. Worse, if the leader leads badly, the team will perform badly.

➤ The effective leader does not micromanage the team. Micromanaging stifles creativity and independent thinking.

➤ The concept of the team is based on the principle that its members all work together to achieve the desired results.

➤ The basis for any relationship, on or off the job, is trust. If it is lacking, the team will never get off the ground.

➤ Whether you are the team leader or a team member expressing your views, you have to be alert to how you come across to others.

➤ Successful team leaders make it a point to listen to their members.

➤ It's important to reward individual superior performance, but equally important to supplement, and sometimes replace it, with rewards for team achievement.

Chapter 3

Laying the Foundation for Team Success

In This Chapter

➤ Opposition to change

➤ Team goal-setting

➤ Structuring the work

➤ Making job descriptions meaningful

➤ The elements of team success

In order for a team to be successful, the team leader and team members have to rethink their jobs. Past methods and processes must be reevaluated in light of the new structure. Ideas, held sacred by some, must be scrapped, and new concepts, often strange and frightening, must be adopted. It takes trust, faith, and courage to move into unknown areas, but the payoff will make it worth the effort.

Overcoming Resistance to Teams

When any change is made in the way an organization operates, the people in the organization are scared. Change of any type is scary, and when people fear that the changes may affect—even jeopardize—their jobs, their hackles go up and they're ready to fight it.

Getting Top Management's Support

You'd think that the senior managers of an organization would be savvy enough to recognize the advantages of teams, and, having read about the success of teams in other organizations, knowledgeable enough. Yet, they often resist converting to teams. Why?

In a team setup, the team leaders and team managers make decisions that are currently made by senior managers. Some may resent this loss of control; others may not have confidence in the abilities of lower ranking employees to make good decisions.

FYI

Some of the companies that have been most successful in implementing team systems are Boeing, Unisys, Proctor and Gamble, GE, Harley-Davidson, Xerox, and Blue Cross/Blue Shield.

There's no way the changeover to teams will work unless top executives in the organization are convinced of its value and give it full support.

Here's a good example of how I handled such a situation. The CEO of a housewares distributor attended a seminar I conducted and was sold on the concept of using teams. He retained me to assist the company make the change. Despite the CEO's enthusiasm, the other senior executives were opposed to changing a system they considered to be working well.

Knowing that unless these executives were as excited about the change as the CEO the program would never get off the ground, I spent the first few weeks concentrating on them.

First, I gave them articles from trade and professional journals describing successful team programs. I arranged for each of them to visit an executive of a firm in which teams were operating, and observe them in action.

Second, I asked them to identify some specific situations on which they were currently working, and we discussed how teams could deal with them.

Third, to deal with these situations, we set up three teams to work on a three-month trial period. I arranged for intensive training of the team leaders and team members in the process of how teams operate and then put them to work.

The executives were able to see the teams in action, note their approaches, and measure results. At the end of the trial period, all were enthusiastic about teams.

Fighting Supervisors' Fears

First-line supervisors have another dimension of concern. Many fear that their roles will be diminished and perhaps their jobs abolished. Most of the supervisors at the housewares company had worked long and hard to merit promotion to management and looked at the new program as a diminution of their status.

Team Builder

Assure new team leaders that if they lead rather than boss, their members will become more productive, so the leader will be able to spend more time on creative endeavors and less time putting out fires.

After an orientation session in which the team concept and examples of successful team programs were described, I had meetings with the individual supervisors to answer specific questions and calm qualms that they had.

Changing from supervisor to team leader is not accomplished overnight. It takes time and is sometimes difficult. First at the orientation meeting, and then in the one-to-one discussions, I pointed out how they would benefit from the change. A frequent comment from supervisors was, "If I let my team make decisions on what to do and how to do it, why do they need me?" I assured them that by delegating these functions, they would have more time to improve overall processes, tackle new projects, and broaden the scope of their jobs. I also assured them that I, along with their senior managers, would be available to help them over the hurdles of getting this new approach underway.

Overcoming Members' Fears

One concern that team members have is that their personal accomplishments will be overshadowed by the team's. Another concern, particularly among the more productive workers, is that they will be penalized because of the poorer performance of less productive team members.

One ingredient of successful team programs is a rewards and recognition program that does consider both individual and team efforts. If such a program is in place, tell them how it works. If it is still under study, tell them you will keep them advised of its progress.

Many people are concerned about their ability to handle the changes in the way the work is done. They consider themselves experts in the current ways and fear they may not have the know-how or capability to change. Assure them that they will be involved in determining the changes that are to be made and that training and support are built into the program.

Heads Up!

Team members: Don't take a negative attitude. Look upon the changes in the work environment as challenges that will help you grow and increase your value to the company.

If it is a newly created team, there is another concern. They don't know their new teammates. A first step is for the members to get to know each other. At the first meeting, have them introduce themselves, tell about their families, their interests, their professional or occupational training, and their work experience. Give the members the opportunity to talk to one another over coffee or lunch. Like a good host, encourage them to mingle and spend some time with each other.

Setting the Team's Goals

As noted in the last chapter, setting goals and working to achieve them is basic to the success of any enterprise, and teams are no exception. The team may set long-term goals to carry out its mission and short-term goals for specific projects. Team goals must be congruent with the goals of the department the team is part of, and of the overall organization.

The Components of a Good Team Goal

The team's mission or long-term goal is usually broad. It expresses the overall purpose of the team, such as "developing marketing plans," "improving quality," or "reducing workplace accidents."

Long-term goals keep the team focused on its main purposes and enable the members to concentrate their efforts and not digress into other areas.

While a team may set its long-term goals just once, it must frequently set project or short-term goals. A good team goal has several components:

➤ **Purpose of the project:** What is the nature of the assignment? For example: to develop a program to increase the number of sites for placing automated-teller machines.

➤ **Source:** To whom will the finished report be submitted? For example: This project was ordered by the new product marketing manager.

➤ **Performance standards:** How will we know we're successful? For example: This project will have been satisfactorily completed when we have provided a marketing plan, an implementation plan, and a control system.

➤ **Timetable:** When must each phase be completed? For example: Phase 1 research, completed July 22; report completed August 15; Phase 2, research completed September 12; report completed October 10.

Collaborative Goal Setting

If, as the old expression goes, "Two heads are better than one," then ten heads are a lot better than two. When a team is involved in setting goals, suggestions and ideas come from all team members. Not only are more suggestions generated, the interaction of the group increases the quantity and quality of these ideas significantly.

Some other advantages of having the team collaborate in goal setting are

Team Builder

Before you can set a goal, you must have a vision—the ideal that you wish to achieve. A perfect example of a well-stated vision was President Kennedy's pronouncement: "We will put a man on the moon in this decade."

➤ By encouraging members to participate, it gives each member the opportunity for personal learning and growth.

➤ Members have a clear sense of what is expected.

➤ Success of the project is enhanced because when people participate in setting a goal, they are more likely to work hard to achieve it. "It's my goal, I have to make it succeed."

➤ Collaboration reinforces the importance of team members supporting each other in implementing the goals.

➤ As each team member knows what performance results are expected by every other member, he or she can measure progress and take the initiative to correct deviations from goals in a timely manner.

Getting Support for the Process

At a recent goal-setting seminar, one participant complained, "I have trouble getting people to buy in to the big-picture concept. They're so absorbed in the individual phases of their jobs that they can't see beyond their own problems."

Here's how you can overcome this type of situation:

➤ Bring everyone on your team into the early stages of the planning process.

➤ Discuss the major points of the overall plan.

➤ Ask each person to describe how he or she will fit in to the big-picture plan.

➤ Give each person a chance to comment on each stage of the project.

➤ Point out that differing opinions are encouraged and how this leads to a consensus on decisions.

Breaking a long-term goal into bite-size pieces that people can relate to can help people see how their part in a project fits together with the others. It can also help them set overall team goals for the long run.

Setting Realistic Goals

Are you ready to set your goals? To prevent yours from ending up just pipe dreams, make sure that they meet the following three conditions:

➤ **Clear and specific:** It's not enough to state that the team goal is "to improve market share of our product." Be specific. (For example, "Market share of our product will increase from its current 12 percent to 18 percent in five years.")

FYI

"The way to achieve success is first to have a definite, clear, practical ideal—a goal, an objective. Second, have the necessary means to achieve your ends: Wisdom, money, materials, methods. Third, adjust all your means to that end."

—Aristotle

➤ **Attainable:** Pie-in-the-sky goals are self-defeating. If the team can see its progress in reaching its goals, it will have the incentive to continue working to accomplish them; it won't if the goals seem completely unattainable.

➤ **Measurable:** A system by which members can measure progress should be built into the goal.

➤ **Time strictured:** Most goals are expected to be accomplished in a specific time period. Members should be aware of these deadlines so they can work to reach them.

➤ **Flexible:** Sometimes a goal just can't be reached. Circumstances may change: What once seemed viable may no longer be. Don't be frustrated. The team should rethink the situation and adjust the goal.

Project goals should include

➤ Description of the project.

➤ Why the project is important for the team.

➤ Results expected.

➤ How project fits into the overall organization's goals.

➤ Timetable for completion of each phase.

➤ Resources: budgets, information, administrative assistance, materials, equipment.

➤ Each member's role in the project.

Once each member is aware of the objectives of the project and his or her role in it and is committed to its achievement, the project will move along smoothly.

Redesign the Way Work Is Done

When teams are formed, the old manner in which the work had been done is no longer effective. Instead of the focus being on individual jobs, it's now on the job of the entire team. True, there will be some members who will continue to perform specialized tasks, but these will be looked upon as part of the team effort rather than as separate jobs.

Establish Ground Rules

A team that has worked together for a long time usually has developed an understanding of how to get the job done in the most efficient manner. When a new team is created, it may take much trial and error before it reaches a smooth-flowing operation.

To speed up this process, the team should establish a set of ground rules. These should include

➤ **How decisions will be made:** By majority vote? by consensus? by the subgroup that faces the problem?

➤ **Basic work methods:** Decide at the outset which phases will be performed by the entire team, by subgroups, or assigned to individual members.

➤ **How issues and concerns will be handled:** Members should be able to bring their concerns to the attention of the team at regular meetings. Some teams require members to present their concerns in writing via memos or e-mail to the entire team before the meeting. Provision should be made for dealing with emergency matters.

Team Terms

Consensus does not mean unanimous agreement. Consensus results after the problem is expressed by the team and compromises are made. Everybody may not agree on every detail, but members believe it to be a sound decision that they willingly support.

➤ **Resolving differences:** By establishing a procedure for resolving differences, much time and rancor can be avoided. The team leader may mediate or arbitrate disagreements (see Chapter 11) or in self-directed teams (see Chapter 24), a third person can be chosen to help resolve the differences.

Heads Up!

Don't assume that what has worked well in the past is the best approach for the present or the future, or that just because an approach isn't new, it's outdated or useless.

Challenge the Status Quo

Shifting from work groups to teams involves change. As pointed out, most people resist change and will find any excuse to keep things the way they are.

Often, when faced with changes in the way work is performed, the reaction is, "But we've always done it this way."

Complacency with the status quo is pervasive. People look for any excuse to keep things the way they always have been. To make changes in the way work is done, members have to be sold on the benefits of the changes.

Another reason people may give for keeping things the way they are is, "If it ain't broke, don't fix it," or its companion comment, "Don't mess with success."

There's no question that many of the processes, procedures, and methods in which work has been done has been successful. Change should not be made just for the sake of change. The point is that, even if the process "ain't broke" and works fine, it should be looked at to see what changes might be made so it will be even more effective when converted to a team activity.

Make Job Design a Team Effort

A team consists of members who possess a variety of skills that can be unified to achieve the team's objectives. Who does what should be clear, consistent with the direction of the team. All members should know where they fit into the overall picture and how, by working together, they will accomplish much more than they could as individuals.

In designing the jobs that the team will perform, the team leader should take advantage of the know-how and experience of all of the members. Just as team goals are more effective when determined by the entire team, so is the design of the job—the processes and methods used to carry out the goals.

In their best-selling book *Reengineering the Corporation,* Hammer and Champy note that in reengineering, the most important phase is the process in which work is done. They define process as a collection of activities that takes one or more kinds of input and creates an output that is of value to the end user.

Since the beginning of the industrial revolution, work was broken down into its simplest tasks and each task assigned to a worker. In most companies today the focus is still on the individual tasks in the process, and team members often lose sight of the purpose of their tasks, which is to provide a satisfactory product or service to the customer. Individual tasks within the process are important, but unless they contribute to the success of the total process, the objectives will not be met.

The team concept lends itself to designing work that has the process in the forefront and looks at individual tasks as components of this process.

Once the team members are oriented to appreciate the subordination of their individual tasks to the entire process, the team is on the way to reaching its goals.

Team Terms

The fastest growing segment of the work force is **knowledge workers.** Instead of manufacturing products, keeping records, or selling merchandise, they invent products, innovate changes, develop systems, create concepts, plan projects, and keep their organizations ahead of the pack.

One way to start getting members to think "process" instead of "task" is to involve them in the writing of the job descriptions for each of the jobs the team performs.

Traditional job descriptions are task oriented. They indicate how a job should be done step by step. To fit the job description into the team concept, instead of listing tasks, it should focus on the desired results. Once this is clarified, the steps needed to attain these results and the criteria by which they will be measured should be specified.

More details on how a team can prepare job descriptions will be found in Chapter 7.

In today's business world, more and more jobs fall into the category of "knowledge work." Unlike manual laborers and clerical workers, whose jobs can easily be categorized and broken into tasks, the contribution of the *knowledge worker* is difficult to quantify. Job descriptions for such people must focus on results desired, as there is no way to specify tasks. Teams of knowledge workers must clearly define the expectations they set for themselves and specify how each member can contribute to it.

The Four C's of Team Success

How can you recognize a successful team? It has four basic qualities.

Collegiality

Members of successful teams work as colleagues. Each respects the intelligence and capabilities of the other members.

When DBC, an industrial equipment manufacturer, formed its customer service team, it had high hopes the team would improve the company's relations with its customers.

Here was the problem: Customers were complaining that orders were not being received when promised, and that often accessories that were supposed to be shipped with the equipment were not included. In addition, it often took several calls before the customer could arrange for shipment of the missing items.

Investigation uncovered several problems: Sales reps would promise delivery without checking with the production department. Orders for accessories were processed separately from the order for the equipment. Shipping of orders was not coordinated.

The solution: Form a task force consisting of sales reps, production schedulers, order processors, and shipping clerks for each region. Then, have them set up and implement a system to correct the problem.

What happened? The team never really got off the ground. The team members couldn't see eye-to-eye on anything. Members representing each department cast aspersions on the capabilities of the other departments.

I was retained to help work this out. It didn't take long to see that the members perceived their roles as defenders of their departments, and the other members as the enemy. My first move was to get them to agree on the team's purpose. I then asked them to spend 10 minutes with each of their fellow team members, as a start on getting to know each person as an individual.

The immediate result: Once they accepted each other as colleagues working to solve a problem, not as competitors, or combatants defending themselves against the others, the air cleared and we were able to start working.

Team Builder

When team members are drawn from several departments, it's essential for them to understand that, for the team to succeed, they must put the goal of the team ahead of protecting the interests of their respective departments.

Long-term result: A new system was developed to overcome the problems. Permanent teams were established for each region. Their members, like those in the task force, coordinated the processing of all orders, from initial sale to final delivery.

One year later, the CEO told me that customer complaints had dropped significantly, and that the teams were working so well he was planning to establish similar teams for other company activities.

Collaboration

Once team members are melded into a team of colleagues, they are prepared to *collaborate* in working toward the achievement of the team's goals.

Most of the inventions of the premodern age were developed by one person: a Thomas Edison, a James

Watt, an Eli Whitney. In our much more complex age, most of the major inventions and discoveries come from collaborative efforts. The engineers at Bell Labs created the transistor; the unraveling of DNA was a collaborative effort of Francis H. Crick and James D. Watson; the joint work of Steven Jobs and Steven Wozniak led to the Apple computer.

When people collaborate in working on a problem, the interaction stimulates the thinking of every member of the team, resulting in a wide range of ideas and many options for resolving problems.

The effective leader of a collaborative team encourages each member to take an active role in discussions, to share information and suggestions, and to participate fully in making decisions.

Coordination

Remember the example of the rocket in Chapter 2? Even if every component of that rocket functions perfectly, in order for it to blast off, everything must be synchronized; in other words, coordinated.

The team is like that rocket. Part of the team leader's responsibility is to hone the skills of each team member, but an equally important responsibility is to coordinate the activities of the team. This is the test of true leadership. The ideal team works together seamlessly to achieve its goals.

Coordination starts with each member knowing his or her role and how it meshes with the roles of the other members. In a well-coordinated team, members can anticipate every action teammates will take and be prepared to react to it. Look at a championship sports team for an example of perfect coordination. Watch the basketball or the hockey puck pass from player to player on the way toward scoring a goal.

Team coordination is not as dramatic in the business world, but it is just as important. Coordinated teams move smoothly toward their goals; lack of coordination results in conflicts, wasted time and effort, and eventual failure.

Coaching

To bring the first three "C's" together is the function of the fourth "C," coaching. The team leader is the team's coach. The main function of the team leader is to propel the team toward its goals.

Team Terms

Collegiality: The working together of two or more people as colleagues, each considered as equal to the other.

Collaboration: The act of working together by sharing information, ideas, and actions.

Coordination: Synchronizing the activities of the team for smooth flow of its actions toward the ultimate goal.

Team Builder

The best way a team leader can "sell" ideas to the team is to present them as the skeletons of an idea and ask members to flesh them out. In this way the team plays a significant role in developing the concept.

To do this, the coach guides the team to set its goals, trains the team in the skills needed to achieve those goals, works with the team to coordinate the members' actions, and motivates them to work creatively toward those goals. In a collaborative, *collegial*, coordinated team, coaching is not limited to the team leader's province, but is part of every member's job.

In truly collaborative teams, the team leader is the first among equals—a colleague, not a boss. Coaching becomes a function of every team member. If a member needs special training, the team leader can ask another member to coach her. If another member seems to be losing motivation, the team leader may delegate coaching him to another member, who, perhaps, had overcome a similar problem in the past.

Using all members as coaches expands the value of coaching and supplements the team leader's efforts to keep the team in tip-top shape.

How the leader can function as a coach is discussed in Chapter 8.

See if your team is on the road to success. Answer these questions:

Yes	No	1. Is the team's mission clear to all team members?
Yes	No	2. Is the purpose of the project or assignment understood by members?
Yes	No	3. Are individual roles clearly defined?
Yes	No	4. Are timetables set for each phase of the project?
Yes	No	5. Do all team members know and accept the performance standards set for their work?
Yes	No	6. Are processes and methods periodically reexamined and adjusted if desirable?
Yes	No	7. Is there a procedure established for making decisions?
Yes	No	8. Is there a procedure established for resolving disagreements among members?
Yes	No	9. Are all team members committed to working collaboratively?
Yes	No	10. Is the team leader functioning as a supportive and inspirational coach?

You can't be a successful coach unless you first determine the specific coaching needs of each of your team members. Work on them. It will pay off, not only in the better performance of members, but in the overall performance of the entire team.

The Least You Need to Know

➤ For a changeover to teams to work, top executives in the organization must be convinced of its value and give it full support.

➤ When first-line supervisors fear that their roles will be diminished and perhaps their jobs abolished, show them how they will benefit from the change.

➤ Team members must be carefully oriented about their new roles and assured that they'll get training and support to master them.

➤ Long-term goals keep the team focused on its main purposes and enable the members to focus their efforts.

➤ When all team members make suggestions and help set goals, more and better suggestions are generated by the group interaction.

➤ Breaking a long-term goal into bite-size pieces helps people see how their part in a project fits together with the others, and with overall team goals.

➤ To be realistic, goals should be clear and specific, attainable, and flexible.

➤ To make changes in the way work is done, members have to be sold on the benefits of those changes.

➤ Just as team goals are more effective when determined by the entire team, so is the design of the job: the processes and methods used to carry out the goals.

➤ In the team concept the process is in the forefront, and individual tasks are components of that process.

➤ Members of successful teams work as colleagues. Each respects the intelligence and capabilities of the other members.

➤ In truly collaborative teams, the team leader is the first among equals—a colleague, not a boss. Coaching is a function of the leader, but also of every team member.

Part 2

Molding a Group Into a Working Team

You're a team leader. Should we congratulate you or commiserate with you? You have your work cut out for you. It's no easy task to mold a group of individuals—each with his or her own skills, experience, philosophy, and mindset, into a creative, contributing, collaborative team.

What do you need to get started? You have to learn to lead. The old days, when the boss gave orders and expected subordinates to carry them out, have long since passed. Today's leader is not a boss, but a facilitator, coordinator, and above all, a motivator.

The seeds of success have been planted in all of us. Now it's up to you to cultivate those seeds so they grow into flourishing plants. The food you need to fertilize these plants is the knowledge of the tools of leadership.

In the following chapters you will find this fertilizer—the basics of molding a team that will be a productive contributor to your organization's success.

Chapter 4

Communication: The Lifeblood of Team Success

In This Chapter

➤ The importance of exchanging ideas

➤ Communicating effectively

➤ Learning to listen

➤ Barriers to communication

It has been said that communication is the lifeblood of organizations. If this is true, then the blood vessels in most organizations are clogged with cholesterol. In order for ideas, data, instructions, and other essential information to flow smoothly, those conduits must be cleared out.

Everybody in the organization is a communicator. Whether you are a top executive, a middle manager, a team leader, or an associate on one of the teams, you can do your part in making communications more effective.

In this chapter you will learn some of the strategies and tactics that will help reduce the clots that block your communications to your team, and equally important, communications from your team to you—a major step in becoming a more successful team leader.

The Team That Talks Together Walks Together

One of the key factors in team success is conversation. This is more than just chit-chat, more than just sharing job-related data, more than just exchanging ideas. It is all of these put together plus that intangible aura of mutual trust and confidence that permeates the truly collaborative team.

Team Terms

Communication takes place when persons or groups exchange information, ideas, and concepts.

Did you ever work in a setting where everybody concentrated on his or her own assignments, speaking to others only when absolutely necessary to get or give information? Sure, the work gets done, but that's all that's accomplished. No creative concepts, no new approaches, no synergism. This is a work group—not a team.

Now visualize an office where seven team members are seated at desks and tables. Computer screens are flashing, telephones are ringing. Some get up and talk to other associates, in twos or threes or more. Chaos? Not at all. They are engaged in projects in which intrateam *communication* is essential. Result: not just a smooth-working team, but an innovative, enthusiastic crew.

The Interactive Workplace

Scott Adams, who worked in his cubicle at a major corporation for many years before becoming a world-famous satirical cartoonist, has poked fun in his "Dilbert" comic strip at the foibles and idiosyncrasies of corporate America.

One of his chief targets of ridicule is the partitioned cubicle in which a great percentage of employees in the lower levels of the corporate structure work.

Why cubicles? They do serve a functional purpose. Before the cubicles existed, most office employees worked in large offices with desks lined up in rows. There was no privacy. Telephone conversations could be heard by everybody in the vicinity. Workers were discouraged from leaving their desks. The supervisor's desk was in the front or back of the room so he or she could observe the employees. Some years ago, the open workplace was redesigned with cubicles.

Team collaboration is best accomplished on a face-to-face basis. Meetings are one obvious way to achieve this, but informal chats are often more convenient, and because they are unstructured, more likely to develop constructive results.

In the high-tech companies in Silicon Valley and elsewhere, the cubicle has been replaced with a team-friendly office layout. Let's visit the office of a software developer in San Jose.

FYI

The cubicle was created as a boon to the employees. It provided them with a modicum of privacy and a space they could call their own. It even gave them some freedom from constant surveillance by their boss.

No cubicles. No private offices. In the center of the room is a conference table. Around it several people are discussing a problem. Other men and women are working at desks scattered around the room. Where's the team leader? the group manager? They're there, among the team members. Instead of having elegant private offices, they have the same type desks and computers as their associates. They participate in group discussions. There are no physical barriers or officious secretaries to keep team members from speaking to them. There is a continuous flow of associates around the room. If privacy is needed for conferring with clients or for training sessions or special meetings, several conference rooms are available.

This allows easy access of all team members to all other team members. It encourages chatting and idea sharing. It breaks the barriers between team members and team leaders.

Get Everybody Into the Act

Charlie J. complained to his buddy Sal, "I can't figure it out. When I ask my team members to come up with new ideas, I rarely get one that's any good. In fact, most of the guys never even make a suggestion. And you tell me your team members are constantly bringing up stuff. How do you do it?"

Sal replied, "Charlie, I've watched you over the years. You barely listen to team members; you squash their ideas without giving them a chance to discuss them; and when a good idea is given, you pooh-pooh it and say you'd already thought of that. You gotta recognize that even though you are the leader, this is a team of bright men and women who want to help, if you'll only give them a chance."

Team Builder

To create an interactive communicative climate, continually ask team members, "What would you do if you were in my position?" Listen to their responses and encourage them to keep thinking about the problems and bringing you additional suggestions.

47

Charlie is typical of many old-school supervisors. They feel that their position requires them to be the idea-generator, and that the others should just accept what the supervisor says and do the work. This is not the case with teams. Charlie should emulate Sal.

Here are 10 valuable tips on how to develop an open and participative climate for your team:

1. Share all pertinent information with your team.

2. Encourage all team members to share information with each other.

3. At meetings, elicit ideas and information from all attendees.

4. Keep an "open door." Team members should feel free to bring you problems and suggestions.

5. Expect team members to bring you bad news as soon as possible, and don't "shoot the messenger."

6. Let team members know in a timely way about information that affects them.

7. Encourage team members to express disagreement or differing viewpoints.

8. Don't express disapproval of their comments either verbally or nonverbally. When appropriate, rebut in a nonconfrontational manner.

9. Answer questions and comments as soon as possible and as fully as possible.

10. Reinforce your commitment to open communications by expressing appreciation for their participation, their suggestions, and their critiques.

Once the team members recognize and accept that their input is not only welcome but is sincerely encouraged, the quantity and quality of their ideas will increase significantly.

Heads Up!

Don't be like Samuel Goldwyn, the movie mogul who once said, "I don't want to be surrounded by yes-men. I want people to express their opinions—even if it costs them their job."

Communications: A Two-Way Radio

On one radio a person sends a message; the person on the second radio receives it. At any time, however, the roles can be reversed. The receiver becomes the sender, the sender the receiver. They talk back and forth.

Effective communication requires that the receiver gets that message clearly and understands it. As with a radio, interference may distort the communication, causing the receiver to misunderstand what is being sent. The sender may not realize that the message is not being received as intended.

The source of the interference lies with the transmitter, or with the receiver, or between the two. Just as in radio transmission, the interference is referred to as "static" or "noise."

The following chart shows some of these statics over the channels of communication between sender and receiver:

From Sender	From Receiver
What Is Said	*Listening*
Lack of information	Hearing only what you expect
Poor organization of ideas	*Prejudice*
Failure to know audience	*Halo effect*
How It's Said	
Poor articulation	
Poor word choice	
Nonverbal Signals	
Failing to read or understand body language	
Attitude of Sender	
Lack of Sensitivity to Receiver	

Now let's explore them and how they can be overcome.

Our Body Talks, Too

People communicate not only through words but also through their facial expressions and body movements. If there were only a dictionary of body language, we could easily interpret what those signs signify. But because body language isn't standardized like verbal language, no such dictionary could be written.

The way we use our body is influenced by our cultural or ethnic background, the way our parents expressed themselves nonverbally, and other individual experiences. Body language differs from one person to another. Some gestures—a nod or a smile—may seem universal, but not everyone uses body language in the same way. When you're dealing with a specific person, you can't be sure that he or she is giving signals you have come to expect.

Team Terms

The **halo effect:** If you greatly admire the speaker, you put a figurative halo over his or her head and are inclined to accept whatever he or she says. The opposite is called the **pitchfork effect** (the symbol of the devil). If you fervently dislike the speaker, you'll discount anything that's said.

FYI

Did you know that listeners get at least 65 percent of a message through body language? Experts say that body language can cancel or reinforce what words say. "Great communicators" like Ronald Reagan paid special attention to their gestures, facial expressions, and body movements when they spoke.

As you talk, your listener is nodding. Good, you assume that she's agreeing with you. Not necessarily so. There are some people who nod just to acknowledge that they're listening. When someone folds his arms as you speak you might think his action is a subconscious show of disagreement, but it could simply be that she's cold! There is danger in misreading nonverbal cues.

Take the time to learn each person's body language. Study the body language of people with whom you work. You may notice that when John smiles in a certain way, it has one meaning; a different smile, a different meaning. Or maybe when Jane doesn't agree, she wrinkles her forehead. Make a conscious effort to study and remember people's individual body languages.

Listening: More Than Just Hearing

Let's say that one of your colleagues brings a problem to you and asks for help. At first you listen attentively. But it's not long before your mind begins to wander. Instead of listening to the problem, you're thinking about other things: the pile of work on your desk, the meeting you have scheduled with the company vice president, the problems one of your children is having at school. You hear your colleague's words, but you're not really listening.

Does this happen to you? Of course, it does. It happens to all of us. Why? Our minds can process ideas 10 times faster than we can talk. While someone is talking, your mind may race ahead. You complete the speaker's sentence in your mind—often incorrectly—long before the speaker does. You "hear" what your mind dictates, not what's actually said.

This is human nature. You must anticipate that it will happen, and you must be alert and take steps to overcome it so that you can learn to truly listen.

Picking Up the Pieces

Now suppose that your mind was wandering and that you didn't hear what the other person said. It's embarrassing to admit that you weren't listening, so you fake it. You pick up on the last few words you heard and comment on them. Sometimes you get back on track, but often you may have missed the real gist of the discussion.

When you haven't been listening, you don't have to admit, "I'm sorry, I was daydreaming." One way to get back on track is to ask a question or make a comment about the last item you did hear: "Can we go back a minute to such-and-such?"

Team Terms

An **active listener** not only pays close attention to what the other party says, but asks questions, makes comments, and reacts verbally and nonverbally to what is said.

Another method is to comment this way: "To make sure that I can better understand your view on this, please elaborate."

Listening Actively

One way of improving your listening skills is to be an *active listener*. Instead of just sitting or standing with your ears open, follow these guidelines:

➤ Look at the speaker. Eye contact is one way of showing interest, but don't overdo it. Look at the whole person, don't just stare into his or her eyes.

➤ Show interest by your facial expressions. Smile or show concern when appropriate.

➤ Indicate that you are following the conversation by nods or gestures.

➤ Ask questions about what's being said. You can paraphrase "So the way I understand it is ..." or ask specific questions about specific points. This technique not only enables you to clarify points that may be unclear but also keeps you alert and paying full attention.

➤ Don't interrupt. A pause should not be a signal for you to start talking. Wait.

➤ Be an empathic listener. Listen with your heart as well as your head. Try to feel what other people are feeling when they speak. In other words, put yourself in the speaker's shoes.

Team Builder

In presenting your views, follow the TEAM acronym:

Tell what is expected.

Explain reasons.

Answer questions from the team.

Motivate team to action.

Five Strategies to Make You a Better Listener

You can become a better listener. You can stop some of the main causes of ineffective listening before they begin. All you have to do is make a few changes in your work environment and in your approach to listening: a small effort with a big return.

1. **Shut off the telephone.** The greatest distraction is probably the telephone. You want to give the speaker your full attention—and the phone rings. Answering the call not only interrupts your discussion but also disrupts the flow of your thoughts. Even after you've hung up, your mind may still be pondering the call.

   If you know that you'll be having a lengthy discussion at your desk, arrange for someone else to handle your calls or set your voice mail to pick up all calls right away. If this isn't possible, get away from the telephone. Try an empty conference room: The phone there won't distract you, and no one knows that you're there—so it probably won't ring.

2. **Hide the papers.** If your desk is strewn with papers, you'll probably sit there skimming them until you realize too late that you're reading a letter or memo instead of listening. If you go to a conference room, take only the papers that are related to the discussion. If you must stay at your desk, put the papers in a drawer so that you won't be tempted to read them.

3. **Don't get too comfortable.** Some years ago I was discussing a situation with another manager. As was my custom, I sat in my comfortable executive chair with my hands behind my head. Maybe I rocked a little, but fortunately, I caught myself before I dozed off.

   Ever since then, rather than take a relaxing position when I engage in discussions, I've made a point of sitting on the edge of my chair and leaning forward rather than backward when engaged in discussions. This position not only brings me physically closer to the other person, but also enables me to be more attentive, and helps me to maintain eye contact. It also shows the other person that I'm truly interested in getting the full story he or she is relating and that I take seriously what is being said. And because I'm not quite so comfortable, there's less of a tendency to daydream.

4. **Don't think about your rebuttal.** It's tempting to pick up one or two points that the speaker is making and plan how you will respond to them. Do this and you'll probably miss much of the balance of what is being said, often the really important matters. Concentrate on what is said through the entire process.

5. **Take notes.** It's impossible to remember everything that's said in a lengthy discussion. Jot down key words or phrases. Write down figures or important facts, just enough to help you remember. Immediately after a meeting, while the information is still fresh in your mind, write a detailed summary. Dictate it into a recorder, enter it into your computer, or write it in your notebook, whichever is best for you.

Evaluate Your Listening Skills

Yes	No	1. Do you keep interrupting when somebody is trying to tell you something?
Yes	No	2. Do you look at papers during the discussion?
Yes	No	3. Do you come to conclusions before you hear the whole story?
Yes	No	4. Does your body language signal lack of interest?
Yes	No	5. Do you hear only what you want to hear and block out everything else?
Yes	No	6. Do you show impatience with speaker?
Yes	No	7. Do you spend more time talking than listening?
Yes	No	8. Does your mind wander during the discussion?
Yes	No	9. Do you think about your rebuttal or responses while the other person is speaking?
Yes	No	10. Do you ignore nonverbal signals from the speaker that will tell you the speaker wants you to respond?

If you answered "yes" to any of these questions, you should concentrate on improving your listening skills.

You Think You're Communicating—But Are You?

Some of the major statics that impede communication are psychological, not physical. You may have perfect articulation and choose your words wisely, but the static develops in intangible areas: assumptions, attitudes, and the emotional baggage each of us has.

Check Out Your Assumptions

You've seen this situation repeatedly. You have a pretty good idea about what causes a particular problem and how to solve it. In discussing it with others, you assume that they know as much about it as you do, so what you say is based on the assumption that they have know-how that they don't have. The result is that you don't give them adequate information. Static!

What's Your Attitude?

Another barrier to communication is the attitudes of the sender and the receiver. A team leader who is arrogant will convey this feeling in the way directions and information are given. He or she may appear to be talking down to team members. This causes resentment, which blocks communication. In order for the message to be received, it must not only be understood but accepted by the receiver. When resentment develops, acceptance is unlikely.

Watch for Preconceptions

People tend to hear what they expect to hear. The message you receive is distorted by any information you have already heard about the subject. So if the new information is different from what's expected, you might reject it as being incorrect. Rather than actually hearing the new message, you may be hearing what your mind is telling you.

What does this mean to you? Keep your mind open. When someone tells you something, make an extra effort to listen and to evaluate the new information objectively, instead of blocking it out because it differs from your preconceptions.

In communicating with others, also try to learn their preconceptions. If they are people you work with regularly, you probably know how they view many of the matters you discuss. When you present your views to them, take into consideration what they already believe. If their beliefs differ from yours, be prepared to make the effort to jump over those hurdles.

Prejudices and Biases—Yours and Theirs

Your biases for or against a person influence the way you receive his or her messages. We listen more attentively and are more likely to accept ideas from somebody we like and respect. Contrarily, we tend to blot out input from people we don't like, and reject their ideas.

Biases also affect the way subject matter is received. People turn a deaf ear to opposing viewpoints concerning matters about which they have strong feelings. Carol is a good example of such a person. As company controller, she is fixated on reducing costs. She won't even listen to any discussion that might increase costs no matter what the long-term benefits may be.

Be Aware of Your Emotional State

Heads Up!

Perception is reality in the mind of the perceiver. Unless your perception and team members' perceptions of a situation are congruent, you will be working at cross-purposes.

Did you ever have a bad day? Of course, we all do. And on one of those bad days, one of your team members comes to you all excited about a new idea. How do you react? Probably, you think, "I have enough on my platter now, who needs this?" Your mind is closed and the message doesn't come through.

It works both ways. An important assignment comes up and you go over to two of your team members, Dan and Joan, to discuss it. Joan is enthusiastic about the job; Dan is skeptical. Why? Dan is annoyed because he is busy working on another project and he wants to concentrate on it. He feels you are inconsiderate to assign him to this job.

Always test the temperature of the water before you step into the tub. A brief conversation with Dan and Joan about their current activities would have brought out how much time Dan was spending on his current project. When you present the new assignment, you make the point that what he is doing now is important, and you are happy with his progress. Show that the reason you chose him for the new assignment is that it won't interfere with, but will complement his current work.

Team Builder

Often, when two teams are working on a project together, much time and trouble can be saved if, on routine matters, members bypass team leaders and deal directly with their counterparts on the other team.

Channels: The Static Between Sender and Receiver

In communication the major source of interference and distortion is the path the message takes from sender to receiver. In many large organizations, communication must flow through set channels. The more extensive the channels, the more likely that distortion will occur. This can be illustrated in the popular party game where one person tells an incident to his or her neighbor, who repeats it to the next person, and this continues around the room. By the time it is retold to the originator, the story is completely different.

It is not unusual for a piece of information passed orally "through channels" to be distorted at each station, so that what the receiver receives is not at all what the sender sent.

One way to alleviate this difficulty is to use written communications. Writing is more difficult to distort, though interpretation of what is written may vary from station to station. Even so, writing has certain disadvantages: Many matters can't or shouldn't be communicated in writing. Writing is time consuming. For rush matters and matters of transient interest, writing is not appropriate.

A more effective way is to shorten channels and allow for bypassing where feasible. The fewer stations along the way, the less chance for distortion. The main reason for channels is to ensure that people who are responsible for a project are kept aware of everything that applies to it. This makes sense, but it is usually overdone. If a matter involves policy decisions or major areas of activity, channels are important. But a great portion of the communication in companies concerns routine matters. Using channels for these not only may distort the message but will slow down the work.

The Feedback Loop

The sender must always be sensitive to how the receiver receives and accepts the message. One way of checking on how messages have come across is the feedback loop.

One way feedback can be obtained is by asking questions. But you have to ask the right questions. The most commonly asked question is, "Do you understand?" But that's not a good question because the answer can be misleading. Most people will say yes. But this doesn't mean that the receiver really *does* understand. He or she may be ashamed to say no for fear of being considered stupid, or may honestly believe he or she does understand, but actually comprehends only part of the message, or interprets it quite differently from how it was intended.

The sender sends information to the receiver. The receiver responds. Reaction to the message is immediately fed back to the sender, who makes appropriate corrections and adjustments. The message is revised and a new message is sent. The sender continues to get feedback until there is assurance that the communication is clearly completed.

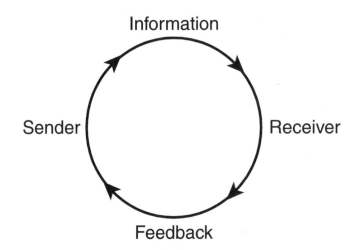

A better approach is to be more specific. Ask, "So that we both understand what you are going to do, let's go over it again," or, "Tell me how you view this." Another approach is to ask questions about the key points, to ensure that they are fully understood.

The Least You Need to Know

➤ Establish an interactive work environment by creative office layout and an atmosphere of open communication.

➤ Whether you're presenting your ideas to a group or to just one person, prepare what you're going to say before you say it.

➤ Speak clearly and distinctly so that you'll be easily understood. Speak with enthusiasm so that your audience doesn't fall asleep.

➤ Listen! Train your mind to listen actively and empathetically. Put yourself in the other person's shoes.

➤ Communication can be distorted by preconceptions, biases, and the emotional state of the participants. Be aware of these factors and be prepared to deal with them.

➤ Open up the channels of communication so that they can be bypassed for routine matters.

Chapter 5

Say It Right—
Write It Right

In This Chapter

➤ Preparing to communicate

➤ Say it right

➤ Write it right

➤ KISS—Keep It Simple, Stupid!

➤ Cybercommunication

➤ Composing impressive reports

Whether you are a team leader or a team member, a good portion of your work involves communication with others in the organization and with outsiders, such as customers, vendors, and subcontractors. Some of this will be done orally, either in one-to-one conversations or at meetings where you will address several people. Some will be done in writing. You'll write letters, memos, faxes, and e-mail. In this chapter we'll explore how to communicate most effectively both orally and when, as they used to say, you put pen to paper.

Communication Effectiveness

Whether the communication is oral or in writing, preparation is important. To be most effective follow these guidelines.

Know Your Subject

Learn as much as you can about what you are communicating. Here are some tips on starting the assignment:

➤ Gather all possible information about your topic. Jot down ideas, key words, and phrases.

➤ Use all research sources within and outside the company to saturate yourself with information.

➤ Be sure to learn about the latest developments in the area you will discuss.

➤ Identify the major points you wish to make.

➤ Organize facts to support your main points.

➤ Prepare notes to ensure you cover every point.

➤ Be aware of the objections to your ideas and be prepared to discuss and rebut them.

Know Your Audience

Even the most skilled orator or writer has failed to communicate effectively if the audience didn't understand the message. Whether your audience is just your own team or a large group, choose words that your listeners or readers will easily understand. If the people you're addressing all come from a technical background, you can use technical terminology. Your listeners and readers will clearly and readily understand these special terms. But if you present technical subject matter to an audience unfamiliar with it, skip the technical language. If your audience can't understand your vocabulary, your message will be lost.

It's easier to communicate with your own team. You all speak the same language, use the same terms, and usually have good knowledge of the subject. Within the team, tailor your message to their interests and know-how by using analogies to which you know they'll relate. For example, you can compare the new project with one they had previously worked on or refer to accomplishments or problems experienced in the past that will help them understand the matters being discussed.

When Communication Is Oral

In oral communication it's not just what you say but how you say it that determines how your message is received. Have you ever listened to a talk where the speaker was terrible? You strained to hear what he was saying, and even then couldn't understand every word. You fidgeted in your seat and couldn't wait for the end.

Do you come across that way to others? Few people realize how they sound because we don't hear ourselves as others hear us. In a public-speaking course I ask the students to give a brief introductory talk about something they really know and want to talk about. You'd think they would get up and breeze along with a fluent and interesting talk. Wrong! I tape the talks and play them back. The students are shocked. They never realized how they sounded.

Watch out for word-whiskers, those extra sounds, words, or phrases such as "er," "uh-huh," "y'know," and other extraneous noises. I once clocked a speaker who interjected "er" 12 times in five minutes. This is very distracting to your audience. Listen to yourself and shave off those "whiskers."

Here are some tips on the most common problems speakers experience and how to deal with them:

Team Builder

Use voice mail to hear how you sound to others. In many voice mail systems, you are given the option to listen to the message you left. Do it! The more often you listen to yourself, the more opportunity you have to learn to speak more clearly.

➤ **Mumbling.** The speaker swallows word endings, making it difficult to figure out what is said. This is easily overcome. Don't speak with a half-opened mouth. Open your lips fully when talking. Try practicing this in front of a mirror. It won't take long to correct this.

➤ **Speaking too fast or too slow.** Do you race ahead? Whoa! Give people a chance to absorb what you're saying. Or do you poke along? Your audience will jump ahead of you, anticipating what they think you are going to say. Keep speaking too slowly and you'll put them to sleep. Practice your talk. Time it. A good pace is between 130 and 150 words per minute. And don't forget to slow down when you want to make a point, and speed up to generate excitement.

➤ **Speaking in a monotone.** This is another sleep inducer. Modulate your voice. Vary volume, pitch, and pace.

➤ **Standing like a statue.** Use gestures to emphasize points.

➤ **Mispronouncing words.** If you're not sure of the pronunciation, look it up. If it's a person's name, ask that person what the correct pronunciation is.

➤ **Failing to observe and react to audience.** Are the troops getting restless? Pause. Change pace, introduce an interesting anecdote to get them back.

➤ **Listen to your voice.** We don't hear ourselves as others hear us. When we talk, perhaps our ears are too close to our mouths or our brains are too busy concentrating on the talking to pay attention to the hearing. Once you know your speech weaknesses, you can work on correcting them.

When the Communication Is in Writing

Most people consider written communication more formal than spoken. How often have you sat down to write something (a memo, a letter, or a fax, for example), knowing exactly what you wanted to say, but the right words just wouldn't come? It happens to everyone. Experts advise, "Just write it the way you would say it." Good idea, but when you boot up your computer, your mind goes blank.

TAB Your Thoughts

A good rule to follow is to carefully plan what you want to say before you write a single word. This simple process will help you plan your letter or memo. It can be summarized in the acronym TAB, which provides clues to help you think clearly about what you want to write before starting to writing it.

Think about the situation: Why am I writing this?

Action: What do I want to accomplish?

Benefit: How will this be of value?

Ask yourself these questions. Jot down the answers on a scratch pad. By "TAB-ing" your thoughts before you do the writing, you'll get a clear idea of what you want to convey. The list will help you organize all the information concerning the situation you're writing about; it will indicate what you want done, how to deal with it, and how those actions will benefit your readers.

Team Builder

Be precise. Be concise. Think of your memo, e-mail, or fax as a cable for which you must pay a dollar a word.

The Three C's

Once you've thought out the message, begin to formulate the way you'll write it. Keep in mind the three C's of good communication. Anything you put in writing must be

Clear: Easy to read and understand

Complete: Cover all the points

Concise: Keep it brief and to the point

For example, if you're writing a memo concerning the status of an order, be sure to respond to any specific questions. Include the order number, date of the order, identification of materials, and other pertinent information. Avoid going into extraneous details.

FYI

Lincoln's Gettysburg Address contained only 272 words—each word a gem.

Get to the Point

Steer clear of complex sentence constructions or extravagant phraseology. Keep it as brief as possible, but make it punchy. One way of making your points stand out is to write the item in the form of a bulletin:

Heads Up!

The "spell-check" feature in your word-processing program is a great help, as it catches most typos and misspellings, but you still have to reread the document carefully—spell check can't catch all of the mistakes.

➤ Headline your main point—use **bold** print.

➤ Break the body of the letter or memo into separate sections, one for each subsidiary point.

➤ Use an asterisk (*) or bullet (➤) to highlight key points.

➤ Where appropriate, use graphs, charts, or other visual aids to augment the impact of your words.

Watch Your Grammar and Spelling

You can't always depend on a secretary to correct your grammar, sentence structure, and spelling errors. Today, most team leaders don't have secretaries or administrative assistants. They write their own correspondence. Even if you're one of the lucky few who has an assistant, you should still check everything that goes out with your signature on it. If you are weak in grammar or spelling, seek out a colleague to be your in-company "editor" for constructive review and suggestions.

Write the Way You Speak

I'll bet you've never received a letter that read like this:

Pursuant to our telephonic conversation of even date, transmitted herewith are the invoices for the work completed through the ultimate month.

But that was how a typical business letter was written in the early part of the twentieth century.

Because many people believe one must be more formal when putting ideas on paper than when communicating them orally, they still use stilted language in letters. Formal language comes across as artificial and often insincere. Your message will be clearer and more easily accepted by the reader if you just write the way you speak.

That letter would have been much clearer if it had been written this way:

As promised when we spoke on the telephone, here are the invoices for the work completed through this month.

"Talk" Your Ideas onto Paper

As the old saying goes, "Keep it simple, stupid!" Pretend you're talking face-to-face or on the phone with the person who will read the letter. Be informal. Relax. Here are some suggestions to make your writing sound more like you.

➤ **Speak your thoughts** in your usual manner, with the vocabulary, accents, idioms, and expressions you usually use. You wouldn't normally say, "Please be advised that because of the fire in our plant there will be a 10-day delay in shipping your order." Instead you'd get right into the message: "Because of the fire in our plant, your shipping order will be delayed 10 days." So why not write just that?

➤ **Use contractions.** You rarely use full phrases such as "I do not want this" or "I will not be able to go." More likely, you say "I don't" or "I won't." Use these commonly used contractions in your writing. It makes your letter come across in a sincere and personal manner. Naturally, avoid slangy contractions like "ain't." You shouldn't use such language when speaking, either.

➤ **Ask questions.** Oral conversation isn't one sided. First, one person speaks, then the other comments or asks a question such as, "If we do that, how will it affect sales to the food chains?" Why not do this in your writing? By interjecting questions in your letter, you focus the reader's attention on specific points. For example, instead of writing "If you desire, we can incorporate additional applications in this software," write "What additional applications would you like to have incorporated in this software?" This gives the reader a chance to reflect on your message in terms that are specific to his or her needs.

➤ **Personalize your letter.** When we speak we use the pronouns I, we, and you all the time. They're part of the normal give and take of conversation. But when we write as representatives of our company we tend to use the passive voice. We rarely write "we," never write "I," and even avoid the straightforward "you." Instead we use such phrases as "It is assumed," "It is recommended," or sentences such as: "An investigation will be made and upon its completion a report will be furnished to your organization." Why not clearly state: "We're investigating the matter and when we obtain the information we'll let you know."

Usually, when writing for an organization, there isn't too much opportunity to be personal and write "I." However, you should use "I" when you express feelings or thoughts that are your own. It's better to say "I'm sorry" or "I'm pleased" than "we're sorry" or "we're pleased."

Another way of personalizing a letter is to use the addressee's name in the text. If you're friends, use the first name; if just business acquaintances, the last name. Instead of writing: "This will result in benefits for your organization," write "So you see, Beth (or Ms. Smith), how this will benefit you."

Team Builder

Double check your grammar and spelling. Reread everything you write. The appearance and correctness of your correspondence affects the image both you and your company project.

➤ **You can use a preposition to end a sentence with.** The rule you learned in grade school about ending sentences with a preposition is passé. In speaking, we don't even think about such things. But when we're writing, we restructure sentences to fit this rule. Don't. It makes the sentence, and therefore the letter, sound awkward. Put the preposition at the end whenever it sounds right to do so. Instead of writing: "The claimant is not entitled to the benefits for which he applied," it's okay to write: "The claimant isn't entitled to the benefits he applied for."

Another grammatical superstition tells us to avoid split infinitives. "To successfully reduce costs, we should take the following steps" sounds more powerful than, "To reduce costs successfully, we should take the following steps."

➤ **Keep sentences short and uncomplicated.** The ordinary reader can take in only so many words before his or her eyes come to a brief rest at a period. If a sentence has too many words, chances are the full meaning will be missed. Studies show that sentences of no more than 20 words are easiest to read and absorb. It is usually quite clear where one idea leaves off and another begins. Limit each sentence to one idea. Remember your objective is to get the idea across to the reader—not to create undying prose. It is also helpful to use short rather than long words. Of course, in writing on technical matters to technically trained people, technical language is appropriate. However, when writing to people who may not have the background in an area that you have, avoid language and jargon that they are unlikely to possess.

➤ **Avoid business clichés.** Instead of using overused and often meaningless business terminology, use simple terms.

Here are some commonly used clichés:

Instead of writing	Write
At a later date	Later (or exact time)
At the present time	Now
Despite the fact	Although
For the period of a year	For a year
In accordance with your request	As requested
In the near future	Soon (or in May)
Is of the opinion that	Believes
Made an adjustment	Adjusted
The undersigned or the writer	I
We are herewith enclosing	Enclosed is
We are not in a position to	We cannot
With the exception of	Except

Give your letters just the right human touch. Express your natural feelings. If it's good news, say you're glad; if it's bad news, say you're sorry. Be as courteous, polite, and interested as you'd be if the addressee sat in front of you.

Write This the Way You Say It

Re our telephone conversation _____

In accordance with your request _____

Per the chairman's letter _____

In lieu of _____

Upon receipt of your order _____

Owing to the fact that _____

Until such time as _____

All that is necessary for you to do _____

To meet our quality guidelines _____

Costs the sum of _____

Reduce to a minimum _____

In view of the above _____

Inasmuch as _____

Pursuant to _____

Peruse _____

Aforementioned _____

Comprised _____

Heretofore _____

The E-mail Explosion

You must give as much attention to writing e-mails as you do to the composition of standard letters and memos. Remember that e-mail is a form of written communication. Many people think of it as a substitute for a phone call rather than a letter, so they dash off their messages with little or no consideration of style or even content. Unlike the phone call, e-mail can be kept either electronically or as a printout, so it should be carefully planned and composed.

FYI

More and more inter- and intraoffice communication is now done via e-mail. According to a poll conducted by Ernst & Young, 36 percent of respondents use e-mail more than any other communication tool, including the telephone.

Make Your E-mail Exciting, Expressive, Engaging

Here are some tips to help you write better e-mail:

➤ Think carefully about what you write. If the message is more than just casual chitchat, plan it as carefully as you would a formal letter. Put yourself in the place of the reader. If you're giving instructions, make sure the reader knows just exactly what action you're requesting. If you're answering an inquiry, make sure you've gathered all the information necessary to respond appropriately to the questions asked.

➤ Use a meaningful subject line. Your correspondent may receive dozens, even hundreds, of e-mail messages each day. To ensure that your message will be read promptly, use a subject heading that will be meaningful to the addressee. For example, instead of "re your e-mail of 6/25," use the subject line to refer to the information you provide in your e-mail (for instance, "Sales figures for June.")

➤ Follow the suggestions given earlier in this chapter on writing letters and memos. Use the three C's, and the TAB approach. Use short, punchy sentences. Keep to the point and be brief.

➤ If you attach files to the e-mail, specify in the text which files are attached, so the reader can check to make sure they came through.

➤ Read the message carefully and spell-check it before you click "Send now." If you are not happy with the message, don't send it. Postpone the transmission. Review it, then rewrite it. Make sure it's okay before it is sent.

Team Terms

SPAM is the computer equivalent of junk mail. Sometimes it's tough to identify SPAM by its source or subject, but with a little experience, most can be picked out and deleted.

E-mail Clutter

How many e-mail messages do you receive each day? Some people are so bogged down with e-mail, they have no time to read it and still get other work done.

In many companies, employees spend an inordinate amount of time on the computer e-mailing jokes, personal messages, offerings ("I have six cute kittens looking for a home"), and information that is usually unimportant to most recipients. Some companies alleviate such clutter, or SPAM, in their regular e-mail by setting up a special "classified ad" or bulletin board e-mail address for these messages.

Another example of clutter is sending an e-mail to an entire mailing list when only a few people on the list need the information. For example, some people planning to take a day off announce their plans to the "Everyone" list, thereby alerting 35 people when only five or six people really need to know. Perhaps they do so to puff up their own sense of self-importance, or more likely, they're lazy. They find it easier to send a message to everyone than to figure out who really needs to know and just click on those names.

Team Builder

E-mail glut can result in your message being ignored or inadvertently deleted. Ask the receiver to acknowledge receipt of your e-mail. If the matters involved are very important, follow up with a telephone call to ensure that the message was received and understood.

"Who's reading my e-mail?"

How private is your e-mail? Not very. Sure, you may have a password and assume that it ensures privacy, but hackers have shown that they can easily break through even sophisticated systems. Assume anything you e-mail can be intercepted. If confidentiality is required, maybe e-mail is not the medium to use.

Remember that any e-mail sent via the company computer can be read by anybody in the company. Over the past few years there have been cases in which employees were fired because of e-mails they sent that violated company rules. The courts threw out their employees' claims of invasion of privacy.

More serious are the cases of people who have made comments or jokes in their e-mail which were considered sexually or racially harassing. Printouts of such e-mail have been entered as evidence in suits against employees' companies, even though company officials weren't aware of the messages. This has led to termination of the senders, as well as legal action against both the senders and the companies.

E-mail vs. Phone Calls or Visits

Many people tend to resort to e-mail rather than make a phone call or a personal visit. Using e-mail is often an easy way out. You don't have to leave your desk, and it's less time consuming than a telephone call. There's no time wasted in small talk or lengthy discussion about a project. All that's sent is the basic message. But often, that small talk and pro-and-con discussion is important. In addition, the phone call allows for instant feedback. It not only helps clarify the message, but it ensures that both you and the other person understand the matters involved in the same way.

Heads Up!

Don't replace phone and personal contacts with e-mail. Voice-to-voice or face-to-face contact with people you deal with on a regular basis strengthens the personal relationship that is so important in building and maintaining rapport.

Charles Wang, the CEO of Computer Associates, found that e-mail's alleged efficiencies were ruining the interpersonal dynamics that had made his company so successful in the first place.

People stopped having face-to-face meetings and stopped speaking to each other altogether. His simple but shocking solution: Turn the whole system off for most of the day and force people to communicate in person. He follows this himself. When he wants you, he comes down the hall and finds you.

A Dozen E-mail Do's and Don'ts

Do carefully plan your e-mails.

Do read and reread your messages before clicking "send now."

Do inform recipients when your e-mail doesn't require a reply. It will save both of you time and clutter.

Do use bullets instead of paragraphs. It makes it easier to read and grasp key points.

Do respond promptly to e-mail you receive, especially when immediate attention is required. Speed of communication is the chief advantage of this medium.

Do check whether important e-mail has been received by asking the respondent to acknowledge it and/or by following-up with a phone call.

Don't send off-color jokes or stories on company e-mail.

Don't use e-mail to replace telephone or personal contacts. It is important to maintain voice-to-voice and face-to-face relationships with the people you deal with.

Don't play e-mail games, or send or respond to chain letters or similar time-wasters on company time and on company computers.

Team Builder

To save both your time and that of the receivers of your e-mail, indicate whether the message is sent just for their information or if it requires action or a reply.

Don't download on company computers pornographic material or items that are derogatory to either gender or to any racial or ethnic groups. Remember that your e-mails can be read by anybody and may offend other people in the organization. It could lead to embarrassment and possibly charges of sexual or racial harassment.

Don't spread gossip or rumors through e-mail. It's bad enough when gossip is repeated on the telephone or in person, but e-mail exponentially expands the number of people receiving such information.

Don't send a message to your entire list unless the message applies to everyone on it.

Writing Reports That Hit the Mark

If you're a team leader, you are often required to submit reports to your bosses or to other managers in the organization. In some cases you may be the sole writer of the report, but often it is a team effort, and as leader, you'll coordinate the team's preparation and composition of the report.

Many people shortchange themselves by submitting poorly developed, poorly thought out, and poorly written reports. Why? Perhaps they believe that presenting the basic data is adequate. A good report must be far more than basic information. It should enable the reader to obtain enough knowledge of the subject covered so that he or she can make whatever decisions are needed. The report should be written in a clear and concise manner so the reader does not have to go through a jungle of irrelevancies to get to the key areas of concern.

Before You Write a Single Word

Consider the following points before writing a single word:

1. **Define the problem or issue.** Discuss the objective of the report with the manager who gave you the assignment. Much time, effort, and money have been wasted by people compiling reports without knowing what managers really wanted. Unless the report writer is entirely clear on how the report will be used, he or she might spend more time than necessary on secondary aspects of the situation without addressing the really important areas.

2. **Give team members their assignments.** If it's is a team project, pick the team members who will be involved and break down the project into the segments each person will handle. Appoint one member to coordinate and record the findings.

3. **Get the facts.** Have team members assemble all the information needed. For example, if the report will cover information about some new software, team members should speak to the people in your organization who will use the software and learn what they really want to accomplish by using it. They should obtain literature about the software, read what the technical journals say about it, and speak to people in other organizations who use that product. Information should be sought from the supplier's sales representatives and from representatives from competing software vendors. Get all the information you can.

4. **Analyze the facts.** Once the information is accumulated, the facts should be correlated and analyzed. One way is to list the advantages and limitations of the software under consideration and make similar lists for other software that also might be viable.

Many hours of sorting and assembling information can be saved by filing it immediately in a dedicated folder or envelope instead of throwing it all together and sorting it when you are ready to write the report.

Know Your Reader

The language and form of your report should be tailored to the person or persons who will be reading it. As pointed out earlier, an engineer writing a report for nontechnical managers should try to couch it in language that is as nontechnical as the subject permits. If the use of technical language is essential to the report, the writer should define and clarify the meaning of the technical terms the first time they are mentioned in the report.

It's advantageous to know what your reader expects in terms of language, details of content, graphic material, and the like. When writing a report for your boss or another manager with whom you have regular dealings, you probably know whether he or she prefers terse, precise reports or a great deal of detail; whether that person prefers graphs or charts to statistical tables or likes to see both; whether rounded approximations are preferred to exact dollars and cents. If you are not sure, ask.

A Format That Tells and Sells

Who should write the final report? It is usually best to assign only one person to do the actual writing. This could be the team leader or one of the team members. The writer will compose a draft of the report. This will be read by the other associates, who will make suggestions, and then a final version will be written. Although there is no ideal report style, the following guidelines will help make the report easy to read and understand:

➤ **State the purpose.** "As you requested, here's the information about the XYZ software programs."

➤ **Summarize your findings and recommendations.** State your recommendations at the beginning of the report.

➤ **Provide supporting material.** Include the details that support your summary and recommendations. Use charts, graphs, and tables if they clarify or reinforce the information in the report.

Watch your language. Keep it clear and to the point. The variety of fonts and styles now available in most word processing software enables you to present your reports in very attractive and interesting formats. Take advantage of this option, but use fonts that are easy to read.

How long should a report be? Long enough to tell the whole story—and not one word longer. Avoid repetition. A common fault in report writing is stating the same idea over and over in different words.

FYI

The "team" that developed the Declaration of Independence consisted of Thomas Jefferson, John Adams, Benjamin Franklin, Robert Livingston, and Roger Sherman. But one person, Jefferson, was assigned to write the document.

The Final Step

Before submitting the report, proofread it carefully. Even a good report loses credibility when it has spelling errors, poor grammatical structure, or sloppy typing. Figures should be checked carefully. Reread it. If possible, have other team members read it. Make whatever changes are needed. Read it once more to ensure you are satisfied.

The Least You Need to Know

➤ Whether your audience is just your own team or a large group, choose words that your listeners or readers will easily understand.

➤ In oral communication it's not just what you say but how you say it that determines how your message is received.

➤ Watch your grammar! Watch your spelling! Your writing style reflects your intelligence, personality, and authority.

➤ Talk to your reader. Relax. Write it as you would say it.

➤ Give as much attention to writing e-mail as you do to standard letters.

➤ Before writing reports, get all the facts, analyze the situation, and understand what the person(s) who requested the information really wants and how he or she wants it presented.

Chapter 6

Meetings: Time-Wasters or Productivity Tool?

In This Chapter

➤ Objectives of the meeting

➤ Who should attend

➤ Set the stage

➤ Make meetings interactive

➤ When meetings bog down

➤ End with a bang

➤ Get the most out of meetings you attend

As a team leader, you are certainly going to have to run a meeting. As a team member, you will probably be called upon to plan and chair several meetings each year.

By this time in your career, you've probably attended countless meetings and have often left feeling that they were a waste of your time.

When you run the meeting, it's up to you to ensure that the meeting will be worthwhile. In this chapter you will learn how to make every meeting an effective learning experience for all participants.

Set the Stage for Successful Sessions

The main purpose of a meeting is to bring several people together to discuss a specific matter. To prevent meetings from becoming time-wasters and morale downers, carefully prepare and organize them.

FYI

In a survey conducted at Dun & Bradstreet's Business Education Services management seminars, more than 70 percent of the people interviewed felt that they had wasted time at the meetings they attended.

Why Meetings?

Some of the reasons for holding meetings include dissemination and discussion of information. There are lots of ways of giving needed information to the team. You can send a memo or letter. You can hold one-to-one conferences with each team member. You can include the information in a bulletin or manual. However, a meeting is the best way of giving information to the entire team at the same time. This allows the team to discuss it as a group, ask questions, obtain ideas and opinions from all the members, and develop a consensus about the issue.

Meetings can be especially productive in the following areas:

➤ **Explaining or reviewing procedures and solving problems.** Areas of confusion can be identified by the questions asked and resolved by answers from the leader or from other team members.

➤ **Idea generation.** Meetings provide the time and tools for brainstorming new ideas and developing innovative approaches to problems faced by the team.

➤ **Setting goals.** A meeting is an effective way to establish goals for either short-term projects or long-term objectives of the team.

➤ **Training.** Meetings can assist people in developing the skills needed to do their work. Such meetings can be used to provide basic skill training, supplement on-the-job training and refresh skills in follow-up sessions after basic training is completed.

➤ **Building morale.** Getting people together at meetings enables them to share ideas and strengthen working relationships. It helps overcome misunderstandings that may occur if the team's mission is not clear.

➤ **Motivating the team.** By meeting together, the members develop team spirit. It molds the members into a collaborative work group. It creates enthusiasm for the work.

Following are some ways in which meetings can be made even more motivational:

➤ Use the meeting to give members recognition and reward for outstanding work.

➤ Have members report on their successes. This sets an example to the others and encourages them.

➤ Have pep talks given by the leader or by invited guests.

Team Builder

Avoid wasting time at meetings by setting and sticking to time limits. One suggestion is to schedule meetings for one hour to end at lunchtime. If some of the members want to continue the discussion, they can do it over lunch.

Who's Invited?

Invite only appropriate participants. This is of particular concern when meetings include people from teams other than your own. Most team meetings are limited to team members, but when projects involve more than one team, it may be advantageous to include representatives from the participating group.

Quite often, many of the people who attend a meeting are not involved in the matters that are discussed. Not only does this waste their time, but their obvious boredom puts a damper on the meeting for everyone. Invite only individuals who have knowledge and ideas that you know can contribute to the discussion or those who can learn something that they should know in order to perform their work.

Getting Organized

The key to the success of any meeting is the agenda. What will be discussed at the meeting must be carefully planned before it is even scheduled. Determining in advance not only what subjects will be addressed but also the order in which they will be covered will make the meeting run smoothly.

In establishing the sequence of topics, put the most important or complex at the beginning of the program. People come to meetings with clear minds and are able to approach these serious matters more effectively early in the meeting. If scheduled for later, not only are people likely to be less attentive, if it's a key matter, they may be thinking about it while other matters are being discussed, and not give adequate attention.

Team Terms

An **agenda** is a list of things to be done at a meeting. Effective meeting leaders carefully prepare the agenda and control the meeting to ensure the agenda is complied with.

Clarify the objective of the meeting. Objectives vary. Some meetings are of a general nature covering a variety of matters that are related to the team's work. Others are called to discuss a specific project or problem. Some meetings are devoted to training in new skills or refreshing old skills. Still others are to motivate the team.

The *agenda* should be directly related to your objective. One of the most common reasons for meeting failure is the inclusion of nonrelevant subjects in an agenda. If the meeting's objective is to discuss cutting costs in a procedure, don't include an item on the company's forthcoming bowling tournament.

Any member of the team may be asked to prepare the agenda. If you're the one chosen for that chore, here are some suggestions:

1. Determine the purpose of the meeting from the person who gave you the assignment.
2. Enlist the other team members in preparing the agenda.
3. Learn what they know about the subject and what they want to learn.
4. Estimate how much time will be needed for each item in the agenda.
5. Anticipate the questions you may be asked.
6. Send the final draft of the agenda at least three days before the meeting to all team members and others who will attend.

The focus of a meeting should be on expanding, demonstrating, and clarifying information. If brand-new concepts, particularly technical or complex material, are to be introduced, give participants written information before the meeting so they can study it and be prepared to discuss it.

Preparing Visuals

An old Chinese proverb says that a picture is worth a thousand words. People remember more of what they see than what they hear—and they remember even more of what they see and hear simultaneously. If your audience sees visuals that reinforce your message, your presentation becomes clearer, more exciting and more memorable.

Let's look at some types of visuals that can augment your presentations.

➤ **Chalkboards:** Good when there are only a few participants, such as your team. Using the chalkboard helps clarify or illustrate information when it is being presented. Be sure the chalk used can be read from the back of the room. Use different colored chalk for emphasis. Many meeting rooms are equipped with white boards on which you can use a variety of colored marking pens. Chalkboards or white boards are best used for items that are not needed for later reference and can be erased.

➤ **Flip charts:** In addition to being used in the same way as chalkboards, flip charts can be prepared in advance. Charts, graphs, diagrams, or key points can be preprinted and can be referred to at the appropriate time. Another advantage is that sheets can be removed from the pad and posted around the room for reference.

➤ **Overhead projectors:** If the presentation is to be given in a large room where chalkboards or flip charts cannot be easily read by the audience, use an overhead projector. Transparencies can be prepared in advance to illustrate key points. In addition, blank acetate film, which you can write or draw on in the same way you would on a chalkboard, can be placed on the projector.

➤ **Slides:** Colorful and dramatic slides can emphasize important points. Be sure the slides are in the carousel in the proper order and right-side up. Check them personally each time before using them.

➤ **Videos:** Some subjects can be illustrated by showing videos. For example, if the meeting concerns the use of a new piece of equipment, the manufacturer can often provide a video demonstrating its use.

➤ **PowerPoint:** All your visual aids can be prepared on your computer in advance of the meeting and used in place of slides or transparencies.

Provide handouts of diagrams, flow charts, statistical tables, or whatever data you bring to the meeting. Distribute the handouts at the beginning of your discussion of that item. If the material is complex, distribute it far enough in advance of the meeting to enable team members to study it.

Make the Meeting Interactive

At too many meetings, the meeting leader dominates the discussion. When that happens the others are an audience, not participants. Especially if the meeting involves just one team, it is essential that everybody on that team participate. There is no place for passive listeners in team activity.

Every participant should have received a copy of the agenda before the meeting and should be prepared to comment, contribute suggestions, and ask questions. But often, this does not happen. Why? It may be that the person running the meeting dominates the discussion, and directly or indirectly discourages others to participate. Another reason: The members are not adequately prepared; they don't know enough about the subject. It also may be that some members are too shy to open their mouths.

Encourage All Members, Even the Shyest, to Participate

Ask questions that stimulate discussion. Be open to questions and dissension. It's better to have members bring up problems at a meeting than let them stew over them over a long period of time.

Keep the group small. If possible limit it to six to 10 people. A good way to get members to take part in the meeting is to assign individuals in the group to report on specific aspects of the subject. This gives them an important role in the meeting. It is also an excellent way to get those men and women who are reticent to present their views at open meetings to take an active role. Giving them the assignment ensures that they will participate.

Going around the room and asking each person for his or her ideas is a frequently used approach to get everybody into the act. List the ideas on a flip chart. Defer discussion until all have contributed.

Keep Blabbermouths from Dominating

Don't you hate it when one person tries to dominate a meeting? It's usually the same one or two people who always have something to say—usually not important, often a personal pet peeve, and always distracting. Here are some tips on how you, as a meeting leader, can attempt to keep them quiet.

Take the blabbermouth aside before the meeting and say, "I know you like to contribute to our meetings and I appreciate it, but we have a limited amount of time, and some of the other people want a chance to present their ideas. So let's give them a chance to talk, and you and I can discuss your issues after the meeting."

If the blabbermouth still talks too much, wait until he or she pauses for breath—which everyone inevitably must do—and quickly say, "Thank you. Now let's hear what Sue has to say." Announce that each speaker has only three minutes to make his or her point. Be flexible with others, but be strict with the blabbermouths.

Similar to the blabbermouths are the digressors. Like the blabbermouths, their hands are always waving. But when you do recognize them, their comments are usually about a fringe aspect of the subject or some entirely different area. Why do they do this? It's possible they didn't know or forgot the objective of the meeting, but more likely it's their way of getting attention.

The best approach is not to respond to the comment. Point out that this is not on the agenda and time is limited. If the person wishes to discuss it, suggest that you will be glad to do it privately after the meeting or, if it has some merit, place it on an agenda for a future meeting.

"You're wrong!" Dealing with Dissidents

Another type of meeting disrupter is the dissident. This person always finds something to disagree with. Sometimes this is based on a legitimate difference of opinion, but often it is the member's way to gain attention.

If the objection can be rebutted, provide additional facts or clarify the areas of confusion. If it will take more time than is available at the session, arrange for a one-to-one discussion after the meeting to ensure the member understands the points raised.

Heads Up!

To control some members from dominating meetings, select some object like a small flag or baton and require that no participant can talk unless they are holding it. The meeting leader controls the flag, allowing only one person at a time to talk.

On the other hand, if the person raising the objection is a constant interrupter, one who always finds something to disagree about, tactfully cut it short. You might say, "Ted, that's an interesting comment. Thank you for presenting your view." And then go on without further discussion.

Keep Your Big Mouth Shut

You have been chosen to conduct a meeting. You spend time researching and preparing information. When the meeting gets underway, you make a lengthy presentation, suggest some solutions to the problems, and then sit back and wait for comments. Typical? Yes, but not the best way. What you have done is conduct a lecture, not a meeting.

Of course you have to present the results of your research. But once you've done this, shut up. Even if you have what you consider great solutions, don't bring them up until the participants have a chance to ask questions, discuss the subject, and bring up their suggested solutions.

Sure, you have more knowledge of the subject as a result of your research, but as the meeting leader, your objective is to stimulate discussion from which ideas that can lead to the best solution will be generated. If you present your conclusions first, you inhibit the creative thinking of the other participants. This is especially important if you are a team leader or manager. Participants may be reluctant to disagree with ideas presented by their boss.

Hold back presenting your views until after the discussion. If the group comes up with the same solution as you have, congratulate them on their thinking and give

them the credit for it. If, out of the discussion, new or
better ideas evolve, accept them easily and don't feel
forced to withdraw or defend your original position.

End Meetings with a Bang

By the time the meeting ends, participants should be
clear about the subjects discussed. Give them a chance
to ask questions. The leader should summarize what
has been accomplished and check to ensure that if any
team members received assignments during the meeting, they understand what they will do and when they
will do it.

Get Questions from Team Members

Most team meetings are informal, and questions from
participants are encouraged at any time during the
meeting. However, there are occasions when meetings
may be more formal, and a question-and-answer period is held at the end. This gives
the meeting leader the chance to clarify points, reemphasize the message, and, if necessary, rebut arguments from opponents.

Following are some suggestions to make this period more effective:

➤ Set a time limit. This gives you control over the duration of the session.

➤ People are often reluctant to ask the first question. Raise your arm and ask,
"Who has the first question?" If nobody volunteers, prime the pump. "When I
discuss this subject a question I often hear is …"

➤ Keep answers brief. This is not the time to make another full presentation.

➤ If a person disagrees with you, don't get defensive. Respond to the question.
Comment that you respect the right of others to have their own viewpoint.

➤ If you don't know the answer to a question, admit it.

At the end of the question period, invite questions from those who didn't have a
chance to ask any.

Make Assignments

If decisions are made at the meeting, members should be assigned to put them into
action. The leader may ask for a volunteer or may appoint a team member to carry
out the assignment.

FYI

"Perhaps Hell is nothing more than an enormous conference of those who, with little or nothing to say, take an eternity to say it."

—Dudley C. Stone, *Journal of Systems Management*

Be sure to divide the easier and more difficult assignments equitably. Don't play favorites. Don't depend on volunteers. Some members never volunteer.

To ensure that all such assignments are understood and accepted by the member, at the end of the meeting the leader should reiterate what assignments have been made, set timetables, and arrange for follow-up.

Team Terms

The meeting **recorder** is not an electronic taping device, but a team member who keeps the minutes of a meeting.

Keep a Record

Appoint one of the team members to be *recorder*. He or she will take notes during the meeting. A detailed description of the entire discussion is not necessary, just a summary of what has been decided and what assignments have been made so that there will be no misunderstandings.

After the meeting, copies of these minutes can be distributed to all attendees and to others in the organization who may be affected by what transpired.

Close the Meeting Positively

It's important to close the meeting with a positive message. It may take the form of a summary. It may be some inspirational comments. It may be a call to action—asking members to take specific steps.

Here are some suggestions for positive closings:

➤ Summarize the key points and point out that applying them will benefit the team.

➤ Challenge the participants to do something about the matters discussed.

➤ Ask the team members to write the one thing they feel most strongly about as a result of the presentation, post it on his or her desk, and reread it every day until project is completed.

➤ Make a final motivating statement to inspire the participants to take the actions resulting from the meeting.

The way in which the leader conducts a meeting can mean the difference between it being a valuable tool or a waste of time. The following quiz will help you determine how effective your meetings are.

Meeting Self-Evaluator

Before the meeting

_____1. Did you prepare an agenda for the meeting?

_____2. Did you distribute agenda to participants in advance of meeting?

_____3. Did you set starting and ending times for meeting?

_____4. Did you prepare visuals and/or handouts?

_____5. Did you assign segments of the program to team members?

_____6. Did you appoint a member to be the recorder of the meeting?

_____7. Did you arrange for all needed equipment and supplies:

_____ Chalkboard and chalk

_____ Flip chart easel

_____ Flip chart pads and markers

_____ Computer & projector for PowerPoint

_____ Overhead projector

_____ Slide projector

Other

_____

_____

During the meeting

_____1. Did you stick to the agenda?

_____2. Did you obtain participation from all members?

_____3. Did you keep blabbermouths and domineers under control?

_____4. Did you distribute assignments equitably?

_____5. Did you refrain from expressing your ideas until members expressed theirs?

_____6. Did you encourage questions from members?

_____7. Did you encourage other participants to answer questions asked by team members?

_____8. Did you summarize key points at the end of meeting?

_____9. Did you verify members' understanding of their assignments before adjourning the meeting?

_____10. Did you end the meeting with a motivational statement or a call for action?

After the meeting

_____1. Did you distribute minutes of meeting to all participants and others who may be affected?

_____2. Did you follow through on assignments made?

_____3. Did you gather feedback from participants about meeting?

The more "yes" answers, the more effective the meeting leader.

Get the Most out of Meetings You Attend

When you lead the meeting, you have control over how well it runs, but most of the time, you are not the leader, but a participant. By taking active steps before, during, and after the meeting, you can make every one you attend a valuable learning experience.

When It's a Team Meeting

When you are notified of the meeting, don't just enter it on your calendar and forget it until the scheduled time. It's worth taking the time to prepare for it.

Keep the following points in mind before the meeting:

➤ Study the agenda. Review the subjects that are listed. Even if you are knowledgeable about them, you still want to be sure you are up-to-date on them. Review your files so you know what's been done up to now. If pertinent, read articles in technical or trade publications that cover the matters.

➤ If it is a new area or one with which you are not familiar, carefully study the material provided. This is too important to just give it a cursory scan and expect to pick up the details at the meeting.

➤ Make notes on comments, ideas, or questions you have about the subjects.

At the meeting

➤ Participate. If you have comments, ideas, or questions, don't hold back. Caution: Don't just talk for the sake of talking. Make your points succinctly.

Team Builder

Build your network. When outside speakers address a meeting, note their names and addresses. You may want to contact some of them for more information. Also list the names and addresses of people you meet at these events. They may be a source of information or guidance in the future.

➤ Deal with disagreements. It's likely that some other team members may disagree with your view. Don't take it personally. In responding, stick to the facts. It's a discussion, not an argument.

➤ Work toward consensus. If the objective of the meeting is to solve a problem, contribute toward the solution. Listen to other views. They may be better than yours. Be ready to reach compromises to attain satisfactory solutions.

➤ Don't dominate the meeting. Sometimes it's hard to hold back when you have ideas you want to express. Give the others a chance to talk.

➤ Take notes on key decisions that were made, or on new information that you have learned.

➤ If the meeting results in assignments to the participants, volunteer immediately for the assignment that most appeals to you. If you hold back, you may wind up with a job that is not as interesting and which you may not enjoy doing.

After the meeting

➤ Review your notes. Take action where required.

If you were given an assignment, discuss it with the leader to be sure you understand what is wanted and when it is expected.

When You Attend Outside Meetings

Whether you are a team leader or an associate, you will probably attend meetings other than those limited to the team. These may be within the company or outside the company, such as conferences or conventions sponsored by trade associations or professional organizations.

Here are some suggestions to help you make these meetings worth your time and attention:

➤ **Prepare for the meeting.** Most conferences and conventions are announced months in advance. Prepare for this meeting in the same way you would for a team meeting as suggested above. Usually an agenda accompanies the announcement. Study it carefully. Does any subject listed require special preparation? You may want to read up on unfamiliar subjects to help you comprehend and contribute to the discussion. You may want to reexamine your company's experience in that area so you can relate what is being discussed to your own organization's problems.

➤ **Meet new people.** Don't sit with your colleagues. You can speak to them any time. If attendees are seated at tables, make a point of sitting with different people at various stages of the meetings. Often at luncheon or dinner discussions, you pick up more ideas from your table mates than from the speakers. In addition, you can make new contacts who may be valuable resources for information after the conference ends. Keep an open mind. To get the most out of what a speaker says, keep your mind open to new suggestions. They may be different from what you honestly believe is best, but until you hear it all and think it through objectively, you don't really know. Progress comes through change. This does not mean that all new ideas are good ones, but they should be listened to, evaluated, and carefully and objectively considered.

➤ **Be tolerant.** Have you ever listened to a speaker who turned you off immediately? You didn't like his or her appearance, clothes, voice, or regional accent so you either stopped listening or rejected what he or she said. Prejudice against a speaker keeps many an attendee from really listening to what is discussed or from accepting the ideas presented.

➤ **Take notes.** Note-taking has two important functions. It helps organize what you hear while you are at the meeting, resulting in more systematic listening. It also becomes a source for future reference.

➤ **Keep an aha! page.** Use this page in your notebook to list exciting ideas that you pick up at the meeting. These are items you want to make sure you don't forget.

➤ **Ask questions.** Don't hesitate to query a speaker when the opportunity arises. But don't waste the time of the meeting with trivial questions. Avoid prefacing your question with lengthy comments. Be clear. Be brief.

➤ **Be an active participant.** Contribute ideas. In most meetings there are people who willingly share ideas and information. Others just sit and listen. When asked why they didn't participate more fully, people commonly respond: "Why should I give my ideas to these people? Some of them are my competitors and I won't give away my trade secrets."

Heads Up!

During a formal presentation, it is not appropriate to interrupt the speaker. If you have a question, jot it down on the last page of your notebook. This will be a reminder so you will not forget the questions you want to ask when the opportune time comes.

Nobody expects you to say anything that would damage your firm or its competitive position, but most discussions are not of this nature. They're designed to promote the exchange of ideas that are of value to most of the attendees. The experience of one organization helps the others. By contributing ideas, you provide richer experiences for others, which in turn in turn results in a more fulfilling experience for yourself.

After the meeting

➤ **Summarize what you learned.** Review your notes while the meeting is still fresh in mind. As soon as possible after you return to your office, write or dictate a report on the conference for your permanent files.

➤ **Report on what you have learned.** Send a memo or brief report to your boss or others in your organization who might find the information of valuable. Discuss it with the members of your team. By sharing what you have learned, you add to the value your firm receives from sending you to the convention.

➤ **Put it into practice.** If nothing is done with what you learned at the meeting, it's been a waste of time and money.

A meeting can be an effective tool or a big waste of time—it's up to you.

The Least You Need to Know

➤ Every meeting should have a purpose, and the meeting leader should make sure the purpose is accomplished.

➤ Several days before the meeting, prepare an agenda and distribute it to everybody who is expected to attend.

➤ Prepare materials and arrange for equipment you intend to use in advance.

➤ Establish a participative climate, facilitate participation by shy or reticent members, and don't allow blabbermouths to dominate the meeting.

➤ Give everyone a chance to ask questions, summarize what has been accomplished, and end the meeting with a call for action or an inspirational message.

➤ You can get the most out of meetings or conferences you attend by following the suggestions made in the last section of this chapter.

Who's Gonna Do the Work?

Whether the function of the team is to market a product, manufacture a component, design a system, service a customer, or any of the multitude of activities performed in the organization, each member of the team performs both as an individual and as a collaborator with the entire team.

In addition to the routine work, each person performs daily, special projects are assigned from time to time to meet the goals of the organization.

Assigning the Work

There are some teams in which every member of the team performs the same routine tasks. For example, all the members of the check clearance team in a bank work at identical work stations, doing exactly the same type of work. In some teams, the workers do different but related work. For example, in an insurance claims team, one or more people may work on one aspect of the claim, then pass it to other members to work on another aspect, and so on. In an engineering team, each phase of the project may be handled by a specialist. In multifunction teams (to be discussed later in

this book), team members come from different disciplines with very different job functions, but work together to accomplish an objective.

Delegating Responsibility

Whether only one or several team members perform these standard jobs, the determination of what should be done is usually made when the job was created or revised and is formalized in a job description.

Usually, the job description is the result of an analysis of the job by industrial engineers, systems specialists, or members of the Human Resources Department who analyze the job and come up with a job description.

As these "experts" are usually not as familiar with the job as the team leader and the members who perform the job, job descriptions often do not reflect the real work being done. This can be overcome if the team leader takes an active part in writing them. In a team-oriented organization, job descriptions are best made by the team itself.

If you are the team leader or part of the team that will write job descriptions for the work the team is performing, here are some guidelines that will help you:

➤ **Observe.** For jobs that are primarily physical in nature, watching a person perform the job will provide most of the information needed to write the description. If several people are engaged in the same type of work, observe more than one performer.

Even a good observer, however, may not understand what he or she is observing. Sometimes the job involves much more than meets the eye. For jobs that are not primarily manual, there is little that you can learn from observation alone. Just watching someone sitting at a computer terminal, for example, isn't enough to learn what's being done.

➤ **Question the performer.** Ask the people who perform a job to describe the activities they perform. This technique fleshes out what you're observing. Most team leaders know enough about the work, of course, to be able to understand what's being said and to be able to ask appropriate questions. However, in a team there are often specialists who do work the leader is not thoroughly familiar with. In these cases, the specialist should write his or her own job description.

➤ **Have team members participate in writing the job descriptions.** Start by asking each member to write the description of his or her own job. Next, each should observe the jobs performed by other team members and interview them about their work. Encourage the team members to discuss the job among themselves before putting the job description into final shape.

One problem with job descriptions is that they get out of date. Too often, in this dynamic world, the jobs change over time, but the job description may stay the same and in time become unrealistic. In such cases, the job should be re-analyzed and a new job description written.

To keep job descriptions current, team members should have periodic meetings dedicated to discussing their current perceptions of their roles and the work they do.

Heads Up!

For the team to function effectively, every job description should be reviewed periodically. If it no longer accurately reflects the work that's being done, revise it, or risk problems ahead.

Another problem is that job descriptions tend to stifle creativity and innovation. There are some people who take the job description too literally and are unwilling to do anything that is not specifically indicated.

How often have you asked someone to do something other than his or her routine work and heard the response, "It's not in my job description!"? All job descriptions should include the phrase "and any other duties that are assigned." The inclusion of this phrase doesn't mean that you can order any team member to do any job that pops up. It means that you can assign duties that are not specifically listed but that are job-related.

Spread the Work Equitably

In some jobs the routine work takes up a great deal of the time for most team members. In others, although standard work must be done, most of the team members' efforts involve special assignments. The team leader usually decides who will do what.

In the team environment, it is best to give the members some control over their work assignments. This will encourage them to take charge of their jobs, resulting in more interest, more commitment, and more enjoyment from their work. This, in turn, will lead to more productivity.

Some ways a team leader can accomplish this are

➤ Provide associates with the training and knowledge to master their work. Encourage them to read books, take courses, and attend seminars that will enrich their job knowledge.

➤ Work with associates to set goals and develop plans to reach those goals. Jointly establish standards against which progress can be measured.

Team Terms

When someone makes a practice of studying a job and asking "Can it be performed with less effort?" "Can it be done at lower cost?" "Can it be improved in any way?" he or she is practicing **constructive discontent.**

➤ Encourage collaboration with other team members in determining methods and procedures, solving problems that arise, and making decisions on job-related matters.

➤ Welcome suggestions and ideas. Maintain a climate of creativity and innovation. Promote an attitude of *constructive discontent* so that members continually review their work and seek ways to do it better.

➤ Meet on a regular basis with associates to discuss their current perceptions of their roles and the work they do.

There are jobs that are unpleasant, physically or mentally strenuous, boring, or just no fun. Somebody has to do them.

When you give one of your team members a job like this, you're likely to get groans, objections, or even outright rebellion. They come up with all kinds of excuses:

"I'm no good at that."

"I did it last time. It's someone else's turn."

"You always pick on me."

"My skills are better used in more important work."

If the team is to succeed, everybody on the team must pull a share of these dull, dreary, sometimes demeaning tasks. The ideal situation is to find ways of eliminating the work by more efficient procedures, but this is not always possible. Teams of highly skilled or technically trained specialists really should not waste time on drudge work, and their team leaders should fight to farm them out to other groups.

But this is not always possible. If the work has to be done, the team leader should rotate the work among all members with no exceptions. Even senior members and team leaders take their turn.

Sometimes it's not just a part of a job that nobody wants; the team is assigned a project nobody likes. The team leader, instead of commiserating with the team, should present the project as a problem to be solved, not a crummy job the team is stuck with. Bring the team together. Ask for their ideas on how to deal with this. By sharing the responsibility with them, you let them know that even though it's a crummy assignment, you're all in it together.

It's not only assigning unpleasant tasks that causes problems. Team leaders often delegate the more interesting or complex projects to the same few members because they know they can be trusted to do good work. How do you think the selected few feel? Are they happy they were chosen? Probably not. They may resent being given so much work. They may burn out from overwork.

Equally important, how do you think the other associates feel? Are they happy because they don't have to work so hard? Probably not. They may feel neglected. Most people want to do good work. They want to be presented with challenges. This is the way they learn.

Some team leaders rationalize this practice by claiming that their chief responsibility is to produce quality work. To do this, they are obligated to give the work to the best qualified people. Wrong! The team leader's long-term goal should be to build up a team in which all members can contribute quality work. Dividing the work among all members gives the less skilled associates the opportunity to grow.

Heads Up!

Even though team members' talents differ, don't give in to the temptation to give all the challenging assignments to your best people. Not only will these stars feel you're taking advantage of them and resent the heavy workload, your average performers will feel neglected and lose the opportunity to build their capabilities.

Plan the Work

When the work is routine, little special planning is necessary. Many companies have *SOPs* (standard operating procedures) or they may call them SPs (standard practices), that detail company plans and policies. Although some companies restrict their SOPs to such matters as personnel policies, safety measures, and related matters, many companies either incorporate specific job methods and procedures or publish them in accompanying "instruction manuals." Providing policies and procedures for routine activities obviates the need to plan anew for them every time they occur. Because SOPs set standards that everyone must follow, all employees working with the manuals can refer to them at any time. This ensures consistency in the way these tasks will be performed.

If you develop SOPs, keep them simple. Too often, they become complicated because managers want to cover every possible contingency. It can't be done. Team leaders often have to make decisions based on unforeseeable factors. SOPs should cover the common issues in detail, but give team leaders (or team members, where appropriate) the flexibility to make spontaneous decisions when circumstances warrant them.

SOPs should also be flexible. Don't make them so rigid that they can't be changed as circumstances change. Plans may become obsolete because of new technologies, competition, government regulations, or the development of more efficient methods. Build in to SOPs a policy for periodic review and adjustment.

Team Terms

SOPs (standard operating procedures), sometimes called "the company bible," include detailed descriptions of practices and procedures followed by the organization.

In developing SOPs

➤ Clearly state what is to be accomplished.

➤ Provide guidelines for acceptable deviation from procedure.

➤ Be specific about areas in which no deviations from the procedure may occur.

➤ Before making the SOP final, test it on the job to ensure that it's "the one best way."

Standard operating procedures are just one phase of planning. As mentioned, it's best if SOPs cover only broad policy matters so that specific plans can be designed for every new project as it's created.

FYI

One reason so little is really accomplished in a bureaucracy is that the emphasis is on compliance with SOPs and related regulations, rather than on achieving results.

Your entire team should be involved in developing the team's plans. The team leader coordinates and leads the process. Particular aspects of the planning should be delegated to the associates who know the most about each particular phase. The team should discuss

➤ What is the project?

➤ Why must this project be done?

➤ When must it be completed?

➤ Who else is working on this project?

➤ How does this project fit in with the company's goals?

➤ What can we do to make this assignment a success?

Team leaders coordinate the process and work with the team to achieve consensus.

Sometimes it's best for the planning to be done by the team leader; other times by the entire team.

Using the entire team to plan is best when

➤ Full acceptance of the plan is necessary for effective implementation.

➤ Some members of the team have specialized knowledge of the subject involved.

➤ Creative ideas need to be generated.

➤ There is adequate time for a collaborative effort.

The team approach may not be appropriate when

➤ The plan involves a routine or simple task.

➤ The plan must be developed quickly.

➤ Most of the team members are likely to agree.

➤ Implementation is easy.

When the entire team is involved in the planning process, the team leader's role is to coordinate the meeting without superimposing his or her ideas on the group. The leader's efforts are best used to help the team reach consensus.

Here are six steps the leader can take to help the team reach a decision:

1. Encourage all team members to participate fully in the discussion. Follow the suggestions made in Chapter 6 on how to overcome domination by a few members and reticence by others.

2. Make sure the team members all understand and agree on what the problem under discussion really is. If the team members don't agree on the problem, they'll never agree on a solution.

3. Elicit positive suggestions. Participants tend to emphasize their disagreements about the subject. This is okay if they lead to solutions, but when the discussion concentrates on the negatives, the leader should turn it positive by saying, "I see your point, but let's think about how we can make this work."

4. If after a lengthy discussion, no consensus can be reached, break the deadlock by conducting a nonbinding poll. Ask them to vote on the basis of the information they have so far. This often impels participants to bring the discussion to a conclusion.

Team Builder

To stimulate discussion on a specific aspect of a problem, pose an interactive exercise. Example: "Let's take two minutes to see how many ideas we can come up with on this."

5. Sum up areas of agreement. There are usually many more areas of agreement than disagreement. Once consensus is reached on any aspect of the discussion, write it on a flip chart. Commend the team for making the decision and move on to the next point.

6. If areas of disagreement exist at the end of the meeting, depending on when the plan must be completed, either arrange for another meeting, or if there is no time, make the necessary decisions yourself. Explain your reasons to the team and deal with any objections.

The Team Leader's Role

In the traditional organization, the supervisor or manager makes all the decisions and assigns the work to the people in the work group. When teams replace work groups, the team leader works in collaboration with the associates to get the work done. But, the team leader doesn't just facilitate, coach, and coordinate. He or she still has a significant role in assigning work.

Who Does What?

One of the basic functions of the team leader in giving assignments to team members is to get to know each team member. All associates are individuals and the team leader must consider their individualities rather than deal with all members in the same way. Let's use the word *PEOPLE* as an acronym to provide hints on how to assign work that will give each of the people in our team the opportunity to succeed and to grow.

Personality: Learn what turns each associate on—or off. People react differently to different approaches. Some need lots of attention; others look upon attention as prying or condescending. There are people who need frequent reinforcement; others need only an occasional pat on the back. Learn the patterns of behavior of each team member and tailor the way he or she is dealt with to those patterns.

Exceptional characteristics: Look for those traits that make each associate stand out from others. For example, Laurie is very creative. When you appeal to her creativity, Laurie can be motivated to tackle difficult projects and to contribute ideas and suggestions that may help solve problems. Gary is a perfectionist. Give him assignments where quality is paramount.

Opportunity: Many team members want to expand their knowledge and acquire new skills. Assigning them work that will give them this opportunity will increase their enthusiasm for the job, and their overall performance will be enhanced.

Participation: Let the associates participate in deciding what to do and how to do it. As pointed out earlier in this book, when team members participate, the team benefits in two ways: (1) they generate ideas derived from the experiences and knowledge of several people, and, (2) because the members were involved, they are likely to be committed to the project's success.

Leadership: When assigning work, rather than giving orders to associates, the effective team leader discusses the assignment, answers questions, provides the resources needed, and motivates the members to successfully perform the job.

Expectations: The team leader lets the members know the performance standards that are expected and how they will be measured.

Give Directions, Not Orders

The old-school supervisor gave orders. At times the team leader may also give orders, but for most matters, it's best to use less dogmatic approaches to making assignments.

Giving a direct order—"Do this!"—should be limited to emergency situations or cases where special emphasis is called for. When given, the order should be clearly stated in a calm manner and no louder than necessary to be heard by the member. Unless its a matter of life or death, orders should not be shouted or bellowed.

Some more effective approaches are

➤ **Requests:** Politely ask the member to undertake an assignment. "Chris, will you please make a cost analysis for the new project?"

➤ **Suggestions:** The suggestion plays up the team member's sense of responsibility. Use it when dealing with sensitive persons. It gives the associate a feeling of control over the job. For example: "It's important for the boss to have this report when she comes in tomorrow morning. It would be great if you could finish it before you leave tonight."

➤ **Sell the idea:** Give reasons wherever possible. If the member understands what is behind a request or suggestion, he or she will respond with greater willingness. It arouses the interest of the person in getting the job done. "Pat, the deadline for submitting the bid is June 15th. We need the business so anything you can do to expedite the estimates would give us a head start in preparing it."

In issuing instructions or directions to your team members, do you

Yes	No	1. Speak clearly and select words that are understood by the team member(s)?
Yes	No	2. Give instructions in an orderly, logical sequence?
Yes	No	3. Make sure the member understands what is expected and the criteria on which it will be judged?
Yes	No	4. *Assign* the task to a member who has the skill and know-how to perform the task or can learn it rapidly?
Yes	No	5. Avoid sarcasm or condescension in assigning the work?

Yes	No	6. Clarify instructions by demonstrating or using visual aids?
Yes	No	7. Give only one assignment at a time to avoid confusion?
Yes	No	8. Refrain from micromanaging?
Yes	No	9. Unless there are special reasons for the team to follow specific procedures, allow the members to work out details of how the job is to be performed?
Yes	No	10. Follow through? Arrange for periodic feedback sessions to ensure the work is going smoothly?

The effective team leader should have answered "yes" to all 10 questions.

Team Terms

There is a difference between just assigning tasks and delegation. When you **delegate,** you not only **assign** work, you give the associate full responsibility to carry out the project.

Delegation Dynamics

Your team has lots of work to do. What will you do yourself, and what will you *delegate* to other team members?

Effective delegation means that a team leader has enough confidence in his or her associates to know that he or she will accomplish an assignment satisfactorily and expeditiously.

You Can't Do It All by Yourself

Sure, you're responsible for everything that goes on in your team, but if you try to do everything yourself, you'll put in 12 or more hours a day. That can lead to burnout and ulcers, or even heart attacks and nervous breakdowns.

There are certain things, of course, that only you can do, decisions that only you can make, critical areas that only you can handle. That's where you earn your keep. Many of the activities you undertake, however, can and should be done by others.

Here are some of the reasons you may hesitate to delegate and rationales for why you should reconsider:

➤ You can do it better than anybody on the team. That may be the case, but your time and energy should be spent on more important things. Each of your associates has talents and skills that contribute to your team's performance. By delegating assignments, you give team members the opportunity to use those skills.

I'm sure you often have thought, "By the time I tell a member what to do, demonstrate how to do it, check the work, find it wrong, and have it done over, I could have completed it and gone on to other things." Showing someone how to perform a certain task will take time now, of course, but once your team member masters the task, it will make your job easier later.

➤ You get a great deal of satisfaction from that aspect of the work and hesitate to give it up. You're not alone. All of us enjoy certain things about our work and are reluctant to assign them to others. Look at the tasks objectively. Even if you have a pet project, you must delegate it if your time can be spent handling other activities that are now your responsibility as a team leader.

➤ You're concerned that if you don't do it yourself, it won't get done right. You have a right to be concerned, but you won't have to be afraid of delegating work to others if you follow the principles described in this section.

Delegating to the Right Team Members

You know the capabilities of each of your associates. When you plan their assignments, consider which person can do which job most effectively. If you're under no time pressure, you can use the assignment to build up an associate's skills. The more team members who have the capabilities to take on a variety of assignments, the easier your job becomes. If no one on your team can do the work, then of course you'll have to do it yourself. So that you can delegate such work in the future, you should train one or more team members in that area.

Get Feedback

After you give detailed instructions to one of your associates, your usual question is probably, "Do you understand?" And the usual answer is yes.

But does the associate really understand? Maybe so. But maybe that person just thinks so but actually isn't quite sure. So in good faith he says, "I understand." Or maybe the person doesn't understand at all but is too embarrassed to say so.

Rather than ask "Do you understand?" ask, "What are you going to do?" If the response indicates that one or more of your points isn't clear, you can correct it before the member does something wrong.

Team Builder

To persuade a team member to take an unwanted assignment, say, "This is a critical job and you have the talent to do it. I need you to come through and generate the results I know you're capable of producing. Your willingness to accept this assignment will not go unnoticed."

When it's essential for an employee to rigidly conform to your instructions, you should make sure that he or she thoroughly understands them. Give a quiz. Ask specific questions so that both you and your team member completely agree about what he or she will do. When it's not essential for a delegated activity to be performed in a specific manner, just ask broad-scope questions to ensure basic understanding.

Tailor the way you present the assignment to the preferences of the person to whom you're delegating. Some people like to have responsibilities spelled out explicitly, perhaps in the form of a written list of items. Others prefer simple, concise instructions. Some people prefer e-mail, and others would rather have you delegate in person.

Understanding Is Not Enough!

Instructions must be not only understood but also accepted by your associate. Suppose that on Tuesday morning, Janet, the office manager, gives an assignment to Jeremy with a deadline of 3:30 that afternoon. Jeremy looks at the amount of work involved and says to himself, "No way." It's unlikely that he will meet that deadline.

To gain acceptance, let the team member know the importance of the work and get him or her into the act. Janet might say, "Jeremy, this report is needed for an early morning meeting of the executive committee. When do you think I can have it?" Jeremy may think, "This is important. If I skip my break and don't call my girlfriend, I can have it by 5 P.M.."

Why did Janet originally indicate that she wanted the report by 3:30 P.M. when she didn't need it until the following morning? Maybe she thought that if she said 3:30 P.M., Jeremy will would knock himself out and finish it by the end of the day. But most people don't react that way. Faced with what they consider to be an unreasonable deadline, most people won't even try. By letting people set their own schedules within reasonable limits, you get their full commitment to meeting or beating a deadline.

But suppose that Janet really did need to have that report by 3:30 P.M., so that it could be proofread, photocopied, collated, and bound. To get the report completed on time, she may have had to assign someone to help Jeremy or allowed him to work overtime so that the report would be ready for the early morning delivery.

Heads Up!

Be realistic when you assign deadlines. Don't make a practice of asking for projects to be completed earlier than you need them. They won't be. Team members will stop taking your deadlines seriously.

Control Points: Your Safeguard

Set *control points* at strategic times during the work on a project. This will help you catch errors before they blow up into catastrophes.

A control point is not a surprise inspection. Team members should know exactly when each control point is established and what should be accomplished by then.

Suppose that Gary, a team leader, gives a project to Kim on Monday morning. The deadline is the following Friday at 3 P.M. They agree that the first control point will be Tuesday at 4 P.M., at which time Kim should have completed parts A and B. Note that Kim knows exactly *what* and *when*. When Gary and Kim meet on Tuesday, they find several errors in part B. That's not good, but it's not terrible. The errors can be corrected before the work continues. If Gary and Kim had not scheduled a control point, the errors would have been perpetuated throughout the entire project.

Team Terms

A **control point** is a spot in a project at which you stop, examine the work that has been completed, and, if errors have been made, correct them.

Give Team Members the Tools and Authority

Nobody can carry out an assigned project without the proper tools or the authority to get the job done. Providing equipment, materials, and access to resources is an obvious step, but giving the associate *authority* is another story. If a job is to be done without your micromanagement, you must give the people doing the job the power to make decisions.

If they need supplies or materials, allot them a budget so that they can order what they need without having to ask for your approval for every purchase. If a job may call for overtime, give them the authority to order it.

Be Available

Team members almost always have questions, seek advice, and need your help. Be there for them, but don't let them throw the entire project back at you. Let them know that you're available to help, advise, and support, but not to do their work.

When people bring you a problem, insist that they bring with it a suggested solution. At best, they will solve their own problems and not bother you. At the very least, they'll ask, "Do you think that this solution will work?" which is a much better response than, "What do I do now?"

Delegation: A Team Activity

When the team members who will do the job have a say in what they're going to do, they approach their work with enthusiasm and commitment.

A good way to delegate is to present the project in its entirety to the team. Discuss how it should be assigned and break the assignment into phases. Determine together which phase each associate will handle. Most members will choose the areas in which they have the most expertise. If two associates want the same area, let them iron it out between themselves. If it gets sticky, step in and resolve the problem diplomatically: "Burt, you did the research on our last project, so let's give Carol a chance to do it this time."

As team leader, be sure that every member of your team is aware of not only his or her own responsibilities, but also of the responsibilities of every other associate. In this way, everyone knows what everyone else is doing and what type of support they can give to or receive from others.

FYI

If you have a difficult task, assign it to a capable but lazy person. He or she will find an easy way to do it.

To keep everyone informed, create a chart listing each phase of the assignment, the person handling it, deadlines, and other pertinent information. Break down the assignments and list them on a chart with the name of the person assigned to each phase, deadline dates, and other pertinent information. Post the chart in the office for easy referral.

The Least You Need to Know

➤ For the many routine tasks a team performs, write meaningful job descriptions.

➤ Spread the work equitably. All associates should share unpleasant assignments as well as participate in challenging ones.

➤ Enlist the entire team in the planning process.

➤ When planning a project, help team members reach consensus so all will understand it and be committed to its success.

➤ Don't give orders: Request or suggest that associates perform a job.

➤ Delegation is more than just assigning work. It is giving the team member the authority and responsibility to complete the project.

➤ Set control points to allow for feedback at key phases of the project so that errors can be corrected before they impact on the entire project.

➤ To keep the team informed on the progress of a project, post a chart listing each phase of the assignment, the person handling it, deadlines, and the current status.

Be a Leader, Be a Coach

What Makes a Leader?

Whether you are a permanent team leader or are chosen to lead the team for a special project, your work is cut out for you. You have to mold the members of the team into a dynamic, interactive, high-performance unit.

How do you do it? By helping the members of your team develop their talents to optimum capacity. You have to keep your team aware of its goals and work with it to reach those goals.

Do you have what it takes to be a leader? It has often been said that leaders are born, not made. Indeed, many of our great leaders displayed the characteristics of leadership from their early childhood. But there are countless examples in government, the military, and industry where men and women were promoted into positions of leadership due to seniority, proficiency in their work, or technical skill. The reason for their promotion had no relationship to ability to lead, nor did the achievement of higher position ensure success in leadership. They had to be taught to lead—and although some never made it, the great percentage became good and sometimes great leaders.

FYI

Shakespeare said, "Some are born great, some achieve greatness, and some have greatness thrust upon them." The same is true of leaders. There are born leaders, but many work hard to achieve it; still others, when put unexpectedly into a leadership position, take the ball and run with it.

The Qualities of Leadership

What traits do most *leaders* have? In his book *Dynamic Leadership Training*, Dr. Franklin C. Ashby, a long-time observer of business leaders, identified 10 characteristics that make great leaders:

1. Outstanding leaders have enthusiastic followers.

Often people in positions of authority can compel subordinates to follow orders by dint of the power of their jobs. But such people are not true leaders. Yes, the orders will be followed, but that is all that will happen. True leaders develop confidence and trust in their associates. (Note that they think of team members as associates, not subordinates.) This engenders a desire not only to follow that leader, but to initiate, innovate, and implement ideas of their own that fit into the goals established.

Many business leaders have built up enthusiastic and loyal followers who put in extra hours, sacrifice personal desires, and stretch their thinking powers to help achieve the goals set by a leader they respect and admire, and to whom they relate. When Steve Jobs was asked to return to Apple Computer after the company had suffered a series of major disasters, he agreed to do so with the understanding that he was not looking to take over the company but to just work to bring it back to profitability. He set an example by working day and night to turn the company around. With a leader like that, his associates at all levels pitched in and pushed the company forward to achieve its goal—the development and marketing of the highly successful iMac computer.

2. Outstanding leaders take a constructively discontented view of the world.

Good leaders aren't complacent. They're constantly on the alert for making innovations that will improve the way work is done, ensure continuing customer satisfaction, and increase the profitability of the organization.

Their minds are open to new ideas, and they welcome suggestions. Even after changes and improvements are made, they still look for even better ways to accomplish their goals.

Leaders like this are never fully satisfied. They review practices and procedures on a regular basis to fine-tune them. They do not fall in love with their own ideas, but are open to criticism and innovation.

3. Outstanding leaders consider themselves a work in progress.

Just as effective leaders are constructively discontented about their departments, they are never entirely satisfied with themselves. They attend seminars and self-improvement programs, purchase and listen to motivational tapes, and read books and periodicals to keep up with the state of the art in their fields and to improve their knowl-

Team Terms

Being a **leader** is the art of guiding people in a manner that commands their respect, trust, confidence, and wholehearted cooperation.

edge and understanding in a variety of areas. Great leaders don't limit their talents to their jobs. They take active roles in professional and trade associations, not only to keep in touch with new developments, but to share their ideas with colleagues from other organizations. They attend and participate in conventions and conferences and develop networks of people to whom they can turn to obtain knowledge or ideas over the years.

4. Outstanding leaders demonstrate a good understanding of human nature.

Great leaders understand people—what causes them to act and react the way they do. They make an effort to learn as much as they can about the members of their teams—not only about their skills and professional competence, but their interests, goals, and desires. They treat each person as an individual who has a personal life not just a company life.

5. Outstanding leaders expect more from themselves.

The best leaders set high standards for themselves and then work hard to achieve their goals. They are also lifelong learners. Like everyone, they make mistakes; and when they do, they view these mistakes as learning experiences and try to turn them into successes. If you've never made errors, you've never made decisions.

6. Outstanding leaders rely on some fixed, unwavering set of convictions or beliefs that serves as their guiding light.

Sir John Templeton, the founder of the Templeton Fund, one of the most profitable mutual funds, has this philosophy of business: The most successful people are often the most ethically motivated. He says that such people are likely to have the keenest understanding of the importance of morality in business and can be trusted to give full measure in all of their dealings.

But the most ethical principles, Templeton insists, come from what goes on in the mind. "If you're filling your mind with kind, loving, and helpful thoughts, then your decisions and actions will be ethical."

Team Builder

Take a sincere interest in the people with whom you interact. As Dale Carnegie pointed out: "You can make more friends in two months by becoming genuinely interested in others than you can in two years by trying to get others interested in you."

Hard work combined with honesty and perseverance are key in the Templeton philosophy. Individuals who have learned to invest themselves in their work are successful. They have earned what they have. More than simply knowing the value of money, they know their own value.

7. Outstanding leaders have both a "tough hide" and an ability to laugh at themselves.

Great leaders have a sense of humor and do not always take themselves seriously. A good example of this is Victor Kiam, now owner and CEO of the Remington Shaver Company. He tells this story about when he was a salesman selling Playtex girdles. He came up with what he thought was a great marketing gimmick. Knowing that girdles frequently were hard to clean, he offered a special promotion: Women who brought in their old, worn-out girdles could buy a new Playtex model at a discount. The plan worked a little too well. So many dirty girdles were turned in at a New York department store that he was nearly arrested for violating health codes.

8. Truly outstanding leaders are not deterred by disappointment, failure, or rejection.

One very successful leader who didn't let failure get him down is Tom Monaghan, who created and grew Domino's Pizza from a one-store pizza parlor to a chain of several thousand home-delivery outlets over a period of about 30 years. In 1989, he decided to sell his hugely successful company to concentrate on doing philanthropic work. His plan, however, did not work out. After two and a half years, the company that purchased the chain failed to maintain the momentum that Monaghan had built. In order to save the company, he was forced to come back.

It took much work and persistence to first rebuild and then expand the organization. The dogged determination that enabled Monaghan to rise from a childhood of deprivation, poverty, and abuse to becoming a great entrepreneur enabled him to not only return Domino's to its original prominence, but to expand it to 6,000 stores—of which 1,100 are in countries other than the United States.

9. Great leaders are positive thinkers.

The practice of positive thinking increases one's ability tremendously, for two reasons. First, because it discovers ability that before was locked up, calling out hitherto unknown resources; and second, it keeps the mind in harmony by killing fear, worry, and anxiety, destroying all the enemies of our success, of our efficiency. It puts the mind in a condition to succeed. It sharpens the faculties, makes them keener, because it gives a new outlook upon life, turns one about so that he faces toward his goal, toward certainty, toward assurance, instead of toward doubt, fear, and uncertainty.

10. Outstanding leaders put the focus on getting things done.

We've all come across people in management positions who appear to have all the attributes of a good leader, but somehow never quite succeed. Somewhere along the line, they have missed the boat. Why does this happen?

One example: A large consumer products distributor hired a regional sales manager, about whom they were extremely enthusiastic. He had come to them highly recommended. During the selection process, he had impressed the interviewers with his thorough knowledge of their markets, his innovative ideas on how to increase business, and his charming personality. During the first several months on the job, he developed a creative and comprehensive marketing program. He spent weeks fine-tuning the program, writing materials and creating graphics for it, and making presentations to management and to his sales force. And that's where it ended. He never was able to actually get out and make the program work. He was one of those many people who are thinkers and creators, but do not have that key trait of leadership—getting things done.

Training for Leadership

For many years, training for management positions was limited to people who were on a special management track (sometimes referred to as a *cadet corps*). They usually were hired as management trainees after graduating from college or graduate school and went through a series of management training programs within an organization, often supplemented by seminars, courses, and residencies at universities or special training schools.

One of the most commonly used management training programs was job rotation. After basic orientation, the trainees were assigned to work for a short period in each of several departments. The ostensible objective was to provide the trainees with an overview of the company so that when they moved into regular positions, they would have a good concept of the entire operation.

Make sense? Sometimes. In many companies, the time spent in each training assignment was not long enough to give the trainees any more than superficial knowledge. They never got their feet really wet. They wasted the time of the department heads, who had to divert their energies from working with their own teams. The regular team members, knowing that the trainees would be gone shortly, often resented their intrusion. This was compounded by the team members' attitude that these trainees

Team Terms

A **cadet corps** consists of a select group of men and women chosen (usually right from college) to undergo intensive training in management.

were a privileged class who would someday be their bosses without having worked their way up. Their real training began when they were finally given regular assignments.

Every Team Member Is a Potential Leader

In recent years the special management track has been supplanted by team development, in which training for management is open to any team member. And why not? Even the military has learned that graduation from military academies isn't essential for top leadership. (Two of the recent chairmen of the Joint Chiefs of Staff, Colin Powell and John Shalikashvili, weren't West Pointers.) Companies have recognized that latent leadership talent exists in most people and can be developed in them.

In a well-developed team, every team member will at some time be assigned a leadership role. It may be to head up a project or to chair a meeting. Not only does this give the member an opportunity to expand his or her skills, but such assignments are excellent training for promotion to team leadership and career advancement.

However, just throwing the member into a leadership role without training is like trying to teach somebody to swim by throwing him into the pool. Many companies have their own formal leadership training programs and there are many such programs offered by training organizations. A list of organizations that provide training in leadership is included in Appendix B.

Team Builder

Rather than pinpoint one or two associates for leadership training, provide training for the entire team. Some members may not make the grade; others may not want to be leaders, but those with leadership potential will learn the basics and some may surprise themselves by recognizing talents for leadership they didn't know they had.

The Training Process

If you are going to conduct the training yourself, here are some suggestions:

➤ **Determine what you want to teach.** From programs you have taken, select those areas you found most rewarding. Ask team members what they want to learn.

➤ **Plan the logistics.** Determine how much time youcan allot, when is the best time, where the training should be given.

➤ **Decide who will do the training.** Will you as team leader be the sole trainer? Will you invite other company personnel to help in the training program? Will you bring in outside experts?

➤ **Decide the best methods to use.** Do your team members respond best to lecture and discussions? reading material? demonstrations? role plays?

➤ **Prepare training materials.** Assemble audiovisual aids, articles, and books that will be helpful. Develop case studies and role plays, and computer or Internet supplements to the training.

➤ **Plan implementation.** After a subject is covered, arrange for members to apply it on the job. Have them report on their experience at next session.

Heads up!

In developing case studies, rather than use the generic cases you find in textbooks, create cases that are relevant to the job. Make them complex and challenging. Design them so that to solve them the team must work collaboratively.

What Kind of a Leader Are You?

If you've been working for any length of time, you probably have had several bosses—each with his or her own style of managing. Most new leaders tend—consciously or subconsciously—to emulate the style of one of their former bosses. Let's look at two common leadership styles.

The hard-boiled supervisor: Terri Tompkins was tough. She believed that one had to crack the whip to get the work done. Her favorite expression was, "I'm the boss. You get paid to work, so get going." She rarely gave praise and often bawled out employees in front of the whole department. She earned the sobriquet "Terrible Terri."

The result: Sure, she got the work out. But at the expense of resentment, which showed up in lower production, higher turnover, more absenteeism, numerous grievances, and generally poor morale.

The easygoing leader: "Happy Harry" Wadsworth was proud of the fact that he was the most popular team leader in the company. He didn't want to jeopardize his popularity, so he hesitated to enforce rules or correct minor errors in work. When a reprimand was called for, he stalled for so long that the reason for it was almost forgotten. Praise was so common, it lost its significance.

The result: A pattern of mediocre work, often behind schedule. Everybody "loved" Harry, but they knew they could get away with laziness and shoddy production.

Even more disturbing, when Harry's boss called his attention to the team's unsatisfactory performance, Harry made an abrupt about-face. He began to get tough and demanding. This only confused his team members. The work picked up for a while, but as strictness is not the nature of Happy Harry's personality, once things straightened out, he reverted to his old self.

Frequent changes in leadership style are more demoralizing than sticking to one style—good or bad. When there is no consistency in the way a leader behaves, morale is poor and production suffers.

The ideal team leader is somewhere in between these two extremes. Leadership is grounded on understanding human behavior and applying this knowledge in working with the team.

The ideal team leader praises associates for good work, but does not throw praise around lightly. Reprimanding, where called for, is done in private and in a calm manner. Members know that high standards are expected in their work and what those standards are. The leader listens to team members, helps them solve the problems that arise in the work, and coaches them to improve their performance.

Great leaders are not wishy-washy, easygoing characters or tyrants. They are neither ignored nor feared by team members. They have earned the confidence and respect of their team.

The Team Leader as a Coach

Probably the most challenging part of the leader's job is molding the individual team members into a dynamic, interactive, high-performance unit. This is the main function of a coach of an athletic teams, and that's your job now.

How to do it? By helping the members of the team develop their talents to optimum capacity. Keep your team alert to the organization's goals and to the latest methods and techniques that will enable them to reach those goals. Help them learn what they don't know and to perfect what they *do* know.

Helping Team Members Take Charge of Their Jobs

The team is made up of individuals. Each person in the team contributes to the success of the team's mission. To do that each member must be skilled in the work he or she performs and motivated to do it superbly.

If team members were given more control over the work they do and encouraged to take charge of their jobs, they would have more interest, more commitment, and more enjoyment from their work. This leads to higher individual productivity and in turn to superior team performance.

How can the leader/coach help members gain that control? These suggestions have worked for many leaders:

FYI

"It matters not how strait the gate
How charged with punishments the scroll
I am the master of my fate
I am the captain of my soul"

—E. Henley, *Invictus*

➤ **Encourage team members to master their jobs.** When members know their work well and perform it in a professional manner, they are on the track toward mastery of their work life. The coach not only trains new members in the basics of their jobs, but works with all members to keep them on the cutting edge of the latest technology, methods, and innovations. In addition, the leader encourages members to take the initiative in adding to their knowledge—to read, to take courses, to attend seminars, to learn from others—not just about specific aspects of the functions currently performed, but to broaden their knowledge of their profession or skill area. This gives the associate a feeling of comfort and confidence when faced with new challenges that arise.

➤ **Aim for excellence.** Are there members of your team whom you know can perform better? They do satisfactory, even good work, but you see in them a potential that is not being reached?

Cathy, team leader of a market development team, felt that one of her associates, Christine, was one of those persons. She set up a meeting with Christine and told her, "Your work is good, I have no complaints about it, but I know that you could and should do better. Had you been less bright, I would be satisfied with what you've been doing, but I see in you the capacity to be one of the very best people in this company. By being satisfied with mediocre performance, you're not aiming high enough. Let's together develop a plan to help you achieve what you are capable of achieving."

They jointly set goals and a plan to reach them. Standards were established so they could measure how close Christine was getting to those goals. They met periodically to evaluate her progress. Within a few months, Christine was doing significantly more effective work and was on her way to an exciting and satisfying career.

Heads Up!

Don't give up on a member easily. Mistakes will be made. Use them as tools to improve the work. When people learn from their mistakes, they are unlikely to repeat them.

➤ **Get the member to participate.** As discussed earlier in this book, it has been shown that when people participate in decisions that affect them, they're more likely to work to achieve their goals.

When a new project is assigned, instead of telling the assignees how to do it, work together with them in setting the procedures. Giving them some control over the way it will be done is another way of helping them take charge of their jobs.

➤ **Encourage creativity.** Most people feel they have some control over their jobs when their suggestions and ideas are taken seriously. Nobody expects that all their suggestions will be accepted, but they do expect that they will be given serious consideration. Create a climate of innovation. Give associates the opportunity to criticize current practices and come up with ideas for improvement. Keep an open mind to new ideas. The old adage "If it ain't broken, don't fix it" must be replaced with "If it works now, it's probably obsolete."

Encourage every team member to rethink their job and know that their views—no matter how radical they may appear—will be listened to.

Ten Tips for Coaching Individual Team Members

1. Meet with each team member on a regular basis to identify what that member can do to become more effective and what you can do to help.

2. Don't wait for a formal performance review to confront poor performance. Take action to correct it as soon as you notice it.

3. Keep a running record on each associate's progress. Include examples of successes and failures. Note areas where improvement is needed. Specify recommendations for that member's growth.

4. In training members, keep in mind that people master tasks in small steps. Build the training by first giving the member small tasks and working up to more complex tasks.

5. Encourage slow learners by praising their efforts and reinforcing the training to help them catch up.

6. Rather than working to achieve several goals at the same time, help team members build their skills by working on one goal at a time. Once they're on the way to meeting it, add another goal.

7. Be a role model to associates by your own pursuit of learning and your application of new approaches to the work.

8. Pass on tips, information, and ideas that you acquire to team members. This may take the form of articles you read and clip, Internet resources you e-mail to them, or sharing new concepts orally.

9. Assign associates responsibility for all or part of a project and give them the leeway to do it without your interference.

10. If the coaching session didn't result in improvement, ask yourself these questions:

    ➤ What was the purpose of the coaching session?

    ➤ What did I do to achieve the purpose?

    ➤ What action resulted from the session?

Have the team member answer the same questions, and compare the results.

For details on the tools and techniques of training members, see Chapter 23.

Coaching the Team

Training each member of the team to perform superbly is just one aspect of the coach's responsibility. Equally important is melding the group into a coordinated working unit.

For a new team, it starts with a thorough orientation on the objectives of the team—what is expected from each associate and from the team as a whole. This can be done in group sessions or, when a new member is added, one on one.

Let's look at Erica Frost, leader of an information technology team. When the team is assigned a new project, Erica spends the first day or more of the assignment discussing it with team members—both individually and as a group. She commented, "The more time I spend up front, the better the success rate." She draws on the experience that various team members have had with similar projects and together they plan the entire operation. As the project proceeds, she keeps tabs on each associate's progress and jumps in with assistance, added training, or whatever is needed to make them more effective on the job.

Team Builder

Create your own training guide book. Include ideas that specifically apply to your company. Encourage associates to add their original ideas and those they learn from their own research to this book. Make it available to all team members at all times.

Just as the coach of an athletic team gives pep talks to the team before the game and during breaks, team leaders find that pep talks stimulate production and reinvigorate members when their enthusiasm wanes.

Pep talks help push the team forward for the short term—and often that's enough to pull it out of a rut. For more lasting effect, keep the team alert to its progress. Praise every accomplishment, celebrate reaching interim goals, give recognition to team members who do outstanding work.

FYI

B. F. Skinner, the eminent psychologist, proved in his experiments that by praising the good in people and ignoring the bad, the good is reinforced and the bad withers away.

Good leaders recognize every improvement and good point. When special achievements are accomplished, the leader praises the team and reiterates how the cooperative efforts of the team members contributed to the achievement. Erica Frost makes a practice of having an impromptu pizza or ice cream party when a significant part of a project is successfully finished. When a particularly complex project is completed, she and her husband host a barbecue at their home for all members and their significant others.

Successful coaches work with members to keep up their spirits when they are depressed, to retrain them when they need to hone their skills, to glory about their triumphs with them, and to build an esprit de corps in the team.

Mentoring: The Two-Sided Training Experience

It's a well-known fact that when a high-ranking manager takes a younger employee under his or her wing—becomes that person's *mentor*—the protégé not only has a head start for advancement, but will acquire more know-how than others about the work, the workings of the company, and the "tricks of the trade".

Mentor, Mentor, Who's the Mentor?

Why shouldn't everybody have a mentor? Why leave it to the chance that some senior managers choose a protégé while others do not? Why not make mentoring a job requirement—not only for senior executives, but for all experienced team members?

By structuring a mentoring program, and assigning the best people on your team the responsibility of mentoring a new associate, you take a giant step forward in making the newcomer productive and on the way to personal growth.

Team leaders are busy people. Often they just don't have enough time to give to associates, particularly newcomers to the team. One solution: Appoint an experienced team member to mentor the newcomer. Don't always select the same member; every associate should have the opportunity to undertake this role.

> **Team Terms**
>
> A **mentor** is a team member assigned to act as counselor, trainer, and "big brother" or "big sister" to another member.

A structured mentoring program requires that people chosen to be mentors be willing to take on the job. Compelling someone to be a mentor is self-defeating. Everybody is not interested in or qualified for it. However, if in your judgment the person who declines the assignment is really qualified, but is shy or lacks the self-confidence, have a heart-to-heart talk about how—by accepting the task—both the member and the team will benefit. New mentors should be trained by experienced people in the art of mentoring.

Both the mentor and the person who is mentored benefit from the process. Obviously, those who are mentored learn much from the process, but equally important, the mentors gain by sharpening their skills in order to pass them on. It heightens the mentors' sense of responsibility as they guide their protégés through the maze of company policies and politics. It also makes them more effective in their interpersonal relationships.

Ten Tips for New Mentors

When a team leader appoints a mentor, give that person a thorough orientation on the art of mentoring. If they have had a successful personal experience with a mentor, use that as a model. If not, suggest that another member who has been a successful mentor become the team member's mentor in mentoring.

Here are 10 things for a new mentor to keep in mind:

1. **Know the work.** Review the basics. Think back on the problems you've faced and how you dealt with them. Be prepared to answer questions about every aspect of the job.

2. **Know your company.** One of the main functions of a mentor is to help the trainee overcome the hurdles of unfamiliar company policies and practices. More important, as a person who's been around the organization for some time, you know the inner workings of the organization—the true power structure—the company politics.

Heads Up!

Some people learn more slowly than others. This does not mean they're stupid. If the person you are mentoring does not catch on right away, be patient. Slow learners often develop into productive team members.

3. **Get to know your protégé.** To be an effective mentor, take the time to learn as much as you can about the person you are mentoring. Learn about his or her education, previous work experience, current job, and more. Learn his or her goals, ambitions, and outside interests. Observe personality traits. Get accustomed to the person's ways of communicating in writing.

4. **Learn to teach.** If you have minimal experience in teaching, pick up pointers on teaching methods from the best trainers you know. Read articles and books on training techniques.

5. **Learn to learn.** It is essential that you keep learning—not only the latest techniques in your own field, but developments in your industry, in the business, community, and in the overall field of management.

6. **Be patient.** Your protégé may not pick up what you teach as rapidly as you would like. Patience is key to success in mentoring.

7. **Be tactful.** You are not a drill sergeant training a rookie in how to survive in combat. Be kind. Be courteous. Be gentle—but be firm and let the trainee know you expect the best.

8. **Don't be afraid to take risks.** Give your protégé assignments that will challenge his or her capabilities. Let her know that she won't succeed in all the assignments, but that the best way to grow is to take on tough jobs. Failures may occur, but that's how we learn, after all.

9. **Celebrate successes.** Let the trainee know you are proud of the accomplishments and progress he makes. When he achieves something especially significant, make a big fuss.

10. **Encourage your protégé to become a mentor.** The best reward you can get from being a mentor is that once the need for mentoring is done, your protégé carries on the process by becoming a mentor.

The Least You Need to Know

➤ To be an effective leader, you must earn the respect, trust, confidence, and support of your associates.

➤ Training for leadership should not be limited to a few.

➤ Leadership skills are trainable. You don't have to rely only on your own know-how or even your company's training capabilities. Take advantage of the many fine training programs that are available.

➤ The ideal leader understands human nature and applies this knowledge to keeping the team moving steadily toward its goals.

➤ Probably the most challenging part of the leader's job is molding the individual team members into a dynamic, interactive, high-performance unit.

➤ Both the mentor and the person who is mentored benefit from the mentoring process.

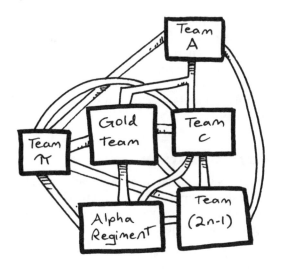

Your Team Is Not Alone

Teams do not exist in a vacuum. They are part of an organization with its own mission and goals. The purpose of any team is to help that organization achieve its goals. The team's goals, therefore, must fit into the overall goals of the organization.

There are situations where a team will work alone—almost as if it was an independent entity—but most of the time the team's work must be coordinated with the activities of other teams or units.

Your Niche in the Company Structure

Teams are created for specific purposes. Most often it is to perform a special function within a department. For example, an engineering team's function might be product design; a financial team, budgeting; a human resources team, recruiting; a marketing

Team Builder

Meet regularly with team members to reinforce their understanding of the team's goals and how those goals fit in with the company's overall objectives.

team, sales forecasting, and so on. As noted earlier, temporary teams may be formed to handle one-time problems, such as preparing a move to a new location or investigating and recommending new equipment. As a team leader, your responsibility is to ensure that your team's mission and objectives are consistent with those of the organization.

The Team's Mission

When the team is organized, the team leader should meet with the department head for input on the department's objectives and what is expected of the team to support those objectives.

In establishing the team's goals, test each proposal by asking, "How does this measure up against the overall goals of the department and the company?"

As you evaluate the team's progress over time, check to make sure that what is being done is in line with the organization's overall objectives and is contributing to meeting its goals.

Another important part of the team leader's job is to coordinate the team's work with other teams. Communicate your team's goals to other team leaders. Learn their goals and convey them to your team members. When members of every team are aware of the goals and activities of other teams in the company, all move forward in a consistent manner to achieve the organization's mission.

Team Terms

A **mission statement** is more than just an indicator of the company's objectives. It is its credo, its raison d'être, the philosophy upon which the company conducts its business.

Help the Team Grow, Help Yourself Grow

There are team leaders who are perfectly happy to lead a team that consistently achieves its goals. But is that enough? Doing a good job is what is expected. The superb team leader works with higher level managers to get assignments for the team that will make it stand out above other teams in the organization. To do this, the leader has to know a good deal more than just the work of the team. He or she must learn as much as possible about the business. Not only will this help the team, it will prepare the leader to move up the corporate ladder.

Following are some suggestions to increase knowledge of the company:

➤ Get basic information about the company by reading the annual report, obtaining research reports about the company on the Internet or from a stockbroker, and studying articles about the company in business journals.

➤ Study the company's *mission statement.* Make sure you fully understand its implications. Discuss it with your boss.

➤ Ask your manager to add your name to distribution lists for memos, bulletins, and reports that will keep you abreast of developments in the company.

➤ Subscribe to trade publications. Learn what competitors and other companies are doing.

Team Builder

Cultivate long-time employees. These men and women know the ins and outs of the company and can fill you in on company history, advise you on company politics, and give you insight into the strengths and weaknesses of the organization.

➤ Attend meetings of trade associations and report information and ideas you picked up to your managers.

➤ Share information about the company with team members. Encourage them to discuss it.

➤ Develop a contact with someone in your company's corporate planning department to learn more about long-term plans and new developments.

➤ Volunteer to participate in committees or task forces that are formed to deal with company problems.

Coordinate with Other Teams

In order for any organization to succeed in meeting its goals, it must be well balanced. It's the team leader's job to coordinate interteam activities.

There are three aspects of coordination:

1. **Coordinating individuals in a team:** This aspect was discussed in Chapter 3.

2. **Coordination among groups of an organization:** Each team must know what other teams are doing; each department must know what other departments are doing—and coordinate their action. If the Sales department plans to push the sale of a specific item, Manufacturing must be prepared to produce it, Purchasing must buy the needed raw materials, Accounting and Finance must make arrangements for funds to be available, and Human Resources must recruit people to make the goods. Teams within each department must be given their assignments. All must be coordinated so the process will be accomplished as planned.

3. **Coordination among various organizations:** In today's complex economy, businesses become dependent upon one another. Companies subcontract work to independent businesses—often in faraway cities or even other countries. Your team may work interactively with a team at another location—people they never see in person. To coordinate work with such teams is another challenge for the team leader.

Coordination starts with planning. All plans must be interrelated and designed to fit in with the plans of the other teams. This is usually done by the team leaders, but in more and more situations—especially when teams are in the same location—the entire team meets to jointly work out the plans.

The team leaders work together to coordinate the implementation of the plans. It is essential that every member be thoroughly committed to them. If everybody knows what's been planned and has had a hand in developing it, there will be little difficulty in coordinating the activities of the teams.

Another way of facilitating coordination is to consider the relationships among teams when laying out the facility. If teams that frequently work together are housed in the same building—even on the same floor—it makes coordination much easier.

As noted in Chapter 4, channels of communication can be a major barrier to the interchange of information and ideas between teams. By setting up procedures to bypass channels, coordination between the two teams can be eased.

FYI

Old aphorisms provide conflicting messages. There's an old joke that says that a camel is a horse designed by a committee. But camels are superior to horses in the desert. Do committees bog down because "too many cooks spoil the broth," or do they benefit because "two heads are better than one"?

When several teams are engaged in a project, a committee made up of representatives of each team may be appointed to coordinate the endeavor. The team leader may represent her team, but quite often an associate is assigned. In some coordinating committees, one member serves as chairperson; in others, each member takes a turn as chair.

Following are some suggestions to make the coordinating committee work smoothly:

➤ Each member of the committee should be given a specific assignment.

➤ Each member should submit a plan and timetable for his or her phase of the project.

➤ After the plans are approved, they are forwarded to each team, where team members determine how they intend to proceed.

➤ Team leaders report progress to the committee on a predetermined basis.

➤ Depending upon the projected length of the project, the committee meets one or more times a week to report on progress and resolve problems that arise between teams.

➤ Upon completion of the project, the committee is dissolved. If the same group of teams starts another project, it's a good idea to form a new committee. This gives different team members the opportunity to benefit from the experience.

Internal Customers and Suppliers

To foster a better relationship among the various teams in an organization, team members should treat the teams with which they interrelate as either customers or suppliers.

Internal customers are the teams or other units of the organization that your team serves. *Internal suppliers* are teams from which your team obtains what it needs to do its job. For example, the market research team supplies the sales department with data it needs to make sales decisions. If the market research team thinks of the sales department as its customer, the members of the team will do all they can to provide it with the best service. If the sales department looks at the market researchers as suppliers, they will deal with them more objectively.

Team Terms

Internal customers are persons or units in the organization to whom a team provide materials, information, or services. **Internal suppliers** are persons or units in the organization that provide the team with materials, information, or services. A team will be a customer in some aspects of its work and a supplier in others.

Your mindset is different when you look at the people, other teams, or departments that you service as customers rather than just another part of your company. You become more alert to their needs; you take the time and effort to provide them with quality service; you go out of your way to keep them happy.

Review in your own mind how you deal with the people in units your team serves. Ask yourself these questions:

Yes No 1. Have you and the internal customer jointly assessed what is wanted from your team?

Yes No 2. Has your team discussed the best ways to meet the internal customer's needs?

Yes No 3. Does your team develop standards for the products or services you provide that meet or surpass the internal customer's requirements?

Yes No 4. Do you make a point of looking at things from the customer's point of view?

Yes No 5. Do you set priorities on the basis of what is important to the internal customer?

Yes No 6. Do you get regular feedback from internal customers on how you're doing?

Yes No 7. Do you hold periodic meetings to discuss ways of being of even greater service to customers?

Yes No 8. Do you reward team members who provide over-and-above-the-line-of-duty service to the team's customers?

Yes No 9. Have you established a means of easy communication between your team members and the internal customers?

Yes No 10. Do you take immediate steps to investigate and follow through on complaints from internal customers?

If you answered "no" to any of the preceding questions, take steps to correct it.

Project Management: A Team Challenge

When companies are faced with special types of projects, usually one-time tasks (such as introducing a new product to the market, moving to a new location, or developing a new product or service), rather than assign it to one or more operating teams, they often create a project management team. These teams may be full-time activities for major projects, but often are part-time. The members continue to do their jobs in their regular teams in addition to working on the projects.

Project Teams Are Interdepartmental

This new group is chosen from several departments and is given the responsibility of handling all matters related to the project. Project team leaders have the authority to obtain from various departments in the company the personnel, information, equipment, and anything else needed to perform the assignment.

The person chosen to be *project manager* is usually an experienced team leader who has expertise in the activity the project involves. Some of the project manager's first tasks are listed here:

➤ Assemble a multidepartmental team that includes representatives from various parts of the organization to plan and implement the project.

➤ Together with these representatives, plan the project and set timetables for each phase.

➤ Work with team members to coordinate the work of everyone involved, from the inception of the design phase to the final distribution to customers. The people involved may include engineers, production personnel, marketing and sales staff, and shipping and distribution personnel.

Team Terms

A **project manager** is a team leader assigned to head up a specific project, such as the design and manufacture of an electronic system or the development and marketing of a new product.

The result is that you get cooperation in place of turf wars. Rather than time-wasting red tape, you get fast decisions. By crossing over traditional departmental barriers, project managers can get quick action, shift gears when necessary, and react immediately to urgent problems.

There are advantages and limitations to being assigned to a project team. Those who are chosen are given the opportunity to expand their knowledge and to take on new and challenging assignments. It often brings them into contact with senior managers and enables them to build networks with members of other teams and departments, which can be an asset in their career advancement.

On the other hand, it takes them away from their regular work. They miss out on some of the team's achievements and, when they return to their regular jobs, may have to struggle to catch up with what the team is doing.

Prioritizing the Work

When one of your team members is assigned to a project team, either full-time or part-time, his or her work still has to be done. Maybe the company will provide you with a temp to help out, but more likely, you will have to spread the work among the rest of the team.

Darlene, for example, is not only working on a project for you but is also on the quality assurance team. Harry, a member of your team, has been asked to work on a special project for another manager. All these assignments are important, but you're responsible for getting the work on your project accomplished.

Heads Up!

Don't be afraid to say no. If your team is already overburdened and some members are working on special projects, turn down the assignment. When you say no, show how taking on the assignment will inhibit completion of other higher-priority projects, and suggest alternative solutions.

What can you do when members of your team have other assignments that are equally important or when your team is facing several high-priority tasks that must be completed in the same time frame?

You can't pull rank. It used to be that you could force your priorities on others because you were higher on the totem pole. Occasionally, this is still acceptable, but in most progressive organizations such power plays are discouraged.

Work it out. Talk to team members and to other team leaders to schedule work that will enable all of you to make the best contribution you can to your organization. This process takes diplomacy and a willingness to compromise.

When one or more members of your team is taken away from regular duties, you have to find ways to get the work done—without overworking the other team members. Many people spend 10 or 12 hours at the office, and then take work home with them at night. There's a limit, however, to the amount of time a person can spend working.

Seek new and creative approaches to your work so that the team works smarter, not harder. Ask yourself: Which kind of work can be eliminated? Which work processes can be reengineered? Which can be delegated? The time you spend learning about new approaches will pay off in better performance.

Joint Ventures: Interteam Collaboration

There are teams that work on specialized projects—doing research or long-term planning—where they have little contact with other teams. Most teams are constantly interacting with others. Their assignments overlap; they exchange ideas and coordinate their work so that each team will meet its goals and deadlines.

Occasionally, a project will be of such magnitude or complexity that more than one team will be assigned to work on it. In such cases, it requires much more than cooperation. It requires a complete integration of the teams for the duration of the project.

Usually the partners in a joint venture will be two or more teams in the organization, but sometimes they may be outsiders, subcontractors, or vendors.

When Sweet Sixteen Cosmetics was preparing to launch its new line of hair-care products, it created a joint venture of its hair-care brand management team and a similar team from its advertising agency.

It started off badly. The ad agency people were much more aggressive, and impatient to get moving fast. The company team was more cautious and wanted to make sure every possible contingency was discussed and prepared for. Fortunately, the team leaders recognized the problem and sat down to work out a modus operandi both teams could live with, and the project went ahead smoothly.

Whether the partners are in the same firm or one is an outsider, the approach to success is the same. Let's say that your team and Lara's team have been assigned to develop a distribution plan for a new product. What can you and Lara do to ensure the joint venture will run smoothly?

FYI

Over the past few years many organizations have downsized and reorganized, sometimes eliminating entire teams and departments by outsourcing the work they performed to independent contractors—often the very people they had laid off. They invite these people to join with the company's teams to share in collaborative planning and actions.

➤ Learn as much as you can about Lara's team. Meet with Lara as soon as possible after the assignment is announced. Share what each of you sees as the objective of the assignment. Discuss the strengths each team can contribute to the project. Make tentative decisions on which team members will perform the various aspects.

➤ Hold a meeting of both teams. Present the overall picture to the members. Obtain input from them on how the project should be broken down.

➤ Arrange for an informal get-together so team members can get acquainted with the members of the other team.

➤ Make specific assignments. Take advantage of the expertise of each member. Instead of breaking the project into separate team activities, make it a true joint venture by pairing members of one team with members of the other.

➤ Project leadership can be shared by both team members, or one can be selected to lead the venture.

➤ Arrange periodic joint meetings to discuss progress and solve problems.

The Least You Need to Know

➤ The team leader's responsibility is to ensure that the team's mission and objectives are consistent with those of the organization.

➤ The leader has to know a good deal more about the business than just the work of the team.

➤ In order for any organization to succeed in meeting its goals, it must be well balanced. It's the team leader's job to coordinate interteam activities.

➤ Look at the people, other teams, or departments that you service as customers rather than as another part of your company, and be alert to their particular needs.

➤ By crossing over traditional departmental barriers, project managers can get quick action, shift gears when necessary, and react immediately to urgent problems.

➤ When an assignment of one of your team members to a special project impacts on your team's progress, work with the team leader(s) involved to schedule work so that all of you can make the best contribution to the organization.

➤ Work smarter—not harder. Seek new and creative approaches to your work. Eliminate, reengineer, and delegate tasks.

Part 3

Can't We All Just Get Along?

Wouldn't it be great if everybody on the team were dedicated workers, cooperative partners, and fun to be with every day? There are some teams like that, but unfortunately, most teams have their share of members who don't pull their weight, who can't get along with other members, and who make life miserable for everybody.

Probably the biggest challenge to a team leader is to bring together a group of diverse human beings—each with his or her idiosyncrasies—and mold them into a collaborative team.

In this section, we'll examine the myriad problems facing the team leader in molding a group of individuals into a smooth working team.

In most teams, members are cooperative and diligent, but there are often those who present problems. Some members don't perform up to expectations; some are sensitive and temperamental; some are too self-centered. Some are just unhappy. Some are stressed or burned out. Some just can't get along with others.

There's hope for many of these people. You'll learn some tips and techniques on how to salvage them. But you can't always win. Some are beyond hope. You'll learn how to deal with that, too.

Overcoming Team Discord

As the team leader, you've done your best to create an effective team. You picked good people. You trained them. You established a collaborative environment—but the team still isn't functioning as it should. Most members are doing their best, but some members exhibit problems that pull down the entire team.

In many teams, there are members who do superior work and resent having to "carry" less effective associates. In some teams there are members who are sensitive or temperamental and are difficult to work with.

In this chapter we'll look at what the team leader can do to resolve some of these problems and help the team move forward.

Members Who Don't Carry Their Loads

Bob is typical of many team members. He has always done work that's just satisfactory—but that's all. When team projects fall behind because Bob's work is slower or less

Team Builder

If one of the team members is keeping the team from achieving its goals, determine the true reason. Both the leader and the other team members should work with the member to overcome it.

accurate, the other associates have to help him catch up. When spoken to by the team leader about this, his work improves for a while—but soon reverts to mediocre performance.

Let's look at some of the ways to deal with this.

Let the Team Leader Fix It

The team leader must first determine why Bob is not performing as well as other associates. There could be many reasons:

1. He may not have the basic skills needed. If this is the case, Bob needs additional training. This can be done by personal coaching in the area where Bob needs help or by sending him to special training programs.

2. He may know the basics, but is not using them properly. The team leader or another member should work closely with him, observing his methods and suggesting how he can correct his faults.

3. He may have the skills, but has a low level of expectations for himself. When in school, Bob probably was satisfied with passing his courses with a "C" and is now satisfied with just meeting minimum standards on the job.

   This is a greater challenge for the team leader. Bob must be made to understand that the team's goal is to achieve higher standards—"A" grades—and Bob must raise his standards to that of the team.

   To do this, the team leader must establish with Bob a plan to get on track. Set daily quantitative and qualitative goals. Take a few minutes at the end of each day to discuss his progress. If he has not met the goals, go over what he has done and determine what must be done the next day so he can improve. Don't expect a rapid turnabout. It takes time to change work habits.

   Involve other team members. They can give added help and moral support. If Bob sincerely tries to improve, the other team members will be patient with him and their initial resentment will be alleviated.

   On the other hand, if he does not improve, he may have to be removed from the team (see Chapter 13).

4. He may have personal problems that are keeping him from concentrating on the job. How to deal with this is covered in Chapter 11.

Let Team Members Handle It

Peer pressure is often looked upon as a negative factor. We read about kids being pressured by their friends to do things parents disapprove of. On the job coworkers put pressure on associates to conform to their work styles—often to the detriment of the organization.

I've heard old-timers tell ambitious newcomers, "Slow down, you're making it bad for the rest of us." The implication is that if they want to be accepted, they follow the informal rules laid down by the group.

Team Terms

Peer Pressure: When team members exert their combined efforts to influence associates who are not meeting expectations.

But peer pressure need not work against the organization. A team member whose poor work habits are holding the team back can be pressured to improve by the rest of the team.

It's often done in a negative manner. "Bob, if you want to be one of us, you have to shape up." Failure to comply could lead to being ignored by associates, not invited to partake in after-work activities, or ostracized in the lunch room.

Negative peer pressure may work, but positive peer pressure is far more effective.

Here is a four-step approach a team leader can take to set the stage for positive peer pressure:

1. Review the expectations of the team. Sometimes the reason the Bobs in your team are not performing as desired is that they don't fully understand what is expected of them. Review with the entire team what each person is required to do to meet the standards. Emphasize timeliness, follow-through, cooperation, and individual responsibility.

2. Give the team an exercise in team building. Ask each team member two questions: "What do you expect from your teammates in order to meet team goals?" and "What can they expect from you?" Lead a discussion on what was brought up and reach a consensus as to the qualities that make up a "good" team member. Play up the importance of each team member helping others—not to do their work for them—but to teach them improved techniques, motivate them to overcome bad habits, and work cooperatively with the team.

3. Ask members how they believe they match the "good" team member profile. Congratulate them on their strengths and ask how they can help associates who are weak where they are strong. Ask what help they may need to build up their limitations. Offer your assistance, and suggest other team members who may give them support.

4. Follow through. At the end of every project, review how the team functioned. Discuss both group and individual performance. Praise their successes. Ask for

133

suggestions on how they could do an even better job on the next project. If one or more of the members did not meet expectations, enlist the support of the team to identify and correct the problem.

Exercises like this not only build up team spirit, but incorporate peer pressure as an integral part of team activity. Members expect their colleagues to demand the best from them and respond positively to their suggestions.

Team Troublemakers

Teams are made up of people. In many teams there are people whose difficult personalities hamper teamwork. They may be overly sensitive, temperamental, self-centered, negative, or just unhappy. Let's look at some ways to deal with these troublesome members.

Team Builder

Keep a success log for your team. Enter in it the special achievements of each of your team members and of your team as a whole. Encourage each team member to keep a personal success log. When things don't go well or when you and your team members are feeling low, have everyone reread the log.

People with Low Self-Esteem

Self-esteem is the way people feel about themselves. If you think of yourself as a success, you will be a success; if you think of yourself as second-rate, you will always be second-rate—unless you change your self-perception—and it can be done.

People with low self-esteem show it in the way they talk about themselves. They're more likely to complain about their failures than to brag about successes. They rarely express opinions that differ from those of other team members, and when they do, they preface it with an apology. When pressed to express their thoughts or ideas, they start their answers with, "I'm not sure about this," or, "I'm probably wrong, but ..." They never volunteer to lead a discussion, and they take charge of a project only when the leader assigns it and then they express doubts about their ability to do it properly.

To make this member a full participant in team success, the team leader has to help build up that self-esteem. Focus on that member's successes, not on failures. Most people don't loathe themselves, but they may have temporary self-esteem slumps and need bolstering. If they don't deal with those slumps, however, more serious consequences can occur.

Give the member positive reinforcement for every achievement, and praise for progress made in the work. Be specific. Use examples of his good work and how it benefited the team. Equally important, be positive when he or she comes up with a good idea or makes meaningful contributions to team discussions and activities.

People with low self-esteem need to be continually reminded that you, the team leader, respect them and have confidence in them.

Make assignments that you're sure the member can handle, and provide added training, coaching, and support to ensure success. The taste of success is a surefire way to build self-esteem.

Overly Sensitive Team Members

No one likes to be criticized, but most people can accept constructive criticism. However, there are some people who resent any criticism. Even the slightest criticism of their work causes them to get defensive.

Let's look at an example of how fear of criticism kept one team from meeting deadlines.

One of the team members, Kevin, is so concerned about being criticized that he's overly cautious in all areas of his work. Rather than risk a slight error, he checks, double-checks, and then rechecks everything he does. This process may minimize his exposure to criticism, but it's so time-consuming that it slows down his entire team. In addition, because of this fear, Kevin hesitates on making decisions. His excuse: "I need more information before I can decide."

Heads Up!

When criticizing sensitive people, begin by praising the parts of assignments that they have done well. Then make some suggestions about how they can do better in the unsatisfactory areas. Caution: Instead of following phrases with the negative *but*, use *and*. For example, say, "Your presentation made your point, *and* adding a visual will make it excellent."

If members of your team behave the way Kevin does, follow these guidelines to help them overcome their fears:

➤ Assure them that, because of their excellent knowledge in their field, their work is usually correct the first time and doesn't have to be checked repeatedly.

➤ Point out that occasional errors are normal and that they can be caught and corrected later without reflecting on the ability of the person who made them.

➤ If you feel that team members need more information before making a decision, guide them toward resources to help them obtain it. If you feel that they have adequate information, insist that they make prompt decisions.

➤ If the team member asks you what to do, reassure him that you believe he has the capability to make the decision and insist it be made quickly.

Team Members Who Can't Keep Their Cool

Terry is a good worker, but from time to time he loses his temper and hollers and screams at his coworkers and even at you. He calms down quickly, but his behavior affects the work of the entire team, and it takes a while to get back to normal performance. You've spoken to Terry about his temper several times, but it hasn't helped.

It isn't easy to work in an environment in which people holler and scream, particularly if you're the target. When this occurs, not only the persons screamed at but the entire team may be unable to work at full capacity for several hours afterward. Situations like this cannot be tolerated.

Here are some suggestions for dealing with someone who has temper tantrums:

➤ After the person calms down, have a heart-to-heart talk. Point out that you understand that it's not always easy for someone to control his or her temper but that such behavior isn't acceptable in the workplace.

➤ If another outburst occurs, send the person out of the room until he or she can calm down. Let the person know that the next offense will lead to disciplinary action.

➤ Recommend the old adage, "Count to 10 before opening your mouth."

➤ If you have an employee-assistance program (see Chapter 11), suggest that the team member see one of its counselors.

Team Builder

If the person you're criticizing begins to cry or throw a tantrum, say that you're leaving and you'll return after he or she calms down. Wait 10 minutes, and then try again. *Note:* It's best not to conduct potentially emotional meetings in your office—use a conference room instead.

The Information Hoarder

Iris was a hoarder. You'd think that every piece of data she had, every source she uncovered, every detail she worked with was proprietary—owned by her and held close to her vest.

Why did she hoard? Often the reason for this behavior is insecurity. She may fear that if others had her "know-how" she might be looked upon as expendable. Her "knowledge" is her security blanket. Or perhaps she liked to hold things to herself so she could look good to the boss when she brought them out in solving problems.

Whatever her reason, the result was devastating to the functioning of the team. Projects were stalled, associates were stymied, errors were made due to the lack of information needed by the rest of the team.

Set up a system for distribution of all information. Hold a meeting to discuss the rules so there can be no misunderstanding. Require all team members to follow the rules. Caution all associates that failure to follow the system is a serious violation of team rules and could lead to disciplinary action.

The Naysayer

Do you have an associate who always opposes the rest of the team? Whenever you're for something, she's against it. She always has a reason why what you want to accomplish just can't be done. She'll tear down your team with pessimism.

Why is she like that? It may stem from some real or perceived past mistreatment by your company. If that's the case, look into the matter. If she has justifiable reasons for being negative, try to persuade her that the past is past and to look to the future. If misconceptions are involved, try to clear them up.

Negativity is often rooted in long-term personality factors that are beyond the ability of any team leader to overcome. In that case, professional help is necessary.

Heads Up!

Tread lightly when dealing with negative people. Acknowledge their arguments and persuade them to work with you to overcome their perceived problems so that the project can move along. Make the person part of the solution rather than an additional problem.

When you present new ideas to negative people, get them to express their objections openly. Tell them, "Those are interesting points and as we move into this new program, let's carefully watch for those problems. But let's give this new concept a try. Work with me on it, and together we'll iron out the kinks."

The Know-It-All

This is the team member who thinks he has all the answers to all the problems. If it's not his idea, it isn't going to work. Often this member may have excellent background in the area involved and does have ideas that can be useful. But in most cases he only thinks he's right but is way off.

Here are two suggestions to help deal with those who think they know it all and help them benefit from those who truly have the answers:

➤ Insist that the member prove his point. Ask him to provide data to back up his statements—facts and figures, sources of information, documentation. If it's all in his head, he will backtrack rapidly.

➤ If you feel the person has good ideas, give her a significant role in the project. Have her research the areas in which she has reservations and report on her findings. Enlist her assistance in training less knowledgeable members in areas of her expertise.

The Prima Donna

This is the member who thinks some of the work assigned to her is beneath her dignity to do. "I'm a marketing specialist, not a clerk. Somebody else should keep those records."

In a team, everybody has to share in both the challenging projects and the routine work. This should be made clear at the outset and be reinforced from time to time.

Following are some ways to deal with this:

➤ Rotate routine tasks among all team members.

➤ Do your own share of "drudge" work. It may not be fun for you either, but you set a good example for the prima donnas.

➤ Make the job more enticing. True, it's not always possible to enrich drudge work, but by giving the member some leeway in performing the job, it can become more desirable. For example, allow the member to work at home on an assignment or tie in the necessary routine work with a more challenging assignment.

FYI

The kid who was the class clown in school is likely to be the team clown on the job. Back then, he or she had the class in stitches with his humor, but could be nasty in playing tricks on the teacher and classmates. The team clown can lighten the boredom of a meeting or break the tension in the team with humor. But beware if the humor is barbed and sarcastic and is aimed at a teammate or the team leader.

The Peacock

In every organization there are people who just can't help but celebrate even the smallest of successes by bragging and strutting. They want everybody to know that they're the greatest. This is not so bad if he or she does this occasionally. But when this peacock "displays his feathers" over and over again, other team members will become annoyed.

Following are some tips on dealing with peacocks:

➤ **Give them special attention.** The reason for strutting is to gain attention. If the team leader recognizes this and praises each and every accomplishment, there will be less reason to strut in front of other members.

➤ **Take the time to listen to them.** Peacocks have big egos and need to talk to others—particularly higher ranking people like team leaders.

➤ **Don't challenge them in front of others.** Often in their bragging, they exaggerate their achievements. Consciously or subconsciously, they need to appear greater than they really are. That doesn't mean you should let them get away with unfounded opinions. When confronting them, have solid facts to back you up—and do it in private.

➤ **Use their talents.** When assigning work, let them know you believe they have what it takes to perform superbly. They "know" they're good, but they'll appreciate hearing it from you and will work hard to prove that you have displayed good judgment in giving them the assignment.

The Obnoxious Associate

Have you ever had a coworker who not only disagrees with everything you say, but expresses dissent in a nasty, sarcastic, even cruel manner. "That's the stupidest idea I ever heard." After several such encounters, you may want to kick him off the team. But that's not always possible.

Following are some ways to squash this fool:

➤ Ask him to repeat his comment. If it was inane, he'll look even more foolish when it's repeated.

➤ You repeat the comment. Then ask, "Did I hear you right?" If the ideas lack merit, he may quickly back away.

➤ Ask for solutions. If he confirms your understanding of his remarks, ask, "How would you deal with it?" This forces him to defend his position and come up with logical solutions—which he has probably not thought out.

Stress and Burnout

Stress is built into the human physiology to protect us from danger. When primitive man faced a tiger in the jungle, his body reacted immediately to the stress. Blood flowed into his muscles, his lungs absorbed more oxygen, his glands pumped adrenaline—all giving him strength to fight or flee. Today the tigers we meet are not jungle beasts but frustrations, unrealistic deadlines, domineering bosses, demanding customers. The body reacts to the stress, but we cannot fight or flee. This results in headaches, ulcers, heart attacks, or just unhappiness. Stress, a reaction meant to be positive, becomes *distress*.

All jobs have their share of stress. This is not all bad. Stress often leads to creativity, added energy, and motivation. It's when *stress* becomes *distress* that problems occur. The stress may show up in the way behavior changes. People who had always been patient become impatient. Calm people become tense. Team members, who have

139

always been cooperative, rebel. All these signs show up when people are under stress.

"There's just too much work to do."

When a team survives downsizing and reorganization, the remaining members may have to work longer and harder. The boss piles more and more work on the team, and the team just can't handle it. As team leader, you decide that you have to speak to your boss about this.

Before you approach your manager, thoroughly analyze the jobs your team is doing. Indicate how much time team members devote to each project, and determine each project's importance to the accomplishment of the team's goals. Reexamine your boss's priorities. Decide with your team what it can do to work smarter rather than harder.

If you still feel after this analysis that your team has more work than it can handle effectively, meet with your boss to review its results and try to reorder your team's priorities. Your boss may agree to defer certain time-consuming jobs because others are more important, reassign some jobs to other teams, or authorize additional personnel.

Sometimes the pressure comes from other teams or departments with whom you're collaborating. You and the leader of the other team should try to work out a schedule that alleviates the pressure. If you can't agree, take it up with the manager who supervises both teams.

Team Terms

Dr. Hans Selye, a pioneer in studying stress, defines **distress**, or **bad stress**, as the chronic state of anxiety caused by unremitting pressures of job, personal, or societal problems.

Heads Up!

Learn to say no when you're asked to take on a special assignment. If it won't help you meet your goals, decline diplomatically. Explain that you realize it's an important project but that you're already involved with several high-priority assignments and, as much as you want to help, you just can't.

When the Pressure Gets Too Great

You're working on an assignment and the pressure keeps building up. You have a headache, your stomach is tense, you just feel overly pressured:

➤ **Take a break.** If possible, get away from your workplace—get out of the building. If you work in a city, take a walk around the block. If you work in an industrial park, walk around the parking lot. If the weather is bad, walk around inside the building. In 10 or 15 minutes, you'll feel the stress dissolve and be able to face your job with renewed energy.

➤ **Exercise.** If you work in a crowded office, it's obviously not expedient to get up in the middle of the room and do jumping jacks or push-ups, but you can choose from several relaxation exercises without being obtrusive. Books and videotapes are available to show you how. If your company has an exercise room, get on the treadmill for five minutes (not enough to work up a sweat, but enough to relax your mind).

➤ **Change your pace.** Most people work on more than one project at a time. If the pressures are too great on your current project, stop for a while and work on another one. When you return to your original assignment, it will go much more smoothly.

FYI

If you want more information on managing stress, read *The Complete Idiot's Guide to Managing Stress,* by Jeff Davidson.

Managing Stress

When the stress on the job is pervasive, steps must be taken to manage it. Some physicians treat stress with tranquilizers and other medication. However, you can often manage your stress yourself:

➤ **Keep in tiptop shape.** Watch your diet, and engage in a regular exercise program.

➤ **Learn to relax.** Participate in meditation or programmed relaxation exercises. Be sure to reserve time to spend alone.

➤ **Learn to love yourself.** People with high self-esteem are less likely to be adversely affected by pressure from others.

➤ **Explore your spirituality.** Whatever your religion, spiritual experience can guide you toward peace of mind.

➤ **Keep learning.** The experience of ongoing learning keeps you alert, open-minded, and stimulated.

➤ **Develop a support team.** Avoid major stress by having friends and family members available to back you up when things don't go well.

➤ **Accept only commitments that are important to you.** Politely turn down other projects that drain your time and energy.

➤ **Seek new ways of using your creativity.** By rethinking the way you perform routine tasks and developing creative approaches to new assignments, you can make them less stressful to handle.

➤ **Welcome changes.** Consider changes as new challenges rather than threats to the status quo.

➤ **Replace negative images in your mind with positive ones.** There's proof that there *is* power in positive thinking.

➤ **Give yourself permission to have a life.** Enjoy activities with family and friends. Don't feel guilty when you're not thinking about your job.

Heads Up!

If your hobby or leisure activity makes you even more tense (competitive sports or tournament bridge), drop it. Substitute one that is truly relaxing.

Burnout

People are not light bulbs. A light bulb shines brightly and suddenly—poof! It burns out. People burn out slowly and often imperceptibly. Although some burnouts result in physical breakdowns such as a heart attack or ulcers, most are psychological. Team members lose enthusiasm, energy, and motivation, and it shows up in many ways. They hate their job, can't stand associates, distrust the team leader, and dread coming to work each morning.

Burnout can be caused by too much stress, but that's not the only cause. Some other reasons are frustration, promises made that weren't kept, or being passed over for an expected promotion or salary increase. Some leaders and managers burn out because of the pressures of having to make decisions that, if made poorly, can cause catastrophic problems. Others just burn out from having to work excessively long hours or do unrewarding work.

Often the only means of helping someone recover from burnout is to suggest professional help (see Chapter 11). There are some things you, as a team leader, can do to help put a burned-out team member on the road to recovery:

➤ **Be a supportive person.** Demonstrate your sincere interest by encouraging the member to talk about his or her concerns and put them into perspective.

➤ **Consider changing job functions.** Assigning different activities and responsibilities or transferring the member to another team changes the climate in which he or she works and provides new outlets that may stimulate motivation.

➤ **Give the member an opportunity to acquire new skills.** This not only helps him or her focus on learning rather than on the matters that led to the burnout, but also makes the person more valuable to your company.

If, despite your efforts, he or she doesn't progress, strongly suggest professional counseling.

The Job's B-o-r-r-r-ing

Some jobs are basically boring, but any job can become boring when you do it over and over again, day after day, year after year. In many companies, jobs are enriched to minimize boredom. By *job enrichment*—adding new functions and combining several simple tasks into a more challenging total activity—jobs can be made less boring.

Here are some ways to prevent jobs performed by your team members from becoming boring:

Team Builder

If a team member is constantly fatigued from work, suggest that he or she see a physician for a thorough medical examination to rule out physical causes and for suggestions to relieve fatigue and stress.

➤ Reexamine all routine work that your team performs. Encourage all people who perform the work to suggest ways of making it more interesting.

➤ People performing routine work often get into a rut. They start out every day performing aspect one, and then go to aspect two and three, and so on. Unless it's essential that work be done in a predetermined order, suggest that they change the pattern. Start one day with aspect six, and then go to three or seven or one. Breaking the routine alleviates boredom.

Team Terms

Job enrichment involves redesigning jobs to provide diversity and challenge and to make them less boring.

➤ Cross-train team members to do a variety of jobs so that they can move from one type of work to another and be less likely to become bored.

➤ Encourage members to help associates—particularly new team members—by becoming mentors to them.

Make the Workplace User-Friendly

More time is spent in our workplace than in any other location outside of our home. Studies show that people who try to make work fun actually have more fun at work.

Here are some suggestions to make the working environment more enjoyable:

1. Encourage team members to become more than coworkers—to become friends. Arrange social activities such as family picnics, lunchtime birthday parties, bowling leagues, or similar group activities.

2. Don't take yourself so seriously. If a team leader has a good sense of humor, it permeates the team.

Team Builder

It's amazing what a fresh coat of paint will do to raise morale. Repainting a wall in a cheerful pastel shade instead of institutional gray can make a big difference in the way team members react to their environment.

3. Celebrate successes—not just the big ones, but every one. One team leader commented that she had a gong on her desk and each time a project was completed before deadline, she'd sound the gong and everybody would cheer.

4. Give praise lavishly. Don't stint on recognizing achievements.

5. When a member is out due to illness, encourage associates to telephone or visit the person.

6. When a member returns from vacation, give him or her a chance to tell the team about it.

Making the workplace an enjoyable place to be will pay off in a motivated, enthusiastic, and productive working team.

The Least You Need to Know

➤ If one team member is keeping the team from achieving its goals, both the leader and the other team members should work with the member to solve the problem.

➤ Members respond to peer pressure. Prodding by associates can often impel a marginal member to increased productivity.

➤ When criticizing sensitive people, begin by praising the parts of assignments that they have done well. Then make some suggestions about how they can improve.

➤ When you present new ideas to negative people, get them to express their objections openly.

➤ Be flexible in the way you work with team members. By demanding strict conformity, you may drive away very talented team members.

➤ Stress often leads to creativity, added energy, and motivation. It's when *stress* becomes *distress* that problems occur.

➤ When the pressure gets too great, get away from your desk and do something else for a while.

➤ Enrich boring jobs by adding new functions and combining several simple tasks into a more challenging total activity.

Chapter 11

Maintaining Harmony Within the Team

In This Chapter

➤ The importance of a collaborative atmosphere

➤ Disagreements about the work

➤ When members don't get along

➤ The team leader's role as a counselor

Teams give people a chance to enjoy and benefit from the interaction of joining together in solving problems. But, team members don't always see eye to eye. Misunderstandings, disagreements, and personal conflicts come up which can hinder team success. It's the job of the team leader to resolve them.

Creating a Collaborative Atmosphere

When the team works in an environment in which cooperative interaction is the norm, there is less likelihood of conflicts among team members. Building such an atmosphere is not a one-time event. It involves an ongoing effort on the part of the team leader.

The Team Leader Conducts the Band

The team leader is the key person in creating the type of environment that is conducive to a harmonious atmosphere. He or she is the conductor of the "band" and provides the beat to which the team marches. Following are some suggestions:

Team Builder

Be alert to differences and step in to resolve them before they fester into major problems. Establish a system to deal with such situations rapidly and equitably.

➤ Encourage cooperation, rather than competition, among team members.

➤ Bring the entire team into decisions relating to the team projects. Give subgroups within the team autonomy in designing their projects.

➤ Don't dominate the team. Don't micromanage their work.

➤ Set up a system for measuring team performance as well as individual performance (see Chapter 12).

➤ Reward team achievements as well as individual accomplishments (see Chapter 16).

➤ Show that you value the work of every team member. Some teams are made up of a combination of highly skilled technicians and lesser-skilled associates. Irrespective of their skill level, each contributes to the team's success.

➤ Discourage "we-versus-they" thinking. This is particularly important when members are drawn from different departments in the company. They often consider teammates from other departments as rivals.

The Members Make the Music

In a truly harmonious team, the leader sets the beat, but the members provide the music. The members, like the musicians in an orchestra, must play a harmonious melody.

Sometimes, however, individual team members may disagree. Unlike the orchestra, where the conductor decides who or what is correct, team members are encouraged to resolve their own differences.

To ensure that harmony is maintained within the team, all members must be willing to work out their differences amicably.

Here are some suggestions for team members when dealing with disagreements with associates:

➤ Listen to the associate's story without interrupting. Wait until he or she is finished before presenting your side.

➤ Pause before you respond. This gives you a chance to think before you speak.

➤ Respond calmly. A loud or angry voice can block your message. Anger only generates anger, and the disagreement is exacerbated.

➤ Back up your arguments. Present evidence. If it's just an opinion that can't be proven, back off. It's no shame to say, "I'll have to check into this."

➤ Be willing to compromise. Both of you may have good points.

➤ If you can't settle the disagreement, bring it to the team leader to be resolved according to team procedures.

When Members Disagree About the Work

Disagreements and discord among team members primarily arise from two sources: They disagree on work assignments or there are personality conflicts between members.

Disagreements caused by different views on dealing with job problems are easier to deal with than personality clashes. Let's look at how Mark, a team leader, handled a conflict of ideas between team members Andy and Candy.

After being given an assignment, Andy and Candy discuss the project and cannot agree about how it should be pursued. They both come back to Mark, the team leader, to resolve the problem.

Mark can use one of two approaches: He can arbitrate it or he can mediate it.

Heads Up!

Don't gloat. If your associate backs down and agrees you are right, give the associate an opportunity to save face. Say, for example, "I can understand why you felt that way before you had a chance to get all the facts." Remember you have to work with this associate over the long haul.

Team Terms

In **arbitration**, both parties present their side of a problem and an arbitrator decides what should be done. In **mediation**, both parties present their side of a problem and the mediator works with them to reach a mutually satisfactory solution.

Mediation Is Not Medication

Mediation is the preferred approach because it's more likely to result in a win-win compromise. Mediation is not medication. It's not a dose that you give a patient to cure an ailment. It's a process that takes time—and often there isn't much time to solve the problem.

Let's see how Mark would mediate this dispute. To make a mediated conflict resolution work, all parties involved must be fully aware of the procedure to be followed. Unless both parties have a clear understanding of the approach, it cannot succeed.

First, Candy tells how she views the situation. You might think that the next step is for Andy to state his side—but it isn't. Instead, Andy is asked to state Candy's view as he understands it.

The reason for this step is that when Candy is presenting her view, Andy, if he is typical, is only partly listening. He's probably thinking about what he plans to say to rebut her argument. By being aware of having to repeat Candy's views, he knows he has to listen carefully.

By having Andy repeat Candy's side of the story, any areas of misunderstanding can be clarified before Andy presents his views. It's amazing how often conflicts are caused by these types of misunderstandings. The same process is then followed with Andy stating his views and Candy restating them.

During this discussion, Mark (as the mediator) takes notes. After Andy and Candy present their sides of the argument, Mark reviews his notes with the participants. Mark might comment: "As I view this, you both agree on 80 percent of the project. Now let's list the areas in which you disagree." Most disputes have many more areas of agreement than disagreement. By identifying these areas, Mark can focus on matters that must be resolved and tackle them one at a time.

Because time is limited, a time restriction must be set on these meetings. Suppose that two hours are allotted for the first meeting. At the end of the specified time, there may be several more items to discuss. Another meeting should be arranged for that purpose. Candy and Andy should be encouraged to meet in the interim without Mark to work on some of the problems. Often, after a climate of compromise is established, a large number of issues can be resolved before the next formal meeting.

Let's say the next meeting is scheduled for one hour, and more problems are resolved. If the project must get underway, this may be all the time available. If some unresolved problems still exist, Mark will have to change his role from mediator to arbitrator and make the decisions.

Team Builder

Encourage team members to work out their differences on their own. Not only will this save the team leader time, it will build an atmosphere of compromise and consensus in the team.

Arbitration: A Last Resort

When Mark put on his arbitrator hat, he has to change his mindset from that of conciliator to that of judge.

Here are five steps to facilitate the *arbitration* process:

1. **Get the facts.** Listen carefully to both sides. Investigate on your own to get additional information. Don't limit yourself to "hard facts." Learn about underlying feelings and emotions.

2. **Evaluate the facts.** Make your own analysis of the situation.

3. **Study the alternatives.** Are the solutions suggested by the two parties the only possible choices? Can compromises be made? Is a different resolution possible?

4. **Make a decision.** Based on your own analysis and evaluation of the arguments of both parties, decide what action should be taken.

5. **Notify the two parties of your decision.** Make sure that they fully understand it. If necessary, "sell" it to them so that they will agree and be committed to implementing it.

In explaining why you made a decision, treat your associates as adults. It's childish to say, "I'm the boss, and this is what I've decided." Let team members know the reason behind decisions, and clarify misunderstandings before implementing a decision.

When Team Members Can't Get Along

Sometimes the conflicts are not just disagreements about the work, but deep-seated personal antagonisms. If such situations are not addressed, it will affect not only the work of the antagonists, but the morale of the entire team as well. Team leaders must step in and resolve them.

They Hate Each Other

If two people on the team dislike each other so much that it affects their work, the leader has to do something about it. First find out why the two people dislike each other. This type of animosity often stems from a past bitter conflict. In the rough-and-tumble competition for advancement in many organizations, some people stab others in the back to gain an advantage. It's unlikely that these members will ever be able to work together in harmony because a deep-seated antagonism taints their every contact with each other.

If at all possible, transfer one or both parties to other departments in which they'll have little contact with each other. However, that option isn't always feasible because there may not be any other departments in which they can use their skills. You as the team leader have to take steps to overcome this situation.

Speak to each person. If attempts to persuade them to cooperate fail, lay down the law. Say, "If this team is to succeed, all its members must work together. What happened in the past is past. Write it off. I'm not asking you to like each other. I don't care if you never associate with each other off the job. I'm demanding that you work together to meet our goals." If necessary, follow up this directive with disciplinary action.

Team Builder

When you notice that team members have an unexplainable dislike for other members, tell them about minimal cues. Awareness of the psychology underlying this feeling will help overcome a person's irrational attitude.

"The chemistry is wrong."

Often the reason for the dislike isn't based on any specific factor. Have you ever met a person and something about him or her turned you off? Sure you have. You immediately disliked that person. Your reaction: "The chemistry between us is all wrong." It happens to all of us.

For example, Stan, a new team member, is introduced to Rochelle. Rochelle's immediate reaction is, "I don't like him," and it carries over into their working relationship.

Why did Rochelle take an immediate dislike to Stan? Psychologists say that this reaction occurs because something about this person subconsciously reminds the other of some unpleasant past experience. Something about Stan (his haircut, the manner in which he speaks, a mole on his left cheek) reminds Rochelle of a third-grade bully who made life miserable for her that year. So she hates him. These factors, called *minimal cues,* trigger long-forgotten subconscious memories that still influence our reactions to people.

If a team member complains that he or she can't work with an associate because "the chemistry is all wrong," suggest that the complainer do the following:

➤ Analyze why this dislike exists. Answer these questions: *Why don't I like working with this person? Is this a personal problem or a job-related problem?*

If it's work related, try to resolve the differences by discussing the problem openly and, if needed, calling on the team leader to clarify the differences.

If it's personal, it may well be the minimal clues that were noted above, or it may be the way that person works, dresses, or talks that bothers you.

➤ Once you identify a reason, try to deal with it. Look at that person more objectively. Next time you're assigned to work on a project with him or her, decide that at the first meeting you will keep an open mind toward that person—just for the duration of that meeting.

➤ Stop letting your feelings get in the way. Make an effort to overlook those annoyances for the duration of the meeting.

➤ If you disagree with her ideas, deal with it calmly and rationally—not angrily and emotionally.

➤ Try to get over your dislike by finding things about the person you *do* like. Win that person over as a friend. Find something nice to say to him or her.

➤ Sometimes the reason for the dislike is the manner in which the other person treats you. Keep your cool. Don't let anything he does or says rile you. Often when such people realize that their actions don't really stir up their victims, they move on to other people.

If he or she is harassing you to the point of keeping you from performing your job, call it to the attention of the team leader.

When you have to work with someone you dislike, make an effort to find something you *can* like about the person: job skills, sense of humor, or a personality trait, for example. Focus on the good point(s). You'll soon forget the intangible factor that generated your dislike.

The Leader as a Counselor

It takes the coordinated effort of all team members to keep your team operating at optimum capacity. It takes only one member of the team who isn't functioning effectively to prevent your team from achieving its objectives. As coach of the team, you must identify problems in their early stages and correct the situation before it mushrooms into a major problem. Your tool: *counseling*.

When a team leader "counsels" an associate, it's more analogous to that of a coach of an athletic team counseling a player than to a psychotherapist counseling a patient.

Professional counseling should be done by trained specialists, and, as you will learn in this chapter, sometimes referrals to these specialists are necessary. Counseling may be called for when team members bring gripes or complaints to the leader, when they have problems with other members, or often when personal problems are interfering with their work.

Team Terms

Counseling is a means of helping troubled associates overcome barriers to good performance. By careful listening, open discussion, and sound advice, a counselor helps identify problems, clarify misunderstandings, and plan solutions.

Gripes and Grievances

Sometimes it appears that everything is running smoothly. Nobody complains. Everybody seems to be happy—and then there's sudden disruption. You never saw it coming.

Another scenario: You think your team is one happy family, but slowly it falls apart. Some members quit or transfer to other departments; absenteeism and lateness get out of hand; when extra effort is needed, the team doesn't give its all.

Heads Up!

As tempting as it may sometimes be to threaten to fire uncooperative team members, don't do it unless you really can carry it out. Union contracts, company policies, EEO implications, or other factors restrict these actions. Make every effort to salvage the member before resorting to firing.

Team Terms

A **gripe** is an informal complaint. A **grievance** is a formal complaint, usually based on the violation of a union contract or formal company policy.

Grievances and *gripes* that cannot be uncovered and adjusted or clarified fester in the minds of the aggrieved. This may show up in poor work, purposeful slowing down on the job, absenteeism, and high turnover. It could lead to unionization and organized employee antagonism. Some means should be provided for employees to bring grievances to the attention of a person in the organization who has the authority to correct it.

Team leaders must always have their ears and eyes open. To keep gripes from developing into grievances or just festering into long-term discontent, here are some suggestions:

➤ The first step is to ensure that a clear line of communication exists from top to bottom, and equally important, from bottom to top.

➤ All company policies and procedures should be clearly imparted to all employees. This could be done in the form of an easy-to-read employee manual, meetings of supervisors with their people to clarify and reinforce what is in the manuals, and when specific violations occur, personal chats with first-time offenders before disciplinary action is instituted.

➤ Getting information from the top down rarely presents a problem; to get information from bottom to top is not that easy. The key person here is the team leader. This starts with gaining the confidence of the members. Employees must feel that it is not just safe, but helpful to bring their complaint to their supervisor and that it will be dealt with promptly and fairly.

➤ When a member brings you a complaint, listen. Even if the complaint seems to be unfounded, in the mind of the complainant, it's a serious matter.

➤ Investigate all complaints. Don't assume you know all the facts. Take nothing for granted. Look at the record and talk to others who know about the situation.

➤ Report back. If the gripe is unfounded, explain your reasoning to the complainant. If it's substantiated, indicate what you'll do to correct it.

➤ Take action. Do what must be done to correct the problem.

Dealing with Grievances

To deal with gripes that cannot be resolved informally, a formal grievance procedure should exist. Of course when there is a union, this procedure is outlined in the union-management agreement and must be followed. In nonunionized organizations there is frequently no provision to deal with grievances. However, it is a good idea to have either a semiformal system or a formal system that serves as a guideline.

A typical system consists of four steps:

Heads Up!

Don't become complacent if no complaints are made by your team members. It doesn't necessarily mean that there aren't any. If complaints aren't expressed, they'll burst out sooner or later in the form of low morale, reluctance to cooperate, and poor productivity.

1. The aggrieved individual discusses the problem with the team leader. Every attempt should be made to solve it at this level. Most grievances have basis in fact and can either be solved by correcting an inequitable situation or by logically explaining to the complainant why the problem exists and what can or cannot be done to correct it.

   Even if there is no basis for the complaint, it should still be given adequate attention. Investigate to uncover the true facts. Explain to the employee what has been discovered. Remember that to the person making the complaint, it is very important even if it appears trivial to the supervisor. It cannot be ignored or glibly passed over by saying, "I'll take care of it," and then forgetting about it. In settling a grievance, a broken promise is the surest way to break down the entire program of sound employee relations.

2. If no settlement is reached, the individual should be given the opportunity to bring the problem—without fear of reprisal—to the next highest level of management. Here again every effort should be made to solve the problem.

3. The next step, if needed, would be to bring the problem to the human resources manager, the general manager, or another highly placed executive.

4. Usually agreement will be reached at an earlier stage, but if not, the individual and management may agree to submit the grievance to a mutually acceptable third party for arbitration. This is not often done in nonunion organizations, but is an option that management may wish to have available in cases where it is in the best interest of all to solve the problem. Arbitration is a better alternative and usually much less expensive than legal action.

FYI

To locate an impartial arbitrator to settle a grievance that cannot be resolved internally, contact the American Arbitration Association, 335 Madison Ave., New York, NY, 10017. Web site: www.adr.org.

When the Grievance Is Against the Team Leader

Barbara was very upset. Her team leader, Maggie, was constantly giving her unpleasant assignments. Sure, the drudge work had to be done, and Barbara was willing to do her share, but Maggie gave her most of this type work and her "pets" never were never given these "dirty jobs."

If Barbara made a formal grievance, she would have to first take her complaint to Maggie, who would probably ignore it and surely would just make Barbara's life even more miserable.

In such cases the team member should have an opportunity to express the grievance without having to first discuss it with the leader. If this were not possible, many important grievances might never come into the open. Because the first step required the employee to talk to the supervisor—the very person who was the offender—companies did not even know about cases of sex harassment by that supervisor until they were charged with violations of the law.

To overcome this, if the grievance involves the immediate supervisor, the employee should be able to bring the matter to the attention of the human resources department or another designated management person. A complete investigation should be made. If the complaint proves to be justified, steps should be taken to correct it at once. All must be done in a diplomatic way and the complainant should be protected against reprisals.

The best way to handle grievances is to prevent their arising by practicing sound human relations principles in all aspects of the company's activities. Inasmuch as we are all humans and mistakes and misjudgments will be made, a clear line of communications should exist so that grievances can be handled expeditiously when they do arise.

To ensure that grievances are properly dealt with, and to provide documentation for the procedure, keep a record of the entire procedure. If your company does not provide a form for this, write a report covering what has been done and what resulted and send a copy to the human resources department.

Getting the Authority to Correct a Problem

As a result of your investigation, you determine that the complaint is justified, but you do not have the authority to resolve it. Find out who does. Bring the situation to the attention of your boss or whoever can adjust it.

Diana, a team leader, was frustrated. When she described to her manager, Charles, a problem her team members were having, he promised to rectify it—but he never did.

Diana's reminders were rebuffed. She was concerned not only about having to continue to work with this unsatisfactory situation, but also about losing the respect of her team members. She discussed the situation with Elizabeth, a manager who had been her mentor earlier in her career.

Team Builder

You can't please everybody. Don't try. It'll drive you crazy. There are times when you have to say no to a team member. Don't be afraid to do so. But help the member understand your reasons and make sure the entire team feels you acted fairly.

Elizabeth's advice: "Let Charles know how important it is to your team to have someone listen to their complaints and consider them seriously. Remind Charles that you deal with every problem over which you have authority, but that this one is out of your jurisdiction. Point out that you screen all complaints and don't pass on the ones that aren't justified. If there's a reason that action has not or cannot be taken, you want to know so that you can pass on the information to your team. Tell him that they're reasonable people who understand that they can't get everything they want, but that they expect that their complaints will be taken seriously. Then let your associates know what action you're taking and what results from it."

Preventing Grievances

Dealing with grievances is time-consuming and takes you away from more productive work. Here are some suggestions for preventing grievances from developing on your team:

➤ Let all team members know how they're doing regularly. People want feedback on not only their failures but also their successes.

➤ Encourage team members to participate in all aspects of planning and performing the team's work.

➤ Keep an open mind about team members' ideas—even if you do not agree with them.

➤ Make only promises that you know you can keep.

➤ Be alert to minor irritations and trivial problems so that you can correct them before they become serious dissatisfactions.

➤ Resolve problems as soon as possible after hearing about them.

When Personal Problems Interfere with Performance

All of us have personal problems. We worry about our health, about our families, and about money. We always have something to worry about. People carry their worries with them into the workplace, and worries do affect their work.

Team leaders are often reluctant to pry into an associate's personal life—and many people resent prying. Sometimes, it's necessary, however. It's much easier if you, as team leader, have a good personal relationship with your associates and if you've always shown interest in them as individuals.

Heads Up!

Don't give advice about serious personal matters. Team leaders are not trained psychologists. Listen! Help put the problem into perspective. Provide or suggest sources for additional information. Help associates clarify a situation and come to their own conclusions.

If you have this type of relationship, begin the discussion by commenting about job-related matters. Ask a question about the work. It may lead into a discussion of the problems the person is having with the project, which may be caused by personal matters.

Be an empathic listener. Your role as counselor is to give team members an opportunity to unload their problems. Encourage them by asking questions. Don't criticize, argue a point, or make a judgment. Act as a sounding board to help release the pressures that are causing the problem. Help the person clarify the situation so that the solution will be easier to reach.

Counseling isn't a cure-all. There are many areas in which you just can't help. However, when a problem is one you can help by just talking it out, your intervention can be useful. Don't lose patience or give up too easily. Often, more than one session is necessary to build a sense of trust and to get a team member to open up.

When the Problem's Too Tough to Handle

Team leaders may be reluctant or even embarrassed to suggest that a team member see a professional counselor. Many people take umbrage at this suggestion: "Do you think I'm nuts?" Point out that going to a professional counselor is no different than going to a medical doctor. Young people are exposed to counseling beginning in elementary school. The most frequently given advice offered by Ann Landers, Dear Abby, and other advice columnists is to seek counseling when faced with serious problems.

Not all problems that require professional assistance are psychological. They may be caused by a medical condition or serious financial troubles. Often they're marital or family situations.

If the company has an employee assistance program (EAP), making a referral to it immediately relieves the team leader of the burden of suggesting specific counseling (see the following section). If not, the human resources department may help provide referrals. Some sources of help in the community are

➤ **Medical doctors:** If a company doesn't have its own medical department or an employee doesn't have a primary care physician, local hospitals or medical societies can provide a list of qualified physicians.

➤ **Psychiatrists:** These M.D.s deal with serious psychological disorders.

➤ **Psychologists or psychotherapists:** These specialists usually have a degree in psychology or social work and handle most of the usual emotional problems people face.

➤ **Marriage counselors and family therapists:** These professionals deal with marital problems, difficulties with children, and related matters. Obtain from your local family service association or mental health association the names of qualified psychologists, psychiatrists, or marriage and family therapists in the area.

➤ **Financial counselors:** These people help others work out payment plans with creditors, develop budgets, and live within their income. Your bank or credit union can provide referrals.

When you refer someone for professional help, be sure to avoid using the terms *psychiatrist, psychologist,* or *therapist.* They have negative connotations to most people. Tell a troubled person that he or she might benefit from seeing a *counselor* who specializes in a particular area. Back up your advice by explaining how counseling has helped other people.

Team Terms

An **employee assistance program,** or **EAP,** is a company-sponsored counseling service. The counselors aren't company employees, but instead are outside experts retained to help employees deal with personal, family, and financial problems.

Employee Assistance Programs (EAPs)

An *employee assistance program,* or *EAP,* is a company sponsored counseling service. Many companies have instituted these programs to help employees deal with personal problems that interfere with productivity. The counselors aren't company employees, but instead are outside experts retained on an as-needed basis. Initiating the use of the EAP can be done in two ways:

1. An employee can take the initiative in contacting the company's EAP. The company informs its employees about the program through e-mail, bulletins, announcements in the company newspaper, meetings, and letters to their homes. Often a hot-line telephone number is provided.

   One of your team members, Gerty, believes that she needs help. Constant squabbling with her teenage daughter has made her tense, angry, and frustrated. In a brief telephone interview with her company's EAP, the screening counselor identifies Gerty's problem and refers her to a family counselor. Gerty makes her own appointment on her own time (not during working hours—EAPs are not an excuse for taking time off the job). Because the entire procedure is confidential, no report is made to the company about the counseling (in most cases, not even the names of people who undertake counseling are divulged).

2. The team leader can take the initiative to contact the EAP. Suppose that the work performance of one of your top performers has recently declined. You often see him sitting idly at his desk, his thoughts obviously far from his job. You ask him what's going on, but he shrugs off your question by saying, "I'm okay—just tired."

   After several conversations, he finally tells you about a family problem, and you suggest that he contact the company's EAP.

   Even though you've made the referral and the employee has followed through, don't expect progress reports. From now on, the matter is handled confidentially. Your feedback comes from seeing improvement in the employee's work as the counseling helps with the problem.

EAPs aren't new. They began in the 1940s as alcohol rehabilitation programs companies had to protect their large investment in skilled employees. The success of these programs led to their expansion to their present day function of dealing with a variety of personal problems.

Employee assistance programs are expensive to maintain, but organizations that have used them for several years report that they pay off. EAPs salvage skilled and experienced workers who, without help, may leave a company.

The Least You Need to Know

➤ The team leader is the key person in creating the type of environment that is conducive to a harmonious atmosphere.

➤ To ensure that harmony is maintained within the team, all members must be willing to work out their differences amicably.

➤ Resolve disputes between members as soon as they arise.

➤ Mediation is preferred to arbitration because it's more likely to result in a win-win compromise.

➤ If two members of the team dislike each other, try to find out the reason. Work with them to overcome the problem.

➤ Counseling is a means of helping troubled associates overcome barriers to good performance.

➤ If no grievances are called to management's attention, it may mean that there is no mechanism in place to do so.

➤ When counseling a member, act as a sounding board to help the person clarify the situation.

➤ Refer troubled members to the employee assistance program (EAP).

Chapter 12

Measuring Performance

In This Chapter

➤ Appraising individuals and teams

➤ Types of evaluations

➤ How peer appraisal works

➤ The leader's performance interview with the team member

"How am I doing?" Everybody wants to know how he or she is doing on the job—and every team wants to know if it is performing up to the expectations of the team manager—and in turn, of the organization. That's the main reason for performance appraisals.

Some of the other values of a good performance appraisal program are

➤ It ensures understanding of performance expectations by all members of the team.

➤ It builds confidence between the team leader and the team members.

➤ It identifies training and development needs.

➤ It fosters communication and feedback.

There are a variety of systems to measure performance of individuals and of teams. In this chapter we'll look at some of these and how to make appraisals work in improving the team's performance.

Individual vs. Team Appraisals

Conducting formal reviews of the performance of individuals on the job has long been part of corporate procedures. The annual review—often dreaded by both the supervisor and the employee—was looked upon chiefly as the determination of how much (if any) salary increase a person would receive.

FYI

Formal structured performance appraisals were introduced in the late nineteenth or early twentieth century when the U.S. government instituted the civil service system. Before that all hiring, firing, and promotions for government jobs were made on the basis of favoritism, nepotism, or political party affiliation. Under the civil service system, performance appraisal (then called merit reviews) was designed to make these job decisions more equitable.

However, the real reason for such reviews is to look at the performance of the employee and determine how that performance can be improved. Salary adjustment was only part of the program—but it became the part that dominated the thinking of both parties.

Today, companies are moving away from focusing on salary adjustment—often covering it in a separate procedure—and concentrate on the employee's productivity, goals, and personal growth.

When teams replace work groups, although individual performance reviews are still important, they become part of team reviews, in which the members are assessed not only on their own performance, but on the productivity of the entire team.

Setting Standards for Individual Appraisals

All employees should know just what's expected of them on the job. Many companies develop and incorporate *performance standards* at the time they create a job description. In other companies, as the job evolves, standards are established.

In routine jobs, the key factors of performance standards involve quantity (how much should be produced per hour or per day) and quality (what level of quality is acceptable). As jobs become more complex, these standards aren't an adequate way to measure performance. Ideas and innovations that are conceived in creative jobs cannot be quantified, and quality may be difficult to measure. This situation doesn't mean that you can't have performance standards for these jobs, but it does require a different approach, such as the results-based evaluation system described later in this chapter.

Performance standards are usually based on the experiences of satisfactory workers who have done that type of work over a period of time. Whether the standards cover the quality or quantity of the work, or other aspects of the job, they should meet these criteria:

Team Terms

Performance standards define the results that are expected from a person performing a job. For performance standards to be meaningful, all persons doing that job should know and accept these standards. Team participation in the establishment of performance standards is one way to ensure this understanding.

➤ They should be specific. Every person doing a job should know exactly what he or she is expected to do.

➤ They should be measurable. The company should have a touchstone against which performance can be measured.

➤ They must be attainable. Unless the standards can be met, people will consider them unfair and resist working toward them.

One way of setting standards that are understood and accepted by team members is to have them participate in setting them and encouraging them to make a practice of regularly evaluating their own performance against those standards. In this way members don't have to wait for formal performance assessments to discover that they are not meeting standards. They see for themselves where they stand and can take corrective action immediately.

FYI

W. Edwards Deming, the father of the quality movement, strongly opposed performance reviews. He believed that, in most companies, performance was equated with quantity at the sacrifice of quality. This was the case for a long time, but quality standards today are given equal or greater weight in evaluations.

Setting Standards for Team Appraisals

Individual performance standards remain important in the team environment, but they must mesh with the standards by which the team will be measured.

Some factors that must be considered in developing team standards are

➤ Goals and direction the team will take are clear to all associates.

➤ Team members participate in setting standards.

➤ Periodic reviews of team performance are scheduled.

➤ Reviews are conducted by team leader and discussed at team meetings.

Types of Performance Assessments

Most companies conduct formal appraisals of employees on an annual basis. Annual reviews are not enough. Goals change during the year; performance varies during the year; problems that were never dreamed of when standards were set come up during the year. Performance reviews should be conducted at a minimum of four times a year. However, it is too time consuming and expensive to conduct frequent formal reviews. Informal discussions of performance should be ongoing. Semiformal brief meetings can be held with team members or the entire team several times each year.

The formal and sometimes semiformal review is standardized. A system is used so that all employees are measured in the same manner. In this section we'll look at some of the more commonly used assessment systems.

Heads Up!

Evaluating team performance is not a substitute for evaluating individual performance. They are both important. Members should be held accountable for their own actions as well as their part in the collaborative efforts of the team.

Check the Box: The Trait System

You've been rated by them. You've probably used them to rate others. The most common evaluation system is the "trait" format, in which a series of traits are listed in the left margin, and each is measured against a scale from unsatisfactory to excellent.

This system seems on the surface to be simple to administer and easy to understand, but it's loaded with problems. Leaders tend to fall into the following traps when rating members on a trait system:

➤ **Central tendency.** Rather than carefully evaluate each trait, it's much easier to rate a trait as average or close to average (the central rating).

➤ **The halo effect.** Some managers believe that one trait is so impressive they rate all traits highly. Its opposite is the "pitchfork effect" (see Chapter 4).

➤ **Personal biases.** Managers are human, and humans have personal biases for and against other people. These biases can influence any type of rating, but the trait system is particularly vulnerable.

➤ **Latest behavior.** It's easy to remember what employees have done during the past few months, but managers tend to forget what they did in the first part of a rating period.

When you rate your team members, don't be overly influenced by their most recent behavior. Employees know that it's rating time, and they'll be as good as a kid just before Christmas. Keep a running log of their behavior during the entire year.

The best way to overcome deficiencies in the trait system is to replace it with a results-oriented system (described later in this chapter). However, if your company does use the trait method, here are some suggestions to help make it more equitable:

➤ Clarify standards. Every manager and team leader should be carefully informed about the meaning of each category and the definition of each trait. Understanding quantity and quality is relatively easy. But what is dependability? How do you measure initiative, creativity, and other intangibles? By using discussions, role plays, and case studies, you can develop standards that everyone can understand and use.

➤ Establish criteria for ratings. It's easy to identify superior and unsatisfactory employees, but it's tougher to differentiate among people in the middle three categories.

➤ Keep a running record of member performance throughout the year. You don't have to record average performance, but do note anything special that each member has accomplished or failed to accomplish. Some notes on the positive side may say, for example, "Exceeded quota by 20 percent," "Completed project two days before deadline," or "Made a suggestion that cut by a third the time required for a job." Notes on the negative side may say, "Had to redo report because of major errors," or, "Was reprimanded for extending lunch hour three days this month."

➤ Make an effort to be aware of your personal biases and to overcome them.

Results-Based Evaluations

Rather than rate team members on the basis of an opinion about their various traits, in the results-based system the people who do the rating focus on the attainment of specific results.

Team Builder

Keep a record of specific examples of exceptional and unsatisfactory performance and behavior of team members to support your performance evaluation.

Results-based ratings can be used in any situation in which results are measurable. This system is obviously easier to use when quantifiable factors are involved (such as sales volume or production units), but it's also useful in such intangible areas as attaining specific goals in management development, reaching personal goals, and making collaborative efforts.

In a results-based evaluation system, the people who do the evaluating don't have to rely on their judgment of abstract traits, but instead can focus on what was expected from team members and how closely they met these expectations. The expectations are agreed upon at the beginning of a period and measured at the end of that period. At that time, new goals are developed to be measured at the end of the following period.

Here's how this system works:

➤ For every job, the team leader and the associates doing the job agree on the results expected for that job. These are called key results areas (KRAs). Employees must accomplish results in these areas to meet the team's goals.

➤ The team leader and the team member establish the criteria on which the team member will be measured in each of the KRAs.

➤ During a formal review, the results an employee attained in each of the KRAs are measured against what was expected.

➤ A numerical scale is used in some organizations to rate employees on how close they come to reaching their goals. In others, no grades are given. Instead, a narrative report is compiled to summarize what has been accomplished and to comment on its significance.

Some companies request that team members submit monthly progress reports compiled in the same format as the annual review. This technique enables both the team member and the leader to monitor progress. Studying the monthly reports makes the annual review easier to compile and discuss.

Team Terms

A **KRA** (key results area) is an aspect of a job on which employees must concentrate time and attention to ensure that they achieve the goals for that job.

Although results-oriented evaluations can be more meaningful than trait systems, they're not free of problems.

Unless the team leader and the team member take an objective view of what he or she should accomplish, unrealistic expectations may be set. The danger is that they may be set so low that employees attain them with little effort, or so high that employees have little chance of attaining them.

Not all goals are equal in importance. Consider the value of the expectation in comparison to the overall goals of the team and the company.

Intangible goals are more difficult to measure. Even intangible factors, however, have tangible phases that can be identified. For example, rather than indicate that a goal is to "improve employee morale," specify it in terms that are measurable, such as "reduce turnover by X percent" or "decrease the number of grievances by Y percent." Rather than state a goal as "Develop a new health insurance plan," break it into phases, such as "Complete study of proposed plans by October 31" or "Submit recommendations by December 15."

Collaborative Evaluations

To make the results-based format even more meaningful, use the collaborative model. If performance evaluations are based on the arbitrary opinion of a supervisor, they serve only part of the real value of reviews. A results-based model provides a formal evaluation for the purpose of raises or promotions and enables you to tell employees how to improve performance, but it doesn't involve team members in the process.

Heads Up!

If a team member gives himself or herself a significantly higher rating than you do, be particularly sensitive in the discussion so that it doesn't degenerate into a confrontation. Use specific examples rather than statements of opinion to make your points.

The collaborative review can do this more effectively and is particularly useful for evaluating creative jobs such as research and development or jobs in the arts. Team members and their leaders jointly determine the standards that are expected, build in the flexibility to accommodate the special circumstances under which they're working, and agree on the criteria that will be used in evaluating the work.

The team member and team leader then complete the evaluation form. The KRAs and the "results expected" items are agreed upon in advance (usually during the preceding review). The team member and the leader independently indicate the "results achieved."

A variation on the *collaborative evaluation* is having team members evaluate their own performance before meeting with their team leader. Both leader and member complete a copy of the appraisal form. At the meeting, similarities and differences in the ratings are discussed, and adjustments in the ratings resulting from the discussions are reflected in the formal evaluation that's filed with the human resources department. In some companies, if the employee still disagrees with the evaluation after the discussion, a rebuttal may be written and filed along with the team leader's report.

At the appraisal interview (described later in this chapter), the team leader and the team member discuss the comments on the form. During this session, the appraisal begins to move from a report card to a plan of action for growth and teamwork.

Team Terms

In a **collaborative** evaluation, a team member evaluates his or her own performance, and the team leader also evaluates it. The final report results from a collaborative discussion between the team leader and the team member.

Collaborative reviews of performance have the following advantages:

➤ They give team members the opportunity to make a formal appraisal of their own work in a systematic manner.

➤ They allow for a thorough discussion between the team leader and the team member about the differences in their perceptions of both expectations and results achieved.

➤ They enable a team leader to see areas in which he or she may have failed in developing a team member's potential.

➤ They help the team member and the team leader identify problem areas that might easily be overlooked on a day-to-day basis.

➤ They pinpoint areas in which employees need improvement and in which they need additional training.

➤ They provide an opportunity to discuss areas in which a team member can become even more valuable to his or her team.

➤ They provide a base upon which realistic goals for the next period can be discussed and mutually agreed upon.

➤ They help team members measure performance and progress against their own career goals and serve as a guide in determining the appropriate steps needed to move forward.

In-Between-Reviews Appraisals

As noted earlier, limiting reviews to once a year is not realistic. Members need more frequent feedback to keep on the cutting edge of their jobs. One solution is the mini-review—usually conducted monthly, but which could be done more frequently.

Members are asked to evaluate their progress for the past month by responding in writing to a series of questions.

At the appraisal interview the team leader and member discuss the member's responses and develop plans to enhance the strengths, shore up the weaknesses, and set revised goals for the ensuing month.

Peer Appraisals

In the traditional organization, supervisors rate their subordinates. When teams enter the picture, the supervisor, now team leader, usually still evaluates team members, but this is supplemented by team members rating each other. Why? Ratings by several people are likely to provide more objective results. Members work closely with each other. They really know how well associates do their jobs. Because ratings are made by several people, individual biases, jealousies, and personality conflicts are neutralized.

Team Builder

Team leaders should note their comments on the monthly report form and keep copies in their files. Reviewing the monthly reports when making the annual formal appraisal will result in a much more realistic view of the progress of each member.

How They Work

Peer appraisals can take as many forms as the traditional supervisor's appraisal. They can be trait-based or results-based. They can be in numerical or narrative style. The important thing is that they be consistent and that all members be carefully trained in using the system.

At the Jumphigh Trampoline Company team ratings are conducted quarterly. Each team member completes an evaluation form for each of the associates. After the team leader reviews the forms, a meeting is held at which the evaluations are discussed. The team leader reads a summary of what was reported. By keeping the individual reports confidential—members are not told who said what about them—evaluations are more likely to be frank and honest.

At the meeting all members discuss the evaluations and suggest ways of helping each other in the areas where help is needed. The team leader will also meet on a one-to-one basis with each member to add his or her suggestions, and to deal with sensitive issues that may have come up in the reviews, but not been broadcast to the group.

In some companies, all of the original *peer evaluation* forms are kept on file; in others only the team manager's compilation is retained. Peer assessments, along with other assessments, become part of the body of information on which the formal performance evaluation is based.

Team Terms

Peer evaluation: Every member of a team is rated by each of the other members. The evaluations may be discussed in private conversations between the team leader and the member or with the entire team.

Pros and Cons of Peer Evaluations

As pointed out earlier, the chief advantages of peer evaluation are the neutralizing of biases by any one rater, obtaining a variety of opinions on each member's performance, and the opportunity for the entire team to share in identifying weaknesses in the team, and developing and implementing steps to correct them.

By having several reviews of each member's performance, the team leader can write a more objective and more comprehensive formal assessment report.

But peer evaluations have a downside. Let's look at some of the problems:

➤ Some members may consider others rivals for promotion or for more interesting assignments and rate them lower than they should.

➤ Members may rate their friends higher than they should.

➤ Members may take the easy way out and rate associates right down the middle of the scale.

➤ Members may "trade off" assessments with others. "I'll rate you high and you rate me high."

Following are some suggestions on how to overcome this:

➤ Before each peer review period, hold a meeting to review the procedure and to reinforce the importance of providing fair, honest, and unbiased assessments.

➤ If possible, using numerical ratings. Require members to answer specific questions about each associate's performance and give examples.

For example: "When working together on a project, in what ways did the associate help move the project forward? In what ways did the associate hold up the project? In what aspects of the work did the associate excel? In what aspects of the work does the associate need to improve? Give examples of how this affected your work."

➤ If a numerical system is needed, when compiling the results, if one review is significantly higher or lower than the others, delete it in making the compilation. Hold a private meeting with that member to probe the reasons for it.

Discussing Performance with Team Members

Whether the formal appraisal results from an evaluation by the team leader, a combination of ratings by peers, or a 360 degree panel, there is usually a one-to-one sit-down meeting between the team leader and the member to discuss it. In many organizations, the member is also asked to rate him or herself as a prelude to the formal appraisal interview.

Prepare for the Interview

Before sitting down with a team member to discuss a performance appraisal, study the evaluation(s). Make a list of all aspects you want to discuss, not just those that need improvement but also those in which the member did good work. Study previous appraisals, and note improvements that have been made since the preceding one. Prepare the questions you want to ask about past actions, steps to be taken for improvement, future goals, and how the team member plans to reach them.

Reflect on your experiences in dealing with this person. Have there been any special behavioral problems? Any problems that have affected her or his work? Any strong, positive assets you want to nurture? Any special points you want to discuss?

Team Builder

Most people are uneasy about appraisal interviews. Allay these fears by making some positive comments when you schedule an interview. You can say, "I've scheduled your appraisal interview for 2:30 on Wednesday. I want to talk about your accomplishments this year, and discuss our plans for next year."

The Appraisal Interview

Make the team member feel at ease with a few minutes of small talk. Then point out the reasons for the appraisal meeting. Say something like this: "As you know, each year we review what has been accomplished during the preceding year and discuss what we can do together in the following year."

Note the areas of the job in which team members have met standards, and particularly the areas in which they have excelled. By giving specific examples of these achievements, you let team members know that you're aware of their positive qualities.

Encourage team members to comment. Listen attentively, and then discuss the aspects of performance or behavior that didn't meet standards. Concentrate on the work, not on the person. Never say, "You were no good." Say instead, "Your work didn't meet standards." Be specific. Give a few examples where expectations haven't been met. This is more effective than to just say, "Your work isn't up to snuff." Ask what the team member plans to do to meet standards and what help you can provide.

If the member's problems aren't related to performance, but rather to behavior, provide examples: "During the past year, I've spoken to you several times about your tardiness. You're a good worker, and your opportunities in this company would be much greater if you could only get here on time all the time." Try to obtain a commitment and a plan of action to overcome this fault.

Heads Up!

An appraisal interview isn't the leader telling the team member, "This is what you did well, and that is what you did poorly." It's a two-way discussion about performance.

Encourage Discussion

Throughout the interview, encourage the team member to comment on or make suggestions about every aspect of the review. Of course, he may have excuses or alibis. Listen actively—you may learn about some factors that have inhibited optimum performance. For example, you may find out that someone has an older-model computer that has started crashing several times a day ever since the company upgraded the software. You may not have been aware that this recurring problem was affecting the member's job performance. With this new information, you can take steps to correct the situation by budgeting for a computer upgrade. By giving the associate the opportunity to express his or her reasons or arguments, you can take steps to correct the situation.

Even if a team member's excuses are superficial and self-serving, allowing them to be voiced clears the air. Then you both can be prepared to face real situations and come up with viable ideas.

Make Criticism Constructive

Many team leaders find it difficult to give criticism. Here are some guidelines to help deal with this sensitive area:

➤ Begin with a positive approach by asking the team member to assess the successes achieved and the steps taken to achieve those successes.

➤ Encourage him or her to talk about projects that didn't succeed and what caused the failure.

➤ Ask what might have been done to avoid the mistakes.

➤ Contribute your suggestions about how the matter could have been handled more effectively.

➤ Ask what training or help you can provide.

➤ Agree on the steps the associate will take to ensure better performance on future assignments.

Develop an Action Plan

At the end of the interview, ask the team member to summarize the discussion. Make sure that the person fully understands the positive and negative aspects of his or her performance and behavior, plans and goals for the next review period, and any other pertinent matters. Keep a written record of these points.

Ask the member to develop an action plan to implement the changes that are to be made. This plan should be specific, listing actions in each pertinent area and timetables specifying when the plan will be started and completed. If new goals are set, list the goals and note when and how they will be achieved.

In many companies, team members who disagree with an evaluation are given the opportunity to write a rebuttal to be attached to the appraisal. When salary adjustments are based on ratings, some organizations provide a procedure for appealing a review.

End the interview on a positive note by saying, "Overall, you've made good progress this year. I'm confident that you'll continue to do good work."

In most companies the appraisal form is sent to the human resources department to be placed in the employee's personnel file. Some companies require that a copy be sent to the next level of management—the person to whom the team leader reports.

Team Builder

If you're a team member who disagrees with your review, send a polite memo to the team leader a few days after the meeting. Point out some recent achievements that may have been overlooked in the review. Although this may not help in the current appraisal, it will be in your personnel file to be noted if interim reviews occur before the next formal appraisal.

Even if it's not a formal practice in your company, it's a good idea to give a copy of the appraisal to the team member. It serves as a reminder of what was discussed at the appraisal interview and can be referred to during the year. And, if it includes goals the employee and you have agreed upon for the year, the employee can reread it from time to time to keep motivated.

Ten Tips for Reviewing Performance

1. Know exactly what you want to achieve. Let your team members know what is expected of them.

2. Keep a log of each member's performance from which to cite specific examples.

3. Discuss the written evaluation with the team member.

4. Listen to team member's comments, then ask questions to stimulate thought.

5. Focus on the individual. Do not compare him or her with other members of the team.

6. Show that you care about the member's performance and career.

7. Reinforce good behavior. Be specific in your criticism. Give examples from their performance record. Ask them how they can do even better. Add your own suggestions.

8. Focus on the behavior, not on the person.

9. Don't be afraid to give honest criticism. Most team members want to know where they stand and how to improve.

10. Help team members set personal goals that are congruent with the goals of the team and the company and develop a plan of action to reach those goals.

Performance appraisal is an essential tool in team leadership. Not only does it enable the leader to keep tabs on each member's performance, but more important, it encourages members to evaluate their own performance on an ongoing basis and take steps to work toward improvement.

The Least You Need to Know

➤ The chief reason for performance reviews is to determine how that performance can be improved.

➤ When teams replace work groups, the members are assessed not only on their own performance, but on the productivity of the entire team.

➤ Have team members participate in setting their standards and encourage them to evaluate their own performance against those standards.

➤ Annual reviews are not enough. Problems that were never dreamed of when standards were set come up during the year.

➤ Keep a record of specific examples of the exceptional and unsatisfactory performance and behavior of team members to support your performance evaluation.

➤ The team leader's appraisal of members, when supplemented by peer appraisals, is likely to provide more objective results.

➤ When discussing with a member areas in which expectations haven't been met, give specific examples. Ask what the member plans to do to meet standards and what help you can provide.

➤ At the end of the interview, ask the team member to summarize the discussion. Keep a written record of the points that were agreed upon.

When Team Members Don't Make the Grade

It's going to happen. No matter how good a team leader you may be, there will be team members who don't meet standards and pull down the team's effectiveness. Just as the coach of a professional sports team is alert to changes in the behavior of all of his players, so the team leader must be sensitive to any changes in his or her team that portend trouble in the making.

In this chapter we'll look at why some team members don't succeed, suggest steps that might correct the situation, and, if that doesn't work, how to discipline and, if necessary, terminate unsatisfactory team members.

Identify Potential Problems

"An ounce of prevention is worth a pound of cure." This old adage sums up how to deal with problems better than any modern dictum. By looking for early indicators, poor performance, deteriorating work habits, or conflicts between members, problems can be identified and steps taken to avert them before they become really serious.

Heads Up!

Team leaders who don't keep their fingers on the pulse of all the members are asking for trouble. Watching for signs of behavior or attitude change is the only way to prevent problems from getting out of hand.

This does not mean that the leader should jump in at the first sign of a problem, but he or she should note it and watch that member carefully. It often may be a temporary aberration that will go away without intervention.

When Members Signal Problems

Most people don't change suddenly from good workers to poor producers. The change is usually slow and sometimes imperceptible until it's almost too late to stop it. Team leaders should look for *amber lights*—warning signs—and intervene as early as possible. If it is not dealt with at that time, the amber light will turn red—danger—and it may be too late to handle it without taking drastic steps.

Following are some amber lights that members turn on:

➤ **Drop in productivity.** Everybody slows down from time to time. Joe has a bad cold, his work suffers; Maria's in a bad mood, she barks at her teammates; Lil's mother is ill, she can't concentrate on her work. These kind of slowdowns will happen in any team. Usually when Joe's cold is cured, Maria's mood changes, and Lil's mother recovers, each goes back to normal productivity. However, if Joe's productivity continues to decline—perhaps slowly over several weeks—there is probably a more serious reason, one that must be addressed or the work of the team will be affected.

➤ **Decline in quality.** Sarah has always been a meticulous individual. She rarely turned in work that wasn't letter perfect. Over the past several weeks, two of her reports had to be redone because of errors, and her current assignment is overdue because she misunderstood a key instruction.

➤ **Increase in absence and lateness.** Chuck, who rarely was absent, called in sick four times last month—each on a Friday. Pat, who lives 10 minutes from the office, was late twice last week and once this week—with flimsy excuses.

➤ **Change from positive to negative attitude.** Carol, who had always been optimistic about team projects, is nitpicking and finding fault with every assignment.

Team leaders who recognize these symptoms can take action to identify the reason the individuals involved have changed behavior, and work with them to overcome the problem.

When the Team Signals Problems

Sometimes the problems that may be signaled relate to teamwork. Sure, they are manifested by individual members, but involve more than their personal performances. If only a few members exhibit the following indicators, treat it as an individual situation. However, if a significant number of members are involved, it should be dealt with on a full-team basis.

Some signs of potential team troubles are

Team Terms

The **amber light** signifies caution. Amber light situations develop slowly and if caught in time by an alert leader can be neutralized. The **red light** indicates danger. The leader may have to take drastic action to resolve the problem.

➤ Members put their personal agendas ahead of the team's. They seek individual recognition and promote themselves at the expense of other members.

➤ Members are pressured to go along on decisions to which they object. The pressure may have been applied by the team leader or by more dominant team members. The result: Their resentment may lead to an implosion in the team.

➤ Some members sit back and let others carry most of the team's work. They never volunteer and only do what the leader orders them to do.

➤ Some members make it a point to find fault with every decision and, if they lose the battle, go along with the project halfheartedly.

➤ Some members consistently fail to meet deadlines. This may be due to lack of enthusiasm for the project, or it may be that the team is really overburdened with work.

➤ There is constant bickering among team members.

Salvage the Situation

Once the problem has been identified, the team leader must take action to alleviate it. Start with the member who has the problem. Even team-wide problems can be overcome if the key members who have caused the problem are targeted.

When the Problem Is Technical Competence

One of the common assumptions in making assignments is that the members who will do

Heads Up!

Watch out for cliques that may develop in the team. If the group separates itself into subgroups, it leads to rivalry, discord, and even sabotage of team efforts. Nip cliques in the bud.

the work have the capability of performing it—and this is usually true. Members are chosen primarily because of their job knowledge. But often, as projects become more complex, there may be members who are weak in some areas. Some may have not have kept up with the technology; others may have concentrated on some phases but have only cursory knowledge of others. The team leader must quickly identify the limitations of each member.

Asking the members if they're able to take on the assignment is not enough, Many people—especially if they've worked in related areas—may think they have the know-how, but don't. Others may be reluctant to admit lack of knowledge.

These type situations can be minimized by

➤ Making a practice of quizzing each member assigned to a new project on his or her knowledge and experience in that area. By making it a routine practice, when members are quizzed they will not feel you are doubting their capability.

➤ Before starting on the project, conduct a refresher program covering the type of work involved and the methods and procedures to follow, and give members the opportunity to ask questions without fear of being looked down upon as unqualified.

➤ Determine which members need shoring up in some aspects of the project and arrange for special training or coaching right from the beginning. This will prevent errors, slowdowns, and potential problems.

➤ Monitor the project carefully during the first phase. Observe which members are having problems and what type help they need—and provide it.

> ➤ If one or more members need more personal attention than you have time for, ask some of the more knowledgeable associates to mentor them.
>
> ➤ If several members are having difficulties with the assignment, arrange for added training—even if it requires training sessions after normal working hours.

Coaching and mentoring were covered in detail in Chapter 8. A discussion of training methods will be found in Chapter 23.

When the Problem Is Personal

There's no way that personal problems can be totally divorced from job performance. When people come to work, they can't store all of their personal worries in their lockers and forget about them until they check

Team Builder

Team leaders should be sure that members have the skills, knowledge, and training to tackle any new project the team is assigned. If you're not sure, test the members to identify weaknesses and take steps to provide the training that will enable them to perform up to the expected standards.

out at the end of the day. These worries and concerns are with them all of the time—and they do affect the way they work.

Refer to Chapter 11 for some specific steps that can be taken by team leaders in dealing with personal problems.

When the Problem Lies Within the Entire Team

Most of the time team problems are caused by ringleaders—domineering team members who influence their associates to follow their agendas.

If the team leader can win over the ringleaders, much of the dissension will end. This is not easy. Members of this ilk are usually difficult to persuade. But it's worth a try.

Here's how Bonnie, team leader of a customer service team, dealt with Clyde, a team member who dominated her team.

Clyde had persuaded several of his associates that they were being treated unfairly when they were asked to learn the jobs of other members. He argued that if every member could do the work of every other member, they wouldn't need as many people and some would be let go. Clyde, as their spokesman, told Bonnie that the members would refuse to take the training.

Bonnie could have ordered the training and insisted that all members participate. She could have disciplined or even fired Clyde for insubordination, but she took a different path. She recognized that disciplining Clyde would only exacerbate the situation. She chose to win Clyde over.

Over the next few days, she spoke to other team members, who expressed their feelings of insecurity and told her how they admired Clyde for pointing the negative consequences out to them.

Bonnie arranged a private meeting with Clyde. She asked him to express all of his concerns about the program and in a calm way refuted most of them. She showed him a plan for expansion of the team's activities that would enable all members to grow. She pointed out how the cross-training was the first step in a long-term team development program. She wound it up by asking him to give further thought to it before a team meeting about the proposed training that she was scheduling for the following week.

During the week, Bonnie noted a change in the team's attitude. At the meeting, Bonnie presented the entire program to the team. She held her breath when Clyde raised his hand, but to her joy, he endorsed the plan. By bringing Clyde into the whole picture, Bonnie converted him from a ringleader of dissidents to the cooperative informal leader of his associates.

This, of course, doesn't always work. If ringleaders become antagonistic and interfere with team progress, remove them from the team if possible.

FYI

When you hear or see the word *discipline*, the first thing that usually pops into your mind is punishment. Look at that word again. Notice that by dropping just two letters in the last syllable (*i* and *n*), it turns into disciple, which is a synonym for *student*. Both words are derived from the Latin word meaning "to learn." If you look at discipline not as punishment, but as a means of learning, both you and your associates get much more out of it. You are the coach, and your associates are the learners.

Formal Disciplinary Action

When team members violate company rules, most companies follow a standard procedure to try to get them back on track, or if this doesn't succeed, to punish the offender. This is generally referred to as progressive disciple.

Typically, progressive discipline is a five- or six-step procedure:

1. An informal warning or reprimand. The team leader talks to the offender, usually at his or her work station; discusses the problem; and cautions that it should not be repeated.

2. A formal disciplinary interview. This is usually held in the team leader's office or a conference room and the offender is put on notice that future violations will not be tolerated.

3. A written warning is given to the offender. Copies are placed in appropriate files. This step is sometimes included as part of the formal disciplinary interview.

4. Probation. The employee is told to shape up over a specified period of time.

5. Suspension. The member is suspended without pay for a specified period of time.

6. Termination. Bye-bye, member.

How these steps are implemented is discussed below.

Effective Reprimands

When you, as team leader, note a member's violation of rules, let's say, tardiness, you call it to the member's attention in a casual way. These chats are friendly, but firm, and are not part of the progressive discipline procedure.

The first official step in the *progressive discipline* system is often called the oral, or verbal, warning: You take the team member aside and remind him that the two of you have previously discussed his lateness and that, because he continues to come to work late, you must put him on notice that tardiness cannot be accepted on your team. Inform him of the next steps you'll take if the behavior continues.

When preparing to reprimand someone, to ensure that the reprimand is conducted in the most effective manner, study the following guidelines:

Team Terms

Progressive discipline is a systematic approach to correcting rule infractions. A typical program has six steps, beginning with an informal warning. If the warning doesn't succeed, the following steps are taken, in order: Disciplinary interview, written warning, probation, suspension, and termination (if necessary).

➤ **Time the reprimand properly.** As soon as possible after the offense has been committed, call the member aside and discuss the matter in private.

➤ **Never reprimand when you're angry.** Wait until you've calmed down before talking to the member.

➤ **Emphasize the what, not the who.** Base the reprimand on the action that was wrong, not on the person.

➤ **Begin by stating the problem and then ask a question.** Don't begin with an accusation: "You're always late!" Say instead, "You know how important it is for all of us to be on the job promptly. What can you do to get here on time from now on?"

➤ **Listen!** Attentive, open-minded listening is one of the most important factors in true leadership. Ask questions to elicit as much information about the situation as you can. Respond to the associate's comments, but don't let the interview deteriorate into a confrontation.

➤ **Encourage the team member to make suggestions for solving the problem.** When a person participates in solving a problem, there's a much greater chance that the solution will be accepted and achieved.

➤ **Provide constructive criticism.** Give the team member specific suggestions, when possible, about how to correct a situation.

➤ **Never use sarcasm.** Sarcasm never corrects a situation; it only makes the other person feel inadequate and put upon.

➤ **End your reprimand on a positive note.** Comment on some of the good things the person has accomplished so that he or she knows that you're not focusing only on the reason for this reprimand, but are addressing total performance. Reassure the person that you look on him or her as a valuable member of the team.

Disciplinary Actions

If an employee repeats an offense after receiving a verbal warning, the next step is the disciplinary interview. In some systems the written warning is given as part of this step; in others it is a separate step taken if the member repeats the offense yet again.

This interview differs from a reprimand in that it is more formal. The verbal warning is usually a relatively brief session, often conducted in a quiet corner of the room. A disciplinary interview is longer and is conducted in an office or conference room.

A disciplinary interview should always be carefully prepared and result in a mutually agreed-upon plan of action. Whereas a plan of action after a verbal warning is usually oral, in a disciplinary interview the resulting plan should be put in writing. It not only reminds both the leader and the team member of what has been agreed upon but also serves as documentation.

In administering the disciplinary interview, follow the same guidelines as suggested for the reprimand. However, as this is more formal, comments, questions and the suggested plan of action should be written, with a copy given to the member, a copy kept in the team leader's file, and a copy sent to the human resources department for the member's personnel file. This is important because if any legal action should ensue from the disciplinary action, this report will serve as documentation to support the position of the team and the company.

Similar distribution should be made of any written warnings—whether issued as part of the disciplinary interview or at a later time.

Probation and Suspension

Until now all attempts to correct a team member's performance or behavior have been positive efforts by the team leader, who has provided advice and counsel. If nothing has worked, the next step is to put the team member on probation.

Heads Up!

To protect your company from potential legal problems, check any forms or letters concerning discipline with your legal advisors before giving them to team members.

This step gives the associate one more chance to shape up before some form of punishment is invoked. Most people take probation seriously.

The two primary reasons progressive discipline is necessary are poor performance and poor conduct. If performance is the problem, probation is the last step before termination. If despite all the retraining, counseling, and coaching the team member fails, probation is one last chance to overcome the problem over a definite period. If this doesn't help, suspending the member won't help. If the member can be transferred to a more suitable job, do so; if not, there is no other choice but to terminate him or her.

Probationary periods vary from as few as 10 days to the more customary 30 days and sometimes even longer. If an employee makes significant progress, the probation can be lifted. If he or she reverts to poor performance after the probation is lifted, you can reinstate the probation or resort to the next step.

When the reason for probation is not job performance but violation of company rules, such as absenteeism, tardiness, or other misconduct, most companies invoke some sort of punishment.

Up to now in the progressive discipline system, there has actually been no punishment. Each step has been a warning with the implication of potential punishment. If probation hasn't solved the problem, the most commonly used form of punishment, short of termination, is suspension without pay.

Team Builder

It's not a good idea to extend a probationary period. If a team member makes some progress by the end of the probationary period but his or her behavior still isn't up to expectations, you can extend the time period—but only once. Continuous probation is bad for morale and rarely solves the problem.

Although team leaders often have some leeway in determining the length of a suspension, most companies set specific suspension periods depending on the seriousness of the offense.

Because suspension is a very serious step, union contracts often require consultation with a union representative before an employee is suspended. But even when companies aren't unionized, it's good practice to require approval for suspensions by both the manager to whom the team leader reports and the human resources department. There should be appropriate documentation specifying the reason for the suspension and the exact period of time involved should be made, signed by the appropriate manager, and acknowledged by the suspended employee.

If an employee returns from a suspension and continues to break the rules, your next step may be a longer suspension or even termination.

Discipline and termination are fraught with perils. Test your knowledge of some of these dangers. Check your responses with the answers that follow the quiz. Careful! Some of these questions are a bit tricky.

Yes	No	1. A member who is fired can sue both the company and the team leader.
Yes	No	2. A team leader can fire a team member if he feels that the member doesn't fit in with the team.
Yes	No	3. Even the most informal reprimand should be documented.

continues

continued

Yes	No	4. One way to motivate marginal workers is to keep them on extended probation.
Yes	No	5. Absenteeism and tardiness can be reduced by rigid adherence to company rules.
Yes	No	6. To make firing an employee less painful, tell him or her the reason is "reorganization" or "downsizing" rather than the true cause.
Yes	No	7. To reduce the company's unemployment insurance ratings, make life unpleasant for the member so he or she will quit.
Yes	No	8. It's wise to overlook excessive lateness if the member is a highly productive worker.
Yes	No	9. To protect yourself and the company, keep secret files on members' foibles.
Yes	No	10. It's a violation of a member's privacy to tell other team members why an associate was fired.

Now let's look at the answers. For many of these situations, the answer could be either "yes" or "no," depending on circumstances.

1. **Yes.** Under the American jurisprudence system, anybody can sue anybody else. That doesn't mean he can win the case. However, in cases where the court has found that the firing was the result of violations of the civil rights laws or was retribution for the employee's "whistle-blowing," companies and sometimes immediate supervisors have been found liable.

2. **Yes.** Unless it can be shown that the reason the member allegedly doesn't "fit in" is because of race, religion, national origin, age, sex, or disability.

3. **Yes.** Other than routine conversations about the work, any discussion of unsatisfactory performance or behavior should be documented to protect the company in case formal complaints or litigation develops.

4. **No.** Probation should be a temporary expedient. If the performance does not improve after a reasonable time, the member should be removed from the job.

5. **Yes.** But that's not enough. The reasons for these infractions should be identified and steps taken to alleviate the problems.

6. **No.** Employees should be told the real reason for termination. If not, they may later use your lie as evidence that it was a subterfuge for some illegal reason for the termination.

7. **No.** Such actions have been interpreted as "constructive discharge," a legal term meaning that the circumstances that led to the resignation were so bad that it is equivalent to being fired.

8. **No.** Nobody wants to lose a good producer, but allowing one member to get away with excessive tardiness sets a bad example for the team. An alternative is to set up a flexible-hour schedule.

9. **No.** The purpose of discipline is to help members improve performance or behavior. They should know what complaints you have about them. Many firms give copies of all forms, memos, or other documents to the member.

10. **No.** Unless the reason is of a personal or sensitive nature. For example, if it's made public that a member was fired for stealing, unless he is convicted of the crime, he could sue you for defamation.

Termination—The Last Resort

Members should never be surprised when they're fired after progressive discipline. Presumably, at every step along the way they were told what the next step would be.

Because the issue of firing employees is such a sensitive one, it must be done diplomatically with full awareness of any legal implications. Ask the human resources department for advice about dealing with the situation.

Some team leaders get more upset about having to fire someone than the person who is being fired. Here are some suggestions to help prepare:

➤ Review all documents so that you're fully aware of all the reasons and implications involved in the decision to terminate the team member.

➤ Review the problems you have had with the person and how you have dealt with them in the past.

➤ Review any personal problems you're aware of that the member has.

➤ Review any problems you've had in firing other employees, and map out a plan to avoid those problems.

➤ Check the company's policy manual or discuss any company rules that apply with the human resources department.

➤ Relax before the meeting. Do whatever helps you clear your mind and calm your emotions. If you've done your job correctly, you've made every effort to help the team member succeed. The progressive discipline system has given the person several chances to change, so you don't have to feel guilty about the firing.

Team Builder

If an employee raises his or her voice, lower yours. Most people respond to a raised voice by raising their own. By responding in a soft voice, you disarm the other person. It has a calming effect.

Spontaneous Termination

Occasionally, termination without warning is permitted. These occasions are rare and usually limited to a few serious infractions that are clearly delineated in company policies. Serious offenses include drinking on the job, fighting, stealing, and insubordination. Because these charges aren't always easy to prove, be very careful before making the decision to fire someone without progressive discipline. Have solid evidence that can stand up in court. Law books are loaded with cases in which people who, because of a rash firing decision, have sued former employers for unlawful discharge, defamation of character, false imprisonment, and whatever else their lawyers could dream up.

Insubordination, which is one of the most frequent causes of spontaneous termination, isn't always easy to prove. If an employee simply fails to carry out an order, it's not enough grounds for termination. Unless a failure to obey instructions can lead to serious consequences, it's better to use progressive discipline. On the other hand, if a team member becomes unruly in his or her refusal to obey, spontaneous discharge may be appropriate.

When someone is fired after progressive discipline procedures fail, an entire series of documents is on file to back it up. In spontaneous termination, however, there are no documents.

Immediately after a spontaneous termination, write a detailed report describing the circumstances that led up to it. Get written statements from witnesses. If possible, get the member to sign a statement presenting his or her side of the story. In the event that this discharge is challenged, having the terminated employee's immediate comments will protect the company in case he or she presents a different version of what happened.

Legal Implications

Because of the concerns companies have about the legal implications of discipline and termination, team leaders should learn as much as possible about the pertinent laws.

Most leaders are familiar with the civil rights laws that prohibit discrimination based on race, religion, national origin, sex, age, and disability. These laws are discussed in Chapter 20. To ensure compliance, check with the company's human resources department or legal advisors before taking action that can lead to termination.

The Termination Interview

When the time comes to let the member know he or she is fired, do it diplomatically. Find a private place to conduct the meeting. Your office is an obvious spot, but it may not be the best one. A conference room is better because, if the fired employees breaks down or becomes belligerent, you can walk out.

Most people who are fired expect it and don't cause problems. They may beg for another chance, but this isn't the time to change your mind. Progressive discipline gives people several "other chances" before they reach this point. If the employee gives you a hard time, keep cool. Don't lose your temper or get into an argument.

It's a good idea to have another person in the room at a termination meeting. A person being fired may say or do inappropriate things. Sometimes the team leader may become upset and say something that's best left unsaid. The presence of a third person keeps both the team leader and the employee from losing control and from saying or doing something that can lead to additional complications.

Heads Up!

As angry as you may be about the trouble an employee has caused or how nasty he or she may be, don't use the termination meeting to tell the person off. A termination is a business decision, not a personal one.

The best "third person" in a termination meeting is a representative from the human resources department. If such a person isn't available, call in another manager or team leader. If the employee belongs to a union, the union contract usually stipulates the presence of a union delegate.

Having a third person in the room when terminating an employee also provides a witness if an employee later sues the company. Suppose that a former employee files an age discrimination suit several weeks after being fired for poor performance. He or she claims that during the termination meeting, the team leader stated that the company needs younger people in order to meet production standards. Although the claim is false, the company will have to spend time, energy, and money to defend against the charge—and it's never certain which side will be believed.

If a third person attends termination meetings, former employees will be less likely to file false claims because they know that they'll be refuted by a witness.

Effect on Other Team Members

A team is more than just a group of workers. Members usually develop close personal relationships and tend to support each other. When a member is terminated, there can be serious repercussions for the remaining members.

When the team is highly motivated, the need for discipline becomes superfluous. Each member of the team becomes a support person and a motivator to other members.

If a team member is slow in some aspect of his or her work, other team members can share their working shortcuts; if someone arrives at work late or frequently takes extra time at lunch, his or her colleagues can explain that it affects their activities. The team leader often doesn't have to reprimand or engage in formal disciplinary measures.

If everyone on a team is committed to meeting its goals and is given the tools to measure their own and the team's progress, they become self-controllers. The need for formal discipline fades into the background and is used only rarely, when all other means have been exhausted.

When a Member Is Fired

There will be times when the team's efforts don't succeed in salvaging a member and he or she must be terminated. If the reason is poor performance, the other members probably have long since recognized that the associate was in jeopardy. As they have tried to help him improve, and have seen their efforts fail, they know that the leader has no choice but to remove him from the job.

FYI

Did you know that most companies fire people at the end of the workday on Friday afternoon? But this is changing. Some companies are now terminating employees in the middle of the week so that they have a chance to begin looking for a new job the next day and not brood about the firing over the weekend.

If the reason for the termination is an infraction of company rules, there may be some dissent if the members consider the rules to be unfair or inequitably administered.

Before making the final decision on termination, speak to the informal leaders and tell them that the member has had her last chance. If the infraction is repeated, she will have to be fired. They may volunteer to work with her to overcome the problem or they may already have given up on her. If they want to help, give them a time limit. If the offender does not change and is let go, they will feel that the decision was fair.

"Is my job secure?"

When a member is terminated, other members may feel insecure. "If Millie was fired, am I next?" If the members were aware of each of the steps taken with Millie—how every effort was made to help her improve her performance or correct her behavior, they will be less likely to worry.

Job insecurity is more serious when members quit or are downsized. This is discussed in the next chapter.

The Least You Need to Know

➤ Poor performance, deteriorating work habits, or conflicts between members should be identified and addressed early on.

➤ Team leaders should be sure that members have the skills, knowledge, and training to tackle any new project the team is assigned.

➤ Showing concern and listening to a member's problem is often enough to get the member back on track.

➤ The first step in disciplining is an oral reprimand.

➤ A disciplinary interview should always be carefully planned.

➤ Firing employees is sensitive. It must be done diplomatically with full awareness of any legal implications.

➤ If you follow the guidelines for disciplinary action in this chapter, most people who are fired will expect it and not cause problems.

Chapter 14

Bye-Bye Buddy

In This Chapter

➤ When a team member quits

➤ Finding the real reason a member quits

➤ How team leaders downsize effectively

➤ Survival tips for downsized team members

It's rare today for a person to join a company after graduating from high school or college and remain with that organization until retirement. Most people have several jobs during their work life. Sometimes the reason for changing jobs is a personal decision; sometimes, it's involuntary—the worker is fired, as discussed in the previous chapter, or, more often, due to reorganization or downsizing, the job is eliminated.

Every time a member leaves a team, whether it's voluntary or involuntary, the team suffers. Productivity is curtailed until a replacement can be found and trained. Often, the job will not be refilled and the work has to be done by the surviving team members.

Dealing with these problems is a major challenge for team leaders.

"I quit."

Nothing is as frustrating to a team leader as having one of her best team members quit. It has often taken months or years to bring that person up to optimum productivity—and now suddenly he leaves.

Heads Up!

Team leaders: Be alert to signs of discontent among your members. Take their threats to quit seriously. Try to identify the problem and deal with it before the member really starts to look for another job.

Not only does this disrupt the momentum of the team's work, it has negative effects on the other members—unless, of course, the member who quit is universally disliked.

Why Members Say "I Quit"

You ask the member why he or she quit. Often your answer will be that it's for personal reasons. Carl decided to go back to college; Vicki's chosen to be a full-time mother; Sam's father's illness requires him to take over his business; Jane's spouse is transferred to another city.

Or the answer indicates a career move. Ben has gone as far as he can in your company; Gerri is offered more money by another firm; an opportunity arises in a different field—one in which Tom is particularly interested. Hilary's going into her own business.

But often the reason given is not totally true. Yes, Tom did go to an industry in which he has particular interest, but would he have made that decision if he were obtaining job satisfaction in his current job? Gerri's leaving for more money. Sure, she would like more money, but perhaps she wouldn't have even looked for a job if she were not unhappy with the way the team leader ran the team.

The Real Reasons People Quit

Every time a person quits, it's important to determine the true reason. This isn't easy because it may not even be clear to the member who leaves. It may be deeply imbedded in the culture of the company and subtly has made the member discontent.

Members may feel they are not making the progress they had hoped for, that their salary is too low, that working conditions are unsatisfactory, or that the job has become boring. Members are often reluctant to divulge the real reason for deciding to quit. This is particularly true if the real cause of discontent lies with the team leader or other team members. Not only is it embarrassing to tell their boss they don't like him, but they may be concerned about getting a poor reference.

Retaining good people is essential to the success and stability of your team. Team leaders should do their best to establish a climate that will lead to satisfied members, who will remain with the organization. Of course, team leaders don't have complete control over these conditions. Much rests with higher ranking managers and with the long-term corporate culture.

The following quiz will give you a chance to evaluate the retention potential of your organization.

FYI

If you decide to quit, it's only fair to give your team leader adequate notice. In addition, here are some suggestions that will make your leaving less painful for the team: Discuss with the team leader how the other members will be notified about your departure. Inform the team leader of the status of all projects on which you are working. Offer to assist whoever will take over your work. If your work involves dealing with customers, subcontractors, or other outsiders, notify them whom to contact after you're gone. Keep in contact with the team leader after you leave to answer questions. It pays to maintain a good relationship.

Test Your Retention Quota

Examine your personnel practices to determine some of the reasons that your retention rate is not as high as you would like.

Yes   No   **1.** Is the company's compensation program (salary plus benefits) at least on a par with competitors for the same types of personnel?

Yes   No   **2.** Do you make members feel that their work is vital to the company's success?

Yes   No   **3.** Do you provide training to keep your members at the cutting edge of the technology needed in their work?

Yes   No   **4.** Do you send members to professional development programs on a regular basis?

Yes   No   **5.** Do you keep in mind members' personal goals and provide opportunity for them to achieve these goals?

Yes   No   **6.** Do you encourage members to contribute their ideas and suggestions?

Yes   No   **7.** Do you provide opportunity for members to assume more responsibility—and pay them accordingly?

Yes   No   **8.** Do members see the career paths open to them and what steps you are taking to help them move along those paths?

Yes   No   **9.** Do you give both private and public recognition to each member's accomplishments?

Yes   No   **10.** Do you sense a feeling of pride in the work and the company among the members?

Review your responses. Any "no" answer is an indicator of a problem that may lead to the loss of some of your good employees.

The Separation Interview

Too often companies do not know why they lose good employees. *Exit* or *separation interviews* are designed to probe for the real reasons people leave a job and obtain from the employee information about the job or the company that may be causing discontent.

I have witnessed a number of exit interviews in which the questions were of such a superficial nature that no significant insight was developed. In order to get meaningful information that will enable the company to identify and correct problems that have caused turnover, a well-structured interview must be conducted.

Team Terms

Separation interviews or exit interviews give organizations insight into the real reasons people quit their jobs.

It is best that this interview *not* be conducted by the team leader of the member who is leaving. A member of the human resources staff or another manager should conduct it.

Just as in an employment or appraisal interview, it is best to start a separation interview by building rapport. Questioning should begin with a general type of question that will not put the member on the defensive. The question of why he or she is leaving the company should never be the first one asked. A better start might be: "Tell me about the kind of work you've been doing in your most recent assignment." This will get the conversation going, but will also enable the interviewer to evaluate whether this is the kind of work one might expect to do in that job. One reason people leave jobs is that it was not what they thought they'd be doing. A market researcher might be spending all her time on statistical compilations when she expected to be doing depth analyses.

Here are some important questions that should be asked in a separation interview and some clues as to what should be looked for to interpret the responses:

1. Questions about the job

What did you like most and least about the job?

Are these job factors or personal factors? The answer provides insight into the job by the pattern of answers obtained from people who leave it.

How do you feel about your compensation?

Many people leave their jobs for another with higher pay. Others feel they should have made more money even though they were being paid the going rate for the work. This will enable the interviewer to compare the methods used to give increases with those of other companies in the area or your industry.

FYI

A recent survey of managerial and professional personnel by the U.S. Chamber of Commerce showed that the 40-hour work week was dead for so-called knowledge workers. Most respondents said that they worked nine-hour days, another hour or more at home, and at least two hours on weekends.

How do you feel about the progress you've made in this company?

A good number of people claim they have left their jobs because of lack of opportunity for advancement. Often this masks the real reasons for leaving. However, it's important to examine what a person might have expected in terms of growth in the company and relate it to the real opportunity for advancement in the job she or he held.

How do you feel about working conditions?

Companies have picked up information from this question about matters that were unimportant in their eyes, but that annoyed employees to the point of causing them to leave. Often these are easily correctable.

2. Questions about supervision

What did you like most (least) about your team leader's style of managing?

As many of the problems existing in organizational life are due to problems with supervisors, it's important to probe this factor, particularly if there is a large turnover in that department. It will bring out whether the team leader is dogmatic, stubborn, or authoritarian, and whether he or she encourages participation.

Probe further to learn about how the team leader dealt with complaints. Some leaders tend to be defensive and take any complaint as a personal affront; others take time out to discuss even the most far-fetched grievances.

It also helps learn the good points of each team leader so that they can be reinforced when you report back to the leader.

Does your team leader tend to favor some employees or act unfairly to others?

Favoritism on one hand and bias on the other are major causes of discontent. The question can also point up blatant areas of cronyism or, at the other extreme, prejudice and discrimination. If this bias is based on racial, religious, national origin, gender, or age factors, it might alert you to serious potential legal problems and give the organization a chance to correct them.

195

Heads Up!

An unbiased, objective separation interview shouldn't be conducted by the team leader or supervisor of the employee who is leaving. The interview should be conducted by a member of the human resources department, another management-level person, or an outside consultant.

3. Questions to sum up the interview

If you could discuss with top management exactly how you feel about this company, what would you tell them?

This open-ended question often results in some interesting insights. Let the person talk freely. Avoid leading questions that might influence the response. Encourage him or her to express real feelings, attitudes, suggestions, problems, fear, and hopes about the organization.

If the applicant has accepted a job with another company, ask

What does the job to which you are going offer you that you were not getting here?

The answer may repeat some of the facts already brought out, but it may also uncover some of the ways the firm failed to meet the person's hopes, goals, or expectations.

If the answers to the above questions have not brought out the true reasons for the employee's leaving, ask specifically

Why are you leaving at this particular time?

Some of the problems that have come out at the interview may have been in existence for a long time. Some of them have seemed unimportant until now. Find out what precipitated the resignation at this time. Have things become worse? Is there anything that can be recommended to management that will prevent them from becoming even more serious and causing more turnover?

A good separation interview can take an hour or more, but it can provide insight into how employees who have quit really feel about the organization, and how these negatives can be overcome and the positive aspects of the work environment reinforced.

Effect on Remaining Members

Whenever a member resigns, there will be some disruption of the team. In addition to the shifting of workloads and the breaking in of a replacement, there is the psychological impact on each person.

Some members may just shrug their shoulders and get on with their jobs. However, there are others who may think, "If Gerri is getting more money in her new job, maybe I should see what I can get."

Another member may realize that the real reason Tom quit was not that he wanted to go into another field, but that he was bored with this job—and "it's no longer a challenge for me either."

FYI

No law requires employees to give notice when they quit, but it is customary to give two weeks notice as that enables the team leader to make a smooth transition. In some cases, team leaders feel that the continued presence of a member who has given notice is disruptive to the team. If so, it's okay to arrange for an immediate separation.

After a member quits, the team leader should take the time to speak to the others individually, probe them about any concerns they have, and work with them to alleviate sources of unhappiness. It may not be possible to solve every problem, but bringing them out in the open clears the air and often deters people from thinking seriously about leaving the organization.

When a Team Is Downsized

Layoffs have always been a factor in the world of work, particularly among blue collar workers. Business slows down and workers are furloughed. When business picks up, the laid-off workers are likely to be rehired.

In recent years many companies have resorted to reducing their company payroll, not only when business was poor, but as a means of increasing profits. These layoffs are usually referred to as *downsizing* or even *rightsizing*.

Downsizing differs from traditional layoffs in that total job categories may be eliminated. There's little chance that people who have held these jobs will ever be rehired. Downsized positions are increasingly white collar and managerial jobs.

Who Goes? Who Stays?

The decision is made to downsize the department. You, the team leader, are ordered to cut two people from the team. Which two?

There are several ways in which downsizing is implemented. Many companies offer an early retirement option. Employees who have been with the company for a specific number of years

Team Terms

Downsizing involves the reduction in the workforce of an organization by eliminating or reducing the number of employees in various job categories. Some firms euphemistically call this **rightsizing**.

Heads Up!

Be careful about how early retirement offers are made. If the implication is "accept early retirement or you'll be laid off anyway," the company would be in violation of the age discrimination laws.

are offered a financial settlement to retire early. For example, José has been with the company for 22 years. He is 60 years old and can retire on full pension at 62. He is offered full pension benefits if he retires now. Rebecca is 50, but she's been with the company for 20 years. Under the pension plan, she could retire at age 50, but receive a much smaller pension. She's offered a bonus if she opts for early retirement.

Seniority is often the company policy in determining who is downsized. In most union-management contracts layoffs must be based on seniority. Last in, first out. Even when there is no union contract, many firms follow this practice.

This means that as a team leader, you have no choice but to lay off the most recently hired team members. Because this practice could eliminate an entire team—if they were all relatively new employees in the company—most organizations using teams do not follow a rigid company-wide seniority program. However, team leaders may be compelled to lay off members with the least seniority.

In most companies the team leader must make the decision. Let's say that nobody in your team opts for early retirement. You have to determine which members will go. It's never easy to do this. You want to keep your most valuable members—those with the most skills, the most knowledge, the most collaborative ability. By rating your members on their value to the team, you can select the two least valuable to be downsized.

It is never pleasant to lay off people. It's particularly difficult when the downsized members are basically good workers with whom you have developed a good relationship. But that's one of the drawbacks of being a team leader.

Dealing with the Survivors

Downsizing can devastate the morale of a team. The laid-off workers are naturally distraught. Survivors worry about their job security, the changes in their work assignments, and increases in their workload.

As a team leader, you have to anticipate and deal with these concerns. When major organizational changes occur—especially when they are out of your control—make a point to acknowledge them and take action to get the team back on track. The feelings and confusion of your team members is a normal reaction, but unless it is assuaged early on, it can fester into a permanent sense of distrust.

Here are some suggestions to help pull the team together:

➤ Acknowledge the situation. Some leaders feel it's best to erase the memory of the laid-off workers. They never talk about them, and act as if they'd never existed.

This is playing ostrich—hiding one's head in the sand. Openly talk about the people who were downsized. Let the members know that you miss them. Encourage the remaining members to express their grief over the loss. The team's challenge now is to regroup and develop ways to keep the momentum going.

Heads Up!

If any team member exhibits unusual stress as a result of the downsizing, take the time to counsel him or her. If that doesn't help, refer that member to the employee assistance program.

➤ Conduct a meeting to plan the reorganization. Review the way the work was distributed before the change. Post on the wall a list of the activities each of the members has been doing before the downsizing. Go over all tasks to see if any can be eliminated or combined with other tasks. Rank the remaining items.

➤ Redistribute the jobs. Let members choose which of the tasks formerly done by a laid-off member they'll take over. Adjudicate any disagreements at the start to prevent later conflicts. In reorganizing the work of the team, it's better to reevaluate each job and rewrite the job description than to just tack on additional duties to the current job description.

➤ Congratulate the team on the way it has acted under the circumstances. Assure members that you appreciate it and will work with them to ensure that the new plan will work smoothly.

Morale Problems

After a downsizing surviving members may feel a temporary sense of relief—they still have their jobs—but deep down there is the concern about the future. If the company did it once, they fear it will probably do it again.

Not only do they worry about insecurity, they know that when teams are reduced in size, it inevitably means that fewer people have to do more work. They may be concerned about being overworked.

Unrest in the Ranks

There's no way a team leader can guarantee that the recent downsizing was the last one. Particularly if there have been previous layoffs—even if they had not affected the team, it's natural to worry about one's job security.

Team Builder

One way to help employees cope with downsizing and reorganization is to institute stress reduction programs. Also, let team members know that, as business improves, temporary, and eventually permanent, staff members will be added to the team to ease the workload.

Some members will polish up their resumés and start a job search immediately. As a result, the team will lose good people when it needs them most. Less aggressive members may sulk and mope, and not accomplish much work. On the other hand, there are some members who may take this as an opportunity to prove they are indispensable. They'll work hard and smart so that, if there is a next time, they'll be less likely to be downsized.

As a team leader, you must do your best to protect your team. Jeremy was a team leader who handled this well. After his team reorganized and was moving along satisfactorily, he met with his boss, Sheila, and brought her up to date on his team's progress. He pointed out that any further layoffs would make it impossible to meet company goals. He asked what more he could do to protect his team from future downsizing. Sheila commented that the company was now over the hump and moving ahead. She assured him that further downsizing was unlikely, and she was confident that his team members were secure unless circumstances got much worse than was anticipated.

Jeremy reported this to his members and although the concern about layoffs wasn't completely gone, it became less dominant in their thinking.

"More work for me."

Smaller teams mean more work for each member. Suppose a team of nine people is reduced to seven. Most likely the amount of work has not decreased in proportion. Work done at a leisurely pace must now be rushed. Members who went home at 5 P.M. now work regularly to 6 or 7. Everyone feels the pressure. Morale is low.

How to motivate members who work longer hours under constant pressure is the primary challenge team leaders face. There are no easy answers. Some leaders counter complaints by telling team members that they're lucky to have a job. This answer isn't a good one. Negative motivation has limited value.

By encouraging the team to find shortcuts to better production, to eliminate unnecessary paperwork, and to come up with creative innovations, the time spent on completing assignments can be reduced and morale improved.

Surviving Downsizing: Tips for Team Members

In your company, other teams have been downsized. You're concerned that sooner or later, it will hit your team. Here are some things you can you do to stand out as a valuable employee and have a greater chance of surviving.

Be Good at What You Do

The first requirement is efficiency. This is basic to all other suggestions. Unless you do your job well, all the plans you can make to survive will fall apart. Learn all you can about your job and the other functions of the team, and work to help the team meet its goals. Study the work. Make suggestions as to how it can be improved. Above all, set high standards for yourself and for any people that you supervise.

Keep Up with the Technology

In the dynamic world in which we live, things are always changing. This is obvious in technical and professional work, but all people—not just the knowledge workers—must keep up with the state of the art in their fields. Subscribe to journals in your field. Attend industry conventions and trade shows. Join and become active in a trade or professional association.

Expand Your Job

Take on added responsibilities outside of your regular work. Volunteer to work on special projects. Learn to perform work done by team members who are not in your specialty. Make yourself knowledgeable about every aspect of the team's work.

Be Visible

Many good team members are not known to anybody other than their team leader. When Tracey's team was consolidated with another team, her team leader was transferred to another location. In order to determine which of the members of her team to keep, the new team leader discussed the qualifications of each of the members of the old team with senior managers of the company. None of them really knew Tracey. Despite her good work, she was let go.

To become visible, make sure that managers other than your team manager know you. One way to become visible is to speak up at meetings. Many people remain invisible because they are reticent to participate actively in meetings and keep their ideas to themselves. Another way is to volunteer for assignments that enable you to meet other team leaders and managers, such as projects that require interaction between teams.

Act Positive

When Shirley heard that the company was planning to downsize, she became totally negative. She assumed that because she was relatively new to the team, she would be laid off. This negativity was reflected in her work and her attitude. She slowed down, made more errors, and criticized everything suggested by her team leader. In other words, she quit in anticipation of the layoff.

Her teammate, Vicki, hired around the same time as Shirley, was more positive. She thought, "I'm a good worker, so I'll probably be kept on." She worked harder and more effectively. When special work was needed, she didn't hesitate to do it. She continued to contribute the same effort, energy, and commitment to her job that she always had. There was little question in the mind of the team leader which one to keep.

FYI

One way companies have reduced the stress of downsizing on both the laid-off employees and those who, although retained, are concerned about future downsizing is to institute outplacement programs. By counseling and aiding the laid-off people in locating new jobs, companies show they are concerned about them as human beings. Those who survived this downsizing see that the company doesn't totally abandon its people even when it must let them go.

Be Flexible

Elliot had managed his store for two years and was proud to be a manager. Unfortunately, due to economic conditions, the company found it necessary to close several stores including Elliot's. Elliot was a member of a team of store managers and assistant managers that operated in the northern New Jersey area. Although several team members were laid off, his team leader offered Elliot a position as assistant manager of another store. "How can I take a reduction in position?" Elliot thought. "How can I tell my friends I'm no longer a manager? Maybe I should look for a manager's job with another chain?"

After careful thought, Elliot realized that as one of the few managers of stores that had been closed who was not laid off, he was respected and appreciated by his present company. By being flexible he could survive this temporary setback until he could resume the career path his company offered.

Sometimes being flexible means relocating to another city; sometimes it means a cut in salary, or as in Elliot's case, a reduction in rank. If you have confidence in the long-term growth of the organization, being flexible is usually better than having no job at all, or moving to a company where you are an unknown quantity and have to start from scratch.

Prepare to Move If Necessary

Because there are times when no matter what you do you cannot prevent loss of your job, be ready to seek a new one. Prepare a resumé and keep it up to date. Use the contacts you have developed in your present job to develop a network that can lead you to other jobs.

As a mature adult, you should be able to face both the good and bad in your career. By careful planning and attention to the possibility of downsizing you can do your best to maximize your possibility of survival.

The Least You Need to Know

➤ Nothing is as frustrating to a team leader as having a valuable team member quit.

➤ Uncovering why the employee really is leaving can benefit the company, enabling it to better attract new employees and retain existing ones.

➤ Retaining good people is essential to the success and stability of your team.

➤ Exit or separation interviews should be used to gain useful information from the employee about problem areas in the job or company.

➤ Whenever a member resigns, there will be some disruption of the team's workload as well as a psychological impact on every member.

➤ Downsizing can devastate the morale of a team. As a team leader, you have to anticipate and deal with it.

➤ Encouraging the team to find creative innovations to speed and improve production will reduce the time spent on completing assignments and improve morale.

➤ If your company is contemplating downsizing, take affirmative steps to make yourself as valuable a member as you can be, and you'll be more likely to survive.

Part 4
T-E-A-M—Yay TEAM!

Look at the word motivation. Two other words that begin with the same three letters are motion and motor. We call the motors in our cars "internal combustion engines." Each of us has an engine inside of us "combusting" to move us forward.

Just as our car cannot move without fuel, neither can people move unless provided with the proper fuel. Your job as a team leader is to provide each of your team members with the fuel that will start their "motors" and keep them going.

But we must keep in mind that all cars don't use the same kind of fuel. Some use gas, some use diesel oil, some run on electricity. So it is with people. What motivates one person may not work for another. To be able to help your team move forward, you have to know what kind of fuel to feed to each of your members, how and when to use it, and what reaction you can expect. Tough job? Sure, but it's worth the effort.

Let's look at the various "fuels" you can choose to motivate your team.

Chapter 15

Power, Power. Who's Got the Power?

In This Chapter

➤ What empowerment means

➤ What empowerment can do

➤ Dealing with problems of empowerment

➤ How empowerment can work in the team

If you've been around management circles for any length of time, you've been exposed to buzzwords—phrases everybody knows and uses. You go to trade association meetings and these terms are the main topic of discussion. They pop up in casual conversations among businesspeople, and they're featured in every business publication.

Empowerment is the buzzword these days. It's not easy to empower people. Some leaders don't want to give up their power, and some team members don't want to take the responsibility that goes with power. This chapter looks at how empowerment works in practice and how it can make you a more effective team leader.

The Meaning of Empowerment

Empowerment means different things to different people. To some managers, it means sharing authority with subordinates, but maintaining control. To other managers, empowerment is just a new way of encouraging subordinates to share their ideas, but not giving up any real authority to them. To many rank-and-file workers, empowerment is a meaningless term designed to make them feel important—but nothing really has changed.

All of these are true with regard to the way empowerment is perceived, but none state the real meaning of this term. Empowerment, if truly implemented, is a new framework for the relationship between managers and subordinates. Indeed, it blurs the line between these categories. The team is the ideal vehicle for empowerment. An empowered team is one in which the team leader and team members share authority and responsibility.

Team Terms

Empowerment means sharing the power you have with the people over whom you have power. Team members are given the authority to make decisions that previously were reserved for managers.

Who's Got the Power? Who Gets the Power?

Power is held by the people who make the decisions that govern how a company, a department, or a team operates. In most companies, power is in the hands of management. In a typical hierarchy, the power flows downward from the CEO through the layers of management. Each layer has power over the one beneath it.

In the traditional power structure, your boss gives you, the supervisor, an assignment. You look it over, determine how it should be done, and assign various components of the job to your team members. Then you follow it through until it's completed.

Empowerment changes this process. You—no longer a "supervisor," now a team leader—share with your team the power to make decisions about an assignment. Rather than tell team members what each of them will do, you work together to plan and execute the entire project.

The concept of empowerment isn't entirely new. For years companies have engaged in a variation called "participative management." Empowerment carries participation one step further. Team members not only participate in decision making but also are authorized to make decisions on their own without seeking approval from higher-level managers.

Here's an example of empowerment in action. The installation of a new communications system at the Environmental Protection League was the biggest job that Beck Communications had ever received. Dick, the owner-manager, had just attended a management seminar on empowerment and thought that this project was a good chance to put into practice what he had learned in the course.

A few weeks before the job was to begin, Dick called a meeting to discuss the job. He outlined the project and asked for ideas about how to proceed. One associate suggested that the first step should be a survey of the facility to see where units should be installed. Another volunteered to examine the current system to determine which parts, if any, could be incorporated into the new system.

At their next meeting, the team planned the entire job and agreed on who would complete each part. When the work began, the team went to work full of enthusiasm. As they had been completely involved in the planning, they were committed to successfully completing the job.

During the installation, as problems arose, the team members were empowered to make decisions to correct them without having to get Dick's approval every time.

Heads Up!

Don't be afraid to share power with team members. In a successfully empowered team, members build up their skills, their productivity, their confidence. If the team does well, you look good to your bosses.

Dick reported that this process worked well. Previously he would have done all the preparatory work himself. He then would have assigned the work to his team members and required them to come to him to solve every problem. This would have taken longer and cost more, and the workers involved would have looked at it as just another job.

Is It for Real?

The key to success of an empowered team is mutual trust, respect, and openness. It's not always easy for these to be developed. Some team leaders believe that their subordinates don't have the capability to make decisions. Some members have had bad experiences with their past or current leaders and don't trust or respect them.

It sometimes takes a long time for people to develop the trust and credibility that are essential for empowerment to work. Some ways to do this will be discussed later in this chapter.

Many team leaders give lip service to empowerment, but still run the team arbitrarily. As one member commented: "They call us a team; they dub me an 'associate,' but things are run exactly the same as before the name changes."

Team leaders are sometimes not even aware of their reluctance to share power. Let's see how Dave faced this situation.

Dave's concept of empowerment was to hold a meeting, tell his team what to do, and ask for comments and suggestions. It didn't take the team long to figure out that Dave only half listened to their ideas and then ordered them to do the job the way he had outlined.

At that time, I was engaged in a consulting assignment at that company, and had occasion to speak to several associates in various departments about morale problems. In speaking to some of Dave's team, I sensed their frustration. This led to a meeting with Dave, who was surprised to learn of his team's reaction. He agreed to hold a team meeting to discuss it.

At the meeting, over which I presided, I suggested that instead of criticizing or complaining about past problems, the members should discuss in which ways they were ready to take on the additional responsibilities that come with empowerment.

Dave was impressed with their knowledge of the work to be done, their commitment to its success, and their willingness to cooperate with him and each other. The immediate result was empowering the team to handle the next project in a truly collaborative manner.

This led to the development of that mutual trust and respect that turns a group into an effective empowered team.

FYI

Taking risks is an essential ingredient of empowerment. Unless members know it's okay to try something new and that failure will not lead to punishment, they will play it safe and never innovate. In companies where team members are afraid to take any action without first checking with higher authorities, any attempts to be empowered will be resisted. Where team members feel comfortable initiating action and accepting responsibility for that action, empowerment begins to work.

The Advantages of Empowerment

Why bother with empowerment? Will giving people more power really help or is it just another gimmick to make people think they are getting more than they really are? Companies that have empowered their teams have generally been more than satisfied with the results. Productivity increases, quality improves, but much more happens.

Ideas: The Whole Team Contributes

People who work on a job know a great deal more about what's going on in their working environment than many managers realize. They see things that are done inefficiently, and they have ideas for improvement. By eliciting their input about new projects and assignments, you're likely to pick up ideas that may not have occurred to you.

When Ruth's team was given the assignment of developing a marketing plan for a new product, she outlined the project and provided each member with a detailed marketing research report. When they met to discuss it, so many ideas were presented that the team was able to develop an outstanding plan of action.

Synergy: The Whole Is Greater

When a team meets to generate ideas, a suggestion one participant makes can trigger ideas from another person that he/she would never have come up with alone. This process adds considerably more new ideas than any one individual might have thought of alone.

This process of *synergy* isn't limited to generating ideas, however. Synergy, defined as "two or more units (people, in this case) working together to achieve a greater effect than individuals can by themselves," is exactly what happens in an empowered team.

Team Terms

Synergy: Two or more people working together so that the individual contributions enhance the results. The whole is greater than the sum of its parts. **Ownership** is the feeling of being a full partner in the development and implementation of a project and being committed to its successful achievement.

If each of Dick's communications specialists had worked alone to perform a specific phase of the system installation, the job would have been completed, but it would have taken longer, and most likely errors that had to be corrected later would probably have occured. By working as a team, each person knew what the others were doing and, if help was needed, could pitch in.

When all members of an empowered team are engaged in the same type of work, each person should be trained to do all aspects of that work. Some teams are cross-functional—they consist of people from different disciplines. Although no member of a team made up of marketing, engineering, and finance specialists can be expected to do the jobs of their colleagues in other areas of expertise, their total involvement in the planning process lets everyone know exactly what each other team member is doing. The results are a coordinated effort and goals that are easier to achieve.

Ownership—"It's Our Project"

When people participate in planning a project, they identify with the project. Because *their* ideas are being implemented, they're committed to its success. They have the feeling of *ownership*.

Gail looked at her job as routine and dull. She did what she had to do and no more. When her boss informed the department that the company was changing its structure to team empowerment, Gail was skeptical. "It's just another gimmick to get us to work harder," she thought.

When the first project under the new system was introduced, Gail sat quietly and listened. Instead of being told what had to be done, the group was asked how they thought the project should be approached. Gail was alert and interested. After a while she timidly raised her hand and made a suggestion that everyone thought was a good one. She was not only given the authority to use the idea in her assignment, it was implemented in other phases of the project. By the time the meeting ended, Gail and her associates were excited about the job and were eager to get to work and make it a success.

Problems of Empowerment

Empowerment can be a great way to motivate people to accomplish superior work, but it doesn't always work. Why not? Let's look at some of the major problem areas.

Team Builder

Not everyone is thrilled to be empowered. Sometimes you have to sell them on the idea.

"Give up my power? Never!"

Men and women who have worked hard to be promoted to managerial positions often believe that empowering their team members will lower their own positions. Here are a couple of the reasons that they may feel this way:

➤ **Status.** Whether you work as a traditional manager or as the leader of an empowered team, you don't lose your status by sharing power with the team. It's a difference not in rank or position, but in methodology. Rather than "boss," you teach, inspire, and motivate your team. Being the leader of an empowered team is a high-status position. People often fear that their status will be lowered as that of others is raised.

➤ **Control.** Some managers ask the question, "I'm still responsible for this department—how can I give up my power without losing control?" You don't have to lose control when you share power. You're a member of the team. You're directly in the midst of every activity and know how each team project is progressing. You are aware of this, and so is every member of your team. Control becomes team control. As team leader, you guide your team to meet performance standards.

Test your effectiveness in empowering your team:

Empowerment Quiz for Team Leaders

Often Sometimes Rarely

_____	_____	_____	1. Do I make most team decisions on my own?
_____	_____	_____	2. Am I impatient when members present their ideas?
_____	_____	_____	3. Do team members ask for transfers or quit?
_____	_____	_____	4. Are team members frequently absent or late?
_____	_____	_____	5. Have my team members complained to management about decisions I've made?
_____	_____	_____	6. Do I have to discipline team members?
_____	_____	_____	7. Do I check work in progress of team members?
_____	_____	_____	8. Do I worry about team members meeting team goals?
_____	_____	_____	9. Do team members mumble about unfair treatment?
_____	_____	_____	10. Have my bosses suggested I take additional training in team management?

If your answers were primarily "often," you should seek training or counseling in how to use empowerment as a leadership tool.

"Who needs power? I'm happy just doing my job."

Everybody isn't turned on by getting power. Many people fear having power or just don't want to be bothered. Let's look at what happened when empowerment was broached to Karen's team. Karen thought that her team members would be excited and enthusiastic about their company's move to empowered teams. Instead, she realized that several people were upset. They had these reactions:

"I'm not paid to make decisions—that's your job."

"Just tell me what to do, and I'll do it."

"I work hard enough as it is. I don't want more responsibility."

"What if I make a mistake?"

As team leader of a newly empowered team, your first job involves converting people who think this way into enthusiastic supporters of the new method of working. Here are some suggestions that may help you do this:

➤ **Figure out why people don't want to stretch their brains.** Employees are often happy doing routine work in a routine way. Find the true reason that they feel this way.

Heads Up!

Head off problems before they start. Have counseling available to assist people who have difficulty adjusting to the new techniques.

213

Perhaps they don't believe that they have the ability to do more than routine work. Sometimes you have to work with team members to build up their self-confidence.

➤ **Help team members fully understand their new roles.** Take the time in the beginning to explain the true meaning of empowerment. Time spent in good orientation pays off in better team efforts.

➤ **Train your team members to generate ideas.** Show videos about team participation; teach team members to brainstorm. Have members of another team that has been successful in empowered activities describe how empowerment has worked for their team.

➤ **Get underway slowly.** In the beginning, choose assignments or projects that easily lend themselves to participatory effort. Gradually progress to the point at which team members tackle all projects collaboratively.

Team members: Test your effectiveness as a participant in an empowered team. Think back over your performance in the team over the past six months:

Often	**Sometimes**	**Rarely**	
_____	_____	_____	1. At meetings did you contribute ideas and suggestions?
_____	_____	_____	2. When discussing issues before making decisions, did you present your viewpoints?
_____	_____	_____	3. If your opinion was different from the majority of the team's, did you attempt to persuade others to your viewpoint?
_____	_____	_____	4. When your ideas weren't accepted, did you fully cooperate in implementing the agreed-upon procedure?
_____	_____	_____	5. Did you take part in resolving disagreements among team members?
_____	_____	_____	6. Did you volunteer to chair or take a leading role in a team meeting?
_____	_____	_____	7. When informed of the subjects to be discussed at a meeting, did you study, research, or develop pertinent information?
_____	_____	_____	8. Did you coach or mentor other team members to help make them more effective?
_____	_____	_____	9. Did you ask your team leader to critique your performance and work with him or her to improve?
_____	_____	_____	10. Did you read articles, books, or reports, or attend seminars to keep you up-to-date in your occupation or profession?

An ideal team member would answer "often" to most questions, but few members are ideal. If your answers were mostly "sometimes," you are doing okay. If there are many "rarely" responses, you need to rethink your role as a team member.

FYI

Empowerment often fails when members are reluctant to make decisions for fear of making mistakes. Build trust by pointing out but appreciating honest mistakes as long as they were made in the quest to satisfy a customer or get a job done more efficiently. One company celebrates mistakes with "Mistake of the Month" plaques or some other humorous token. Another company offers a quarterly reward of $100 to employees who admit mistakes. Encouraging people to admit and resolve their mistakes can save thousands of dollars a year in wasted time and lost productivity.

When the Leader's Role Changes

Some team leaders fear that their company will have no need for them after empowerment becomes the way of organizational life. If everyone is involved in what leaders traditionally do, what role is left for the leader?

One solution: Redesign the role of the team leader. This has been done in some organizations. Traditional teams are replaced by "self-directed" teams that have no permanent team leader. In this setup, the team chooses a project leader (or two or more leaders) for each project.

Using self-directed teams may be too radical for many companies, but variations can be adapted to meet special purposes. Subteams can be created to handle different projects on a self-directed basis. The permanent team leader serves the important purpose of coordinating all team activities and providing training and support. How the self-directed team works is discussed in Chapter 24.

In any case, the team leader's role becomes more that of facilitator, coordinator, and troubleshooter. Team leaders have more time to plan, organize, and work with their bosses on long-term projects and act as a consultant to their own team members and to other teams where their expertise can be of value.

Making Empowerment Work in the Team

Empowerment isn't a cure-all for all management problems. Rather, it enhances collaborative efforts to get a job accomplished by giving every member of a team the power to get things done. To do this, management must be willing to give up some of its prerogatives.

Full Support of Top Management

Empowerment works most effectively when a company's CEO empowers its senior management group, which, in turn, passes that empowerment down through the organization.

Many CEOs, like Jack Welch of General Electric and Jerry Junkins of Texas Instruments, have done just that, and the results have been outstanding. Junkins considers the empowerment given to his staff and in turn to 1,900 teams the number one strength of his company.

> **Team Builder**
>
> Empower people who deal with customer problems to make decisions without the need to seek approval from above. For example, at Nordstrom any sales clerk can make exchanges, give refunds, or provide special service. At AT&T Universal Credit Company, requests for credit limit increases are handled by the person receiving the call.

A good example of empowerment in action comes from the General Motors Saturn division. Any assembly line worker can push the button that stops the line if he or she sees something that needs correction.

GM used an example of this in a TV ad. It described the reaction of an employee who stopped the assembly line when he realized that a part had not been inserted properly on a chassis. The correction took just a few seconds, but the employee said that it made him feel good that he had the power to stop the line—an action reserved in most operations for a manager—and that he was able to help maintain the quality of Saturn's cars.

In addition to General Electric and Texas Instruments, many major companies, such as Kodak, Intel, and Federal Express, have reported that instituting empowered teams has made them able to not only keep up but also move ahead in their tough, competitive industries. Thousands of smaller companies relate similar experiences.

Train for Empowerment

Team members and team leaders should be trained in the techniques of empowerment. Because many companies assume that the transition to empowerment is more difficult for team members than for team leaders, they concentrate their training on team members. Because the program is collaborative, supervisors (now team leaders) and employees (now team members) should be trained together by consultants or others who are knowledgeable in this type of work.

Team leaders should be given special training in coaching and counseling, as these functions will become major aspects of their new function.

Team members should be offered programs in problem solving and decision making, creativity, and communications to make them more effective collaborators.

Training should be ongoing. Many organizations have excellent training programs for orienting and starting up an empowered team program, but after the program is underway, they assume that it will work smoothly. It doesn't always work that way. As teams mature, most likely new problems will occur. Hold reinforcement training meetings periodically to discuss and resolve complexities that develop.

Heads Up!

In disputes between a team member and outsiders, assume your member is right unless, after investigation, it's found that the member was wrong. If proven wrong, concentrate on correcting the situation rather than blaming the member.

Build Trust

Empowerment cannot work unless trust exists at every level: team members, team leader, higher managers. Here are some ways to develop and maintain trust:

➤ **Clear and consistent goals.** Trust levels are low when members are uncertain what is expected of them. This is exacerbated when goals change frequently.

➤ **Fair treatment.** Not only do people want to be treated fairly, they expect that their companies will treat everybody fairly. Trust is developed when members know that their leaders are interested in what they say, listen actively to their complaints, and act to resolve them. Trust is maintained when team leaders assign work equitably, help when problems arise instead of resorting to punishment, and are considerate of the opinions of their members.

➤ **Decisiveness.** Most people don't trust leaders who are indecisive. They expect decisions to be made. The frustration of not knowing what course to take is worse than making a poor decision.

When the decision is to be made by an empowered team, the process should be clearly established. If the decision is to be based on consensus, are the steps toward obtaining consensus clear? If consensus cannot be reached, is the decision delayed? made by the team leader? made by higher management? There can be trust only if everybody understands and agrees about the process.

➤ **Loyalty.** Team leaders must support the team members, and team members must support each other. Once a decision is made, each member of the team must work with the others to implement it—even if he or she disagreed with it.

Team Builder

By sharing power with team members the leader will get the job done more willingly, more rapidly, and more effectively. Any concern about losing control is compensated for by the improved motivation and performance of an empowered team.

If things go wrong, the team leader and the entire team take responsibility. Don't point fingers at one or a few members. Blaming each other destroys the team. Be loyal and work together to correct the situation.

➤ **Give credit where credit is due.** Team leaders should lead the team in celebrating successes. Each member should be given recognition for his or her part in the success. Members should be encouraged to acknowledge and praise teammates who have been particularly helpful.

➤ **Stick up for team members.** Team leaders should back up members of their teams if there are conflicts with people in other departments. Leaders have to stick their necks out for members if they want to maintain team loyalty.

Provide Full Information to the Team

All team members should be given full information about team projects, support to acquire necessary skills and techniques, freedom to interact with the team leader and any team member to accomplish the team's goals, and encouragement to use their initiative in planning and implementing projects.

Every Team Member Is a Coach

We've noted repeatedly in this book that team leaders must look upon themselves as coaches. Indeed, every team member may also be required to coach and facilitate certain projects or parts of projects. These members should have the opportunity to take the same leadership training programs that are given to permanent team leaders.

Titles may change, and functions may be altered, but there will always be a role for people who can guide, counsel, and motivate their coworkers. Empowerment doesn't mean giving up power; it means sharing power. It doesn't mean that you abdicate responsibility. Instead, you create a climate in which all team members are as excited about the job as you are.

The Least You Need to Know

➤ An empowered team is one in which the team leader and team members share authority and responsibility.

➤ The key to the success of an empowered team is mutual trust, respect, and openness.

➤ By eliciting input from people who are doing a job, you're likely to pick up ideas that may not have occurred to you.

➤ Ownership is the feeling of being a full partner in the development and implementation of a project and being committed to its successful achievement.

➤ Empowerment enhances collaborative efforts to get a job accomplished by giving every member of a team the power to get things done.

➤ For effective collaboration, team leaders should be given special training in coaching and counseling, and team members should be offered programs in problem solving and decision making, creativity, and communications.

➤ All team members should be fully informed about team projects, free to interact with the team leader and other members, and encouraged to use their initiative in planning and implementing projects.

Chapter 16

Different Strokes for Different Folks

> ### In This Chapter
>
> ➤ Motivating members, motivating the team
>
> ➤ Recognizing team members' achievements
>
> ➤ Techniques of praising
>
> ➤ Keeping up the team's enthusiasm
>
> ➤ Competition: teams vs. teams

If you're a team leader, your chief job is to meld your team members into a cohesive group and work with them to develop within themselves that inner motivation to accomplish the team's goals.

It starts by taking the time to get to know the team members as individuals. Team members are humans, not robots, each with his or her own strengths and weaknesses, personal agenda, and style of working. Learning and understanding each team member's individualities are the first steps in building a team. Once this is accomplished, the focus shifts to blending this variety of personalities into a workable team.

In this chapter we'll look at both these challenges.

Individual vs. Team Motivation

Maybe you think that all you really have to know about your associates is how well they do their work. Wrong! Knowing the members of your team requires more than just knowing their job skills. That's an important part, but it's only a part of their total makeup. Learn what's important to your team members—their ambitions and goals, their families, their special concerns—in other words, what makes them tick.

Look at this picture. What do you see? Ask several friends, colleagues, family members what they see. Some people report that they see two people facing each other; some interpret it as two people about to kiss; some as two people having a confrontation. Others see it as a cup. Some interpret it as a wine goblet, others a chalice. Each of those people was looking at the exact same picture, yet there was a wide variety of interpretations.

Know Your Team Members

What does this mean? Each of your team members may be looking at the same project, the same data, the same program—but each may see entirely different things. The same is true of motivation. What excites one member may turn off another; what's a meaningful reward to one member maybe means little or nothing to another.

Team Terms

A person's **MO** is his or her method, or mode, of operation—the **patterns of behavior** that a person habitually follows in performing work.

If you've ever watched crime shows or read detective stories you've learned about *MOs*—a term for "method of operation." Criminals tend to repeat the same MOs in all of their crimes.

Not just criminals, but all of us have MOs in the way we do our work and the way we live our lives. Study the way each of your team members operates, and you'll discover his or her MO. For example, you might notice that one team member always ponders a subject before commenting on it. Another might reread everything she works on several times before submitting it to the team leader.

Psychologists refer to MOs as *patterns of behavior*. Being aware of these patterns helps you understand people and enables you to work with them more effectively.

By observing and listening, you can learn a great deal about your team members. Listen when they speak to you: Listen to what they say, and listen to what they *don't* say. Listen when they speak to others. Eavesdropping may not be polite, but you can learn a great deal. Observe how your team members do their work and how they act and react. It doesn't take long to identify their likes and dislikes, their quirks and eccentricities. By listening, you can learn about the things that are important to each of them and the "hot buttons" that can turn them on or off.

By observing and listening, you might realize that Claudia is a creative person. If you want to excite her about her role in an assignment, you can do so by appealing to her creativity. You notice that Mike is slow when he's learning new things but that, after he learns them, he works quickly and accurately. To enable Mike to do his best, you know that you'll need patience.

Answer these questions about your team members honestly.

Yes No 1. Do they know what you expect of them in their work?

Yes No 2. Do you provide them with the materials and equipment they need to do their work well?

Yes No 3. Do you give them recognition and praise for good work on a regular basis?

Yes No 4. Do the members relate well to each other?

Yes No 5. Do you take a personal interest in each member?

Yes No 6. Do you provide resources for member's personal development?

Yes No 7. Do you elicit and seriously consider members' opinions?

Yes No 8. Do your members consider their work important to the organization?

Yes No 9. Are your members committed to performing quality work?

Yes No 10. Do you counsel regularly with members about their progress?

The more "yes" answers, the higher the morale in your team.

Develop Team Spirit

After team members understand their new roles, you, as their team leader, must ensure that they begin to apply the team system on the job.

Let's look at how Denise did this. As sales manager, her primary role had been training, motivating, and leading her sales force. Denise discovered that, as in most companies, without the support of the office staff to obtain and maintain sales production, sales were lost and customers became dissatisfied.

The salespeople in Denise's company were paid on a commission basis. They worked hard and long hours to get and keep accounts. They were often frustrated, however, when the order department stalled deliveries by finding petty problems or when customer service representatives antagonized customers by showing indifference to their inquiries.

Denise reorganized the department into five teams, each covering a different sales region. Each team was made up of salespeople, order clerks, and customer service personnel.

FYI

Nobody expressed the meaning of team spirit better than Alexandre Dumas in his book *The Three Musketeers:* "All for one, one for all."

The compensation system was changed. Rather than rewarding only the salesperson for making a sale, bonuses and raises for all team members would be based on the team's productivity.

At the end of the first year, sales had increased significantly. Rather than stall orders because of minor errors on an order form, order clerks went to the source and corrected the errors immediately. Secretaries and customer service reps went out of their way to help customers, and morale in the department grew immensely.

The team leader should always be alert to what motivates his or her team and what factors inhibit motivation. To be sure you know what motivates your team, try this exercise:

➤ Write down what you believe are the top team motivators.

➤ Ask the team members to write down what they believe motivates them.

➤ Conduct a meeting and compare and discuss the lists.

➤ Resolve the differences between the lists and come up with a plan to implement the motivators that really work for the team.

Giving Recognition to Individuals

One of the challenges organizations face when they create teams is how to adjust their rewards and recognition programs to fit the team concept. Traditional rewards such as individual raises and status symbols—a fancy office or a reserved parking space—are no longer viable. If only individual achievements are rewarded, team members become competitive instead of cooperative. If the only awards are group awards, some members may feel that it doesn't pay to knock themselves out when other members just glide along.

Encourage Members to Excel

When the emphasis is on the team, individual members may lose the incentive to do their very best. They feel that their personal contribution will be overlooked. But unless each member is motivated to do his or her very best, the team goals will never be met.

One way to motivate members and build up their confidence is to give them positive reinforcement. Too often, the only feedback employees get is criticism.

Team Builder

By focusing on positive things—by giving attention and appreciation to the good things people do—you reinforce their desire to "do the right thing." You also help build their self-image and create within them positive thoughts that help develop a positive attitude.

When people hear continual criticism, they begin to feel stupid, inferior, and resentful. Although someone may have done something that wasn't satisfactory, your objective is to correct the behavior, not to make the person feel bad.

The famous psychologist B. F. Skinner noted that criticism often reinforces poor behavior (when the only time an offender gets attention is when is when he or she is being criticized). He recommended that we minimize our reaction to poor behavior and maximize our appreciation of good behavior.

Rather than bawl out an associate for doing something wrong, quietly tell the person, "You're making some progress in the work, but we still have a way to go. Let me show you some ways to do it more rapidly." When the work does improve, make a big fuss over it.

Some team leaders provide individual achievement rewards that reward improvement. Instead of basing rewards on who sells most or produces most, they are based on each member's improvement over past figures or on new achievements. Members compete with themselves rather than against each other.

Another approach is peer-driven awards. Team members can reward a teammate for extra effort. Members can give other members a "You Made My Day" card (see the following illustration). This recognition, by itself, is often enough of a motivator, but some companies add tangible rewards. One company gives members who accumulate five cards two tickets to a local movie theater. Others provide similar inexpensive, but meaningful, prizes.

> *You Made My Day Card*
>
> *Date:*
>
> *To:*
>
> *From:*
>
> *What you did:*
>
> *What it meant to me:*
>
> *Signed:*_____
>
> *Copy to Human Resources*
>
> *Copy to team leader*

Praise Members' Accomplishments

Although all of us require praise to feed our egos and help make us feel good about ourselves, you can't praise people indiscriminately: Praise should be reserved for accomplishments that are worthy of special acknowledgment. So how do you deal with people who never do anything particularly praiseworthy?

FYI

Some supervisors fear that giving praise indicates softness on their part. "We don't want to coddle our subordinates." Praise is *not* softness—it's a positive approach that reinforces good performance. When you stop thinking of your team members as subordinates and instead think of them as partners working to reach team goals, appropriate praise will become a natural part of your behavior.

Florence faced this situation in her team of word processors. Several marginal operators had the attitude that as long as they met their quotas, they were doing okay. Praising them for meeting quotas only reinforced their belief that nothing more was expected of them. Criticism of their failure to do more than the quota required was greeted with the response, "I'm doing my job."

Florence decided to try positive reinforcement. She gave one of the operators a special assignment for which no production quota had been set. When the job was completed, Florence praised the employee's fine work. She followed this practice with all new assignments and eventually had the opportunity to sincerely praise each of the word processors.

Make Praise Effective

Some supervisors praise every minor activity, diminishing the value of praise. Others deliver praise in such a way that the manner in which it is given makes it sound phony. To make your praise more meaningful, follow these suggestions:

1. **Don't overdo it.** Praise is sweet. Candy is sweet too, but the more you eat, the less sweet each piece becomes—and you may get a stomachache. Too much praise reduces the benefit that's derived from each bit of praise; if it's overdone, it loses its value altogether.

2. **Be sincere.** You can't fake sincerity. You must truly believe that what you're praising your associate for is actually commendable. If you don't believe it yourself, neither will your associate.

3. **Be specific about the reason for your praise.** Rather than say, "Great job!" it's much better to say, "The report you submitted on the XYZ matter enabled me to understand more clearly the complexities of the issue."

4. **Ask for your team members' advice.** Nothing is more flattering than to be asked for advice about how to handle a situation. This approach can backfire, though, if you don't *take* the advice. If you have to reject advice, ask people questions about their inadequate answers until *they* see the negative aspects and reject their own poor advice (see Chapter 4).

5. **Publicize praise.** Just as a reprimand should always be given in private, praising

Heads Up!

People need praise. If members do nothing that merits praise, assign them projects in which they can demonstrate success and then praise their accomplishments. But beware of overpraising. When you praise every little thing, you dilute the power of praise. Save it for significant improvements, exceptional accomplishments, and special efforts.

should be done (whenever possible) in public. Sometimes the matter for which praise is given is a private issue, but it's more often appropriate to let your entire team in on the praise. If other team members are aware of the praise you give a colleague, it acts as an incentive for them to work for similar recognition.

6. **Give them something they can keep.** Telling people that you appreciate what they've done is a great idea, but writing it is even more effective. The aura of oral praise fades away; an e-mail message, a letter, or even a brief note endures. Even if a tangible award such as cash, merchandise, or tickets to a show or sports event are given, it's worth spending a few more dollars to include a certificate or plaque. Employees love to hang these mementos in their cubicles or offices, over their workbenches, or in their homes. The cash gets spent, the merchandise wears out, the show becomes a long-past memory, but a certificate or plaque is a permanent reminder of the recognition.

FYI

"When I must criticize somebody, I do it orally; when I praise somebody, I put it in writing."

—Lee Iacocca, former CEO of Chrysler

Recognize Team Interaction

Recognizing a team member's accomplishment is important, but it's equally important to recognize and reward successful efforts of the entire team. Shared rewards reinforce team spirit.

Some companies have instituted team-recognition programs. In Xerox's successful program, individuals receive awards for special achievement, and to encourage teamwork, recognition is also given to teams. These awards include honors to teams that perform outstanding work and special recognition to teams for "Excellence in Customer Satisfaction."

Another way in which Xerox recognizes teams is by holding an annual Teamwork Day. The first Teamwork Day was held in 1983 in a company cafeteria in Webster, New York. The objective was to teach managers the results of planning quality-circle activities and fostering a truly competitive team spirit. Thirty teams showed off projects that year. No tangible rewards or prizes were given—just thank yous. It was so well received that the following year 60 teams participated and 500 visitors crowded the cafeteria.

In the third year of Teamwork Day, hundreds of teams wanted to participate, but there was room for only 200 (1,000 people attended the exhibits). In the fourth year the company rented the convention center in Rochester, New York, and 5,000 people attended. In its fifth year, the program expanded internationally; teamwork fairs were held in Rochester, Dallas, London, Amsterdam, and elsewhere. Teamwork Day is now a highly anticipated annual event.

Some other ways teams can be rewarded include

➤ **Teams are given more challenging assignments.** This shows that management has confidence in the team and also offers the team opportunities to express its creativity and be of even more value to the company.

➤ **Teams are given more freedom in determining their goals.** Collaborative goal setting is an integral part of team activity; however, many team leaders are pressured by management to "guide" their teams to set predetermined goals. When teams show that they meet or exceed goals, this "guidance" is minimized or eliminated.

➤ **Higher level management recognizes team's accomplishments in special ceremonies.** The team is presented with awards at celebratory dinners or special meetings. Family members are invited to enjoy the members' recognition.

➤ **Team is invited to attend company's national convention.** In some companies the annual convention is a major event and is held at a resort hotel. Attendance is restricted to senior and middle managers plus a select list of other employees. Outstanding teams may be invited to attend or even participate in the program.

➤ **Teams make a presentation.** Teams that have been particularly successful are asked to make a presentation at the convention, demonstrating how they worked together to accomplish a difficult assignment.

➤ **Teams are awarded plaques.** Teams that are recognized for various achievements are given special plaques. Successful teams may have several plaques to commemorate achievements displayed in the area in which they work.

➤ **Teams are chosen as models for other teams.** Team members may be asked to mentor members of new teams to help get them started on the right foot. Leaders of other teams may be sent to observe the team in action.

Team Builder

Motivation is not a one-size-fits-all process. You must tailor the motivational program for your team to the needs and personality of the team. By keeping alert to what excites your members, create innovative programs that will motivate them to help the company meet its goals.

Make Your Team Self-Motivating

The most motivated team is one that motivates itself. If there is a climate in which members feel free to innovate, to express themselves without fear, to take the initiative, to call on teammates and team leaders for needed resources, the team will stretch itself to extraordinary efforts.

The objective of motivation is to stimulate people to exert more energy, effort, and enthusiasm in whatever they are doing. The best motivation is self-motivation. Your job as team leader is to provide a climate in which self-motivation flourishes.

Train the Team to Work Together

When people are accustomed to working as individuals, it is often difficult for them to put aside their personal agendas for the benefit of team collaboration.

Inasmuch as traditionally employees' careers are made or broken by their individual activities, some members will look at teammates as competitors instead of partners.

Although these members may give lip service to cooperation and collaboration, in the back of their minds they are thinking: "I'm more concerned with my own advancement, so I'd better show the bosses I'm better than my associates."

Sometimes the personal goals are honorable. Sara's goal is to make enough money as rapidly as possible so she can stay at home with her children. To Cora this job is only a stopgap until she can get into law school. Tim's dream is to work as a telecommuter, and he is using this job as a way of making contacts that could help him do this.

In order for the team to operate successfully, the team leader should know the personal goals of each member and try to fit them into the team goals. If a project requires understanding legal implications, assign it to Cora. If research has to be done that could be accomplished at home, Tim or Sara can be accommodated.

Often, personal goals are more devious. In order for George to make himself visible to higher management, he boasts that every success was due to him and every failure the fault of other team members. Maria flatters the team leader to gain special favors. Curtis thinks this team is moving too slowly and is trying to transfer to what he considers to be a more dynamic group.

It's not advisable to accommodate these subversive goals. Leaders must be impervious to flattery and alert to self-serving agendas. Firm action by the team leader can keep these members from disrupting team harmony. If they cannot be brought into line, they should be removed from the team.

Create an Enthusiastic Environment

When we are enthusiastic about something, no matter how difficult it may be, it seems easy. The excitement, the joy, the inner feeling of satisfaction permeates the entire activity. It stimulates one to put all of one's energy and emotion into the project and ensures that the objective will have a strong probability of being achieved. How can we make our team more enthusiastic?

To get the team to be truly excited about something, you as team leader must generate that passion in the team. However, teams are often required to do things about which they don't have that deep commitment. One way that helps develop enthusiasm is to find something in the assignment about which they can become excited. By focusing on this, real enthusiasm will be generated.

FYI

Enthusiasm is the secret ingredient of success of the most successful people as well as the generator of happiness in the lives of those who possess it. Norman Vincent Peale summed it up: "What goes on in the mind is what determines the outcome. When an individual really gets enthusiasm, you can see it in the flash of the eyes, in the alert and vibrant personality. You can see it in the verve of the whole being. Enthusiasm makes the difference in one's attitudes toward other people, toward one's job, toward the world. It makes the big difference in the zest and delight of human existence."

For example, the first phase of the new project requires the time consuming and dull job of researching through several data banks. Most team members dreaded this tedious, but necessary, job. To generate some enthusiasm the team leader divided the work into segments and set time limits for completing each segment. He offered a prize to the team member who came up with the most valuable information from the data bank in each segment within the time allotted. Meeting this challenge made the work more fun, and they tackled it enthusiastically.

Give the team members an opportunity to learn as much as they can about the subject. Learning leads to knowledge and often engenders excitement about the matters learned. When a subject is mastered, people become more enthusiastic about it.

Give the team a pep talk. For years coaches have been giving pep talks to inspire their teams. When you feel the team needs an extra push to accomplish a mission, give them a pep talk.

Team Terms

The term **hidden agenda** describes the secret personal goals of a member that work to the detriment of the team's cohesiveness.

Help the Team Collaboratively Set Goals

As noted previously in this book, one of the key ingredients to team success is setting and working toward goals that have been collaboratively established by the team.

Often, in the pressure to get an assignment completed, team leaders ignore some of the important team goals. The immediate project dominates their thinking. Never lose sight of your goals. There will be temporary diversions, but unless the key goals are always returned to, the team will drift and its energies skewed away from its mission.

Team members should be encouraged to set goals for themselves that are congruent with the goals of the team. As noted earlier, sometimes personal desires and *hidden agendas* may conflict with team goals. The team leader's role is to show members how, through their team activities, they can achieve their personal goals.

To keep the team motivated, it is essential that all members be reminded regularly of the goals to which they are committed and their progress in achieving them.

Here is a quiz to help you determine how effective you are in doing this.

Check Your Goal-Setting Practices

Yes No   1. I make a practice of meeting with each member at least twice a year to review his or her goals and discuss what they have achieved or failed to achieve to succeed in each goal.

Yes No   2. I make a practice of conducting a goal review meeting with the entire team at least once a year to analyze current goals, adapt them to changing circumstances, and/or set new goals.

Yes No   3. I make a practice of not arbitrarily setting goals for the team. The whole team is expected to make those decisions.

Yes No   4. Once goals are set, I allow team members to determine the methods they will use to reach them.

Yes No   5. I invite members to set personal goals to enhance their knowledge and prepare for advancement.

Yes No   6. I make a point of challenging members' personal goals by having them review and report on their relevance to the team's goals.

Yes No   7. I periodically reinforce the importance of the goals in one-to-one meetings with members and at team meetings.

Yes   No   **8.** Important components of my performance reviews of team members are their progress in reaching personal goals and their contribution to team goals.

Yes   No   **9.** I let my managers know the goals the team has set and report periodically to them on progress.

Yes   No   **10.** When the team is pressed to complete assignments that temporarily keep them from working toward established goals, I adjust the timetables, but get them back on track as soon as feasible.

The more "yes" answers, the more focused you are on setting and meeting the goals of your team and its members.

Because at any one time, a dynamic team has a variety of goals to meet, there will be some that have been completed, others that are in the process of completion, and some which are still on the drawing board.

In a busy team, when a goal is reached, particularly when it is an interim goal, it is easy to ignore it and just keep moving ahead. To maintain the enthusiasm and to solidify team spirit, don't let the completion of any goal go unrecognized.

At the Achilles Heel Company, when a team completes a segment of a project on schedule, the team leader strikes a gong. Everybody in the office stops work and congratulates the team members. Sure, it disrupts the work for a few minutes, but everybody on the team enjoys the acclaim; the other teams are inspired to push their projects, and everybody goes back to work with renewed enthusiasm.

Interteam Competition

When most people think of teams, they think of sports. From the time we were children, we either participated in sports as team members or cheered our favorite teams. In high school and college, rooting for the school team was as much a part of our lives as the academic programs.

The excitement and enjoyment of playing or observing sports is the competition. We rejoice in victories and lament losses. But even if our team should lose, the team members and fans shout the rallying cry: "Wait till next year!"

As teams become more and more a part of our work life, can competition among teams get members more enthusiastic about the team's work and result in higher productivity?

Team Builder

Celebrate successes. When a project is completed, have a party, release balloons, take the team to lunch. At the least thank the members for their contributions.

Us vs. Them

Unlike the games played in school, college, and in the professional leagues, work teams don't face a win-or-lose situation. On the job everybody must win. In any contest or competition between teams in the same company, the overall goal is a win for the company. The objective of such competitions is to stimulate every team to higher productivity. The winner doesn't "defeat" the other team(s)—just bests them in attaining the contest's objectives.

Setting Up the Teams

When the Ace Insurance Company initiated competition among its teams, it chose to have regional contests. The company had five regions in three adjacent states in the Midwest. The team in each region consisted of members who were directly involved in sales. On each team were sales reps, who sold the policies; underwriters who determined the insurability of prospects and rates to be applied; and customer service reps who dealt with customers' problems.

The objective of the ongoing contest was to increase total sales. As regions differed in past sales and future potential, the contest could not be judged by gross sales figures. A formula was developed to accommodate for these differences so that every team had an equal chance to win the prize: a cash bonus.

In setting up a team competition, be sure that all members are informed of the objectives of the contest, the rewards, the rules of the contest, and what is expected of each of them.

What's the Score?

Who wins is based on the objectives of the contest. Most often it is scored by increases in sales or production. The winner is the team that sells or produces the most—usually adjusted to special conditions as done by the Ace Insurance Company.

Some of the other objectives of interteam competition are

➤ **Quality improvement:** In their pursuit of improving quality to meet TQM objectives or to comply with ISO 9000 criteria, contests are set up. The team with the highest percentage of reduction in rejects or rework wins the contest.

➤ **Cost reduction:** Some competitions in cost reduction are judged on actual reduction in a team's cost of operation during the contest period. Others are more long-range, with awards based on the team that comes up with the best cost-savings ideas.

➤ **Awards are given to the team that has the fewest person/days lost because of accidents:** A variation on this was instituted by an Arizona trucking company. To reduce the number of traffic violations or accidents, a bonus was offered to the team with the least number of such incidents by members of the team. For each incident by any member of a team, the entire team's bonus would be reduced by $50. Each member of the team with the fewest incidents would receive an added bonus of $100 per member. You can guess the peer pressure put on members by their teammates to drive safely.

➤ **Special projects:** Companies that want to promote a new product or push sales of a slow-moving product can set up competitions among teams. A department store held an interstore competition for promoting its store credit cards.

For example, Radio Shack set up an interstore competition to encourage sales associates to get customers to sign up with a long-distance telephone carrier.

Rewards for Winners

At the Ace Insurance Company, some of the rewards for the winning team included treating the entire team to some special event like a weekend getaway at a resort, a team picnic or beach party on company time, or giving the team time off from work.

Most important is giving the team recognition. Photos of the team in the company magazine, a plaque in the work area, and personal letters to team members from the CEO all add to the value of competition.

Don't forget the runners-up. Nobody should be a loser. Every team should be thanked for participating and given some token to acknowledge its efforts.

The Downside

Team competition can cause problems. Sometimes teams become too zealous to win, to the detriment of the company. At Ace Insurance one team was so determined to win the first quarter's contest that they withheld information needed by another team, causing the loss of a good customer. It's up to team leaders and contest managers to work out ways of preventing this.

The Least You Need to Know

➤ As team leader, your chief job is to make your team members a cohesive group and work with them to develop that inner motivation needed to accomplishing the team's goals.

➤ By observing and listening, you can learn a great deal about your team members. Listen to what members say, and listen to what they *don't* say.

➤ In motivating the team, follow the TEAM acrostic: **Train** members in team interaction; develop **Enthusiasm** for meeting goals; **Assure** members of your support; set goals and let them know how their performance in reaching the goals will be **Measured.**

➤ One way to build up members' confidence and motivate them is to give them positive reinforcement. Too often, the only feedback employees get is criticism.

➤ To maintain team harmony and still give individuals rewards for achievements, instead of having members compete with each other, have them compete against their own previous accomplishments.

➤ People need praise. If members do nothing that merits praise, assign them projects in which they can demonstrate success.

➤ Recognizing team members' accomplishments is important, but so is recognizing successful efforts of the entire team.

➤ The most motivated team is one that motivates itself.

➤ To engender enthusiasm, the secret ingredient of success, develop in all team members a fervent commitment to the team's goals.

➤ Competition among teams can stimulate and excite members to achieve the goals of the contest.

Chapter 17

Show Me the Money!

> **In This Chapter**
>
> ➤ The value of money as a motivator
>
> ➤ Setting the compensation scales
>
> ➤ Incentive pay for the team
>
> ➤ Those "little extras" that make people happy

Everybody wants to get paid. Money buys us the necessities of life, and more money enables us to buy added comfort and enjoyment. But does money motivate people to stretch their efforts to accomplish more on the job?

The answer is "yes and no." In this chapter we'll look at the value of money as a motivator. We'll examine plans to tie money more closely to productivity. We'll also explore the many extras or perks companies offer to make employees happy campers.

Does Money Motivate?

A team of behavioral scientists led by Frederick Herzberg studied what people want from their jobs and classified the results into two categories:

> ➤ **Satisfiers (also called maintenance factors):** Factors people require from a job in order to expend even minimum effort in that job. These factors include working conditions, money, and benefits. After employees are satisfied, however, just

Team Terms

Satisfiers are factors people must have from the job in order to produce at least minimum work. **Motivators** are factors that stimulate people to perform over and above the call of duty.

giving them more of the same factors doesn't motivate them to work harder. What most people consider *motivators* are really just *satisfiers*.

➤ **Motivators:** Factors that stimulate people to put out more energy, effort, and enthusiasm in their job.

To see how this concept works on the job, suppose that you work in a facility in which lighting is poor, ventilation is inadequate, and space is tight. The result: low productivity.

A few months later the company moves to a new site with excellent lighting and air-conditioning and lots of space—productivity shoots up.

The company interprets this as a solution to its productivity problems. Managers assume that by improving working conditions, workers will produce more. They decide to make the working conditions even better. They paint the walls a cheerful color; they place potted plants around the facility; they install Muzak. The employees are delighted. It's a pleasure to work in these surroundings—but productivity doesn't increase at all.

Why not? People seek a level of satisfaction in their job—in this case, reasonably good working conditions. When the working environment was made acceptable, employees were satisfied, and it showed up in their productivity. After the conditions met their level of satisfaction, however, adding enhancements didn't motivate them.

Money: A Satisfier, Not a Motivator

Money, like working conditions, is a satisfier. It's generally been assumed that offering more money generates higher productivity. And it works—for many people, but not for everyone. Incentive programs, in which people are given an opportunity to earn more money by producing more, are part of many company compensation plans. Why should they work for some people, but not for others?

Let's look at one company's sales department. Salespeople usually work on a commission, or incentive basis. If salespeople want to earn more money, all they have to do is work harder or smarter and make as much money as they want. Therefore, all salespeople are very rich. Right? Wrong!

How come? Sales managers wonder about this. They say, "We have an excellent incentive program, and the money is there for our sales staff. All they have to do is reach out—but many of them don't. Why not?"

Psychologists note that most people set a personal salary level, consciously or subconsciously, at which they are satisfied. Until that point is reached, money does motivate them, but once reached, no more. *This level varies significantly from person to person.*

Some people set this point very high, and money is a major motivator to them. They "knock themselves out" to keep making more money.

Others are content at lower levels. It doesn't mean that they don't want an annual raise or bonus, but if obtaining the extra money requires special effort or inconvenience, you can forget it. Other things are more important to them than money.

By learning as much as you can about your associates, you learn about their interests, goals, and lifestyles, and the level of income at which they're satisfied. It is futile to offer the opportunity to make more money as an incentive to people who don't care about money. You have to find some other ways to motivate them.

Team Builder

Team leaders rarely have control over the basic satisfiers: working conditions, salary scale, employee benefits, and the like. These factors are set by company policy, but leaders do have the opportunity to use the real motivators: job satisfaction, recognition, and the opportunity for team members to achieve success.

Different Needs at Different Times

Team members vary in what motivates each of them, and what motivates a member may change from time to time.

For 20 years, Tony, a production worker in a plastics plant, did his job satisfactorily and met his quotas. Despite an excellent incentive plan for higher productivity, Tony never made an effort to earn those production bonuses. He was satisfied with his base pay and annual raises.

Two years ago, Tony's productivity suddenly began to jump. He earned production bonuses every quarter and even asked for added training to enable him to earn even more. What happened? Tony was planning to retire in a few years. His company pension is based on the amount he earned in the last five years. By earning this extra money, not only could he save money for the travel he and his wife planned after he retired, but it would ensure a higher retirement income.

The opposite also occurs. Estelle looked for every opportunity to earn extra income. For years, she'd ask for overtime work; she'd fight to win every production bonus. Her goal was to send her son through college. After he graduated and was off on his own, Estelle no longer felt the incentive to earn more, and it was reflected in her work.

The Basis of Base Pay

Most compensation programs determine how much an employee should be paid by considering the skill level of the job as determined by a job analysis and comparison with similar jobs in the industry and community. From these salary surveys a range is established. The amount paid to individuals performing the same job varies depending on experience, length of service in the company, and raises based on the performance review.

Pay for a Team Leader

When a person is promoted to a higher level position, pay is raised accordingly. Team leaders will get higher salaries than team members. Their bosses will get more pay, and the CEO will get the highest salary.

As teams become more and more collaborative, the leader becomes less of a manager and more the "first among equals." Under these conditions, how should the team leader be compensated? Is it equitable to pay leaders more when their work is much the same as associates'? In the future, as teams become more and more a part of the corporate culture, the base pay of team leaders will be only slightly more than team members' to accommodate the additional administrative details they perform. The real financial rewards will be based on team productivity.

Team Terms

The **going rate** is what companies are paying people with similar backgrounds in the industry or the community. It has also been defined as what you have to pay employees to keep them from going.

Pay for a Team Member

As noted, base pay is determined by the skills of the jobs involved and the market value or *going rate* of a job. If there is a shortage of qualified personnel, salaries will be higher; if there is a surplus, base pay may be lower.

In most companies, employees are reviewed annually and, unless their performance is unsatisfactory, they will usually receive an increase. In many organizations every employee gets at least a cost-of-living increase or an annual raise just for still being on the payroll.

This is changing. New trends in compensation programs are developing. Here are some of these developments:

➤ Rank will not determine pay; contribution and performance are becoming the primary bases for compensation. The sales rep who brings in the most business may be paid more than his boss, the sales manager; the engineer who develops a viable patent may receive a higher bonus than the chief engineer.

➤ Increases in base salary will be reduced. With inflation more or less stabilized, cost-of-living increases have become minimal.

➤ Pay for performance plans are replacing fixed salary increments. Workers who contribute to the company's productivity and bottom line will be rewarded. Marginal and average employees will be given minimal increases or none at all.

➤ Lump sum merit bonuses are gaining in popularity. Instead of raising salary, companies are paying production bonuses. Because bonuses are not part of salary, they do not become the basis on which benefits and future salary adjustments are based.

Because team members will be paid bonuses based on the team's performance, more productive workers will be penalized because of their marginally productive associates. This can lead to discord in the team. Peer pressure from the high producers on the low producers often brings up productivity, but team leaders will have to work hard to keep the team working effectively to build and maintain high performance.

When compensation is performance-based, and some team members pull down the productivity of the team, the high priority of the team leader is to help marginal workers boost their productivity, and if that fails, remove them from the team.

Incentive Pay Plans

Since the earliest part of the Industrial Revolution, companies have used financial incentives as part of their compensation programs. In many companies all compensation was based on "piecework." It was assumed that people would work harder and faster if they received a direct reward for production. This system was carried forward into the period of "scientific management." Frederic Taylor, the founder of this new movement, and his followers believed that people could be motivated by wages based on productivity and developed variations of the "piecework" pay system to achieve their goals.

In an economy that is moving rapidly away from mass production and manufacturing-based businesses to custom-engineered production and service-type industries, pay per piece has little value. New types of incentive programs have had to be developed. This section looks at some old and new incentive pay plans.

Pay by the Amount Produced

Wages based solely on the number of units produced was the primary pay plan in some industries. The harder you worked, the more money you received. In the early days of scientific management, speed of production was the primary factor in determining wages, and this method worked well. Abuse in the piecework system, however, was rampant. Often, when workers mastered their work and produced more than quotas required, companies raised the quota or reduced the price paid per piece to keep their

Team Builder

Money is a motivator for some people all of the time; for others, some of the time; and, if it's combined with other motivators, for everyone all the time.

overall costs down. This practice led to demotivation, in which workers set their own top limits and would only do a fixed amount of work.

I saw how this system worked during the summers of my college years, when I worked in a factory that used this type of program. Because I was young and energetic and wanted to make money to pay my college expenses, I quickly mastered the work and soon exceeded my quota. One of my coworkers pulled me aside and said, "Hey, you're working too fast. You're making it bad for the rest of us." His implication was that if I didn't slow down, he would break my arm.

This, of course, defeated the purpose of the incentive program. As work became more complex, paying by the piece was no longer practical. Because of pressure from unions and, later, minimum wage laws, hourly rates replaced piecework rates in most industries.

In the age of "scientific management" (the 1920s and 1930s), a variation of piecework was introduced. Quotas were established based on time and motion studies, and people who exceeded quotas received extra pay. These types of programs still exist and, properly designed and administered, succeed in motivating some people.

Although in some compensation systems, team members are rewarded on the basis of their individual production, additional bonuses may be given if the team as a whole exceeds production quotas. This gives each member incentive to produce more and at the same time help the team meet its goals.

It doesn't always work. One of my clients, the Sweet Sixteen Cosmetics Company, used this combined incentive system for its packers. Some sharp operators figured out that their personal production bonus would be higher if, instead of helping the slower members improve, they concentrated their efforts on personal productivity. The team bonus would be less or even nonexistent, but they would earn incentives.

FYI

The straight piecework system lives on. In the late 1990s, government agents raided illegal garment factories in which undocumented workers worked in sweatshops for 12 or more hours a day at piece rates that netted them earnings well below minimum wage. It also continues to be used by global companies that have opened plants or subcontracted production in developing countries.

To correct this, I redesigned the program so that time spent in helping other team members was factored into the incentive plan. The result was a significant increase in total team productivity and even higher bonuses for the better workers.

Profit Sharing

Many companies have instituted profit sharing plans as an incentive to their employees. These are plans in which a portion of the profits the company earns is distributed to its employees. Many of these plans are informal. The executive committee or board of directors sets aside at the end of the fiscal year a certain portion of profits to be distributed among employees. Other, more formal plans follow a formula established for that purpose.

In many organizations, only managerial employees are included in a profit sharing plan; in others, all employees who have been with a the company for at least a certain number of years are also included; in still others, the entire work force gets a piece of the profits. Some profit-sharing plans are mandated by union contracts.

A number of profit sharing programs are based on employee stock ownership. In addition to the stock options discussed in the next section, various types of stock-ownership plans are used. Some companies give shares of stock as bonuses or encourage employees to purchase shares.

A growing variation is the employee stock ownership plan or ESOP, whereby employees own so much of the stock that they virtually own the company. Having an ownership stake in the company should be a great incentive. As stockholders, they share in profits by receiving dividends. The higher the profits, the higher their dividends. Alas, it doesn't always work that way. Factors outside the control of employees often affect stock prices and dividends, and as the share of the company owned by each employee is very small, they have no real input in running the organization. ESOPs work well when things are going well, but are of little value when stocks are down.

Stock Options

In an economy where more and more teams work in jobs in which performance cannot be measured by production figures, other types of incentive plans must be developed.

Stock option programs provide opportunity for employees to benefit from an increase in the value of the company's stock. Employees are given "rights" to purchase the stock at a price that is lower than the market price. Let's say the stock is currently selling for $25 per share.

Team Terms

Stock options are rights that enable recipients to purchase company stock at a fixed rate no matter what the market value may be. The incentive: If the market value increases, the recipient can exercise the right and make an immediate profit on the sale.

Options are issued enabling employees to buy the stock at $22 per share. If they exercise the options immediately, they make a $3 per share profit. However, the incentive is to keep the options until the stock rises in value. A year later, the stock is selling at $40 per share. They can still purchase it at $22 and sell it immediately for a profit of $18. In the exploding Internet business, exercising stock options has made millionaires of many employees.

The incentive is to help the company grow through its efforts, and this will result in higher stock prices. The downside is that stock price doesn't necessarily reflect the company's profitability. Other market factors may influence it. If the stock falls below the option price, the rights are worthless.

Until recently, stock options were not offered to lower-level employees. They were chiefly a major part of executives' compensation packages. Over the past few years, particularly in start-up firms, stock options have been a force in attracting and retaining needed technical personnel.

Management by Objective (MBO)

Management by objective is used in many companies as both a management tool and an incentive program. Although there are many variations, the basic idea is that managers and associates determine together the objectives and results expected for a specific period. After a time period is agreed upon, associates work with minimum supervision to achieve the specified goals. At the end of the period, the manager and the associates compare what has been accomplished with the objectives that have been set. In some organizations, bonuses are awarded for meeting or exceeding expectations.

When a company is organized on a team basis, MBO is extended to the team. Rather than individual objectives, team objectives are set by the team leader and the entire team, and the team works collaboratively to meet these objectives. Results are measured against expectations at the end of the period, and the entire team shares the rewards or bonuses.

Special Awards for Special Achievements

Another type of incentive compensation is recognition and extra pay for special achievements of teams and individual members. One example is that of the Footloose Shoe Store chain, which instituted campaigns periodically to emphasize various aspects of its work. One campaign, for example, centered on increasing sales of "add-ons" (accessories for customers who have just purchased shoes at a store). The campaign, which lasted four weeks, began with rallies at a banquet hall in each region in which the chain operated. Staff members from all the stores in the region assembled in a party atmosphere, where food, balloons, door prizes, and music set the mood as the program was kicked off.

Each store was designated as a team. Footloose announced that prizes would be awarded, including $2,000 to be divided among all the team members (both sales and support people) of the winning team. The salesclerk who made the most personal add-on sales in the region would receive $500, and the sales clerk who made the most add-on sales in each store would receive $100. The campaign was reinforced by weekly reports on the standings of each team and each salesclerk.

The result was not only a significant increase in accessory sales for that period, but an increase in regular shoe sales, attributed to the excitement and enthusiasm generated by the campaign. Another party was held to present awards and recognize winners. Footloose runs three or four campaigns every year.

Team Builder

Tailor your incentive plan to what the company wants to accomplish. Create innovative programs that will motivate workers to help the company meet its goals.

Xerox is another company that adds financial reward to recognition. To encourage team participation, special bonuses are given to teams that contribute ideas that lead to gains in production, quality, cost savings, or profits.

Other examples of team incentives come from companies that have instituted total quality management (TQM) programs. Special emphasis is placed on providing high quality products or services to customers. The objective is reinforced by offering financial rewards based on reducing the number of product rejects, gaining measurable improvements in quality, and increasing customer satisfaction.

Perks

In many companies, employees have been given *perks*—those little extras that may not seem like much, but they often are significant additions to the traditional compensation package.

The Perk Buffet

Company perks vary. Here are some of the more commonly provided perks:

Team Terms

Perks (short for perquisites) are goods or services given to an employee in addition to regular salary and benefits as an incentive to attract and retain personnel.

➤ **Company cars.** Cars are leased for executives, salespeople, and sometimes other staff members.

➤ **Memberships in professional associations.** To encourage technical and specialized personnel to keep up with the state of the art in their fields, the company will pay their dues for appropriate associations.

➤ **Subscriptions to professional and technical journals.** Offered for the same reason as memberships in associations.

➤ **Membership in social clubs.** Because much business is conducted on the golf course or over a meal, for years many companies have paid the enrollment fees and annual dues for country clubs and dining clubs for executives and sales representatives. In recent years such memberships have been extended to other employees as an added incentive.

➤ **Subsidized lunchrooms.** I recently had lunch in the cafeteria of a large insurance company. My bill for a salad, entree, coffee, and dessert was less than half of what I normally pay at a restaurant. This is a great savings for employees.

➤ **Coffee and snacks.** Many companies provide a never-empty coffeepot for employees. Often the company offers free doughnuts, bagels, or sweet rolls at break time.

➤ **Child care.** With the great number of families where both parents are working, child care is a major problem. Some companies have child care facilities right on the premises or arrange for child care at nearby facilities and subsidize the cost.

➤ **Transportation.** Vans or buses are made available to employees to bring them to and from work. It's cheaper for the employees to use the company's transportation than to take public transportation or drive one's own car. Some companies will take employees to and from the nearest railroad station or bus depot at no cost to them.

➤ **Tuition.** Companies often pick up the entire bill for courses taken by employees—even if not specific to their job training. If the company doesn't pay in full, it may pay a portion of the cost of education.

➤ **Scholarships.** Some companies provide funds for college scholarships for children of employees.

➤ **Flextime.** A very effective perk is giving team members control over their own time. Some companies have company-wide flexible hours, but others allow team leaders to set the hours for their teams. For example, if the team is facing a lot of pressure to complete a project, don't insist that all members be on the job from 9 to 5. Some team members may be more productive if they can work at home for a few hours before reporting to the office. Others may want to complete work away from the office during the day. Others may do their best work in the evening. Letting each member set time schedules for the project gives that person control over his or her hours and usually pays off in higher productivity.

Now let's look at some of the less common perks that companies give:

➤ **Birthday celebrations.** There are a few companies that give employees a day off on their birthday. That's a nice gesture, but it can disrupt team production. Many more companies celebrate the birthday on the job—at a break, lunch, or after work—with a mini-party: cake (no candles, age is confidential), soft drinks, and a little fun. When teams are relatively small, the whole team may go out together after work for a little party.

➤ **Pets at work.** Bringing pets to the office can be very distracting, especially if they get restless. However, some companies permit employees to bring the dog or cat to work if they are kept under control. One company sets aside one day each week as "pet day" for employees who wish to take advantage of it.

➤ **Casual dress days.** Offices have always been formal places. Men wore suits and ties; women wore conservative outfits. Today many companies—particularly in the high-tech fields—have no dress code. Employees can wear whatever they feel comfortable in—except perhaps beachwear or "indelicate" attire. However, most offices still have traditional dress codes, modified somewhat. Sports jackets and slacks are okay for men and blouse-skirt outfits or slacks for women. To appease and attract the younger generation, companies have instituted casual dress days, usually Fridays, in which men can replace business suits with open-necked sports shirts and slacks and women can wear sporty outfits.

➤ **Exercise rooms.** With so many people engaging in regular exercise routines, many large firms have built complete gymnasiums for use of employees. Smaller organizations, of course, have neither the space nor funds for a gym, but an exercise room with a stationary bike, a treadmill, or other equipment for use by employees is feasible.

➤ **Recreation rooms.** To give employees a chance to relax after work, during breaks, or at lunch, some organizations have recreation rooms. In an article in the *Wall Street Journal,* one firm reported that it provided a billiard table and ping pong table; another beanbag chairs; another a Velcro wall at which employees throw sticky toys.

Heads Up!

If you use flextime, set some ground rules such as the minimum number of members who must be present during business hours and how time schedules will be established for each week.

Team leaders can create their own perks for team members. They need not be time consuming or expensive. All it takes is a little creativity. You may not be able to set up an exercise room or recreation room, but I bet you could incorporate some form of exercise or recreation into your team activity. Why don't you and your team have a brainstorming session to generate ideas for special "team perks" to make your team environment even better than it is now? See the following guide to team perks:

Assessing Perks

List perks you now have:

_____

_____

_____

_____

_____

_____

_____

_____

_____

List perks other firms offer that you would like to have:

_____

_____

_____

_____

_____

_____

_____

_____

_____

How can we adapt these to our team?

_____

_____

_____

_____

_____

_____

_____

_____

_____

Other suggestions:

_____

_____

_____

_____

_____

_____

_____

_____

_____

_____

Perks vs. Cash

Why do perks work as motivators? Why not give the employees cash bonuses and let them purchase or lease their own car, pay their own dues to the country club, or buy what they wish?

Companies have found that most employees like receiving perks. If they did get a cash equivalent, they would probably use it to pay bills or fritter it away. Perks keep reminding them that the company is giving them something. Every time they step into the company car, it reinforces their loyalty to the company. Every time they pass the day care bill to the accounting department, they thank the company for taking that burden off them. The company can benefit as well because it can save money by taking advantage of group rates in leasing cars and purchasing merchandise.

In addition, many perks attract hard-to-find personnel to the company. Marilyn, a skilled operating room nurse, chose to work for South Shore Hospital because it provided a day care facility for her three-year-old son. Ken accepted a slightly lower salary at his new company because he was allowed to bring his dog to work. Sean isn't looking to change jobs because he loves the golf club for which his organization pays his dues.

Do perks give incentive for higher productivity? There are no studies showing that perks motivate productivity, but companies believe that the loyalty and stability perks engender contribute in the long run to the bottom line.

Perks should not be confused with benefits. Benefits such as pensions, health care, and life insurance are part of the compensation package. Today almost all large companies provide these standard benefits. Perks usually are add-ons to make life more pleasant for employees.

FYI

In a study for the American Society of Interior Designers, 41 percent of job applicants said the office environment would affect their desire to accept a job.

Teams That Play Together Stay Together

One way to develop team spirit is to engage in recreational activities as a team. Bowling leagues, softball teams, and other sports activities are frequently sponsored by companies. If team members enter these programs as a team, it could add a little fun to the job and cement the relationship among team members.

Carrie was not much of an athlete, and when her team entered the relay race at the company picnic, she was afraid she would do badly, embarrass herself, and lose the respect of her teammates. She confided her worries to her colleague, Beverly, the informal leader, who reassured her that her teammates would help her. Before the picnic, the team practiced running and gave Carrie some tips on improving her techniques. When her turn came to run, the team cheered her on, and she did fine.

Recreational programs need not be formal. It's not necessary or even advisable for team members to spend all of their free time together. But, occasional parties or attendance at a sports event or concert helps the members know each other as total humans, not just coworkers.

Sandy, a team leader, invited his team each year to a Christmas party and a summer barbecue. The team members looked forward to these events, and Sandy attributed the very low turnover in his team to the personal rapport that was built and reinforced by these parties and other recreational activities in which the team as a group participated.

The Least You Need to Know

➤ Satisfiers are factors people must have from the job in order to produce at least minimum work. Motivators are factors that stimulate people to perform over and above the call of duty.

➤ Money is a satisfier. It's generally been assumed that offering more money generates higher productivity. And it works—for most people, but not for everyone.

➤ Learn as much as you can about your associates' personal life style. Offering the opportunity to make more money as an incentive to people who don't care about it is futile.

➤ Most compensation programs determine how much an employee should be paid by considering the skill level of the job as determined by a job analysis and comparison with similar jobs in the industry and community.

➤ As teams become more and more a part of the corporate culture, the base pay of team leaders will be only slightly more than that of team members. The real financial rewards will be based on team productivity.

➤ Although in some compensation systems team members are rewarded on the basis of their individual production, additional bonuses may be given if the team as a whole exceeds production quotas.

➤ Profit-sharing (ESOPs) and stock option programs are effective incentives that are growing in popularity.

➤ Companies have found that most employees like receiving perks. Perks keep reminding them that the company is giving them something.

Part 5

Staffing the Team—And Getting It Going

Teams consist of people. Sometimes the team leader "inherits" the people. They have been members of a work group that has been converted into a team. In the next chapters, you'll learn how to mold an existing work group into a functioning team.

Sometimes the team is created for special purposes, and the team leader picks the people. They may be drawn from employees currently employed within the organization or recruited from outside. Over time, new members may be added to replace those who leave, or because the team expands.

Whether you're forming a new team or augmenting a current one, choosing a team member can be one of the most important acts a team leader performs. In the following chapters you'll acquire the techniques needed to recruit and select team members who will work well together. You'll also become acquainted with the tools and techniques to hone the skills of your members.

All this takes dedication and effort on your part, and it's worth it. It will help you build a team committed to reaching its goals, and it will make your job more satisfying and rewarding.

Transforming a Work Group Into a Team

In some instances, when a company moves into the team mode, it creates new teams from scratch. This usually occurs when a team is formed to work on a new project. However, most of the time totally new teams are not created. The same people who had been working as a traditional work group are now transformed into a "team."

How does this affect the way the former supervisor, now "team leader," functions? What does this mean to the men and women who are now called "team members" or "associates" instead of workers or employees?

The trauma of this change on both leaders and members will be explored in this chapter.

The New Leader

Earlier in this book I discussed the importance of the team leader abandoning the role of the domineering boss. Despite the efforts of companies to change the habits of their leaders, there are still too many team leaders "bossing" their teams. Why should this be?

Heads Up!

The leader's job is to lead. The role of the leader in participative management is to guide, coach, counsel, and ensure that the goals of the team are accomplished.

Many supervisors have no qualms about stating: "I like being a boss." There's status and prestige in being in charge. There's power in giving orders and having the authority to make decisions, to praise or discipline employees, and to even be able to fire them. When supervisors become team leaders, much of this changes.

It's not easy to give up these "rights." Yet team leaders must be persuaded to accept the change if they wish to succeed in their new role.

From Boss to Leader

Bossy behavior is not limited to men and women who have supervised traditional work groups in the past and find it difficult to change their leadership style. It is also found among many newly appointed team leaders, who have picked up their dogmatic management style from the bosses they worked for in the past.

When the team leader bosses rather than leads, all of the benefits that should accrue from using teams are diluted or disappear completely. If members are treated as subordinates, they will act as subordinates; if the leader uses the team-building techniques that are discussed throughout this book, they will meld into a real team.

Here is a simple comparison between the style of a boss and a leader:

The "Boss"	The Leader
Drives the team	Guides the team
Instills fear	Inspires confidence
Says "Do"	Says "Let's do"
Makes work drudgery	Makes work interesting
Relies upon authority	Relies upon cooperation
Says "I"	Says "We"

Micromanaging the Team

Lisa was one of those bosses who didn't trust anybody in her department to do things right. She spelled out every step of the way the work had to be done. She looked over the shoulders of her subordinates to make sure they did the work her way. She checked and rechecked every assignment. Nobody liked working for Lisa.

When the organization moved into team management, Lisa was oriented on the new approaches required to succeed as a team leader. She nodded agreement to everything—and then began to manage her new team exactly as she had her former work group.

Naturally, the team never got off the ground. When her boss spoke to her about this, she responded, "If I'm responsible for the output of this team, I have to make sure it's right."

Yes, Lisa is accountable for her team's work, but by *micromanaging* the work of her associates, she defeats the main purpose of teams: to encourage participation of all team members. Unless Lisa learns and applies the techniques of team leadership, it's best to remove her from a leadership position.

For advice on how to ensure that the team meets the standards set for good performance without micromanagement of every aspect of the job, refer to Chapter 7.

Team Terms

Some managers **micromanage** every phase of an assignment. That means they look over the team member's shoulder to check that every *i* is dotted and every *t* crossed. This stifles creativity and prevents team members from working at their full potential.

The Future for Team Leaders

The move to downsize companies in the 1990s resulted in eliminating many middle-level management jobs. Opportunities for team leaders to move up to middle management have been curtailed by this flattening of company structures.

New and creative approaches must be found to retain ambitious team leaders and keep them motivated when advancement is much slower than it was for their predecessors.

Of course, normal attrition will create openings. Managers will retire, die, or move to other positions within or outside the organization. Supervisors and team leaders have always been the logical source of promotion to these jobs. This will enable some leaders to advance. However, the elimination of so many positions that previously were stepping stones to the upper levels has made it necessary to think of new and creative ways to reward team leaders when promotion is not viable.

Promotion usually includes salary increases. One way to keep motivating leaders when promotion is not an option is to give them the opportunity to earn more money. Promotion means gaining more status and prestige. Ways can be found to meet this need. Promotion to the next level puts one on the track to advancing his or her career. With fewer places to promote, some other means must be developed to motivate people who are career oriented.

Some approaches that have been used are

1. Project management

Many companies work on a project basis. Teams are assigned projects—some of which are long term, while others are one-shot activities. From time to time, a project is too large for one team, and two or more teams are assigned to the job. One way to reward team leaders is to put them in charge of major projects. They may either be detached temporarily from their teams or manage the project in addition to their regular assignments. The project manager can be rewarded with an extra bonus for successful completion of the project. This may satisfy the need for financial reward.

Project management also gives the project manager status. However, once the project is completed, it may be a letdown to return to being a team leader. Although future project management assignments are likely to be given to them, there is no assurance as to if or when that may be.

The results of the assignment are recorded in the team leader's personnel file and considered by his or her boss in the performance review. This will be taken into account when openings do occur for promotion.

2. Training team leaders

Team leaders who have led highly successful teams may be chosen to train newly appointed team leaders or to coach or mentor less successful team leaders. To be chosen for this assignment is an honor that shows the leader that the company recognizes his or her achievements. Often, added compensation is given for this work.

3. Special assignments

When United Fabricators decided to open a new plant in Puerto Rico, it assigned three of its top team leaders to work with the development task force to set it up. Their job was to plan the team organization, hire and train team leaders, and counsel them until the operation was underway. This gave the leaders the opportunity to use their talents to the maximum. All three were offered management positions in the new plant. One accepted; the others opted to return to their old jobs as team leaders at the main plant. They enjoyed the experience, which taught them a lot and put them in line for eventual promotion.

4. Outsourcing

Another way of rewarding exceptional team leaders is to fire them. Sound crazy? Not if the firing involves setting them up in their own business. Frank was leader of a team at Bradley Transport that prepared all the paperwork needed to meet government regulations. Frank's future at Bradley was limited. The only higher-level jobs in the company were in areas in which Frank had limited experience. He told Mr. Bradley that although he loved his job, he saw no future there and would have to seek another job elsewhere. Mr. Bradley came up with a solution. "You're an expert in the documentation needed in the transport field. Why don't you set up your own company to deal with this. I'll subcontract what your team is now doing to your new company. That will give you a good start—and you'll be free to sell your services to other truckers. Frank accepted the offer. Today he is the owner of a very successful firm servicing several transport companies and growing rapidly.

FYI

Young people entering the work force in the 1970s and '80s could expect to be promoted at least twice during the first five years and move up the corporate ladder relatively rapidly after that. Their younger siblings getting their first job in the 1990s were faced with the "flattening" of companies, which eliminated several layers in the hierarchy. This resulted in far fewer opportunities for rapid advancement.

Overcoming Members' Resistance to Change

Nobody really likes change. We know what we have, and as Shakespeare said, we'd "rather bear those ills we have than fly to others we know not of."

Resistance to change is not logical; it's emotional. Members have deep inner concerns about new ways of doing what they have been doing for a long time in a way that they believe is good. Why should this be?

Breaking Out of the Comfort Zone

Most people resist change of any sort. Once people become accustomed to doing something in a certain manner, we become comfortable doing it that way. Changing takes us out of our *comfort zone.*

A good example is learning a sport. When I was a teenager, my friends and I went to a local park to play tennis. We took no training, but after a while were able to play a respectable game. Years later, to improve my game, I signed up for formal lessons. After watching me play, the instructor showed me the proper way to stand, and how to hold and swing the racket and maneuver around the court. I had been doing it all wrong. Changing wasn't easy. Moving out of the comfort zone in which I had been playing hurt—my muscles ached, my back ached. *It hurts to change.*

If the change is mental, it also hurts. Changing the way you have to approach the work is just as painful as physical pain. Discomfort, headaches, tension, stress—all may result. Moving out of one's comfort zone is never easy.

Team Terms

A **comfort zone** is the place in which we feel most at ease when doing a physical or mental exercise. Our muscles, nerves, brain, and senses are conditioned to being used this way and resist any change from it.

Nobody wants to hurt, so they resist change. Changing from being part of a traditional work group to being a member of a collaborative team is hard work.

Skepticism About Team Effectiveness

Converting to teams is a radical change. Many members are concerned about the effect of such change on their jobs, their careers, their futures. Others just don't want to suffer the aches and pains of leaving their comfort zones. They try to find all kinds of reasons to rationalize their opposition. Let's look at some of them:

1. "We always did it this way."

Probably the most common reason given is some variation of these statements: "If it ain't broke, don't fix it," or "Don't tamper with success."

These are valid reasons if the work has been a great success. But usually, things are not as successful as they might be. There is a need for change. Even when everything appears to be going well, improvements can be made.

2. "I don't want the added responsibility."

There are members who want to avoid taking responsibility for fear of punishment if they fail or make mistakes. Still others may just be shy people who are afraid that their ideas will be lost in team discussions and they will be held accountable for decisions made by a dominant majority.

This can be overcome by careful orientation of members as to the way the team will operate, and by assuring them that mistakes and failures are part and parcel of team growth. Most important is the development of their self-confidence and acceptance of their new role as equal partners with their associates. (How to do this will be explored later in this chapter.)

Heads Up!

Don't take literally what a member tells you about his objections to the team concept. It's often a superficial comment that hides a deeper concern. Determine the real reason by careful questioning and listening, and then deal with it.

3. "Just tell me what to do and I'll do it."

In many organizations, there are "plodders" who really don't want to strain themselves. All they want is to do what they're told to do during working hours and get home. Don't give up on them. Many of these plodders are very good workers. They may be your best technicians or specialists, who do good work, but whose real interests lie outside the job.

Ken is a good example of this. He probably knows more about the intricacies of computer graphics than anybody on your team. Give him an assignment and leave him alone in his cubicle with his computer, and he'll produce top-notch work. But at meetings he never opens his mouth. When asked questions about his work, he'll respond in detail, but when asked to comment on other team projects, he has nothing to say.

What's going on in Ken's mind? He looks upon himself as an artist. He enjoys his work because it's art. He looks upon the other work the team does as peripheral to his creativity and has no interest in it. There's no way his team leader can make him a collaborative team member. People like Ken function better in a traditional environment.

On the other hand, there are members who use this as an excuse to cover up their fear of change. These members can be converted to participating team members by working with them to overcome their concerns.

Team Builder

If there are highly competent specialists on your team who just don't fit in as collaborative members, detach them from the team and work with them as nonteam resources in their specialized areas.

One way of dealing with such people is to phase these members into teamwork. Instead of shifting overnight from the old format, break in slowly. In the first few projects as a team, work with these members as you had in the past. Tell them what to do. During this period, spend time orienting them to the team concept. Let them observe members who are working the team way. Over the first few months, require them to take on more of the decision-making regarding their work. If they continue to resist and just can't function in the team environment, they may have to be removed from the team.

4. "Teamwork won't help my career."

Because the emphasis of teamwork is on the team, not the individual, ambitious members may feel that their competence and potential will be overshadowed by the team. This is especially true when the reward and recognition program primarily rewards teams, not individuals. If the team leader isn't going to move up, what chance of promotion does an ambitious member have?

Members who seek to move up in the organization should be assured that their personal contributions are not overlooked, and as new teams are formed or current leaders move on, opportunity does exist for them. Also, make clear that the performance review and the compensation system rewards individuals not only on their performance, but on their participation as a team member.

Change the Team Member's Self-Image

How the members of a team feel about themselves and about the way they are perceived by their immediate supervisors or team leaders and others in the organization is reflected in the effectiveness of the team. Companies use a variety of approaches to get members to be true believers.

"Employee" vs. "Associate"

When people think of themselves as *employees* or *subordinates,* there is an aura of inferiority surrounding them. The terms themselves connote subservience to a higher authority.

One of the ways companies use to overcome this is to eliminate those terms and replace them with *associate* or *team member.* These terms connote equality of position.

Does changing one's job title really work? The answer, like so many answers to problems of this type, is "yes and no." It works if the change in title is backed up with change in the attitude of management toward the individual and a true change in the job function.

Susan didn't feel that being an associate was such a big deal. She commented that her team leader was still her boss and still told her what to do and how to do it. "Everything is the same as before the title change," she reported. "It's just another gimmick to make us work harder."

Her friend Nancy worked in another company where the title change was more than a superficial gesture. When teams were formed, the members were given a thorough orientation on how the team was to function and what each person's role would be. "Management took it seriously, so we associates took it seriously. And it seems to be working. I'm making more of my own decisions and enjoying my work more."

Nancy's company spent time and money on changing the attitudes of management and of the members themselves as a basic step in getting the program underway.

"Follower" vs. "Collaborator"

Heads Up!

Don't think just changing job titles is enough to make members understand and accept their new role. You have to back it up with good orientation and training and build their self-confidence in their abilities to function as responsible team members.

We pointed out earlier in this chapter that many people are fearful of accepting the responsibility of team participation. They have been conditioned from their earliest work experience to be followers.

There is nothing degrading about being a follower. In fact, one must learn to follow before one is ready to lead. The difference between just being a follower and being a collaborator is one of degree. In traditional organizations, subordinates follow instructions and orders without question. They have little or no say in what they will do. In a team, the member doesn't totally abdicate the role of follower. He or she participates in formulating projects and determining how a job will be done, and then follows the decisions made.

One reason members hesitate to be collaborators is lack of self-confidence. Because they have been followers for so long and have looked to others to make decisions, they're afraid to stick out their own necks. But like the turtle, if they want to move forward, they have to stick their necks out of their shells.

Building members' self-confidence is an important step in making the team concept succeed. Some ways to help build self-esteem were discussed in Chapter 10. In addition,

➤ When the team concept is first introduced, give members relatively easy assignments. Give them only basic instructions from which they will have to develop their own approach to the assignments. If they come to you with questions or ask for your decisions, insist that they solve their own problems. However, don't let them fail. If their actions will lead to failure, intervene by subtly suggesting changes. Reinforce good decisions with praise.

➤ Train them or send them for training in problem solving and decision making. Provide exercises or case studies in which they will be required to make decisions. As these are not on-the-job problems, the fear of failure is removed. The experience will help them become more confident when faced with collaborative decisions on the job.

➤ Take note of each member's talents and strengths. Make a big deal over things they do especially well.

➤ If some members are especially shy or don't make progress, suggest they enroll in courses designed to build self-confidence, such as the Dale Carnegie Course or assertiveness training programs.

Are You a Team Player?

Yes   No   1. Are you willing to cooperate with team members rather than compete against them?

Yes   No   2. Do you volunteer to help team members with tough assignments?

Yes   No   3. Do you praise associates for their good work?

Yes   No   4. Do you participate actively in team meetings?

Yes   No   5. Are you willing and able to express your ideas even if they are different from your associates'?

Yes   No   6. Are you aware of team goals and committed to achieve them?

Yes   No   7. Do you volunteer to take on assignments even if they are not your favorite type work?

Yes   No   8. Do you make a point to welcome new members and help them get oriented to the team?

Yes   No   9. Do you take training seriously and try to apply what you learn on the job at the first opportunity to do so?

Yes   No   10. Do you do your best to get along with other members even if they are unfriendly?

The more "yes" answers, the better you are as a team player. Work on changing your behavior in the areas where you answered "no."

Team Builder

Take these steps to keep alert to what's going on in your team:

Keep your door open.

MBWA: Manage by walking around. Get out of your office and into the area where your team works.

Know each associate as a human being. Know about family, hobbies, interests, philosophy of life.

Encourage team members to share ideas with you and the other associates.

Mold the Group Into a Team

Once team members understand and are committed to their new roles and have overcome their resistance to the change, the team leader is ready to build this group of individuals into a collaborative team.

Here's where the team leader's role as a coach comes into play. Compare this to a high school basketball team. The kids who are picked for the team were selected because they showed promise. Most probably they had been playing basketball in the school yard or the local "Y" and are more than competent players. But they're not a team. The coach's job is to take these youngsters and teach them how to play as a team.

The team leader may have a highly competent group of workers. The job now is to mold them into an interactive, effective, cooperative unit.

Explain New Expectations

Do members know what is expected of them? Are they aware of the changes in the way they behave and perform? Dealing with these matters is a priority job for the team leader.

Following are some ways this can be accomplished:

➤ Focus on results. In orienting the team, put emphasis on results expected from the team's activities rather than on the activities themselves. Let them know that management looks at results and is not concerned with the details of the methods so long as they meet the legal and ethical standards set by the organization. Assure them that they have the expertise to get satisfactory results.

➤ Build commitment. Provide a climate in which members' ideas and suggestions are seriously considered. When members know they are treated as true collaborators, their commitment is solidified.

➤ Give all members opportunity to grow. In assigning work, give every member the chance to lead a project, work on a challenging phase, and take a key role. Develop smaller teams within the team to let less experienced members take charge of a project. Encourage your more skilled members to act as mentors.

➤ Encourage all members to participate in every aspect of the work—even those in which they don't have as much expertise as other members. Their fresh ideas may be valuable, and it helps build up their self-confidence.

Let your bosses know about the progress of each of your members—and let the member know that you have done so. This makes them visible to higher management and may boost their careers. It will boost yours as well if you develop a team of winners.

Provide the Team with Tools and Help Needed

Another responsibility of the team leader is to ensure that the team has the tools it needs to get the job done. This may mean negotiating with management for a higher budget to purchase the latest equipment or software and training the members in the best techniques of doing their work.

More than this, the team leader becomes a source of advice, information, and counsel for the team. Members should feel free to call on the leader for assistance when technical or administrative problems arise.

Effective team leaders don't wait for problems to be brought to them. They take active steps to identify potential problems and deal with them early.

A participant at one of my seminars shared with the class a form he developed to get continuing feedback from his members on areas that they felt needed attention (see the following table). He commented that as a result of using this form, he was able to make his team the leading team in the company.

Team Member Queries and Comments

I read, heard of, or saw the following equipment or material that we ought to purchase:

_____

_____

_____

_____

_____

What it can do:

_____

_____

_____

_____

_____

continues

Team Member Queries and Comments (continued)

How it can help us:

_____
_____
_____
_____
_____

Source:

_____
_____
_____
_____
_____

Cost:

_____
_____
_____
_____
_____

Other comments:

_____
_____
_____
_____
_____

My work could be done more efficiently if

we could eliminate _____

we could change _____

we could add _____

because _____

I anticipate problems with

_____
_____
_____

Suggested solution:_____

Costs could be reduced on _____if we

_____

_____

I am concerned about the safety of _____

In working on the_____ assignment, I learned

_____

_____

A project our team ought to tackle is _____

_____

You can be more effective as our team leader by _____

_____

_____

_____

Build Team Spirit

The best way to build team spirit is by getting members committed to team goals and excited about reaching them. This is not an easy task. People differ, and what excites one may turn off another.

Some team leaders emulate sports teams by having the team pick a name, design a team insignia, and hold team rallies.

At one company, team contests were made more competitive and more fun by giving teams names and colors. In the shipping department there were three teams: "The Movers and Shakers," "The Shipping Sharpies," and "The Packing Pack." Each chose a team color combination, designed flags, and had a good time in friendly competition.

Heads Up!

Team leaders are change agents, but it's not always possible to make the changes desired. They might recite Rheinhold Niebuhr's Serenity Prayer: "Grant me the serenity to accept the things I cannot change, the courage to change the things I can, and the wisdom to know the difference."

At another company, team members in the customer service department purchased blue blazers with the team insignia on the lapel. All the men and women on the team proudly wore their blazers while at work.

There are people who don't relate to this type of hype. They find it childish and silly. Forcing reluctant members to wear the blazer and sing the team song is self-defeating.

It takes patience to get the team working together as a collaborative unit—a team that interacts seamlessly to achieve its goals. It won't happen overnight. Don't give up. Work for your team and with your team in building up the members' confidence in themselves; in you, the team leader; and in the team itself. Work at it. Be persistent. Be patient, and the payout will be higher productivity, better quality, a motivated work force, and a happier workplace.

The Least You Need to Know

➤ If members are treated as subordinates, they will act as subordinates; if the leader considers them participative members, they will meld into a real team.

➤ Team leaders must trust their members. Micromanagement by the leader makes the members feel inadequate and destroys team spirit.

➤ Since positions that previously were stepping stones have been eliminated, when promotion is not viable, new and creative ways must be found to reward team leaders.

➤ Nobody really likes change, because it takes us out of our comfort zone. The transition to new ways of doing things takes time and must be handled with care.

➤ Identify the reasons members are skeptical about teams and their place in the team. Work with them to overcome their fears.

➤ One reason members hesitate to be collaborators is lack of self-confidence. Building members' self-confidence is an important step in making the team concept succeed.

➤ The team leader may have a highly competent group of workers. The job now is to mold them into an interactive, effective, cooperative unit.

➤ The best way to build team spirit is by getting members committed to team goals and excited about reaching them.

Chapter 19

When the Team Is Brand-New

In This Chapter

➤ Determining skills needed

➤ Personality factors in creating the team

➤ Seeking team members within the organization

➤ Putting the team together

Occasionally team leaders have the opportunity of creating their own teams. A new project is undertaken, and new teams are to be formed to work on it. The company is expanding, and some of the work of an overburdened team is to be assigned to one or more new teams. A task force is to be formed to deal with a critical situation.

As team leader, you will have two major challenges in forming your new team. The first is to determine what skills and personal characteristics are needed to fulfill the team's mission.

Once you know what qualities you require in a new member, you have to seek people who possess those qualities. Where will they come from? You may draw some members from within the company—transferring members of established teams or people working in nonteam positions to the new team. Some or all of the new team members may have to be new hires.

In this chapter we'll first look into establishing the job specifications, and then we'll explore the first step in forming the team—seeking members from within the organization.

Establish Criteria for Members

Before criteria can be established for selecting team members, the team's mission must be clearly understood. Obviously, the people you choose must have the skills needed to achieve the mission, but that's not all. Members should have personal characteristics that make for team success. What these are may differ from team to team. It's the team leader's responsibility to make a realistic assessment of what these personality traits should be.

Team Terms

Job specifications are the qualifications a person should have in order to perform a job.

Skills Required

After you develop your job description (see Chapter 7), you can determine which qualities you seek for the person who will be assigned to do the job.

In some situations the *job specifications* must be rigidly followed; others may allow for some flexibility. In civil service jobs or in cases in which job specs are part of a union contract, for example, even a slight variation from job specs can have legal implications. In some technical jobs, a specific degree or certification may be mandated by company standards or to meet professional requirements. For example, an accountant making formal audits must be a certified public account (CPA); an engineer who approves structural plans must be licensed as a professional engineer (PE). On the other hand, if there's no compelling reason for the candidate to have a specific qualification, you may deviate from the specs and accept an equivalent type of background.

Most job specifications include these elements:

➤ **Education.** Does a job call for college? advanced education? schooling in a special skill?

➤ **Skills.** Must the candidate be skilled in computers? machinery? drafting? statistics? technical work?

➤ **Work experience.** What are the types and duration of previous experience in related job functions?

➤ **Personal characteristics.** Does a candidate have the necessary skills in communication, interpersonal relations, and patience? This will be discussed later in this chapter.

One of the most common problems in determining the specifications for a team member is requiring a higher level of qualifications than is really necessary. This knocks out potentially good candidates for the wrong reason. This problem frequently occurs in the following areas:

➤ **Education.** Suppose that the job specs call for a college degree. Is that degree necessary? It often is, but just as often having the degree has no bearing on a person's ability to succeed in a job. Requiring a higher level of education (or, for that matter, any qualification) has more disadvantages than advantages. You may attract smart and creative people, but often the job doesn't challenge them, resulting in low productivity and high turnover. More important, you may turn away the best possible candidates for a position on your team by putting the emphasis on a less important aspect of the job.

Team Builder

When you set up specs for a job, ask yourself, what must the applicant be able to do that other members cannot do? Keep in mind that your team will be stronger if it includes people with different but complementary skills.

➤ **Duration of experience.** Your job specs may call for 10 years' experience in accounting, but why specify 10 years? No direct correlation exists between the number of years a person has worked in a field and that person's competence. Lots of people have 10 years on a job but only one year's experience (after they've mastered the basics of the job, they plod along, never growing or learning from their experience). Other people acquire a great deal of skill in a much shorter period.

It's not that years of experience don't count for anything. Often, the only way a person can gain the skills necessary to do a good job, make sound decisions, and make mature judgments is by having extensive experience. Just counting the years, however, isn't the way to determine that ability.

Rather than specify a number of years, set up a list of factors a new member should bring to a job and how qualified the person should be in each area. By asking an applicant specific questions about each of these factors, you can determine what he or she knows and has accomplished in each area.

➤ **Type of experience.** Another requirement job specs often mandate is that an applicant should have experience in "our industry." Skills and job knowledge often can be acquired only in companies that do similar work. In many jobs, however, a background in other industries is just as valuable and may be even better because the new associate isn't tradition-bound and will bring to a job original and innovative concepts.

➤ **Preferential factors.** Some job specs are essential to perform a job, but other factors, although not critical, could add to a candidate's value to your team. In listing preferential factors, use them as *extra* assets and don't eliminate good people simply because they don't have those qualifications.

Heads Up!

Be sure the person you hire can do the job. The job specs should emphasize what you expect the applicant to have accomplished in previous jobs, not just the length of his or her experience.

For example, it may be an extra benefit if a candidate already knows how to use a certain type of computer software, but because that knowledge can be picked up on the job, eliminating a person who is otherwise well qualified might be a mistake.

Personal Characteristics Required

Personal factors can be as important (or even more important) than some tangible requirements. These factors that make an impression in the hiring process often are the same traits that will make a candidate successful on the job. They are the human factors that enable people to work well with you, their coworkers, and others within or outside the organization with whom they will interrelate.

Here are some of the personal characteristics that determine the way a person will fit in with the team and how you can identify them at an interview:

1. Appearance

In most contacts with people our immediate reaction is to appearance. A person whose physical characteristics, dress, and presence are pleasant, neat, and attractive starts off on the right foot in most interpersonal relationships. This does not mean that you should judge someone solely on appearances, or that you should give preference to handsome men and beautiful women. Neatness, a pleasant countenance, and good taste in dress and grooming are important. Caution: Overemphasis on appearance, making it the key factor, can result in a halo effect. For example, good looks alone will not make one a successful salesperson.

2. Self-confidence

When Phil was interviewed he exuded self-confidence. He was not afraid to talk about his failures, unlike people who try to impress interviewers by bragging about their accomplishments. Phil was matter-of-fact about his successes. He projected an image of being totally secure in his feelings about his capabilities. It is likely that Phil will manifest this self-confidence on the job, enabling him to adapt readily to the new situation.

3. Communication skills

Laura was able to discuss her background easily and fluently. She did not hesitate or grasp for words. When the interviewer probed for details, she was ready with statistics, examples, and specific applications. Not only does this indicate her expertise, it indicates her ability to communicate—an essential ingredient in a participative team.

FYI

There's an old saying in the field of management: "You can only be as good as your people." Staffing your team with top-notch members not only pays off in success on the job, it enhances your organization's reputation among customers and potential customers. In addition, it builds up the company's reputation as a good place to work and attracts candidates for future growth.

4. Alertness

Diane sparkled at the interview. She reacted to your questions and comments with facial expressions and gestures. You could see that she was on her toes. Alert, sparkling applicants are usually dynamic and exciting people who give all to their jobs.

5. Maturity

Maturity cannot be measured by the chronological age of a person. Young people can be very mature, and older people may still manifest childlike behavior. Mature applicants are not hostile or defensive. They don't interpret questions as barbs by a "prosecutor out to catch them." They don't show self-pity or have excuses for all of their past failures or inadequacies. They can discuss their weaknesses as readily as their strengths.

6. Sense of humor

Evan was a sourpuss. At no time during the interview did he smile or relax. Even when you tried to lighten up the interview with a humorous comment, he barely reacted. This may be due to nervousness, but more likely Evan is one of those very serious people who never look at the lighter side of things. They are difficult to supervise and impossible to work with in a team. It is easier and much more fun to work with a person who has a sense of humor. On the other hand, applicants who are too frivolous, who tell inappropriate jokes, laugh raucously, or act inconsistently with the situation, may be immature.

7. Intelligence

Although some aspects of intelligence may be measured by tests, we can pick up a great deal about the type of intelligence a person has at an interview. If the job calls for rapid reaction to situations as they develop (required in sales, for example), a person who responds to questions rapidly and sensibly has the kind of intelligence

Heads Up!

Don't be taken in by glib people. They can talk a great job, but have only cursory experience or knowledge of it. To determine if an applicant is a talker but not a doer, ask in-depth questions and probe for specific examples of their work. Glib phonies cannot come up with meaningful answers.

needed for the job. However, if the person is applying for a job where it is important to ponder over a question before coming up with an answer (research engineer), a slow, but well-thought-out response may be indicative of the type of intelligence required.

8. Warmth

This very important intangible asset is difficult to describe, but you know when it is there. The warm person reacts to you, is empathetic, and shows real concern about the matters discussed. This person will talk freely about interpersonal relations. He or she is comfortable at the interview and makes you feel comfortable. An individual with this type of personality is at ease in any environment and will fit into the team rapidly and naturally. These are likable people and easy to live and work with.

9. Sensitivity to feedback

The applicant who understands what you are projecting not only in your questions and in your comments, but with your body language, will probably do the same on the job. This is an asset that is invaluable in the workplace. Such people are easy to train. They readily accept and implement instruction and criticism and work well with their peers.

10. Naturalness

A person who is natural and relaxed probably is a well-integrated person. However, do not automatically negate a nervous applicant. To reach such a person and determine what latent characteristics may exist beneath his or her uneasiness calls for skill, patience, and determination. Their nervousness during the interview may be masking their real selves.

11. Ability to work with others

Interpersonal skills are essential in a team. There is no place on the team for prima donnas or loners. Query the prospect on what part he or she took in team or group activities in current or previous jobs. Ask about outside activities in which he or she interacted with colleagues. Get specific examples of the part he or she played.

Staffing your team with members who have these personal characteristics, plus creativity, integrity, loyalty, and enthusiasm, is essential to the team's success.

When you list the intangible requirements for a job, however, put them in proper perspective as they relate to the work. If a job calls for communication skills, specify exactly which communication skills you need: for example, one-to-one communication, the ability to speak to large groups, innovative telephone sales methods, or creative letter-writing skills.

If a job calls for "attention to detail," specify what type of detail work. If a job calls for "the ability to work under pressure," indicate what type of pressure (for example, daily deadlines, occasional deadlines, round-the-clock sessions, difficult working conditions, or a demanding team leader).

It's important that new team members fit in with the team. This doesn't mean that they all must have similar education or social backgrounds. It certainly doesn't mean that the team be made up of people with similar ethnic origins. It means that they think along similar lines.

Your new members cannot be clones of old members. Each has an individual personality that is somewhat different from other members'—and that's what makes the team dynamic.

More suggestions on evaluating these personal characteristics are covered in Chapters 21 and 22.

Team Builder

The intangibles that make for success on a job are just as important as education, skills, and experience. In making your job analysis, be as diligent in determining the intangible factors as you are in assessing the tangible ones.

Select Members from Within the Company

In forming a new team, your best source of possible team members is the company itself. Current employees, whether they are members of another team or are working in nonteam activities, know the culture of the company, have skills that are used by the company, and, most important, they're not strangers. The team leader and other members may have worked with them or interacted with them in the past.

It's not always possible to obtain current employees. Many are working on projects from which they cannot be detached. Others are happy in their current assignment and are not interested in changing; still others may be interested but their managers are not willing to release them from their current assignment.

It's worth the effort to form a new team with at least a few current employees to serve as its nucleus and recruit the rest of the team from outside sources (see Chapter 20).

Where to Find Them

In any sizable company there probably are employees whose skills aren't being fully used. David is an accounting clerk, but has picked up a great deal of know-how about computers. He'd be a great choice for a team that needs that knowledge. Rebecca's previous job was in the medical records division of a hospital. Her current job at an insurance company doesn't involve these records. She'd be an asset to a new team formed to work in that area.

Team Terms

The Internet has opened communication to and from people and organizations globally. But there are many matters that concern only the organization and should not be broadcast outside of it. To meet this need, **intranets,** internal Web sites accessible only by people associated with the organization, have been created.

Make friends with the human resources staff. When you need that extra push to fill your job vacancies, you'll be one step ahead of other team leaders.

How can you find the Davids and Rebeccas in your organization?

➤ **Job posting.** When a team is being formed that requires certain skills, a description and specification for the job is posted on bulletin boards, noted in the company house organ, or listed on the company *intranet.*

The purpose of posting is to enable individuals to apply for positions anywhere in the organization. It may be to join a new team, to be considered for a higher level position, or to seek opportunity elsewhere in the organization.

Usually, interested people apply for the posted position through the human resources department, which in turn submits their applications to the team leader.

One major problem with job posting is that employees who are not selected may become disgruntled, which might affect their attitude toward their current job. To avoid this, human resources departments should always explain the reason for rejection and encourage the applicant to acquire skills that will qualify him or her for future openings.

➤ **Personnel records.** If properly maintained, personnel records can be a major resource. Examination of these records may uncover employees working in jobs below their educational or skill levels. It may also reveal persons who have had additional training since they were employed by the company.

Employees should be encouraged to inform the human resources department of their activities. Periodic questionnaires designed to bring the personnel records up-to-date should be circulated. At the annual (or periodic) performance review, any new skills or knowledge members have acquired should be incorporated in the report.

➤ **Skill banks.** Many companies have developed skill banks. The skills and other job factors identified for the jobs the company currently uses or plans to use are coded and stored in a database. As part of the processing of new employees, information about the education, skills, and other job factors they bring to the job are similarly coded. These are kept updated by voluntary reports from employees on their newly acquired qualifications and by reports from supervisors.

When a new team is formed, the job specs that are sought to staff the team can be matched with the job factors in the skill bank. Qualified personnel are quickly identified.

➤ **Recommendation by current team members.** When an opening occurs in your team, ask members if they know people within the organization whom they feel would fit into the team. Members often have keen insight into the qualifications and personalities of their coworkers in other departments. They have seen them in action, worked with them on assignments, and may know them socially.

The danger, as you can guess, is that if the person is rejected, the member who recommended him or her may take it as a personal affront. This can be ameliorated by carefully explaining to the member the reason for rejection, and pointing out that it in no way reflects on the person who made the recommendation.

➤ **Former employees.** When a new team is formed or replacements are sought for members who have left, take a look at employees who have been downsized. Many of these people are excellent workers who, because of lack of seniority or other reasons not related to their competence, were laid off. As they had worked for the company, you can check them out easily. If rehired, they need minimum training and can become productive rapidly.

Questions to Ask Prospective Team Members

When forming an entirely new team or adding members to a current team, the team leader has the awesome responsibility of selecting the right person.

When an outsider is hired, candidates are interviewed in depth by one or more members of the human resources department. They may be given a battery of tests and have references checked—often before the team leader meets them. Before a decision to hire is made, the candidates are interviewed by the team leader and often by team members.

When the prospects come from inside the company, the team leader does most of the screening. The leader has access to the personnel files of prospects, including test results and reference checks made at the time that person was hired. These should be reviewed, but much may have changed during the period the person has been employed by the company. Team leaders should study performance reviews and any other information in the file that will provide up-to-date and pertinent information.

Team Builder

Choose new members carefully. The men and women you select for your team must not only have the technical skills to do the job, but must be able to work in a team environment and relate well to the other team members.

Leaders should not rely on files alone. It is important that the leader interview the prospect carefully. Interviews, when properly conducted, can give the leader a much greater understanding of the prospect's background and, more important, the personal characteristics that are exhibited in a face-to-face interchange. Suggestions on how to conduct effective interviews (whether with outside applicants or internal prospects) are provided in Chapter 21.

In addition to asking questions about education, work experience, and special skills needed for the job, here are 10 questions that will help determine how an applicant has functioned as a team player:

1. **What are your career goals?** Unless the prospect's goals can be met in your team, there's no point in hiring him or her. Marge tells you her goal is to create marketing programs; your team does market research. She'll be disenchanted early on. Ted wants to be a team leader. All members of your team are periodically assigned leadership roles. This will be a good team for him to get the skills needed to meet his goal.

2. **Tell me about a typical assignment in your present job that you particularly liked.** The answer should be in line with the type of work that will be done in your team. Probe for details so you can get a clear picture of what she has done. It also indicates whether the prospect prefers working on her own or on projects where several members are involved.

3. **Now tell me about an assignment you had that you really didn't enjoy doing.** If your job involves a good deal of these assignments, think twice about hiring this prospect.

4. **Tell me about some of the suggestions or ideas you made at company meetings that influenced the decisions that were reached.** The answer will show creativity and participation in meetings.

5. **How did you persuade other team members to accept your ideas?** This will give you insight not only into the prospect's persuasive ability, but also into how he or she interacted with other team members.

6. **What was your greatest disappointment in your present job? How did you deal with it?** Stewart said his greatest disappointment was that his team did not complete a major project on deadline. In fact, they were two weeks late. He said he had knocked himself out to do his part, but the other team members were lazy and unwilling to put in the extra effort and additional hours needed. What does this tell you about Stewart? It could mean he's a hard worker and willing to exert himself. This would be an asset. It could also mean that he is self-centered. He called his associates lazy. He didn't mention trying to help or motivate them. The leader should probe to learn more about his relations with the other members.

7. **What leadership roles did you take on your team?** If the prospect says he or she has never had that opportunity, ask questions on how the team operated.

In some teams, members never get a chance to lead. If the prospect did lead subteams or other groups, learn as much as you can about what was done, how the prospect functioned as leader, and what resulted.

Team Terms

The ability of a person to work as a collaborative member of a team is called **teamability**.

8. **Describe how your job fit in with the team's activities.** Probe to find out how participative the prospect was, what initiatives he took, how he worked with other members, how he reacted to the team leader's management style. Take your time and listen carefully. The answers to this question can give you a good sense of this prospect's *teamability*.

9. **If you join our team, what would you do to get started on the right foot?** The answer should include studying the job description and performance standards, but should also emphasize getting to know the team members—not just as coworkers, but as individual persons.

10. **If you join our team, what would you expect from me as your team leader?** At a seminar I conducted, I surveyed a group of team members about how they would respond to this question. Here are some of their responses:

    ➤ "Solid training in the work I'll be doing."

    ➤ "Respect."

    ➤ "Opportunity to participate fully in team activities."

    ➤ "Fair treatment."

    ➤ "Recognition for my accomplishments."

    ➤ "Interesting and challenging assignments."

    ➤ "Tell me what you want to accomplish and then let me do it."

In evaluating the candidate, you pick the answer(s) that meet your desires.

Questions to Ask Prospect's Current or Past Leaders

Unlike attempting to get reference information from a former employer (see Chapter 22), you are more likely to get complete and accurate information about a prospect from another supervisor or team leader in your own company.

Before sitting down with the current or former leader, read the personnel file. Note any areas in the file you want to explore with the leader. For example, in Jerry's performance review two years ago, a comment was made on his failure to meet deadlines. No similar comments appeared in later reviews. Discuss with the leader whether this has changed. In Eileen's review, you noted that most of her work was of the type

Heads Up!

Don't accept a prospect for your team from within the company—no matter how good he or she appears—without studying his or her personnel file and interviewing present and former supervisors and teammates.

that was done on her own. Is this an indicator of her inability to work with others or just the nature of the work? Explore this with her leader.

To ensure that you obtain all the information you need, interview the current or former leader in a systematic manner. Even if the leader is a close friend, make it a formal meeting, not just part of one of your everyday chats. Here are some questions that should be asked:

1. **Tell me about _____'s job in your team.** This will provide a general background of the prospect and put the rest of the questions into perspective.

2. **Give me some examples of some of the contributions he made to your team's achievements.** From this you can determine what you might expect if you accept this prospect.

3. **What are some of _____'s strong points?** These are factors that may help build your team.

4. **If I were to accept _____ , what are some of the things I should watch out for?** You'll learn about both serious problems, if any, and those little foibles that can be annoying.

5. **How do other team members view _____?** If they enjoy working with him, that's an asset. If they dislike him, he may have difficulty with your members. Don't accept either answer without probing for details. In either case, the circumstances may explain the reason for liking or disliking the prospect. Find out how this affected the team's work.

6. **What are _____'s career goals?** As noted above, if the prospect's goals cannot be met in your team, don't accept him. Often the reason an employee wants to join a new or different team is to further career goals.

7. **What part did _____ take in team meetings and discussion?** If the prospect didn't actively participate in such meetings in the current team, it's not likely she'll be any different on your team.

8. **How did _____ react when his ideas were not accepted by the team?** Some members pout; others act rebellious and refuse to go along with the majority; others give reluctant support; and still others accept defeat gracefully and give full support to the decision.

9. To current team leader: **Why do you think _____ is seeking to change from your team to mine?** To past team leader: **Why did _____ transfer out of your team?** Is the team leader's answer the same as that given by the prospect? Does it show instability or is it a valid reason?

10. **If I accept _____, what can I do to make her a valuable member of my team?** The insights of leaders who have worked with the prospect can be most helpful to getting the new member productive.

The danger in interviewing the prospect's current team leader is that he or she may be reluctant to lose a productive member and give you misleading information. Or, the leader may be anxious to get rid of a troublemaker and fail to tell you about real problems. Try to interview other team members to obtain other viewpoints.

There is no assurance that any new member will succeed. Good screening through interviews with team leaders and team members who worked with the prospect, careful review of personnel records, and thorough interviews with the prospect can increase your chances of making a good selection.

Organize the Team

Once the members have been chosen, arrangements must be made with the human resources department to transfer those selected to the new team. Before the team meets for the first time, the leader should review the backgrounds of each member, determine which job on the team each will hold, and prepare to get the new team underway.

Get to Know the Members

When the team member is notified that he or she has been selected, the team leader should congratulate the member and welcome him or her to the team. The leader should spend some time with each member to get acquainted, chat about the team's mission, and discuss in general terms what is expected from the member and what the member expects from the team.

Some questions you may want to ask in those one-on-one meetings are

➤ **What name do like to be called by?** Some Williams prefer being called "Bill"; others "Will." Some Elizabeths prefer "Liz," others "Beth." Still others "Betty." Some people use nicknames that are not even related to their given names. Make the member feel at ease by using his or her preferred moniker.

➤ **What are your favorite activities outside of work?** This often tells you a great deal about the whole person, not just his or her work persona.

➤ **What do you expect from working on this team?** You may have asked this at the

Team Builder

When orienting a new team member, pick up those little personal tidbits that can be so helpful in getting to know the person.

281

job interview, but now that the member is accepted, get a clearer picture of what he or she is most interested in and what contributions may be expected.

➤ **What sort of things irritated you in previous jobs?** This gives you insight into how to deal with this member and avoid antagonism. It will also give you insight into his or her sensitivity.

➤ **What would you like me and your teammates to know about you so we can get to know you better?** He or she may tell you about family, childhood, schooling, jobs liked or hated, and other things he or she likes to talk about. The more you know about the member, the better it is for establishing rapport and maintaining an easy relationship.

Orient the New Team

The first official meeting of the new team should be devoted to orienting the members to the team's purpose and giving the members a chance to get acquainted with each other. Following are some suggestions:

➤ As team leader, start the orientation meeting by again congratulating the members on being chosen for the team. Then discuss the team's mission. Encourage the members to express their ideas on the mission and suggest interim goals toward achieving the mission.

➤ Get the team to discuss how important it is for the entire team to collaborate in working toward the goals. Ask them what might keep the team from reaching goals and what they can do to minimize those problems. Bring out how essential it is that they work together in harmony.

➤ Point out that you are not there to boss them but to provide help and counsel whenever they need it.

➤ Show members how they can help one another. Note that helping associates learn new techniques, solve tough problems, or overcome disappointments will be considered in their performance reviews.

➤ Emphasize each person's importance to the team's success. Each member has been picked for the team because of his or her special qualifications. Working together will give them the opportunity to not only do their own best work, but benefit from the work of the entire team.

Heads Up!

Don't press members to talk about their families. It's okay if they volunteer information, but some women who were asked about their children or plans to have children have filed discrimination complaints against companies (see Chapter 20).

End the orientation meeting with a free period in which members can chat with each other and get started on knowing their teammates.

FYI

"Managing requires setting aside one's ego to encourage the work of others. It requires a 'big picture' and team perspective rather than an individual achiever perspective."

—Sara M. Brown, management consultant

Members: Get Started on the Right Foot

The team leader alone cannot make a team successful, All associates must take active roles in getting the team going.

Here are some tips for new team members:

1. **Learn your job.** Study every aspect of the job. Ask the team leader and associates for suggestions on articles to be read, courses to be taken, and company materials that may be available to help you get started properly.

2. **Be friendly, but not too familiar with your team leader and associates.** A common concern when joining a team is how you'll get along with the leader and teammates. This is especially true if you join an established team. There's no reason to be jittery. The leader wants you to succeed and has confidence that you will. That's why she hired you. Your teammates need your contributions. They'll welcome you. Caution: Until you know these people better, don't push yourself on them. Don't ask questions about their personal lives and don't tell them all of your troubles. Be receptive to their overtures for friendship, but don't be too aggressive.

3. **Be an active participant.** The essence of teamwork is the participation of every member in setting goals, determining procedures, and implementing the work. One of the exciting aspects of team activity is the interaction among team members and the joy of seeing your collaborative efforts pay off.

4. **Don't try to change things immediately.** If you join an established team, even if you believe you can improve a method or procedure, wait until you're on the job for a while before suggesting it. Hold your ideas until you have earned the right to express them by your performance on the job. On the other hand, if the entire team is starting out at the same time, your suggestions and ideas are as valuable as any other team member's from day one.

5. **Don't align yourself with the malcontents.** In most teams there will be some members who are never happy. They find fault with every decision and complain about everything. They make a strong effort to recruit new members to their clique. Keep away from them.

6. **Be a cooperator.** Teamwork requires cooperation. You'll find most members do cooperate with each other. Help those on the team who need help and are happy to work with you to get you started. Once you have mastered your job, make a point of helping others.

7. **Be a loyalist.** Stick up for your team. Never talk negatively about it to people outside the team. If you have problems or complaints, settle them within the team. Support your team leader and associates in any conflicts with other teams or with senior management. Your loyalty will be appreciated by your leader and help bring the team together in times of crisis.

Being a part of a team can be a stimulating and rewarding experience. Take advantage of this opportunity. You'll learn much, share much, and enjoy the great satisfaction of knowing you were part of a successful team.

The Least You Need to Know

➤ The people chosen for the new team must have the skills needed to achieve the mission, but that's not all.

➤ Personal factors can be as important (or even more important) than some tangible requirements. They are the human factors that enable people to work well with others.

➤ Put intangible factors in proper perspective. If a job calls for communication skills, specify exactly which communication skills are needed. If a job calls for "the ability to work under pressure," indicate what type of pressure.

➤ In forming a new team, the best source of possible team members is from within the company.

➤ Always consider rehiring laid off employees.

➤ To make a good selection: Interview former team leaders and team members who worked with the prospect. Review personnel records, and conduct thorough interviews with the prospect.

➤ The first meeting of the new team should be devoted to orienting the members and letting them get acquainted with each other.

Chapter 20

Recruiting Candidates from Outside the Company

In This Chapter

➤ Planning the hiring strategy

➤ Complying with employment laws

➤ Where to start your search

➤ Nontraditional sources for candidates

Quite often the team has to be staffed partially or in full with people recruited from outside the organization. In large organizations much of this recruiting is done by the human resources department (HR). In smaller firms, team leaders do their own recruiting. But even in companies where the HR department is responsible for recruiting, the team leader can augment their efforts by participating in the process.

In any case, team leaders must work closely with human resources to ensure that they understand what type of experience, skills, and personal characteristics the members hired should possess. It is also important that team leaders be thoroughly acquainted with the laws that govern employment.

This chapter provides an overview of the employment laws and reviews the various sources from which candidates may be drawn.

Team Builder

Keep a file of potential members for your team. Even when there are no openings, accept resumés that are sent to you and interview prospective members. When an opening develops, you have a head start in your search. If the candidate is no longer available, ask the prospect to suggest someone with a background like his or hers.

Heads Up!

When companies use current employees as their primary source of new teams, it tends to perpetuate the racial, ethnic, and gender makeup of the staff. Companies whose employees are predominantly white and male and who rarely seek outside personnel have been charged with discrimination against African Americans, other minorities, and women.

Preparing for the Search

In the last chapter we discussed the advantages of transferring current employees to the new team. But this is not always feasible. More often than not, outsiders must be recruited.

When Hiring Outsiders Is Advantageous

Although the advantages of adding a current employee to your team usually outweigh the limitations, there are also advantages to seeking candidates from outside the company.

➤ If you seek new members only from within the company, you limit the sources from which to draw prospects. There may be many outsiders who are qualified to meet your needs.

➤ People who have worked in other companies bring with them new and different ideas and know-how that can benefit your team.

➤ Outsiders look at your activities with a fresh view, not tainted by overfamiliarity.

➤ Outsiders often possess skills and knowledge that insiders don't have and that are needed for new projects that are being undertaken.

Sometimes when an outsider is brought into an established team, a current team member who desired that position may become upset. The team leader cannot ignore this. Let's see how Don, the leader of a sales team, dealt with this.

When a customer service job became available, Karen, an order clerk on Don's team, applied for the position. It paid a bit more and was a much more interesting job.

Don didn't feel Karen was qualified for that assignment and chose to fill it by hiring an outsider. As soon as Don decided that Karen wasn't right for the position, he sat down with her for a private meeting. He went over the job specs and asked Karen to tell him how she met each of the requirements. It didn't take Karen long to realize she was far short of what was needed. Don reassured her that she was doing a good job as an order clerk and that he would help her pick up some of the skills needed for customer service work so that next time an opening occurred, she'd be better qualified.

Work with the Human Resources Department

If you work for a large organization, the chances are that you do not do your own recruiting. You work through the human resources or personnel department.

Naturally, you're not their only client. Other team leaders and managers are bugging them to fill their jobs. In this job market, they have their hands full.

But that's no excuse, as far as you're concerned. You need to fill those vacancies. Following are some suggestions:

➤ Make friends with the HR staff—not just when you need people, but as a regular practice. If you haven't done this up to now, it may be too late for your current needs, but work on it, and next time you have a job to fill, you'll see the difference.

➤ Offer to help them by contacting people you know. For example, you may be a member of a professional association and can tap its resources.

➤ Offer to screen resumés received as a result of ads that have been placed. This saves them time and work, and you'll have to look at them anyway sooner or later.

➤ Give them prompt reactions to anybody they refer to you. One of the biggest gripes HR people have about team leaders is their stalling on making decisions.

The Laws on Hiring

The laws governing equal employment affect every aspect of your job as a team leader. It begins even before your first contact with an applicant and governs all your relations with employees: how you screen candidates, what you pay employees, how you treat employees on the job—all the way to employees' separation from the company, and sometimes even after that.

The Laws That Affect Employment

The main federal laws that apply to equal employment are shown in this list:

Team Terms

The **Equal Employment Opportunity Commission (EEOC)** is the federal agency that administers most of the civil rights laws. They issue regulations, investigate complaints, and take action to enforce the laws.

➤ Title VII of the Civil Rights Act of 1964, as amended, prohibits discrimination in employment on the basis of race, color, sex, religion, or national origin. The law is administered by the *Equal Employment Opportunity Commission (EEOC)*. The EEOC also administers the Age Discrimination in Employment Act (ADEA) and the Americans with Disabilities Act (ADA).

➤ The Age Discrimination in Employment Act of 1967, as amended, prohibits discrimination against individuals 40 years of age or older. Some state laws cover all persons over the age of 18.

➤ The Americans with Disabilities Act of 1990 prohibits discrimination against people who are physically or mentally challenged.

➤ The Equal Pay Act of 1963 requires that an employee's gender not be considered in determining salary (equal pay for equal work).

Most states have similar laws. Because some state laws are stricter than the federal laws, make sure that you know what your state requires.

In addition, several presidential executive orders require that certain government contractors and other organizations receiving funds from the federal government institute affirmative action programs to bring more minorities and women into the workplace.

Team Terms

Although discrimination against any ethnic, racial, or religious group is prohibited, because of the long history of discrimination against certain groups, the EEOC has designated them as **protected classes**. They are: African Americans, Hispanics, Asian and Pacific Islanders, Native Americans, women, and the disabled.

It's important to remember that an employer isn't obligated to hire an applicant just because he or she is in a *protected class*. An employer can still hire another candidate who is deemed to be better qualified, but the employer cannot use discriminatory information to *exclude* a candidate who otherwise is most qualified for a job or promotion. Team leaders must, therefore, avoid doing, asking, or saying anything that could possibly be construed as discriminatory to avoid the appearance of discrimination, which can be misinterpreted regardless of whether it was a factor in a hiring or promotion decision.

The interpretation of EEO laws comes from both administrative rulings and court decisions. As in many legal matters, what seems simple is often complex. It's strongly recommended that you consult an attorney to clarify any actions you take under these laws.

Are Your Specs Legal?

Suppose that there's an opening in the team and the team leader asks the human resources department to line up some applicants to be interviewed. Let's eavesdrop on how the team leader described the type of person that he believed would fit in best with his team:

"We're an aggressive, hard-hitting bunch of young guys. Get me a sharp, up-and-coming recent college grad. Most of my boys are Ivy Leaguers, so that will be an asset. And, oh yes, I want a clean-living churchgoer."

How many violations of the equal employment laws are in that statement?

Let's review it:

➤ "Young guys." Violates the prohibition of both age and sex discrimination. Avoid terms that even hint at gender preference, such as *guys* or *gals*.

➤ "Recent college grad." *Recent* usually means young. Of course, some people graduate from college in their 40s or older, but they're the exceptions to the norm. Specifying *or even implying* that a candidate be "young" violates the age discrimination laws.

➤ "Ivy-Leaguer." This discriminates against people who, because of their race or religion, have chosen to attend primarily minority colleges or religion-sponsored schools. Also, because minorities are likely to be less affluent and attend less expensive schools, hiring only "Ivy Leaguers" has the effect of discriminating against minorities.

➤ "Churchgoer." This phrase violates the prohibition against religious discrimination. It can be interpreted as discriminating against people who choose not to belong to any organized religion, or as "Christian only," because members of other religions may not attend "church."

"I didn't know I couldn't ask that."

Who does the interviewing? In most companies the human resources department does preliminary screening, but team leaders and often other team members interview applicants.

To function as a manager today, you must be thoroughly familiar with various state and federal laws concerning equal employment opportunity.

Heads Up!

Every team member must be thoroughly familiar with EEO laws because an improper question from any interviewer can lead to a formal complaint.

To help you measure your knowledge of these laws, see the following quiz. It covers only a few of the key factors in the laws but should give you some insight into understanding this important area. To test yourself, check your responses against the answers that follow.

What Do You Know About EEO?

On an application form or in an interview, you may ask

Yes   No   1. What are the names of your nearest of kin?

Yes   No   2. Do you have a permanent immigration visa?

Yes   No   3. Have you ever been arrested?

Are the following help wanted ads legal?

Yes   No   4. Management trainees: College degree; top 10 percent of class only

Yes   No   5. Accountant: Part-time opportunity for retiree

Yes   No   6. Employment Recruiter: Experienced in recruiting at predominantly black colleges

Other areas:

Yes   No   7. Companies may give tests to applicants to measure intelligence or personality as long as the publisher of the test guarantees that it is nondiscriminatory.

Yes   No   8. A company may refuse to employ applicants because they are over 70.

Yes   No   9. A company may refuse to employ an applicant if she is pregnant.

Yes   No   10. A company may ask what provisions a woman has made for child care.

A company may indicate an age preference if

Yes   No   11. It is for a training program.

Yes   No   12. Older people cannot qualify for the company pension program.

Yes   No   13. The job calls for considerable travel.

Miscellaneous questions:

Yes   No   14. A company may ask what foreign languages an applicant speaks.

Yes   No   15. The company may specify that it requires an attractive woman to greet customers and visitors.

The following quiz answers are based on federal law, but some states have interpreted the laws somewhat differently. In addition, because new laws, administrative rulings, and judicial interpretations are promulgated from time to time, the reasoning on which these answers is based may change. Keep in mind the job-relatedness of the questions and whether the questions asked of applicants have a disparate effect on minorities. These are key factors in determining the legitimacy of the questions.

1. **No.** You cannot ask about next of kin because the response may show national origin if the name differs from the applicant's. You may not even ask whom to notify in case of emergency until after you hire an applicant. You don't need that information until the person is on the payroll.

2. **Yes.** Immigration laws require that legal aliens working in the United States have a permanent immigration visa (green card).

3. **No.** Courts have ruled that, because some minorities are more likely than non-minorities to be arrested for minor offenses, asking about an arrest record is discriminatory. You *can* ask about convictions for felonies.

4. **No.** Unless you can substantiate that students from the top 10 percent of their class have performed significantly better than students with lower grades, this ad isn't job-related.

5. **No.** Because most retirees are over the age of 60, specifying a "retiree" implies that persons between the ages of 40 and 60 are not welcome. The Age Discrimination in Employment Act protects persons older than 40 against discrimination because of their age. In some states the age level starts at 18.

6. **Yes.** So long as it does not specify the applicant must be black.

7. **No.** The Supreme Court, in Griggs vs. Duke Power Co., upheld the EEOC's requirement that intelligence and personality tests must have a direct relationship to effectiveness on the job for the specific work for which the test is used. Because only the company using the test can verify this relationship, it must be validated against each company's experience.

8. **No.** The Age Discrimination in Employment Act prohibits discrimination against people who are 40 years or older. There is no top age limit.

9. **No.** Pregnant women may not be refused employment unless the work might endanger their health (such as heavy physical work or exposure to dangerous substances). Employers cannot ask an applicant whether she is pregnant or comment that the company doesn't hire pregnant women. If a pregnant woman was rejected, the company would have to prove that the reason for the rejection was something other than her pregnancy.

10. **No.** Because men aren't usually asked about provisions for child care, it has been interpreted as a means of discriminating against women.

11. **No.** Training programs may not be limited to young people.

12. **No.** Participation in a pension program is not an acceptable reason for age discrimination.

13. **No.** Ability to travel is not related to age.

14. **Yes.** But you may not ask how the applicant learned the language because it may identify national origin.

15. **No.** A company's desire to have an attractive woman as a receptionist doesn't make it a bona fide occupational qualification (see the following section).

Every manager who hires people should, ideally, score 100 percent on this quiz. Failure to comply with any one of these rules may result in complaints, investigations, hearings, and penalties.

Bona Fide Occupational Qualifications (BFOQs)

There are some positions for which a company is permitted to specify only a man or only a woman for the job. Clear-cut reasons must exist, however, for why a person of only that gender can perform the job. In the law, these reasons are referred to as *bona fide occupational qualifications,* or *BFOQs.*

Team Terms

Bona fide occupational qualification (BFOQ). A specific qualification that limits a job to only men or only women. The only undisputed **bona fide occupational qualifications** are wet nurse (for a woman) and sperm donor (for a man).

If a job calls for heavy lifting, for example, is it a BFOQ for men only? Not necessarily. Certain strong women may be able to do the job, and certain weak men may not. It's legitimate to require that all applicants—both men and women—pass a weightlifting test.

And that's not all. Suppose that a job calls for driving a forklift truck and that the operator is occasionally required to do heavy lifting. A woman applicant may be able to drive the truck but not be able to do the lifting. If the lifting is only a small part of the job, you cannot reject her. She is capable of performing the major aspect of the work, and other people can be assigned to handle the lifting.

Suppose that you have always had an attractive woman as your receptionist and that the job is now open. Is this a BFOQ for a woman? Of course not.

There's no reason that a man who has the personality for the position cannot be just as effective.

Avoiding Age Discrimination Problems

Despite federal and state laws, the accent on youth in many companies has kept older men and women from getting and keeping jobs or from functioning at their highest levels in a job. Study after study have shown that mature people are at least as productive and creative, are more reliable, and make better judgments and decisions than their younger counterparts.

Most company application forms no longer ask a person's age or date of birth. Age is omitted in most resumés. Yet, it's still easy to guess an applicant's age range within a few years. A team leader who gives preference to younger applicants may reject potential members who could be of great value to the team, just because of the prospect's age.

Heads Up!

When you interview older applicants, avoid the stereotypes that may keep you from hiring highly qualified people for the wrong reason.

Many team leaders have conscious or subconscious reluctance to hire men and women who are older than the team members. Of course, they don't admit it. Here are some of the "rationalizations" that leaders give for not hiring otherwise qualified older candidates:

➤ **The applicant is overqualified.** The term *overqualified* is often a euphemism for "too old." Some people may have more know-how or experience than a job requires. You may be concerned they will be bored and unhappy in a short time, lose interest, and become nonproductive. Discuss the details of the work with the applicant. Every job gives the holder an opportunity to learn new things. The applicant may be able to contribute to the job some expertise that makes it more challenging. Judge the person as an individual, not as a member of an age group.

➤ **The applicant made more money in the last job than you can offer in this job.** People with many years of experience often have earned more money than those with less experience. If the amount of salary your company can offer is a factor in your hiring decision, discuss it with the applicant. He or she should be the one to determine whether the salary is satisfactory. You may worry that if a better-paying job comes along, the new member will jump to it. That may happen, of course, but a younger person would probably do the same.

➤ **This person won't fit in with the team.** Being of different age levels isn't necessarily a barrier to cooperation and collaboration. Make that determination on the basis of the candidate's personality, not on his or her age.

The team will benefit from a mix of men and women of all ages and various cultural backgrounds—all contributing their talents, expertise, and experience to the team's activities.

Applicants with Disabilities

The newest and probably least understood civil rights law is the Americans with Disabilities Act (ADA). This section discusses some of the highlights of the law and how it applies to you as a team leader. All companies with 15 or more employees are covered by this law.

The ADA makes it illegal to discriminate in hiring, in job assignments, and in the treatment of employees because of a disability. Employers must make *reasonable accommodation* so that these people can perform the essential duties of their jobs.

This accommodation can vary from building access ramps for wheelchair users to providing special equipment for people who are seeing- or hearing-challenged, unless this type of accommodation is an undue hardship for the company. Undue hardship is usually defined in monetary terms. If an applicant who uses a wheelchair applies for a job with a small company, the cost of building an elevator or a ramp to give access to the floor on which the job is located may be a financial hardship. Because of this undue hardship, the company could, if it cannot provide a less expensive accommodation, reject the applicant. If the same applicant applied for a job in a more affluent company, however, it may not be considered undue hardship to do the necessary construction.

Accommodation doesn't always require expensive construction. The hypothetical examples in this list examine some other ways to meet this requirement:

➤ The small company you work for wants to hire a highly qualified accountant, but there's a problem. The applicant uses a wheelchair. The accounting department is on the second floor of the building, which has no elevator or ramp. Constructing one would cost more than the company can afford. This is considered to be an *undue hardship* for the company. You are not required to go to that expense. However, the company may be able to accommodate this person in a less expensive way. Use your imagination. Why not let him work on the ground floor? His work could be brought to him. It may be an inconvenience, but it would qualify as reasonable accommodation, and it would enable you to hire this particular competent accountant.

➤ A highly skilled word processor operator is legally blind and walks with the aid of a white cane. She can transcribe from dictated material faster and more accurately than many sighted people. You want to hire her, but you're concerned that in case of a fire or other emergency she would be a danger to herself and others. The accommodation you can make is to assign someone to escort her in case of an emergency.

➤ An assembler in a factory was badly injured in an automobile accident. His job requires him to stand at a workbench all day. When he returned to work, he was unable to stand for long periods. His team leader sent him home and told him that until he was able to perform the work as he had before, he could not return. The leader was wrong. Accommodations should have been made. Perhaps a high stool could have been provided so that the employee could reach the workbench without having to stand. If that option wasn't feasible, his hours might have been adjusted so that he could work part time on that job and do other work that didn't require standing for long periods for the rest of the day.

FYI

Alcohol and drug users are considered disabled under the ADA. If a person can perform a job satisfactorily, a previous record of alcoholism or drug addiction is not reason enough to refuse to hire. If an applicant is still addicted, however, and it's been manifested by a recent history of poor attendance or poor performance, you can reject him—not because of the addiction, but because of poor work habits.

Sources of Applicants

As was noted earlier, in most companies the human resources department, not the team leader, does the recruiting. So why then should team leaders be concerned? HR serves the entire organization, and your needs are not necessarily their first priority. Team leaders can prod the HR staff to work on their behalf and suggest sources that they may have overlooked. They can also help HR make better use of the sources.

Eileen was able to suggest ways of making help wanted ads more attractive to the type candidate she was seeking. Adam asked permission to speak directly to the employment agency that was working on the opening in his team and clarified some of their misunderstandings of his needs. Nina was able to suggest some sources HR had not thought of. Aaron's team worked in a branch distant from the home office, and he had to do the recruiting himself.

Tried-and-True Sources

Even if a job is hard to fill, don't overlook the standard sources for recruiting applicants—and not all jobs are hard to fill. These are tried-and-true methods:

➤ **Help wanted ads.** The most usual source for seeking applicants for routine jobs is to place ads in local newspapers. These ads are read by local residents who are seeking positions. However, if your job is hard to fill and you are willing to relocate people from other areas, your best bet is to advertise in trade or professional journals.

➤ **Private employment agencies.** Most of these agencies have files of applicants who are immediately available and can match them against your job specs, enabling you to fill the job quickly. As they screen applicants before referring them, you will see only qualified people and avoid the wasted time of interviewing countless unqualified applicants.

Contact employment agencies that specialize in your type of work. You can identify these agencies by studying the ads that they place in newspapers and professional journals. If you note that the agency covers a variety of jobs in your areas of interest, it probably will understand your specs and may have candidates available who fit your needs. Once you've established a relationship with one or two agencies, you will be able to have a ready source of personnel when needed.

Most employment agencies require the employer to pay a fee, which may range from 20 to 30 percent of the annual salary paid to the employee, and even more for technical and management jobs.

➤ **Headhunters.** Executive or technical recruiters differ from employment agencies in that they put their efforts into identifying and going after specific candidates who are usually currently employed and not actively seeking jobs. These firms usually work only on higher paying positions. Some firms charge a flat fee, paid whether they fill the job or not; most take a nonrefundable retainer and a percentage of salary if they succeed in filling the job.

➤ **State job services.** All of the states have a job service that can recommend applicants for your jobs. You certainly should list your jobs with the local office of this agency. Many state job services provide testing and other screening facilities. Some companies have developed excellent relations with these agencies. Other firms have expressed dissatisfaction because state placement services are primarily concerned with finding jobs for unemployed people. These firms believe that the better applicants may be currently employed and not registered with these agencies.

➤ **School affiliated employment services.** An excellent source of trainees is high school, college, and technical or specialized school employment services. Most do not charge a fee and are anxious to place their graduates. These schools sometimes have records of alumni who do have work experience in their files.

Ask for Referrals

Your team members and other company employees are a great source of referrals. Nobody knows as much about the jobs you have to fill in your team than your own team members. Enlist their help in filling vacancies. Many companies offer rewards to employees who refer candidates who are hired. These rewards run from a token cash bonus or merchandise prize to very substantial payments for referring hard-to-find applicants. Referral bonuses as high as $10,000 are not uncommon. This is cheap, considering that if the company had to pay a fee to an agency or headhunter, it would probably cost much more. (Typically a fee for filling a $60,000 a year job is from $12,000 to $18,000.)

Another source is former team members. They know what the team required. In their new jobs they have access to a network of candidates you normally would not know. In some cases, you might entice a former valuable team member to come back just by asking for a referral.

Some employers are asking retirees if they would consider working part-time; others are luring mothers of young children back to the workforce early by helping with day care. Others arrange for two people to share a job—each person working part-time. This allows for continuity in the work and gets jobs done that must be done. These arrangements, usually used by women who need time for family responsibilities, bring to the company talents that would have been lost if full-time work was demanded.

Try the Internet

One of the fastest growing sources for locating qualified personnel is the Internet. There are several computer-based job banks that can be tapped for various job categories. Most job seekers today file their resumés with one or more of these sources.

Many companies have Web sites where job-seekers can learn about the company. Originally designed to attract customers, today many have a job opening section that is kept current. There are also several Web sites that carry classified ads or even match applicants with job openings (for a fee).

If your company doesn't have a Web page, create one. This is a particularly effective tool for recruiting professional, administrative, and technically trained people.

Job Fairs

Job fairs are sometimes organized by trade associations or private recruiting firms. They tend to specialize in specific types of jobs. Companies may rent a booth at the fair to attract the applicants, provide them with job information, and even conduct preliminary interviews.

Some larger firms conduct their own job fairs. Advance Micro Devices (AMD) ran such a fair in Austin, Texas. They promoted the fair in radio ads

Team Terms

Job fairs are like trade shows. Instead of displaying company products or services to customers, participating companies present information about jobs and careers in the organization to prospective employees.

Team Builder

Build your own network. When you meet a person who you feel can be of some value, set up a file noting his or her name, company, position, and any other pertinent information. Get in touch from time to time to keep the contact active.

for weeks in advance, then set up a big tent to supply job information for those who wandered in. The fair was "wildly successful," and AMD hired 30 people. IBM ran a similar recruiting fair in Panama City, Florida, where thousands of college students were partying on spring break.

Explore Your Network

At trade shows, professional association meetings, and even at social events, team leaders have met men and women in their fields on whom they can call for advice, information, and referrals. Quite often these people know viable candidates for your job openings.

When a vacancy for a systems analyst opened in Henry's team, he phoned Arthur, the Management Information Systems (MIS) manager of the bank with which his firm dealt, and asked if he knew a person with the qualifications needed. Arthur didn't know anybody, but suggested that Henry call Joel, an MIS executive at another bank. Joel referred two analysts whom he knew. One was hired for the job.

That's the beauty of having a network—and there is no fee for the service.

The Least You Need to Know

➤ People who have worked in other companies bring to your team new ideas and know-how, and often possess skills and knowledge needed for new projects.

➤ Make friends with the human resources staff. Offer to help them in the search by screening resumés, contacting sources, and giving them prompt reactions to candidates they refer to you.

➤ Learn and adhere to the laws governing equal employment. Keep them in mind when writing job specs, screening candidates, dealing with people on the job, through their separation from the company, and even beyond.

➤ Team leaders must avoid doing, asking, or saying anything that could possibly be construed as discriminatory, regardless of whether it was a factor in a hiring or promotion decision.

➤ When you interview older applicants, avoid the stereotypes that may keep you from hiring highly qualified people.

➤ The Americans with Disabilities Act requires employers to make reasonable accommodation for people with disabilities so they can perform the essential duties of their jobs.

➤ Even when the human resources department does the recruiting, team leaders might suggest sources they may have overlooked.

➤ One of the fastest growing sources for locating qualified personnel is the Internet. Most job seekers file their resumés with one or more Internet job banks.

➤ Develop a network of people on whom you can call for referrals of candidates. These personal contacts often provide the best candidates—and there is no fee for the service.

Chapter 21

Separating the Wheat from the Chaff

In This Chapter

➤ Evaluating resumés

➤ Saving time and expense by pre-screening

➤ Preparing for an effective interview

➤ Good questions, bad questions

➤ Getting meaningful information at the interview

As a result of your recruiting efforts, you've received a number of resumés. Your next job is to determine which applicants are worth bringing in for interviews. Your time is valuable, and good interviewing is time consuming. It's important to study those resumés carefully and pick candidates whose backgrounds appear to be closest to the requirements of the open job.

Although there are other tools used to help choose among the candidates for a job (see Chapter 22), the interview is by far the major technique used in determining if an applicant will be hired. It's critical that team leaders know how to use this tool most effectively.

This chapter will give team leaders guidelines on how to select from the resumés the applicants worthy of interviews and how to conduct an interview that will provide the information you need to make a valid choice.

The Resumé: Don't Be Misled

The applicant writes his or her resumé as a promotional piece telling you why he or she should be hired. It is not necessarily an objective recap of qualifications. Your job is to find among those glowing words, what the applicant has really done in his past jobs and schooling.

Team Builder

Show some flexibility in your "knockout factors." Unless a specific degree is needed for legal or professional reasons, a person who lacks the degree but has extensive experience in a field may be better qualified than a person with a degree and less experience.

Tips on Rapid Screening

You may receive hundreds of resumés in response to an ad. It can take hours and hours of your time to read them and make your preliminary judgments. You can save time and uncover hidden problems in the resumé by following these guidelines:

➤ Establish some "knockout factors." These are job requirements that are absolutely essential to performing the job. They include necessary educational qualifications and/or licenses; for example, a degree in electronics, certification as a plumber, or a pilot's license.

➤ Select key aspects of the job and screen for them. When you have many applicants for a position, you can narrow the field by looking for experience in those key aspects.

➤ Look for gaps in dates. Some people who have had short duration jobs omit them from their resumés. Here's what they do:

1. Indicate just the years rather than month and year. (For example, 1996–1999 for one job and 1993–1996 for the previous job.) It may mean only a short period of unemployment between jobs, but it may also mean that a job held for several months between the listed jobs is not listed.

2. Listing the number of years worked instead of the dates. This may also be a cover-up for gaps in work history. It could also be a means of emphasizing older jobs when the more recent work experience is not relevant to the job being sought. For example, say the job sought is in market analysis. The applicant was a market analyst 10 years ago, but has been working in a different type position since. By placing the marketing experience first in the resumé and not specifying dates, the impression is that the marketing job was most recent.

3. Giving more space on the resumé to past positions. This may be due to the applicant using an old resumé and updating it instead of creating a new one—which could be a sign of laziness. Or it may just mean that the more recent jobs were of lesser pertinence than previous ones.

4. Overemphasis on education for experienced applicants. If a person is out of school five or more years, the resumé should primarily cover work experience. What was done in high school or college is secondary to what has been accomplished on the job. For such applicants, information about education should be limited to degrees and specialized programs completed.

These are not necessarily knockout factors. They simply suggest further exploration in the interview.

Determining Whom to Interview

The resumé is usually the first source of screening applicants. The following guidelines will help you determine which candidates should be invited for interviews:

➤ Study the job specifications for the open position. Prepare a list of key factors that the applicant must have to qualify.

➤ As you read the resumé, check to see if most of these factors are mentioned in the applicant's description of job duties or schooling.

➤ If they are, determine if this experience or training has been acquired in a setting comparable to that of your organization. (For example, cost accounting experience in a chemical company may not be of much value to an automobile parts company as the cost systems are entirely different.)

➤ If these factors are not mentioned, it doesn't necessarily mean that the applicant lacks them. In writing a resumé, an applicant may overlook some important factors in the effort to keep it brief. To avoid eliminating an applicant who has much of what is needed, but has omitted a key factor, phone the applicant to obtain more information.

➤ Determine if the applicant has enough depth of experience to meet your requirements. For example, Barbara's last job was on the staff of the human resources (HR) department of a large organization. All she did was interview applicants for clerical jobs. Stanley was an HR staffer in a smaller company. He not only interviewed applicants for a variety of jobs, but dealt with other human resources functions. However, he worked for a very small company and didn't have the sophistication and knowledge of up-to-date technology needed to work on your team.

➤ Does the resumé show the accomplishments and results attained by the candidate? If the description of the work done is presented in concrete terms, showing achievements, rather than a textbook description of the job duties, it's more likely that the candidate is a clearer thinker and has a results-oriented view of the job.

Heads Up!

Resumés are only pieces of paper, which cannot possibly describe the whole person. If you choose *not* to see an applicant based on the resumé, you will lose this prospect—perhaps the best candidate—forever. If you have any doubts, before placing it in the reject file, telephone the candidate to obtain more information.

➤ Are the accomplishments indicated significant? If the applicant brags about a routine or superficial achievement, it may indicate a low standard of what is important.

Fill Out the Application Form

Most applicants provide resumés of their background and experience. In addition, most companies require all applicants to complete an application form.

You may wonder why an application form is necessary when you have a resumé. You need it! As pointed out above, resumés are an applicant's sales pitch—designed to make you want to hire him or her. A resumé can hide undesirable aspects of a person's background or overplay positive factors. Some applicants write resumés that omit employers the candidate doesn't want you to know about. Others don't give dates of employment, salary history, and other information you may need. An application form provides you with the information *you* need to know, not what the applicant wants you to know.

Because all the information requested on the application form is the same for all applicants, it complies with the equal employment opportunity laws. In addition, it helps you compare applicants' backgrounds when you make your hiring decision. Make sure that all applicants complete the form, even if they provide a detailed resumé.

Like every aspect of the hiring process, an application form must comply with equal employment laws. In today's litigious society, you would think that most companies would be conscious of this situation and have these forms reviewed carefully by legal experts. As a consultant, I have had the opportunity to see countless company application forms. I'm amazed that even now—more than 30 years after the EEO laws went into effect—I still see application forms that ask for age, marital status, number of children, dates of schooling (which can identify age), and other illegal information.

Before you print more copies of your application form, have your legal advisors check it to ensure it complies with the latest regulations of the EEOC and your state's civil rights agency.

Preliminary Interviews

The cost of bringing an applicant from out of town to a company's location can be extremely high. To minimize this cost, many companies start the selection process by reviewing resumés, then sending company application forms to prospects in whom there is some interest. A good start, but often not enough. Before inviting the applicant for a depth interview, conduct a preliminary telephone interview.

Prescreening Out-of-Town Applicants

When a company seeks applicants from outside of its geographic area, it is usually for higher level jobs—technical, professional, managerial positions. You don't want to waste your time and

Team Builder

Some team leaders use telephone interviews for all applicants, not just those from far away. If properly conducted, the leader can obtain enough information to determine whether a face-to-face interview is warranted—saving countless wasted hours interviewing unqualified candidates.

money or the time of the applicants by bringing them in for personal interviews only to find they are not basically qualified or even interested in the job. A thorough telephone interview can provide many of the answers you need to make a preliminary decision on the applicant's viability.

Here are some guidelines that will make these interviews more effective:

1. Give advance notice.

It's probably best to make the phone call in the evening when the applicant is at home rather than call him/her at the workplace. It's advisable to inform the applicant by mail or e-mail that you will phone at a specific time so that the applicant will be at home and be prepared for the call.

Plan the phone interview as carefully as you would an in-person interview. Study the resumé and application form. Note the areas that require elaboration. Don't be afraid to ask hard questions about such things as reasons for wanting to leave the current job, explanations for periods of unemployment, relations with team leaders, and specific details on work background.

2. List what to ask.

Study the job specs carefully. The resumé may show that the applicant meets the required job factors, but often a person may meet some aspects of those factors and not others. Sometimes superficial experience is blown up in the resumé.

Probe to determine if the applicant's experience and skills are close to what you are seeking. Prepare a series of questions that will elicit specific information on duties, responsibilities, accomplishments. Have that list in front of you. If the response does

not give you the information needed, probe more deeply for it. Use some of the suggestions for questioning applicants made later in this chapter.

3. Take notes.

In a telephone interview it's even more important than in an in-person interview to note the answers to your questions. We tend to remember people we see and what they tell us more easily than those who are only interviewed on the phone.

4. Be flexible.

The telephone interviewer who just reads a lot of questions and jots down the answers but doesn't react is like a salesperson who uses a canned presentation on the phone and becomes confused if the prospect doesn't answer as expected. The answer to one question may prompt you to ask questions not planned, enabling you to obtain information—either positive or negative—about the applicant that the prepared questions would not have uncovered.

5. Listen for danger signals.

In addition to noting the applicant's substantive responses to the questions, listen to how he or she speaks. A voice often shows an applicant's confidence or lack of it. Hesitance, equivocation, and long pauses between thoughts often reflect weaknesses. Nervous laughter, frequent digressions, evasions, or nonresponsive replies are danger signals.

If you feel the applicant is not giving you the information you want or seems to be hiding behind vague answers, let him or her talk for a while. Listen closely, giving nondirective responses. If you still don't get the information needed, return to direct questions. Failure to obtain good information is a good reason to terminate the interview and reject the candidate.

6. Discuss salary.

Some team leaders go through an entire telephone interview and invite the candidate to the company without discussing salary. When salary is brought up at the in-person interview, a serious discrepancy in what you are prepared to pay and what the applicant expects may appear. This could have been avoided if the salary situation had been clarified during the telephone interview.

You need not commit the company to a specific salary, but you should ask what salary is expected. If it's within the range, it's unlikely a problem will arise. If you are far apart, a frank statement of this should be made.

7. Close the interview.

Before closing the interview, review your notes to be sure you have all the information you need. If you are sure you want to extend the invitation, set up a date. If you have some doubts or you wish to give it more thought, or discuss it with your associates, tell the applicant when you will be in touch with him or her.

If you've decided the applicant is not for you, how you close the interview will depend on the circumstances. If the reason is clear, such as lack of technical qualifications, it probably was obvious during the interview. Just point out, "I really need a person with more design experience on my team."

If the reason is not clear—for example, you want to compare him or her with other candidates—comment that you hope to make a decision by the end of the month and you'll let him or her know. And do it.

FYI

Personnel experts estimate that every departing employee costs a company 1.5 times his or her salary—a combination of recruiting costs, training time, and lost productivity as coworkers and supervisors pitch in during the transition.

The Quick-Screening Interview

In some situations, a short telephone call can save you countless hours of interviewing time.

Stacey, team leader of a telemarketing firm, was staffing a new team. In response to her ad, she received more than 200 resumes. From them she culled out 50 possible candidates. Rather than spend hours and hours interviewing them, she chose to prescreen them by telephone.

She set up a form (see the following example), which she completed for each applicant whom she telephoned. She estimated a maximum of seven minutes for each call.

Preliminary Screening Guide

Name: _____

Phone number: _____

Questions to ask:

How do you view the job of a telemarketer? _____

What in your background qualifies you for such a job? _____

Tell me briefly about your duties in your current or recent jobs. _____

What would you like to know about the job on my team? _____

What to look for:

Voice: Does the applicant have a good telephone voice? _____

Manner: Does the applicant speak coherently and clearly? _____

Concept: Does applicant understand what telemarketing involves? _____

Experience: Is it applicable to this job? _____

Questions asked: Are they job related or self-centered? _____

General: Did I feel comfortable talking with applicant? _____

Did applicant sound confident about him/herself? _____

Comments:

Invite for interview? _____ If yes, date and time: _____

From these screening calls, Stacey narrowed the list to 22 and hired five for the team.

Team Builder

When there is a rush to fill a job, and you know there are not too many people likely to respond to your ad, bypass asking for resumés. Have applicants telephone you, and conduct a preliminary telephone interview as the first step in screening.

Interviewing Tips

Many team leaders don't know how to conduct an *interview*. They have a pleasant chat with the applicant and hope to learn enough to make a hiring decision. An interview must be more than a casual conversation: Be prepared to ask questions that enable you to judge an applicant's qualifications and give you insight into the strengths and limitations they would bring to the job.

Before we discuss interviewing techniques, here's your chance to check how good an interviewer you are. Answer the questions in the following quiz.

How good an employment interviewer are you?

True   False   1. You should study the application form before inviting the applicant in.

True   False   2. It makes little difference whether or not the applicant has a favorable impression of you.

True   False   3. In the information-gathering part of the interview, you should do about 50 percent of the talking.

True   False   4. A company application form should be completed even if the applicant has a resumé.

True   False   5. The best way to start the interview is to challenge the applicant.

True   False   6. Specific questions should be framed to elicit "yes" or "no" or similar simple responses.

True   False   7. You can obtain additional information from the applicant after they have responded to your question by maintaining silence or making noncommittal remarks.

True   False   8. You should set traps to catch the applicant in lies or inconsistencies.

True   False   9. One way to obtain more detailed information is to ask the applicant for specific examples of his/her experience in the area under discussion.

True   False   10. The applicant's motivation and attitudes are secondary to his/her technical qualifications for the job.

True   False   11. If the applicant fails to meet every job specification, he/she should be rejected.

True   False   12. Nonverbal clues can help you evaluate the applicant.

True   False   13. To be sure that you remember the interview, take detailed notes on what the applicant tells you.

True   False   14. If an applicant has questions to ask you, you should respond: "I ask the questions, you answer them."

True   False   15. You have a responsibility to describe the company and job to the applicant in whom you have interest.

Team Terms

Look at the word **interview**. The first part (**inter**) means between. The second part (**view**) means a look. An **interview** is a look at a situation (in this case a job) between two people. It's not a one-way interrogation.

Now check your answers:

1. **True.** By reviewing the application, you can plan what will be covered in the interview.

2. **False.** The interview is a two-way process. To get the most out of the interview, the applicant must respect you. If you've made a favorable impression, you will increase the likelihood of the applicant accepting an offer if it's made.

3. **False.** This is a major problem with some interviewers. Always remember that nobody can learn anything if his mouth is open. Let the applicant do most of the talking. Keep your part down to about 20 percent.

4. **True.** Resumés are written by the applicant to emphasize his/her strengths and minimize limitations. The company application form is more objective.

5. **False.** This will only make the applicant more tense. A tense applicant is a non-communicative applicant.

6. **False.** Open-ended questions elicit more and better information.

7. **True.** These nondirective techniques can be most effective in getting applicants to tell more than originally volunteered in response to the question.

8. **False.** If you are Perry Mason, this is okay. But not in an employment interview.

9. **True.** Specific examples of the work the applicant has done give you deeper insight into the depth of experience acquired.

10. **False.** Intangible factors are at least as important to job success as technical know-how.

11. **False.** There are few "dream" applicants. Trade-offs often must be made.

12. **True.** Watch body language, facial expressions, and so on. Good interviewers learn to understand and interpret them.

13. **False.** It's best to write down only key factors during the interview. After it's concluded, write comments and evaluation. Too much writing during the interview prevents you from fully listening and inhibits the applicant.

14. **False.** Encourage questions. You can make significant judgments based on the type of questions the applicant asks. Also, your answers can help the applicant decide whether this job is right for him/her.

15. **True.** A good description of the organization and the job can do much to sell the applicant on accepting an offer. If you hire the applicant, it serves as the first step in orientation. Caution: Don't tell too much too soon. See comments on this later in this chapter.

How'd you do? If you had all 15 correct, you have a superior knowledge of interviewing. Otherwise, learn from your incorrect answers and read the balance of this chapter for more suggestions on improving your interviewing skills.

Prepare for the Interview

To ensure that you get the information you want, make a list of pertinent questions before you meet with a candidate:

➤ **Review the job description.** Prepare questions to bring out the applicant's background and experience in the functions of the job for which you are interviewing.

➤ **Review the job specifications.** Prepare questions to help you evaluate whether an applicant's personal characteristics and skills conform with what you're seeking.

➤ **Review the application and resumé.** Some of the information you need may be gleaned from these documents. Prepare questions that expand on what's in those documents.

Team Builder

You can get much more (and more useful) information by asking open-ended questions. Rather than asking, "Do you know how to use Excel?" ask, "Tell me about your experience in using Excel."

Questions You Should Ask

In preparing for the interview develop a list of key questions. Usually they include the following five areas:

1. **Education.** Explore whether the applicant has the requisite educational requirements or other background that would provide the necessary technical know-how.

2. **Experience.** Inquire about the type and length of pertinent experience. Ask not only "What did you do?" but also, "How did you do it?" You can determine from an applicant's answers whether he or she has the type of experience that's necessary for the job.

3. **Accomplishments.** It's important to learn what the applicant has done that makes him or her stand out from other qualified candidates.

4. **Skills.** Learn what special skills the applicant can bring to the job.

5. **Personal characteristics.** The job specifications should indicate the personal characteristics necessary for doing a job. During an interview, try to identify the personality factors that may affect the applicant's compatibility with you and your team members.

The following list of interview questions is to guide you in preparing the questions you want to ask a job candidate. Questions similar to these, tailored to the job involved, can provide a great deal of meaningful information.

311

Interview Questions

Work experience

Describe your current responsibilities and duties.

How do you spend an average day?

How did you change the content of your job from when you started it until now?

Discuss some of the problems you encountered on the job.

What do you consider to be your primary accomplishment in your current job (or in previous jobs)?

(In addition to the above, develop a list of specific questions to determine job knowledge and experience in various aspects of the job for which you are interviewing.)

Qualifications other than work experience

How do you view the job for which you are applying?

What in your background particularly qualifies you to do this job?

If you were to be hired, to which areas could you contribute immediately?

In which areas would you need additional training?

In what way has your education and training prepared you for this job?

Weaknesses

Which aspects of your previous job did you do best?

In which areas did you need help or guidance from your boss?

In which areas of your work have your supervisors complimented you?

Motivation

Why did you choose this career area?

What do you seek in a job?

What's your long-term career objective?

How do you plan to reach this goal?

Of all the aspects of your last job (or jobs), what did you like most? Least?

What kind of position do you see yourself in five years from now?

What are you looking for in this job that you're not getting from your current job?

Stability

What were your reasons for leaving each of your previous jobs?

Why are you seeking a job now?

What were your original career goals?

How have these goals changed over the years?

Resourcefulness

Describe some of the more difficult problems you have encountered in your work.

How did you solve those problems?

To whom did you go for counsel when you couldn't handle a problem yourself?

What's your greatest disappointment so far in your life?

In what way did this disappointment change your life?

Working with others

On what teams or committees have you served?

What was your function on this team (or committee)?

What did you contribute to the team's activities?

How much of your work did you do on your own? As part of a team?

Which aspect did you enjoy more, working alone or as part of a team? Why?

What did you like best about working on a team? Least?

Conducting the Interview

Don't start the interview with a curt, "What makes you think you can handle this job?" If you're looking for a tough, no-nonsense person who will be exposed to constant harassment and pressure, this approach might work. But most jobs aren't like that. Even if applicants aren't intimidated by this approach, they're less likely to be forthright in their responses. It becomes a battle of wits, rather than an elucidating discussion about qualifications.

Most job applicants are nervous or at least somewhat ill-at-ease in an interview. To make an interview go smoothly, put the applicant at ease. Welcome them with a friendly greeting, a smile, and a handshake. Introduce yourself and begin the discussion with a noncontroversial comment or question based on something from the applicant's background. For example, start out with a comment like, "I noticed that you graduated from Thomas Tech—two of our team members are Thomas grads." This assures an applicant that you're familiar with the school and are favorably inclined toward its alumni.

Heads Up!

When you use a list of questions, don't stick only to the questions on the list. Listen to the answers, not only for what an applicant says but, equally important, for what's *not* said. Follow up with probing questions to elicit more detailed information.

After you break the ice, you're ready to move into the crux of the interview and ask the questions you have prepared.

Probe for Details

Have you ever had the feeling that an applicant is hiding something or is reluctant to talk about a particular aspect of his or her background? These three techniques may help open these closed doors:

Team Builder

Elicit from applicants information about what they have done in previous jobs (or other areas of their lives) that they're particularly proud of. Past successes are good indicators of future achievements.

1. **Use silence.** Most people cannot tolerate silence. If you don't respond after someone has finished talking, he or she will usually fill in the gap by adding something more. ("I've had experience with mass-mailing software." [Silence.] "I did it once.")

2. **Make nondirective comments.** Ask open-ended questions, such as, "Tell me about your computer background." An applicant will tell you whatever he or she feels is an appropriate response. Rather than comment on the answer, respond with, "Uh-huh" or "Yes," or just nod. This technique encourages applicants to continue talking without your giving any hints about what you're seeking to learn. This approach often results in obtaining information about problems, personality factors, attitudes, or weaknesses that might not have been uncovered by direct questions. Conversely, it can also bring out additional positive factors and strengths.

3. **Ask probing questions.** Sometimes applicants can be vague or evasive in answering questions. Probe for more detail, as in this example:

Interviewer: For what type of purchases did you have authority to make final decisions?

Applicant: Well, I know a great deal about valves.

Interviewer: Did you buy the valves?

Applicant: I recommended which valves to buy.

Interviewer: Who actually negotiated the deal?

Applicant: My boss.

You learned that the applicant did not have the purchasing experience needed for the job.

Remember the Candidate

One of my most embarrassing moments occurred in my first job as a personnel manager. I interviewed several candidates for a sales position. Two of the candidates had similar backgrounds but quite different personalities. You guessed it. I mixed them up and made the job offer over the telephone to the wrong person. Was I shocked when he walked in the following Monday morning!

It's difficult to remember every person you interview. It's advantageous to record the highlights of an interview and, of course, the decision you made. Taking detailed notes during an interview is neither possible nor desirable; doing so often makes an applicant "freeze up," and, if you're busy writing, you can't fully listen.

Take brief notes during an interview. Write down enough information to be able to remember who each applicant is, what makes one applicant different from another, and how each applicant measures up to the job specs for which she or he has been interviewed. Immediately after the applicant leaves, write additional comments so that you have a complete record of each interview.

When you're evaluating several candidates for the same job, keep good records to help in comparing them. By using a standard interview report form, you can make a comparison more effectively. Often, more than one person interviews an applicant, and if each one reports comments on a standard form, evaluations are easier to interpret.

In the case of investigations by federal or state EEO agencies, good records of an interview can be your most important defense tool. When records are unavailable or inadequate records have been kept, the hearing officer bases judgment on the company's word against the word of an applicant. Complete and consistent records give the company solid evidence in case of an investigation.

Give the Applicant Information About the Job

An important part of the team leader's interviewing process is telling the applicants about the company and the job. Team leaders are often so ill at ease about asking questions that they spend most of an interview describing the duties of the job, the advantages of joining the team, and the benefits the company offers.

There's a time during interviews for these issues—after you have obtained enough information about an applicant to determine whether he or she is a viable candidate.

At the beginning of an interview, briefly indicate the type of job you're seeking to fill. If you divulge too many details about a job, a shrewd applicant will tailor the answers to your questions to fit what you have described.

The best way to give information about job duties is to ask questions about an applicant's qualifications in that area before you give information:

> Interviewer: How much of your previous job involved copy writing?
>
> Applicant: Most of it. I spent at least two-thirds of my time writing copy.
>
> Interviewer: Great, writing copy is a major part of this job.

Heads Up!

Don't give applicants a copy of the job description before an interview. Their responses to your questions will be influenced by what they have read.

Had you first told the applicant that the job was primarily in writing copy, even though they may have had only a minimum of that type experience, it's likely that most applicants would play that up in the interview and give you a distorted concept of their actual experience.

In the next chapter, we'll cover some additional aspects of interviewing and discuss making their hiring decision.

The Least You Need To Know

➤ Screen resumés carefully before calling an applicant for an interview and make a checklist of qualifications the applicant must have.

➤ If the applicant has much of what is needed, but has omitted a key factor, follow up by phone. You may avoid eliminating a qualified person for the wrong reason.

➤ All applicants should complete an application form, even if they have a resumé. The application provides you with the information *you* need to know, not what the applicant wants you to know.

➤ Before inviting an applicant for an interview, send prospects a company application form. After reviewing it, if interested, conduct a preliminary telephone interview.

➤ When there is a rush to fill a job, and you know applicants are scarce, bypass asking for resumés. Have applicants telephone you, and conduct a preliminary telephone interview as the first step in screening.

➤ Be prepared to ask questions that enable you to judge an applicant's qualifications and give you insight into that person's strengths and limitations for the job.

➤ To ensure that you get the information you want, make a list of pertinent questions *before* you meet with a candidate.

➤ Listen not only to what an applicant says, but more important, to what he or she does *not* say. Follow up with probing questions to elicit more detailed information.

➤ To get the interviewee to add more in response to a question, use silence; make nondirective comments; ask probing questions.

➤ Take brief notes during an interview. Immediately after the applicant leaves, write additional comments so that you have a complete record of each interview.

Chapter 22

Making the Hiring Decision

In This Chapter

➤ Have team members interview prospects

➤ Making reference checks meaningful

➤ Testing applicants

➤ Selecting the best prospect

Because the interview plays such a critical role in the hiring process, it's a good idea to have more than one person interview candidates who have passed the preliminary screening. In large companies, human resources department staffers do the initial screening. Those candidates who pass muster are then interviewed by the team leader.

To supplement the team leader's interview, it's smart to have other team members interview the prospects. Because each person tends to look for different facets of an applicant's background, if several people do the interviewing, it will uncover much more about a candidate than any one interviewer can find. It's particularly helpful for team members to interview people who may join their team, because their reactions can help you make a better choice.

In addition to interviewing, before a final decision is made, prospects' references should be checked. In some cases, employment testing may be used.

This chapter discusses these and other approaches to learning as much as possible about applicants before making the hiring decision.

Team Builder

Before making a hiring decision, have an applicant interviewed by other members of the team who will work closely with that person.

Bring Team Members Into the Act

Hiring an employee can be the most important decision you make as a team leader. The people who comprise your team can make or break your endeavors. No matter how good you may be as an interviewer, it's a good idea to seek the reaction of other team members before making a final decision.

Who Else Should Interview the Prospect?

If you're the only person who has interviewed an applicant, get the perspective of at least one other person on your team. The interviewer may be a senior member of the team or, if the team is made up of people with different specialties, a member engaged in the prospect's specialty.

If the new employee will work closely with another team, the opinion of the leader of that team will be meaningful. Many companies require finalists to be interviewed by the manager at the next higher level—your boss.

Because the team concept involves every member of a team, the process of choosing members for your team should be a team activity. Ideally, every member of the team should interview prospects. The downside is that interviewing takes time: If every team member interviews every applicant, no other work gets done.

To save time and give each member a chance to meet and get an impression of the prospect, it's not necessary for every team member to conduct a full interview. Each team member should concentrate on the part of an applicant's background in which she or he has the greatest knowledge. All team members will have the opportunity to size up an applicant and to share their evaluations with the rest of the team.

Other Approaches to Multiple Interviewing

One-on-one interviews are very valuable, but, as noted are very time consuming. Following are variations on this theme that have been used in some companies.

1. Panel interviews

In this setup, the prospect is interviewed by all of the team members at the same time. Typically, they sit around in a circle. The prospect is asked a question by any one of the panelists. Any other team member can follow through with a question to augment the response or to obtain added information.

Some candidates may feel intimidated by the team "ganging up" on them, but if the discussion is kept nonconfrontational, it can develop a good deal of information and, more important, show how the prospect interacts with a group.

After the *panel interview*, the panel members discuss what has been learned and their reactions to the prospect.

2. Assessment centers

Although companies usually use *assessment centers* as a means of evaluating current employees to determine their advancement potential, this approach can be adapted for screening applicants.

Here's how it works. If after interviews with the human resources staff and the team leader there is a serious interest in the candidate, he or she may be invited to participate in the assessment process.

Team Terms

In **panel interviews,** a group of interviewers (often the entire team) sit down with the applicant and collectively conduct the interview. A variation on this is the **assessment center,** in which, in addition to the interview, the candidates are given a series of exercises to perform, and the panel observes them in action.

Members of the assessment group are usually drawn from team members and members of other teams, or higher level management who are knowledgeable in the prospect's area of expertise. A human resources manager or consultant facilitates the meeting.

Assessment center programs are not just repetitions of panel interviews. Candidates will be questioned by the panel on various aspects of their background or their thinking, but this is just the beginning. Most assessment center programs go much deeper.

There are many variations of this process. Some include a series of situational exercises in which candidates must respond to real life problems likely to be faced on the job. They may be asked to prepare and make a presentation of a new project, to study a situation, make recommendations, and then defend their position.

Some companies assess several people in the same session. They may be rivals for the same position, candidates for differing jobs, or current employees being considered for promotion (not necessarily for the same jobs). In these cases, one of the goals of the assessment program is to study the way the various participants interact. The assessors note which people take leadership roles, come up with the most creative ideas, and cooperate with the others; personality traits are also observed.

Although assessment centers provide useful information, often not easily attainable through other means, they are expensive to conduct and should probably be reserved for key positions.

Some teams use a variation of the assessment center as part of the selection process. After initial screening, they give the finalists a participative exercise. A realistic situation is presented to them and they work together to resolve it. The team members observe (sometimes behind a one-way window) how the prospects approach the problem, who takes the lead, how each interacts with the other prospects, and the creativity and logic used in the exercise.

Heads Up!

When the entire team participates in choosing a candidate, it's quite likely some members may strongly oppose hiring a prospect that the majority votes to accept. Hiring such a person may cause friction in the team, and it may be best to look further.

Compiling Opinions

Before a decision is made, the team should meet and discuss their reactions to the prospect.

In some companies, members must complete an interview summary sheet in which they note the information they developed in their interviews. Here's where inconsistencies are uncovered, information missed by the team leader brought up, and other data unfolded.

Each member then lists what he or she views as the strengths and weaknesses of the prospect. From this information, the team can assess the contributions the prospect can bring to the team and in what areas he or she may need help to become fully productive.

Comments by members are evaluated by the team leader, who must make the final judgment. In some teams, the decision is made by consensus.

Checking Applicant's Background

Applicants can tell you anything they want about their experiences. How do you know whether they're telling the truth? A reference check is one of the oldest approaches to verifying a background, but is it reliable? Former employers unfortunately don't always tell the whole truth about candidates. They may be reluctant to make negative statements, either because they don't want to prevent the person from working—as long it's not for them—or they fear that they might be sued. Still, a reference check is virtually your only source of verification.

Sending a Letter or E-mail Request

One way to obtain information is to write a letter or send an e-mail to the former employer. Very often these letters are routine forms asking simply whether the applicant worked there, the job held, dates of employment, and general statements concerning quality of work.

Some HR people send more detailed forms asking a variety of specific questions about performance, personality, and other pertinent data. To make these forms effective, they must be carefully designed and should cover all the things one wants to know.

The problem in sending letters or e-mails—be they simple forms or more complex inquiries—is the reluctance of most people to put anything of an adverse nature in writing. If it gets into the wrong hands, they may face a defamation suit. Even if the letter is true, the company must go through the trouble and expense of defending itself. And if the information is subjective (for example, "he was lazy," "she is stubborn"), it's not easy to prove.

Today, most companies prefer to use the telephone to check references.

Team Builder

Unless your company policy requires that reference checks be made by the human resources department, it's better for the team leader to do it. Team leaders have more insight into the team's needs and can react to the responses to questions with follow-up questions that will help determine whether the applicant's background fits the team's needs.

Effective Telephone Reference Checks

Most reference checks are made by telephone. To make the best of a difficult situation, you must carefully plan the reference check and use diplomacy in conducting it.

See the prototype telephone reference form that follows. Design a similar one that fits the information you seek.

Name of Applicant _____

Person Contacted, Position _____

Company _____

Phone number _____

1. I would like to verify some of the information given to us by _____, who has applied for a job for a (job title). He/she stated that he/she worked for your company from _____ to _____. Is this correct?

2. He/she told us her work involved _____. Is this correct?

3. Can you elaborate on some of his/her duties and responsibilities?

4. (Add here specific questions related to job duties as indicated in the job description.)

5. He/she says her salary was _____ per year. Is this correct?

6. What were _____'s major contributions to your team?

7. If we were to hire him/her as a _____ on our team, in what areas would we have to build up his/her skills?

8. How did he/she interact with other team members?

continues

continued

9. Is there anything else I should know about _____ to make him/her an effective member of my team?

10. If you were building a new team, would you accept _____ as a member of that team? (If not, why not?)

Heads Up!

Be careful to follow the same guidelines in asking questions of the reference as you do in interviewing applicants. Just as you can't ask an applicant whether she has young children, for example, you can't attempt to get this type of information from the reference.

Unfortunately, in this increasingly litigious world, companies have cautioned team leaders and human resources staff not to give any information about a former employee on the telephone. Sometimes they'll verify dates of employment and job title, but that's all.

This makes getting useful information much more difficult—and that information is needed if good hiring decisions are to be made. The following list provides some tips for making a reference check:

➤ **Call an applicant's immediate supervisor.** Try to avoid speaking to the company's HR staff members. The only information they usually have is what's on file. An immediate supervisor can give you details about exactly how that person worked, as well as his or her personality factors and other significant traits.

➤ **Begin your conversation with a friendly greeting.** Then ask whether the employer can verify some information about the applicant. If the person you call refuses to give information, make the comment, "I'm sure that you would want to have as much information as possible about a candidate if you were considering someone. All I really want you to do is *verify* a few facts."

Most people don't mind verifying data. Ask a few verification questions about dates of employment, job title, and other items from the application.

➤ **Diplomatically shift to a question that requires a substantive answer,** but *not* one that calls for opinion. Respond with a comment about the answer, as in this example:

Team Leader: Tell me about her duties in dealing with customers.

Supervisor: (Gives details of the applicant's work.)

Team Leader: That's very important in the job she's seeking because she'll be on the phone with customers much of the time.

By commenting about what you have learned, you make the interchange a conversation—not an interrogation. You're making telephone friends with the former supervisor. You're building up a relationship that will make him or her more likely to give opinions about an applicant's work performance, attitudes, and other valuable information.

If a former employer refuses outright to answer a question, don't push. Point out that you understand any reluctance. Then ask another question (but don't repeat the same one). After the responses begin coming more freely, you can return to the original question, preferably using different words.

What happens if you believe that the person you're speaking to is holding something back? What if you sense from the person's voice that he or she is hesitating in providing answers or you detect a vagueness that says that you're not getting the full story? Here's one way to handle this situation:

"Mr. Controller, I appreciate your taking the time to talk to me about Enid. The job we have is very important to our firm, and we cannot afford to make a mistake. Are there any special problems we might face if we hire Enid?"

Here's another approach:

"If we hire Edgar, he will need some special training for this job. Can you point out any areas to which we should give particular attention?"

From the answer you receive, you may pick up some information about Edgar's weaknesses.

FYI

One of the great paradoxes in reference checking is that companies want full information about prospective employees from former employers, but because of their fear of being sued for defamation, when asked for information about their former employees, they give little more than basic information.

Another way to get more and better information about a candidate is to make a personal visit to the former employer. Obviously, this is expensive and time consuming and is not feasible in most cases. However, if the position is a critical one and the company is nearby, a face-to-face interview with the prospect's former team leader may be very enlightening.

In a personal interview, you not only are likely to get a franker report, but by studying the former boss's body language, you can pick up clues that can lead to significant follow-up questions.

One of the advantages of having a good network in your industry and community is that you are likely to know the former employer. Fred, a team leader for one of my clients, reported that he made a point of sitting next to a prospect's former team leader at a business luncheon and was able to get more information about that prospect than from any reference check he had ever made.

Dealing with Poor References

Suppose that everything about Albert seems fine. In your judgment he's just right for the job. When you call his previous employer, however, you get a bad reference. What do you do?

If you've received good reports from Albert's other references, it's likely that the poor reference was based on a personality conflict or some other factor unrelated to his work. Contact other people in the company who are familiar with his work and get their input.

Lydia's previous boss tells you that she was a sloppy worker. Check it out some more. Lydia's ex-boss may have been a perfectionist who isn't satisfied with anyone.

When you contact Peter's former supervisor, you hear a diatribe about how awful he was. But you notice that he'd held that job for eight years. If he'd been that bad, how come he worked there for such a long time? Maybe his ex-boss resents his leaving and is taking revenge.

Heads Up!

Never tell an applicant that he or she is hired "subject to a reference check." If the references are good but you choose another candidate, the applicant will assume that you received a poor reference. Also, never tell a person that the reason for rejection is a poor reference. Reference information should be treated as confidential.

Use common sense in evaluating references. Take into consideration that the respondent may have a personal grudge against the prospect. There are bosses who never give a good reference. One manager told me that anyone who quits is disloyal and doesn't deserve a good reference.

Employment Tests

Some companies swear by tests; others swear at them. In companies in which tests are used extensively as part of the screening process, the HR department or an independent testing organization does the testing. Except for performance tests (discussed later in this chapter), it's unlikely that in your job as a team leader you will have to administer tests. But, as HR departments usually provide test results to team leaders, it's important that you understand the tests that are used.

Types of Applicant Screening Tests

The most frequently used tests in hiring are

➤ **Intelligence tests.** Like the IQ tests used in schools, they measure the ability to learn. They vary from simple exercises (such as Wunderlich tests) that can be administered by people with little training to highly sophisticated tests that must be administered by someone who has a Ph.D. in psychology.

➤ **Aptitude tests.** These are designed to determine the potential of candidates in specific areas, such as mechanical ability, clerical skills, and sales potential. Such tests are helpful in screening inexperienced people to determine whether they have the aptitude for the type of work in which you plan to train them. Most aptitude tests can be administered and scored by following a simple instruction sheet.

➤ **Performance tests.** These measure how well candidates can do the job for which they apply. Examples include operating a lathe, entering data into a computer, writing advertising copy, and proofreading manuscripts. When job performance cannot be tested directly, written or oral tests on job knowledge may be used.

➤ **Personality tests.** These are designed to identify personality characteristics. They vary from the type of quickie questionnaires you find in popular magazines to highly sophisticated psychological evaluations.

FYI

Personality tests are offered by a large number of vendors. Some are gimmicks that purport to "guarantee" successful hires. Others are more traditional and make no exaggerated claims. To choose among them, talk to companies that have experience with them and learn their results. You can obtain information about approved tests from the American Psychological Association, 750 First St., Washington, DC, 20002. Phone 202-336-5500. Web site: www.apa.org

A great deal of controversy exists over the value of these types of tests. Team leaders are cautioned not to make decisions based on the results of personality tests unless the full implications are made clear to them by experts.

Employment Test Users

In 1998 a survey about workplace testing was conducted by the American Management Association (AMA). Nearly 1,100 human resources managers responded. Nearly half of the respondents said they use some form of psychological testing to assess abilities and behaviors for applicants. Tests that were used measured cognitive ability, interests/career paths, managerial ability, and personality.

The most frequent forms of psychological measurement assess cognitive ability (defined as spatial, verbal, and math skills), according to researchers.

As is true with all forms of testing, smaller organizations are less likely to conduct psychological tests than larger firms (39 percent of firms grossing less than $10 million compared to 54 percent of billion-dollar companies).

Nearly 65 percent of employers test applicants' job skills. This includes skill tests such as word processing, computing, or specific professional proficiencies (for example, accounting, engineering, or marketing).

Comparing Candidates

The interviewing is over, and references have been checked. You now have to decide which candidate to hire. Before you make a decision, review the evaluations of all the people who interviewed applicants. Discuss the finalists with your team members and others who may have interviewed them.

The Candidate Comparison Worksheet

One way you can help make a fair comparison of candidates is by making a comparison chart similar to the final selection worksheet.

Candidate Comparison Worksheet

Applicant	Education	Experience	Intangibles	Other

Common Mistakes in Hiring

In making a hiring decision, make every effort to avoid letting irrelevant or insignificant factors influence you. Some of these are

➤ **Overemphasizing appearance.** Although neatness and grooming are good indicators of personal work habits, good looks are too often overemphasized in employment. This bias has resulted in companies rejecting well-qualified men and women in favor of their more physically attractive competitors.

➤ **Giving preference to people like you.** You may subconsciously favor people who attended the same school you did, who come from similar ethnic backgrounds, or who travel in the same circles as you.

➤ **Succumbing to the halo effect.** As discussed earlier in this book, many people are so impressed by one quality of an applicant they overlook that person's faults, or attribute unwarranted assets to him or her. Because Sheila's test score in computer know-how is the highest you've ever seen, for example, you're so impressed that you offer her a job. Only later do you learn that she doesn't qualify in several other key aspects of the job.

Heads Up!

Don't let anxiety over losing a desirable candidate tempt you to make an informal offer—promising a higher salary or other condition of employment that hasn't been approved—with the hope that you can persuade management to agree to it. Failure to get this agreement will not only cause the applicant to reject the offer, but can also lead to legal action against the company.

In making a final decision, carefully compare each candidate's background against the others' and against the job specs. Look at the whole person. You have to live with your choice for a long time.

Making a Job Offer

You've made your decision, and now you're ready to offer the job to the lucky candidate. A few problems remain, however: negotiating salary, getting an applicant's acceptance, and arranging a starting date. In addition, you must notify the people you interviewed and didn't hire (you might also choose to notify the people who took the time to send a resumé).

In most companies, the final offer, including salary, is handled by the HR department. Usually the HR representative discusses directly with the applicant the starting salary, benefits, and other facets of employment. If you're responsible for making the offer in your company, however, it's a good idea to check all the arrangements with your boss and the HR department to avoid misunderstandings.

Negotiating Salary

Most companies set starting salaries for a job category. You may have a narrow range of flexibility, depending on an applicant's background. But when jobs are difficult to fill, starting salaries are negotiable.

Obtain a general idea of each prospect's salary demands early in this process so that you don't waste time in even considering people whose salary requirements are way out of line.

In negotiating salary, keep in mind what you pay currently employed people for doing similar work. Offering a new person considerably more than that amount can cause serious morale problems.

There are exceptions to this rule, of course. Some applicants have capabilities that you believe would be of great value to your company, and to attract these people, you may have to pay considerably more than your current top rate. Some companies create special job categories to accommodate this situation. Others pay only what they must and hope that it won't lead to lower morale.

The total compensation package includes vacations, benefits, frequency of salary reviews, and incentive programs. All these items should be clearly explained.

FYI

Companies traditionally have used an applicant's salary history as the basis for their offer. Ten percent or 15 percent higher than a person's current salary is considered a reasonable offer. Because women usually have been paid less than men, however, basing the salary you offer on current earnings isn't always equitable. If the job had been offered to a man and you would have paid a higher rate based on his salary history, you should offer a woman the same rate, even though her earnings record has been lower.

Even when the salary you offer is less than an applicant wants, you may persuade that person to take your offer by pointing out how the job will enable him or her to use creativity, engage in work of special interest, and advance career goals.

Getting the Offer Accepted

One of the most frustrating aspects of the selection process is carefully selecting the prospect you want, making an offer, and having it rejected. Why should this happen?

Often it's because you didn't fully "sell" the job to the applicant. In your interviews and subsequent contacts with the prospect, you should ask about what he or she wants from the job and reinforce how this job will meet those desires.

Team Builder

Don't notify unsuccessful applicants until shortly after your new employee starts work. If, for some reason, the chosen candidate changes his or her mind and doesn't start, you can go back to some of the others without having them feel that they were a second choice.

A common reason candidates stall on accepting your offer is that they are considering a job with another firm or are still not sure about leaving their present job.

One way to counteract this is to ask the prospect to write down all the advantages of joining the other company or staying on the present job. Then, you list all the advantages of joining your team. Be prepared to show how your job—which may pay less or have fewer benefits—is still the best bet because of how it will help the prospect meet the goals he or she has set for the future. If this person is the one you really feel will be the best for your team, it's well worth your while to make this effort.

The Least You Need to Know

➤ Because the interview plays such a critical role in the hiring process, it's a good idea to have more than one person interview candidates.

➤ It's not necessary for every team member to conduct a full interview; just concentrate on the part of an applicant's background in which she or he has the greatest knowledge.

➤ Former employers may be reluctant to make negative statements, either because they don't want to prevent the person from working or they fear that they might be sued.

➤ If a former employer refuses outright to answer a question, don't push. Later, you can return to the original question, preferably using different words.

➤ It's important that you understand the evaluations of the tests that are used by your company's HR department.

➤ Before you make a hiring decision, review the evaluations of all the people who interviewed applicants. Discuss the finalists with your team members and others who may have interviewed them.

➤ In making a final decision, carefully compare each candidate's background with the others' and against the job specs.

➤ In negotiating salary, offering a new person considerably more than that paid to current team members can cause serious morale problems.

➤ In your interviews and subsequent contacts with the prospect, ask about what he or she wants from the job, and reinforce how this job will meet these desires.

Chapter 23

Honing the Team Members' Skills

In This Chapter

➤ Picking the right training programs

➤ Making training work

➤ Conducting training meetings

➤ Computer training

➤ Everybody learns every job on the team

Whether you have formed a brand-new team, or added members to a current team, the first step is to train the new members in the skills, knowledge, and techniques the team will use and, most important, how to work together.

But training is not limited to newly formed or augmented teams. Training must be an ongoing function if the team is to accomplish its goals.

In this chapter you will learn how to orient new members and assess the training needs of all members, what the tools and techniques of training are, and some of the aspects of training that are especially pertinent to teams.

Setting Up an Orientation Program

In most companies, before new employees actually start their jobs, the human resources department gives them a briefing about the company. They may be shown

Team Terms

New employees get a better start on the job if they are made to feel they are part of the team from the beginning. Programs designed to give them information, answer their questions about the company and the team, and acquaint them with their teammates are called **orientation programs.**

videos, given a tour of the facilities, receive literature, or attend a lecture. They learn the history of the organization, the benefits are explained, and rules and regulations outlined. This is a good start. The team leader must augment this with an orientation to the team. The quality of the orientation has an impact on the future performance of new members, the manner in which they interact with associates, their job satisfaction, and even their career progress.

What Makes a Good Orientation Program?

Some of the things the team leader can do to make the new member feel part of the team are

➤ Acquaint the new member with the background and history of the team. Tell them about past projects and challenging assignments.

➤ Discuss the team's mission and what is being done to accomplish it.

➤ Describe the functions of other members so that when you introduce them, the new member will have a head start in remembering who does what.

➤ Introduce the new member to the team members. When making the introduction, comment about both parties. For example, "Alice, this is Carla, our expert in state taxes. Carla's been with the company for 10 years and on our team for the past three years. Carla, Alice will be working on developing systems for our new project."

➤ Give the new member a chance to chat with each member. Make a practice of having each team member spend break time or lunch time with the new associate during the first few weeks.

➤ As noted in Chapter 8, you may choose a current member to mentor the new associate.

Formal and Informal Training Programs

New members may need basic training, but training and development aren't limited to newcomers. All members of your team need ongoing training. They should continually acquire new techniques and renew established skills. Always encourage self-development.

If you are a leader and a coach, you are the guide and stimulus to your team's growth. By working closely with each of your team members, you can suggest areas in which additional training will be helpful and recommend skills they should acquire. You can also provide the resources for this process.

Assess Your Training Needs

Many companies only guess as to what type of training is needed. Training in the specific skills required to do the work is obvious, but skills alone do not ensure productivity.

Too often, training programs are instituted that are not needed, while others that could be more valuable are ignored.

Before choosing any training programs, the team leader should conduct a needs analysis. Professional training experts apply systematic approaches to needs assessments, but you can make some basic assessments on your own.

Heads Up!

If your new associate has done similar work in another job, don't assume that training is unnecessary. Observe the way a new employee approaches the job. It may be done differently from the way your team does it. To ensure consistency, retrain the person.

Study the jobs involved and ask yourself questions like these:

1. What is the gap between desired and actual performance?
2. Is the problem caused by lack of technical skills?
3. Is the problem caused by attitudes of the members?
4. Can the gap be closed by personal attention, or does it require special training?
5. If training is needed, which members need the training?
6. Are facilities available within the company to provide the training? If so, who will do it and when?
7. If not, what outside sources are available?
8. What performance results should be expected from the training?
9. What is the cost of the training?
10. What financial benefits will result?

Another approach to assessing training needs is for the team manager to list what he or she believes are the areas in which training is needed. Then ask team members to list the areas where they feel they need training. Compare the lists. If there are significant differences, discuss this with the team and reach an agreement on what training should be done and the order in which it will be given.

Once you have the answers, you can determine the type of program to institute. If you choose to do the training yourself, prepare to be the best instructor you can be. Techniques and tools of effective instruction will be covered later in this chapter. If

Team Builder

Tip for members: As jobs change, people must also change. Anticipate the types of jobs you think your company will eventually need. If your company doesn't provide training in those areas, find your own ways to acquire the necessary skills. Take computer training, enroll in interpersonal relations courses, or learn a foreign language. Take the initiative—your career is in your own hands.

another person in your firm or an outside organization will conduct the program, go over the training needs carefully with that person and make sure that what is required is covered in the proposed program.

Skill Training

Basic skills training has its place in the business world. The fundamentals of a job must be acquired as a start. But we can't stop there. Continued training must be an ongoing concern. Training in new technologies is essential, but even that's not enough. The following list shows five ways to bring your training and development up-to-date:

➤ Instead of teaching employees how to deal with specific problems, teach them how to identify and solve all problems.

➤ Place the ultimate responsibility for learning on the individual (or, in team learning, on the team). The person who conducts the training is a facilitator: Rather than spoon-feeding information to trainees, he or she guides them through the process and summarizes and reinforces the resulting insights.

➤ Make sure that people who will learn together share a common vocabulary, are trained to use the same analytical tools, and have communication channels available so that they can work together and with other people or teams within an organization. A company, through its training department or HR department, should provide these tools.

➤ To learn to solve problems, trainees should be encouraged to tap resources in other departments or from outside the company, such as customers, suppliers, and trade or professional associations.

➤ Enlist people from all job categories (managers, team leaders, human resources specialists, technicians in all fields) to be the facilitators. This not only expands a company's training resources but also helps develop future leaders.

Train for the Soft Skills

Much of the need for training is to improve members' abilities to communicate, to relate with other members, to deal with customers, to sell their ideas, and to develop other intangible assets. These are often referred to as the *soft skills*.

A study of training effectiveness by the American Society for Training and Development (ASTD) in 1999 brought out a startling discovery. Although American companies were spending huge amounts in training employees in information technology over the past five or six years, productivity gains have been only 1 percent to 1.5 percent per year. Why so poor?

The reason many experts offer is that, although we are building technical skills, we aren't investing enough in training the human side—the skills needed to deal with people. Without investing in people, all you have is a lot of machinery. It's essential to train people in the soft skills.

Team Terms

Soft skills are the skills needed to work effectively with other people. They include communications, interpersonal relations, leadership, and personal development.

This is not only true in the areas of high technology, but in every part of the organization. Most training of factory and office employees is on improving performance; most sales training concentrates on product knowledge. Time, money, and expertise must be given to the human side of the team members' activities.

As most team leaders don't have the expertise to conduct their own training programs in the soft skills, such programs are conducted by either the human resources department or outside consultants, schools, or training organizations.

Programs in selling, leadership, self-confidence, communications, public speaking, and more are available as in-house courses, or you can send team members to public seminars or classes. These programs are offered by individual consultants, college professors, training organizations, and others. They vary from one-day seminars to week-long retreats to weekly classes over several months. Charges range from payment of a fee for each attendee to a flat fee for the program.

Tips for Picking the Right Training Organization

If you choose to use an outside organization to conduct the training, choose wisely. A wrong choice will not only be a waste of your members' time and your company's money, but may result in developing habits and attitudes contrary to those you desire. Here are some suggestions:

1. Select a firm with professional credentials. It should be a member of the American Society for Training & Development (see Appendix B) or affiliated with a university or, in technical areas, with appropriate professional associations.

2. Ask managers of other companies for referrals. If they have used training organizations for similar problems, their recommendations will be valuable.

Heads Up!

When considering outside training, steer clear of programs that promise miracles. If they sound too good to be true, they are too good to be true. Your best bet is to use well-established, proven training programs.

3. Check out the firms that you are considering with other companies in your industry or area. Even if they haven't used them themselves, they may know of others who have.

4. Ask for references. Get the names of several past and present clients. Make sure you speak with clients who used the service several years ago. Ask them about the long-term values received from the training. Ask if they would use the firm again.

5. Sit in on a current training class. If the firm gives public programs, either attend a session yourself or send one of your members. If the type of program you want isn't offered publicly, but at another company, ask that company for permission to attend.

6. Ask to see a random selection of past program evaluations. Look for patterns of positive and negative factors. For example, I recently read a batch of evaluations that indicated the instructor was a dynamic, exciting speaker, but also noted that he did not encourage group participation. As participation was key to my client's objectives, we didn't select that trainer.

7. Who is going to do the instruction? Make sure that the instructor is an expert in the field in which you need help. One of my clients needed training in Total Quality Management and retained a prestigious consulting firm. But the trainer they assigned had only a superficial knowledge of that area. Interview the principal of the firm *and* the assigned instructor.

8. Be wary of programs that advertise training "gimmicks" that promise to give your employees motivational or improved interpersonal relations skills. Many of these programs are great fun to attend, but rarely provide long-term benefits. Over the years, programs such as EST, Theory Z, and others have come and gone.

Overcoming Resistance to Training

Team leaders may occasionally have members who resist going for training, especially in the soft skills. They feel it is a waste of time and are reluctant to admit they lack these intangible assets.

Of course, you can compel them to attend the sessions, but compulsion leads to resentment, defeating the purpose of the training.

FYI

According to the American Society for Training and Development, most training concentrates on managerial, supervisory, white-collar, salaried employees. There is still a large percentage of people who work in semiskilled jobs, and they're not getting the training they need to move up into the salaried and growing area of knowledge work. This training is essential if we are to meet the needs of industry for the next decade. Many companies that have a regular need for people with certain skills team up with local community colleges to train people in those skills—often providing financial aid, equipment, materials, and instructors.

Some suggestions to persuade them to accept these programs are

➤ Be frank with the member. Many people have no idea how they are perceived by others. Give them some examples of their behavior that illustrate their need for this training. Point out how similar programs have helped other members.

➤ Change the members' perspective. If they think of it as a waste of time and money, suggest they think of the training as an investment in themselves—a valuable asset that will not just improve their value to the team, but will enrich their lives.

➤ Meet with the member after each session and discuss what he or she learned and how it can be applied on the job.

➤ When they have completed the training, congratulate them in front of the entire team. Let every member know how proud you are of their accomplishment.

Companies should require all employees to take some form of training every year. If this is a standard practice and the programs taken in past years were interesting and productive, there will be little resistance by team members to enrolling in new programs.

Training Tools and Techniques

Training cannot be a haphazard process. To be effective, it must be planned and systematized. There are many techniques used by trainers.

Although some training is done by sending the member to a class or seminar outside the company, most team leaders train their members on the job; that is, they work with them as individuals. In addition, team leaders may conduct training meetings to teach the entire team a new procedure.

Team Terms

Job Instruction Training (JIT), a systematic approach to training people to perform tasks, involves four steps: preparation, presentation, performance, and postwork.

On-the-Job Training

There is an effective and relatively simple method for training members on the job. It's a systematic approach designed to train people to perform tasks. It is a four-step program known as *Job Instruction Training (JIT)*. The steps are the four P's—preparation, presentation, performance, and postwork.

➤ **Preparation.** Preparation is both physical and psychological. All *physical* equipment and facilities that are necessary for training should be in place before you begin. If you're training someone in a computer process, you should have on hand a computer, the software, the training manual, the data, and any other necessary material.

After you begin, you don't want to be interrupted by having to look for items you need. There is also a *psychological* part to this process. Before the training begins, trainees should be told what will be taught, why, and how it fits into the overall picture. When people can see the entire picture, not just their small part in it, they learn faster and understand more clearly, and they're more likely to remember what they've been taught.

➤ **Presentation.** It's no longer feasible to say to a trainee, "Just watch me, and do what I do." Work today is much too complex to learn just by observation. The following four steps can guide you in showing someone how to perform a task:

1. Describe what you're going to do.

2. Demonstrate step by step. As you demonstrate, explain each step and explain why it's done (for example, "Notice that I entered the order number on the top right side of the form to make it easy to locate").

3. Have the trainee perform the task and explain to you the method and reason for each step.

4. If the trainee doesn't perform to your satisfaction, have him repeat the task. If he performs well, reinforce the behavior with praise or positive comments.

➤ **Performance.** Once you're satisfied that a trainee can do a job, leave her alone and let her do it. The member needs an opportunity to try out what she has learned. She will probably make some mistakes, but that's to be expected. From time to time, check out how things are going and make necessary corrections.

➤ **Postwork.** The postwork step is important because people tend to change what they have been taught. Careless people may skip some steps in a procedure, causing errors or complications. Smart people may make changes that they believe work better than what they were taught. Although you should encourage your associates to try to find more effective approaches to their job, caution them not to make any changes until they have discussed them with you. They often may not be aware of the ramifications of their suggested changes.

Schedule postwork discussions of new assignments three to four weeks after the presentation step. At that time, review what the associate has been doing, and, if changes have been made intentionally or inadvertently, bring the person back on track.

Training Manuals—Gobbledygook or the Real Stuff?

Training manuals, or "do it by the numbers" handbooks, are helpful for teaching routine tasks. They make the training process easy for both the trainer and the trainees. Members can always refer to them when in doubt about what to do.

Unfortunately, some training manuals are poorly written and as confusing as the instructions that come with "assemble-it-yourself" products made in some faraway country; others are laced with technical terminology that is intelligible only to the engineers who wrote them.

Because today's jobs are becoming less and less routine, training manuals are often inadequate—to the point that they may even stifle creativity. Members tend to rely on the manual because it's easy, rather than think out new and possibly better approaches to dealing with a problem.

Interactive Training Meetings

Some team meetings are devoted primarily to training. In addition to the suggestions on conducting meetings made in Chapter 6, special steps should be taken to make training meetings more effective:

Heads Up!

Too often, when organizations decide to institute a training program, they pull from their files the training manuals or materials from a program that had previously been used. This is not necessarily bad, but before using existing materials, make sure that they were successful when previously used.

➤ Before calling the meeting, assess your training needs to determine which training is better done at a meeting, individually, or by sending the members to outside programs. Discuss this with the team members. Identify their individual concerns. Determine which members can be called upon to help conduct the training meeting.

➤ Establish the learning objectives. Determine the specific areas that the meeting will focus on. Show how this training will help the team meet its goals. Set up criteria on which the effectiveness of the training will be measured.

➤ Record what has been accomplished at the meeting. Have the team create a training manual based on what has been learned. This will help the team continue to improve and can be built on as new ideas develop.

Although the meeting can be chaired by the team leader, a member who is expert in the area covered may be tapped to run all or part of it. Occasionally, a member of another team, a specialist from another department, or an outside consultant may be invited to conduct training meetings. If nonteam members are used, prepare the team by identifying the background of the guest and explaining why this person is qualified to train the team in that subject.

Prepare the team to participate by giving members an outline of what will be covered. Suggest that they think of aspects of that area in which they are particularly interested and prepare questions for the presenter to answer and the participants to discuss at the meeting.

Computers As a Training Tool

Many companies have developed computer programs to train employees in a variety of areas. Such programs were initially designed for use in schools to enable students to learn at their own pace. Slower learners could take their time and repeat unclear sections until they understood them. Fast learners or students who had more background in an area could move quickly ahead, and students could test themselves as they progressed.

FYI

Online learning is not a panacea for workforce training, and it's highly unlikely it will ever wipe out live seminars or human instruction. But it's rapidly gaining support. The online learning market is expected to grow ninefold by the year 2001, reports *Training Magazine,* capturing a bigger share of the $60.7 billion budgeted this year for workplace training.

Because most companies have their own ways of doing things, generic programs, such as the ones used by schools, haven't been of much value. Some generic programs, however, such as those that teach basic accounting skills and various computer operations, can be a valuable asset to any organization. Check computer software catalogs to determine which programs might be valuable to you.

Some larger organizations have customized programs to meet their own needs. These programs are usually proprietary, however, and aren't made available outside the company that developed them. Perhaps you can also customize programs to meet your own requirements.

Over the past few years, more and more individuals and companies are turning to the Internet as a source for learning. Universities and private organizations offer courses and less formal study programs on hundreds of subjects. You can study a foreign language, learn basic or advanced math, acquire technical know-how, and even obtain a college degree.

New technologies make it possible for companies to provide training to employees located in several locations via the Internet. Team members can review what they learned in a class or on the job by checking a predetermined Web site.

The World Wide Web has made all sorts of education more accessible. The greatest potential for Web-based training is in job training. The convenience of the Internet makes it an appealing tool, both for time-strapped, ambitious workers and cost-conscious, skill-hungry employers. Many companies have ongoing training programs available on their intranet.

Teleconferencing

Sometimes the most effective way to train or retrain staff members is to hold meetings or classes at which employees from several locations are brought together for the training. This is a common practice among national and global organizations. It's also one of the most expensive ways to train. Not only do the participants take time off from their regular work for the training sessions, but there is additional downtime for getting to and from the training site. Travel, hotel, and meals, and often the cost of renting the training facility (for example, a conference center) add to the expense.

Team Terms

Teleconferencing: Using computer and video techniques to enable interactive meetings in which people in several locations participate.

One way to reduce the cost and time involved is *teleconferencing*. Using specially designed computer and TV equipment, participants can see, hear, and interact with the instructor and each other without going far from their bases. Many organizations have teleconferencing technology available in each of their facilities. Other companies use the services of teleconferencing firms that can set up such conferences wherever needed.

Cross-Training

Most teams divide work into special areas, and members are trained to work only in the areas for which they were hired. The advantage is that people become very proficient in their phase of the work, which leads to efficient, cost-effective production.

This may work well in simple operations where there are large numbers of people engaged in routine work, but as jobs have become more complex and sophisticated, and teams replace traditional work groups, one-skill activities are no longer practical.

Enhancing the Effectiveness of Teams

Everybody in the team should have enough knowledge of the work of all members of the team. Sometimes it is not feasible to cross-train every team member in the work of all of the others, but each should be able to pitch in and help others and be fully trained in the skills used by at least one other team member.

When team members have more than just a casual knowledge of the work of the others, they can work more closely with them, coordinate their work more effectively, and even make suggestions that can help team members in disciplines other than their own. When faced with special assignments, such as researching new projects, selecting new equipment or software, or selecting new team members, the training each has in the work of others will enable them to make more meaningful decisions.

Opposition to Cross-Training

Some people do not want to be cross-trained. They don't want to be shaken out of their comfort zones. To motivate these people to enthusiastically support cross-training, they must be shown how it will be beneficial to them. If it will lead to possible advancement, point out how this will be accomplished. (Caution: Do not make promises you may not be able to keep.) Describe how it will make their work more interesting. If there are several areas in which training will be offered, give them the opportunity to express which areas they would like to be trained in.

Some workers feel that if they add additional skills, they should receive higher compensation. Whether these new skills warrant salary increases is up to the company. In most cases, immediate salary adjustments are not merited, but should be considered in future reviews.

Team Builder

Cross-training is an important antidote to downsizing. If the company downsizes your team, other members are able to take over immediately.

Instituting the Program

In setting up a cross-training program, don't overwhelm members by giving them too much to learn all at once. It's best to train the members to perform the work of one associate. After they have mastered that job and practiced it for a period of time, you may start training them in the work of another associate.

Following are some cautions regarding setting up cross-training programs:

➤ **Training too many people in too many areas.** A good first step is to ask each member what additional job he or she would like to train for. It would be nice if every member could do every job, but in most teams that's not feasible.

➤ **Selecting members for cross-training in areas in which they don't have the prerequisite education or skills.** Many jobs require background that the member must bring to the job and that cannot be acquired by on-the-job training.

➤ **Letting team members train other members without training them in how to train.** The characteristics needed to be a good trainer are discussed later in this chapter.

➤ **Requiring members to do twice as much work.** This would include their own work plus taking the training. Adjust their workloads while they undergo training.

➤ **Failing to appreciate the work it took to acquire the new skills.** Recognize the completion of the training by congratulating the member. If the new skills warrant it, recommend a salary increase.

"Okay, I've learned my colleague's job, but when will I do it?"

Another problem in cross-training is that new skills are easily forgotten if not used. A good example of this is what happened when Arlene took maternity leave. Arlene's job in the team was processing orders. She checked the order against current inventory to determine if it could be filled from stock. If not, she sent a replacement order to the production department. Her work kept her very busy. When the team leader instituted a cross-training program, each team member had to teach her job to three other team members. Arlene spent several hours a day for a week training them how to handle her tasks.

After the training, all the members returned to doing their regular work. It was more than a year later when Arlene left on maternity leave for 12 weeks. Her work was divided among the members who had been trained in her job—but as none had even thought about the job since the original training, they all had to be retrained.

Heads Up!

Practice does *not* make perfect. If people practice doing things wrong, they become perfect in doing things wrong. Practice makes *permanent.* When you train associates, periodically check out what they're doing. If it's wrong, correct it immediately, before it becomes permanently ingrained as a bad habit.

To avoid this, the cross-training has to be reinforced over time. Periodic refreshers should be arranged for this purpose. Even better, require all members to work on the job for which they were cross-trained from time to time.

Training As a Team Activity

Just because you're the team leader doesn't mean that you have to train all your team members. The training function should be shared by everyone on the team. Some organizations encourage an entire team to share in the task of training new members; others assign one person to act as a mentor.

Determining who will train new members or be assigned to retrain others depends on what the member is being trained to do. *Caution:* A person who knows the job best isn't always the best qualified person to train others. It takes more than job knowledge to be an effective trainer.

Job know-how *is* essential for the person who will do the training, but it's only part of the picture. Look for these additional factors:

➤ **Personal characteristics.** Patience, empathy, and flexibility.

➤ **Knowledge of training techniques.** If a team member has the personal characteristics, he can learn the training techniques. Some companies provide "Train the Trainer" programs to build up the communications skills in people who will do the training.

➤ **A strong, positive attitude toward the job and the company.** If you assign a disgruntled person to do your training, that person will inject the trainee with the virus of discontent.

Whether the members will function in the future as permanent team leaders or take their turn in leading a self-directed team (see Chapter 24), training will be an essential part of their jobs. Time and effort spent in training members how to train is well worthwhile.

The Least You Need to Know

➤ The quality of the orientation for new members has an impact on their future performance, interaction with associates, job satisfaction, and even career progress.

➤ All members of your team need ongoing training. They should continually acquire new techniques and renew established skills. Always encourage self-development.

➤ Before choosing any training programs, the team leader should conduct a needs analysis.

➤ Trainers should not spoon-feed information to trainees, but should guide them through the process and summarize and reinforce the resulting insights.

➤ Much of the need for training is to improve members' soft skills.

➤ If you choose to use an outside organization to conduct the training, research it carefully and choose wisely.

➤ Companies should require all employees to take some form of training every year.

➤ An effective and relatively simple method for training members on the job to perform tasks is the four P's: preparation, presentation, performance, and postwork.

➤ The Internet makes training feasible for time-strapped, ambitious workers and cost-conscious, skill-hungry employers.

➤ Every team member should be able to pitch in and help others, and be fully trained in the skills used by at least one other team member.

➤ The training function should be shared by everyone on the team. New member training can be shared by an entire team or by one member assigned to act as a mentor.

Part 6

Special Teams for Special Purposes

Teams serve several purposes in an organization. Most teams are regular work groups that perform the routine activities that enable the organization to accomplish its goals. These teams manufacture products, distribute merchandise, handle financial transactions, provide customer service, and perform the day-to-day functions of the company.

Most of these teams have team leaders, appointed by management to guide and inspire the members, coordinate the work, and keep the team on target.

But there are other types of teams. Imagine a team without a leader! You'll learn in this section about teams that direct themselves, and teams that alternate leadership from project to project.

Here's another challenge to team leaders—leading a team drawn from several different departments, made up of members with different backgrounds, different viewpoints, and sometimes conflicting agendas. In this section you'll learn how to mold them into a collaborative team.

As companies spread out geographically, with employees in many remote locations, team members may work far apart from their associates. Later in this section we'll show you how to keep such teams productive.

The Self-Directed Team

Changing a work group into a team is much easier when there is a permanent team leader—a person appointed to organize the team, select the members, guide the team in setting up its mission and goals, and motivate associates to achieve them.

More radical, and much more difficult to implement, is the move to self-directed teams—teams with no formal leaders.

In this chapter we'll explore this newest variation on the team concept.

The Team with No Permanent Leader

At a meeting I conducted I asked what the participants thought would happen if a team did not have a leader. The most frequent response: *chaos*.

In the discussion that followed, concern was expressed that unless there was a person to whom team members could look for guidance, instruction, training, and motivation,

In **self-directed teams,** there are no formal or permanent leaders. Members may work collaboratively on projects or, if appropriate, select an associate to lead a specific project. All members can serve as temporary leaders when and if needed.

the members would each go his or her own way and goals could not be reached. Others were concerned that with no central control, the team would flounder and eventually collapse.

Actually, leaderless teams have existed successfully in various forms for centuries. For example, although most orchestras, marching bands and dance bands have conductors, there are many groups of musicians who play together as teams without formal leaders, such as string quartets and jazz combos. Research projects are usually performed by teams without formal leadership. Each member knows what has to be done and works to do it.

Structure of the Team

Self-directed teams are not structured much differently from leader-led teams—with the obvious exception that there is no leader.

Much depends on the function of the team in the organization. In some teams every member performs the same type of work. For example, a claims processing team in an insurance company is made up of claims clerks, each of whom handles one or more aspects of the process. They have similar backgrounds and do similar, but not identical work.

The accident prevention team in the same insurance company consists of members with different backgrounds: a mechanical engineer, an electrical engineer, a medical technician, a human resources specialist, and others. Each deals with a different phase of the work, but all work together to achieve the goal of reducing accidents.

If either type of team is converted from a traditional work group or a team with a leader to a self-directed team, the structure remains much the same. The job description for each member would not change. Each member knows what to do and how to do it.

Any difference in structure would be in the means of collaboration. In a leader-led team, assignments would be meted out by the leader. In the self-directed team, a system to distribute assignments must be developed by the team. This can be done at periodic planning meetings. Performance standards must be agreed upon, and as there is no leader to check performance, a means of self-evaluation (discussed later in this chapter) must be created.

Clarifying the Team's Mission

As noted earlier in this book, a team's mission should be fully understood and accepted by the team. Whether the team is leader-led or self-directed, the mission should be established collaboratively. It's not good team practice to have the leader dictate the mission to the members. However, due to his or her position, the leader has great influence in the manner in which the *mission statement* is worded and how it is understood by the members.

When there is no leader, there is much more pressure on the members to come up with a mutually satisfactory mission statement.

All team members should participate in developing the team's mission statement. They have to work with it and live by it. The best way to start is to form a committee of three or four members to draft the statement. Then have the entire team review and discuss it and come up with the final version.

Once the mission statement is composed, and approved by the manager, copies should be given to each member and to everybody else who is affected by it—especially customers, both internal and external.

Project Leaders

Many team activities are in the form of projects. Some teams, like the claims team, perform routine work, where projects are not often called for. However, if a new type program is instituted or new equipment is being considered, project subteams may be created to deal with them.

Team Builder

In converting to a self-directed team, modify the current job descriptions to give members more control over making decisions. Specify what matters must be referred to the team as a whole.

Team Terms

The team's **mission statement** indicates the purpose of the team, whom the team serves (its customers), the values it wishes to project about service and quality, and the contribution it aims to make. The **vision statement** is more like a motto—a condensed version of the mission statement.

Other teams, such as the safety team, work primarily on projects. They may be short-term projects, such as investigating an unsafe situation and coming up with suggestions on correcting it. They may be long-term projects, such as developing an entire safety program for a client.

In either case, the manner in which the project is planned and implemented is the same. Let's look at an example.

Heads Up!

Team members should be careful not to let a few team members dominate the team by volunteering to be project leaders for every new assignment. If the volunteer has headed a project recently, another member should be given the chance to lead.

One of the clients of the insurance company has been charged by OSHA (Occupational Safety and Health Administration) with several violations. The client has asked the company to study the problems and suggest solutions. As this falls within the mission of the safety team, it is given the assignment.

A meeting is held to discuss the project. The first step is to appoint a project leader to manage the assignment. Any member can be chosen for this temporary leadership role. In most teams, every member will act as project leader at one time or another.

Who picks the project leader? In some cases, a volunteer is sought. Jim, the mechanical engineer, says, "I've worked on similar mechanical problems at another plant, I'll take the lead." Sally, the HR representative, points out that she's had experience working on OSHA complaints, and she'll be glad to either lead or serve on the project. A discussion is held on which one could contribute the most, and the team agrees that Jim should be project leader and Sally and three other members will make up the project subteam.

In some teams, project leadership is rotated. A member comments, "Jim, you headed the last project, let Sally head this one." Jim agrees to this and will serve as a subteam member.

There are times when nobody wants the assignment. As there is no boss to appoint a project leader, the team has to work it out and persuade a member to take the task.

Project leader is a temporary assignment and there is no added compensation for the role. There are no special benefits. However, it gives the member good experience in leadership and prepares him or her for eventual career advancement.

In addition to the project leader, other members may be given specific roles in the project. In this example, problems are analyzed, and members decide to address the area of plant layout. One member is chosen to evaluate the current layout and research alternatives. One of the problems in the plant layout involves chemical emissions. A member with a background in chemistry is added to the team to work on this. Many of OSHA's complaints concern interpretation of their regulations. Sally's been through this before, so she'll handle it.

The subteam will meet on a regular basis to report on its progress and exchange ideas. The entire team will discuss the project at regular team meetings. Often, team members who are not working on that particular project have experience, or can contribute ideas, that help move the project forward.

Self-Direction Requires Self-Motivation

Without a team leader to prod the members, to coach them, to inspire them, to cheer them on, who's going to motivate the team? They have to motivate themselves.

When things are not going right, each member must be able motivate him- or herself, and give a boost to teammates.

FYI

"A completely diverse group must agree on a goal, put the notion of individual accountability aside and figure out how to work with each other. Most of all, they must learn that if the team fails, it's everyone's fault."

—Douglas K. Smith, coauthor of *The Wisdom of Teams*

Commit Yourself to Achievement

A self-motivated team must be made up of self-motivated members who are dedicated to achievement. They want to accomplish their goals and will work to overcome obstacles. Here are some suggestions to help individual members become self-motivated:

1. Set clear and specific goals and work to achieve them.

Diane had great ideas, but was shy about expressing them to her team. Her personal goal was to be able to get up at a meeting and present her ideas without faltering or stammering.

To do this, she enrolled in a public-speaking course. She was a good student and was able to make several good talks to her class, but when she raised her hand at a meeting, she reverted to her old habits and was unable to talk coherently.

She resolved to overcome this, and after the course ended, at the suggestion of her teacher, she joined the local Toastmaster's Club—a group at which members give short talks at every meeting. This gave her more experience and built up her self-confidence, which carried over into the team meetings. Today she is an articulate participant in team discussions.

2. Make a contract.

A contract is a binding agreement. Rocco, a member of a financial team, knew that an MBA would be a great asset to his career. He registered for evening courses at a local

Team Builder

When the whole team is involved in establishing goals and determining how to reach them, the energy and effort put into achieving them is increased exponentially.

university. The company's tuition reimbursement program would pay all of his tuition if he maintained a B average. At the end of his first semester, he fell short. He had to get at least one A and two Bs in the second semester to get full reimbursement.

To ensure that he would do this, he drew up a contract with himself specifying his commitment to raise his grades and listing what steps he would take to accomplish this. When difficulties arose or he was tempted to slacken his efforts, he reread the contract and renewed his commitment.

3. Share it with another person.

The great writer on self-motivation, Napoleon Hill, recommended that you share your commitment with another person. Rocco gave a copy of his contract to his teammate, Eric, and had him sign it as a witness. Eric promised Rocco that he would keep after him to do the work needed to get those grades. Rocco credits Eric's support with helping him achieve the goal.

4. Give yourself a pep talk.

For years coaches have been giving pep talks to inspire their teams. When you are feeling down, when you need an extra push to accomplish a mission, give yourself a pep talk.

Lisa's goal was to become a medical secretary. She completed the courses required and set out to find a job. After several rejections due to her lack of work experience, she became discouraged. When she went to her next interview, she thought, "What's the use? I'll run into the same thing again." However, she determined that she would fight to get this job. She gave herself a pep talk. "I want this job and I have the technical know-how. I am a diligent and conscientious worker. I can do this job and will be a real asset to this doctor." She repeated this over and over again on the way to the doctor's office. Her self-confidence and enthusiasm manifested itself in her answers to his questions, and she was offered the job.

Some months later the doctor told her that when he saw from her application that she had no work experience, he had decided to give her just a courtesy interview and reject her. But her enthusiasm convinced him to try her. She carried that enthusiasm into the work itself and became a very successful medical secretary.

Team Goal Setting

When members are active participants in establishing the mission and determining the goals, they will be enthusiastic about them.

The team members at a newly created software development company were asked to set the team's goals. Before the first meeting, each member was given a statement of the purpose for which the team was formed and the general areas in which it would function.

1. At the first meeting of the team, they set up a formula as to how they would tackle the assignment.

2. Each team member brought to the next meeting a draft of the goals and expectations that he or she considered should be included in the team goals.

3. The team members evaluated the drafts and, through the consensus process, reached agreement on the goals and determined what should be done to implement them.

4. Several members volunteered to work on performance standards for each phase of the projects planned.

5. After studying the final version of the goals and standards, each member chose the projects to which they felt they could contribute most effectively.

The team moved ahead on its self-chosen assignments with great enthusiasm and alacrity.

Total Team Involvement

An advantage of working in a team is that each team member helps motivate the others. If one member feels low, his colleagues can help him get over it. If another is stressed out, her associates can assist her with stress reduction exercises.

But team involvement is more than just one member helping another. In Chapter 16 suggestions were made on how a team leader can work to make the team self-motivating. Here is a quick review of some of these suggestions and how they can be applied when there is no leader to guide the team:

Heads Up!

Everybody in the team should be included in all team celebrations—not just those on the project sub-team that achieved their goal. This solidifies team spirit and reminds all members that every success within the team reflects on the team as a whole.

➤ Establish a climate in which members feel free to innovate and express themselves without fear. When there is no team leader to criticize innovations or ideas, this climate of free expression is built into the atmosphere. The danger is members' fear of being in a minority and being overruled by a dominant majority. Dissension and expression of contrary opinions is what leads to successful consensus. When members know that their opinions—whether accepted or rejected—are always welcome, it enhances not only their motivation, but that of the entire team.

355

Team Builder

When we are enthusiastic about something, no matter how difficult it may be, it seems easy. The excitement, the joy, the inner feeling of satisfaction permeates the entire activity.

➤ Members must learn to put aside their personal agendas for the benefit of the team. With no leader to keep the team members in line, the team must monitor itself. More time must be spent in team meetings working out internal conflicts and molding the members into a synergistic group.

➤ Provide team rewards for successful achievements. In a leader-led team, it is the team leader's responsibility to recommend raises, decide on bonuses, and set up tangible incentives for members. When there is no team leader, the determination of rewards is more complex. In some firms, the manager to whom the team reports has full control over this, but more and more self-directed teams are creating their own reward programs within guidelines set by the company. This often takes the form of special rewards for reaching or exceeding quotas or meeting or beating deadlines.

As noted earlier in this book, rewards need not be tangible to be effective. Praise by higher levels of management, public acknowledgment of team successes, and similar forms of recognition are good motivators.

Self-directed teams often mark their successes with team celebrations. When a project is completed, the entire team takes an extended lunch hour for a celebratory meal or an afternoon off for a family picnic.

Getting the Self-Directed Team Underway

Before setting up a self-directed team, the company should determine if the work involved can be most effectively performed within that structure. If the team philosophy fits company strategy, and if management is willing to make a long-term commitment to the process, it should proceed as follows:

1. Fill the team with men and women who are capable of thinking and acting as individuals and are not dependent on being hand-fed by a boss.

2. Create accountability for members' work. Standards should be established against which members can measure their own progress. There's no team leader to do it for them.

3. Empower the team. The team must be given the authority to make decisions, carry them out, and accept responsibility for their success or failure.

4. Train members both in the technical phases of their jobs and in how to work together as a team.

New teams often have a hard time getting under-way. Members are not accustomed to working without a leader, and there will be times when they just don't know how to proceed. Companies that have been successful in using self-directed teams recognize that it takes time to make them work. Some companies have a team coordinator on the management staff to help new teams over the fits and starts of maturing. Others retain outside consultants to keep an eye on teams by being available for training, and counsel teams and team members when necessary to keep teams on track.

Heads Up!

Team members: Don't lose heart if things don't work out great from the start. It takes time for a new team to mature. People who have always worked under strict leadership must learn to work as a collaborative group without a boss. Managers: Be patient. Keep supporting the teams. In the long run, it will pay off.

Rethinking the Job

Before you can enter into a new situation, you have to end what used to be. It is difficult to give up the habits, practices, and thought patterns that have dominated your life. Too many such changes is synonymous with loss. You are indeed losing a safe and familiar situation and moving into strange and often frightening circumstances.

But as in any loss, it is necessary to let go of the old. It is never easy to detach oneself from the past. It is unsettling and disturbing. You've grown accustomed to working in one way, and now you must work in an entirely different manner. Some people become angry, others sad, still others confused—many suffer from all of these emotions before they finally let go of the old and embrace the new.

The transition is not easy. You often hear gripes and comments decrying the changes, and expressions of longing to go back to the old, safe, and familiar ways, rather than push forward into unknown territory.

Some members are assailed by doubt, fear, and anxiety. They are not quite certain how they will fit into the self-directed team.

A period of transition is needed to take members through the process of change, enabling them to resolve their doubts and fears. They must redefine their roles, renew their commitments, and re-create their approaches.

Once the transition is complete, new beginnings replace old ways. The members are ready to accept their new status. Fear and uncertainty are replaced by confidence and enthusiasm.

They become accustomed to the new thinking and new approaches to the work. They see that things they thought were not possible are actually happening. This results in renewed self-confidence, a sense of belonging, and excitement. Their role in the self-directed team is embraced, and they make commitments to ensure its success.

Redesigning the Work

When work is done by self-directed teams, the concept of breaking a job down into simple repetitive tasks supervised closely by a boss is replaced by a system of production developed by the team empowered with the authority and responsibility to do it.

Jobs must be redesigned to give the team member enough leeway to approach them with intelligence, innovation, and concern for customer satisfaction.

FYI

Simplifying work by breaking it down into its basic components was initially described by Adam Smith in his *Wealth of the Nations* and brought into modern management by Frederick Taylor, the founder of "scientific management."

Here are some guidelines for redesigning a job to fit into the self-directed team concept:

1. Don't limit the job to a "one-skill" operation. The greater the variety of skills and talents needed, the more opportunity to be creative. If members can be trained in several skill areas, they can work together on all phases of a project.

2. Enrich the job. Instead of individual members performing each phase of a job, design the job so that it can be carried through to completion collectively. For example, in an advertising agency, it's customary for one person to write copy, another to edit it, another to present it to the client, still another to deal with the media in which it will appear. In an enriched job, one member or a team or sub-team would collaborate on all phases of the job from the beginning to the end.

3. Allow team members to do significant work. Sure, every job has its drudge factor—unrewarding work that must be done. By not making that drudge work a job in itself, in which the performers can get no real satisfaction, design it as a small part of a major job that leads to achieving a desired goal.

4. Give members the authority, the freedom, and the discretion to plan, organize, schedule, and perform the work.

5. Set up a self-appraisal system, so that team members always know what is expected of them. That way, they can measure their activities against standards on an ongoing basis and make immediate adjustments if standards are not being met.

Evaluating Performance

In a traditional work group and in a leader-led team, performance appraisal of individual members is done by the supervisor or team leader. In the self-directed team, there is no leader. Who will evaluate performance?

There are several approaches to this. Let's look at a few of them:

Replace appraisals of individuals with team appraisals. This is based on the

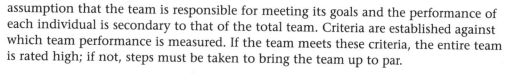

Team Builder

Self-directed teams should establish a feedback system that will enable all members to see, at any time, the progress of every member as it relates to the projects being worked on. Members can keep tabs on their colleagues' progress and avoid being surprised when their own work is held up because of a glitch in a teammate's activity.

assumption that the team is responsible for meeting its goals and the performance of each individual is secondary to that of the total team. Criteria are established against which team performance is measured. If the team meets these criteria, the entire team is rated high; if not, steps must be taken to bring the team up to par.

Team members are expected to help each other. Members with greater knowledge of an area will teach those with less; members will motivate each other and work to build up the productivity of all.

Salary increments and other rewards are based on the team's accomplishments and shared equally among the members.

The danger here is that weak members will depend on their more effective associates to carry the ball. Stronger members may resent this and seek jobs elsewhere.

Self-evaluation. Members appraise their own work. The criteria are set by the team for all the jobs that they are commissioned to perform, and by the project subteams for new projects. Members know exactly what is expected of them and can check their progress on an ongoing basis. If quality is below standards, production behind schedule, or there are other deviations from the standards, corrections can be made immediately.

If the company requires annual or periodic formal appraisals, members report on their own work, matching results against the standards. The member is rated on the basis of the results achieved.

Heads Up!

Although self-evaluation is an important component of the self-directed team, to obtain comprehensive appraisals of a team member's effectiveness, also use some form of peer evaluation.

The downside of self-evaluation is that, although it works well in measuring tangible results, it doesn't take into consideration the member's soft skills. One cannot objectively rate one's own abilities to relate with other members, communicate effectively, or participate effectively in team activities. Self-evaluation has to be supplemented by another opinion.

Peer evaluation can take several forms. In Chapter 12, I discussed peer appraisals in some detail. As noted in that discussion, some companies require all members to appraise all other members, and the evaluations are discussed at an open meeting or in private sessions between the team leader and the member.

Open meetings tend to put the member whose appraisal is being discussed on the defensive. He may feel everybody is ganging up on him. Negative comments are blown out of proportion, and constructive advice is not listened to. A member may resent what another member says, destroying any rapport that existed between them.

In the leader-led team, this can be obviated by having the team leader present a summary of the appraisals without mentioning who said what, which can have a constructive result. But in the self-directed team there is no leader to do this.

One of my clients had a team of 14 members. The amount of time it would take for all members to evaluate each of the others and then conduct a meeting to discuss all the evaluations would be excessive. I suggested that instead of a total peer evaluation, each member be rated by three other members. The raters were chosen by lot. After the evaluations were made, one of the raters was chosen by the group to discuss the evaluation with the member. This reduced the time significantly and was very effective as an appraisal approach.

I used a variation on this for a smaller team—only six members. Here all six rated the other members, but instead of a total team meeting, one member was chosen by the team to study the evaluations of another member and discuss it with her.

The Successful Team

Successful self-directed teams differ in many ways. Each has its own goals and aspirations. Each is influenced by the personalities of its members. But all have some characteristics in common:

1. The members are enthusiastic about the team.
2. They have clear-cut goals to which they are committed.
3. Members participate actively in team meetings and other team activities.
4. Ongoing training in both technical and soft skills is a regular team procedure.

5. Members mentor each other.

6. The team sets standards for its jobs, and means of measuring them.

7. The team looks at projects creatively and approaches them with intelligence and innovation.

8. All members are involved in hiring and disciplining.

9. All members are given opportunity to lead projects.

10. The team's first priority is satisfying its customers—whether they are internal or external.

The Least You Need to Know

➤ Self-directed teams have no formal or permanent leaders. Members may work collaboratively on projects or select an associate to lead a specific project.

➤ In converting to a self-directed team, modify the current job descriptions to give members more control over making decisions.

➤ In most teams, every member will act as project leader at one time or another.

➤ Projects are discussed at regular team meetings. Often, team members who are not working on that particular project can contribute ideas that help move it forward.

➤ A self-motivated team must be made up of self-motivated members who are dedicated to achievement.

➤ When members are active participants in establishing the mission and determining the goals, they will be enthusiastic about them.

➤ An advantage of working in a team is that each team member helps motivate the others.

➤ Companies that have been successful in using self-directed teams recognize that it takes time to make them work.

➤ To obtain comprehensive appraisals of a team member's effectiveness, some form of peer evaluation should be used in addition to self-evaluation.

Chapter 25

Cross-Functional Teams

Most teams are made up of people working in the same department and performing closely related work. However, from time to time situations develop that are best dealt with by forming a team composed of representatives of several departments. Often these are temporary teams that are dissolved when the project is completed. As a team leader you may be asked to head up such a team from time to time.

Sometimes they are permanent teams designed to deal with an ongoing situation in which expertise from several departments is required. Such teams may be led by a permanent team leader or may function as a self-directed team.

In this chapter we'll look at how these teams operate, some of the problems that arise, and what the team leader can do to convert such diverse groups into collaborative teams.

Team Terms

Cross-functional teams, sometimes called **multidepartmental teams,** work on assignments in which the expertise of members of diverse departments is needed. For example, they may be composed of representatives of finance, marketing, engineering, and human resources.

Forming Teams for Special Projects

Many teams work regularly on routine activities. They assemble products in the factory, handle customer relations over the telephone, process mortgages in a bank—in other words, perform the daily tasks needed to make an organization operate smoothly. From time to time they may be assigned special projects related to their regular work. For example, the customer relations team may be assigned a project to solve a persistent problem bothering a customer.

Other teams work on a project basis. A team in an advertising agency may work on designing a marketing campaign for a client. When it is completed, the team is assigned another marketing project.

Ad Hoc (Temporary) Teams

Occasionally, situations arise in an organization that require know-how from several departments. Teams may be formed, often on a temporary basis, to deal with it. These teams are referred to as *cross-functional teams* or *multidepartmental teams.*

Let's look at how the Simmons Distributing Company planned and executed its move to a new facility a few miles away.

In 1998, Harry Simmons, founder and CEO of an auto parts distribution and warehousing company, decided to move from his crowded space in downtown Pittsburgh to a new building in an industrial park a few miles out of town. He selected a task force to plan the move. Because of the multitude of aspects to such a move, he drew the team from several departments.

The team consisted of one representative each from operations, shipping, marketing, finance, and human resources. He appointed Andy, his executive assistant, team leader.

At the first meeting, Harry gave a short presentation of what he wanted accomplished and turned the meeting over to Andy. The objective was to move the entire company into the new building over the weekend of April 3 and 4 and be ready to get into full operation Monday, April 5, with a minimum of downtime.

The team broke down the operation. Each member would look into what had to be done in his or her special field. The finance member would negotiate the cost of the move, the marketing person would plan how to deal with customers to accelerate or delay shipments during the move, the operations member would arrange for setting up the plant layout, and the HR member would arrange the work schedules.

Because the work involved would take all of their time, the members were relieved of all other duties until the move was completed.

Over the next few months, the team met regularly to report progress and get assistance from other members whenever they ran into a problem in which another team member had know-how.

In the week before the move, all desks, equipment, and other items to be moved were labeled and coded. Locations in the new building were numbered, and employees were given maps showing where to report on Monday. On Friday evening, the team checked everything at both facilities, and on Saturday the movers moved the furniture to the new location. On Sunday a team of workers put everything in place, and on Monday morning, everybody reported to the new building and was ready to work a normal workday.

Team Builder

In creating a temporary cross-functional team, make sure each member knows the capabilities of the other members and feels free to call on them for help when needed.

A week after the move, the team met for the last time to summarize its work and make a final report to Mr. Simmons, who thanked them and dissolved the team. Members returned to their regular work with a feeling of satisfaction about their accomplishments.

What did we learn from the Simmons experience? When a group of dedicated members collaborates with each other—even in areas that are outside of their regular activities—seemingly difficult and complex tasks can be accomplished.

Sometimes temporary teams are formed for much less demanding assignments. One of my clients, a real estate management firm, created a temporary cross-functional team to deal with a special situation. The tenants at one of their malls wanted to run an open-air fair to attract customers on a summer weekend when business was usually slow. The management firm agreed to cooperate.

The team consisted of five members: two from sales, and one each from operations, marketing, and human resources. The fair was scheduled for the third weekend in July. The team met for the first time in May and chose the member from the marketing department as team leader. Each member was given a choice of assignments and asked to spend about two hours a week on the project. They met weekly, and brainstormed ideas to make the program successful. The sales members acted as liaison with the store owners; the other members drew from their experience ideas for promoting the fair, staffing the exhibits, coordinating with the stores, and arranging for the mayor and other political leaders to put in an appearance.

The fair came off on schedule and was a great success. The team members were able to continue to do their regular work and enjoyed this diversion from the routine.

Permanent Teams

In some situations, cross-functional teams are established on a permanent basis. They are usually not full-time assignments, but additions to the members' regular work.

Many companies have cross-functional teams to search for and develop new products or services. Such teams work on an ongoing basis, meeting periodically (usually monthly) to examine suggestions that are referred to them by fellow employees, the company research and development departments, or outside organizations.

Because any new product or service must be looked at from all angles, the team will have members drawn from engineering, finance, marketing, and manufacturing or, in a service business, operations. Each can contribute his or her expertise to the analysis and make recommendations to senior management.

Participation in this team takes relatively little time from the members' regular assignments, and they continue to serve in their regular teams or departments.

Heads Up!

Don't keep picking the same people to serve on part-time teams. It's not fair to their regular team leader, and it's not fair to them. Give others the opportunity to serve.

Creating the Team

When a cross-functional team is formed, the members are usually chosen by a member of management to whom all of the departments from which members will be selected report. This often is the CEO or an executive vice president.

Often this executive will select the team leader, who will work with him or her in picking the team members. In some cases the team leader is chosen after the team is formed from among the members. In other cases the members elect their leader.

In selecting the team, these guidelines should be followed:

➤ **Know the job.** Before selecting a team member, clarify just what the job calls for. In most cases, this will not be a full-time assignment. The team needs people who can contribute a specific type of expertise.

The person or group that is forming the team should write a statement of what the team's function will be and what is expected from each member. This tentative analysis will help determine the makeup of the team. Once the team is formed, they will study it and fill in the details.

A tentative job description should be designed to indicate what will be expected of each member.

➤ **Know a good deal about the people selected.** In a smaller organization, the senior executive may know most of the employees. She knows that Christine's background is marketing to retailers or that Joel's knowledge of electronics would add value to the team.

In larger firms it's not likely that the executive who selects the team knows the potential members personally. She would have to get recommendations from knowledgeable people.

One source is the human resources department. If there is a job bank, each employee's skills, experience, and other background information can be retrieved by searching it. If there is no computerized job bank, the HR staff can pick out personnel records of possible choices for consideration.

Probably the best approach is to ask for recommendations from the team leader or department head of the team(s) in which the type member that is being sought is most likely to be working.

➤ **Select the best candidate.** From the various sources used, select several prospects in each function. Review their records. Interview them. Talk to their team leaders. Pick the ones you feel can contribute the most to the team's mission.

➤ **Persuade the team leader.** Team leaders are often not willing to release any of their valuable members—even for short-term assignments. Successful team members are usually busily engaged in work for their regular teams. Taking them away from it cannot help but affect the team's productivity.

The senior executive to whom this new team will report should discuss the assignment with the team leader of the prospective member's current team. This delicate job should *not* be done by the new team's leader. It needs the clout of the senior manager.

Point out the importance of the assignment. Specify how much time will be needed away from the regular work. If necessary, agree to provide a temp worker or in some other way help the leader make up for lost production.

➤ **Persuade the member.** Members chosen for part-time teams are not necessarily thrilled. It means more work and it rarely, if ever, leads to more money. Explain the team's mission to the prospect; show how important it is to the company. Emphasize how much fun the job is, and what it will mean to his future in the company and his career.

Develop Collaboration

When any new team is formed, it takes time to develop that spirit of collaboration that is essential for it to succeed. In a cross-functional team, this is even more difficult, as the members come from different departments, have different backgrounds, and think differently from one another.

FYI

Although they don't refer to it by that name, senior management for all companies operate as cross-functional teams. The CEO is the team leader, and the members usually are vice presidents of marketing, manufacturing, finance, operations, human resources, and other major areas.

A good way for the team leader to get started is to bring this up at the first meeting. Ask the members about their perception of the departments the others come from, the fears they have, and how they may resolve them.

I attended an early meeting of a team that was made up of finance, sales, and technical members. Here are some comments that were brought up:

> Sales member: In my dealings with the technical people, I find they take much too long to make decisions. We need action, and we need it ASAP.

> Tech member: It's more important to do it right than do it fast.

> Finance member: But don't forget costs. We must stay within budget.

The team leader has to find a means of getting each member to see and understand the viewpoints of the others, and then help find a mutually satisfactory solution. It's never easy, but with patience, willingness to compromise, and innovative approaches, collaboration can be attained.

Assign Work

In any team, the work is broken down and various members are given assignments. In a cross-functional team, it's logical to assign those aspects of the work that are in a member's special area of expertise to that member. That's the main reason for having cross-functional teams.

However, there are times when it is advantageous to assign more than one member to a segment of the job. Sometimes, there's only one specialist in that field on the team. If the job requires additional specialized knowledge, a person who knows that area but is not on the team may be enlisted to help. But often, the specialized member can be aided by a team member from another specialty. This gives the member a chance to see the task from a different view and acquire new knowledge. It also helps develop the collaborative efforts so important to team achievement.

Barriers to Cross-Functional Teams

Making any team succeed is hard work; it's even harder when members come from diverse and often conflicting backgrounds.

What Problems?

Let's look at some of the problems that impede cross-functional teams:

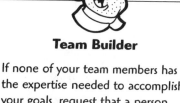

Team Builder

If none of your team members has the expertise needed to accomplish your goals, request that a person with that know-how be added to the team for the duration of that project.

➤ Members tend to look upon themselves as representatives of their department or discipline, instead of as team members. When problems are discussed, their focus is, "How will this affect my department?" rather than, "What's the best solution?"

➤ Members, when dealing with a problem in their special area, often make decisions without consulting other team members. For example, a sales member in a customer relations team may make commitments to customers that cannot be fulfilled. Had she discussed it with the team, she would have learned that key resources were not available to keep the commitment.

➤ Team members tend to express themselves in their own jargon, not realizing that other members misunderstand their comments, or don't understand them at all. When communication fails, team collaboration fails.

➤ Some members will not share information with other members because, as they come from a different discipline, they believe they're not competent to understand it.

➤ Members move too quickly to accept an early suggested solution rather than encourage exploration of other solutions.

➤ Members tend to denigrate members of other disciplines. For example, engineers may feel marketing people are not as "professional" as they are in examining problems.

➤ Members talk too much and listen too little. This is particularly true of members who talk for a living, such as salespeople and public relations staff.

To overcome some of these barriers to team success, members must first become aware of their own negative behavior patterns and take steps to learn and use different approaches to team activity.

FYI

It's normal for members to carry over into a cross-functional team the philosophy and behavior developed in their regular teams. Team leaders must recognize this and show the members that, although the teams' goals may differ, they are still working for the same organization. To accomplish what the organization desires, they must rethink their perception of their roles and change behavior accordingly.

So, How Do We Solve Them?

Building team spirit in a cross-functional team is not much different from building team spirit in any team, with a few additions. If you are team leader of such a team, here are some suggestions:

1. Review all of the previous chapters. They're loaded with ideas on building a collaborative team.

2. Once the team develops its goals, the team leader should draw out from each member his or her perception of the goals. The entire team should have the same understanding of the goals. If not, lead a discussion on the differences and work up an acceptable consensus.

3. From the very first meeting of the team emphasize the need for all members, no matter what discipline they were trained in, to think in terms of the team's mission and objectives—not those of their previous or current full-time team goals—when working on this team's projects.

4. If controversies develop between members from different disciplines (for example between members from sales and those from finance), settle them rapidly.

If you don't, members from the other disciplines represented on the team will take sides, and the collaborative effort will be stalled or even destroyed.

5. If there are a few members who don't understand their roles in a cross-functional activity, work with them to change their concept. Ask a member whose background is similar to theirs to take an active part in training them. For example, if the problem member is from a technical area, have a member from the technical side assist in the training.

Heads Up!

Never forget the purpose of the team. Don't let the team get bogged down in minutia and nit-picking. Keep all members alert to the goals, and work with them to accomplish them.

6. Welcome diverse opinions. When members know that their ideas are welcomed, they become more participative and more willing to collaborate on final decisions. Seeing things from the team viewpoint does not mean that all members should see things in the same way. As long as the objectives are the same, differing opinions on analyzing and solving problems can result in better decisions.

7. Maintain mutual esteem. One of the ingredients of a good team spirit is that all members respect their associates and recognize their capabilities. This is especially important in a cross-functional team, where members from one discipline may feel superior to members of others.

Engineers are notorious for looking upon members from other disciplines as inferior, and denigrating their ideas as "soft" or "simplistic." College grads may think of themselves as superior to skilled craftsmen, who in turn look down on anyone on the team who "never got his hands dirty getting out the work."

No matter what the education or skill level of a team member, each has much to contribute, or he or she would not have been appointed to the team. Team leaders can help change these attitudes by praising the suggestions and accomplishments of each member at team meetings, and letting each person know he or she is respected. As the other members begin to recognize the assets of their teammates, the snobbishness will be ameliorated.

8. Sharpen intrateam communications. Team leaders should make it easy for team members to communicate with each other. If all the members are in the same location, informal minimeetings can be called at a moment's notice to deal with a problem. If members are dispersed over several locations, e-mail and the company intranet can keep them in touch. Members should be encouraged to meet one-on-one or in small groups at any time.

9. Coordinate with the members' full-time team leaders. As many cross-functional teams are part-time assignments, the members spend most of their time doing their regular work in their full-time team. The work of the special team takes them away from their regular job periodically. As noted previously, their regular team leaders agreed to this when the members were selected for the team.

   In most cases, weekly or monthly team meetings are held on a regular basis. Much of the team's work can be done after regular working hours or at times when things are slow in the permanent team.

   However, there are times when the work of the cross-functional team does require additional time off from the members' regular work. When this happens, the cross-functional team leader should speak to the leaders of the members' regular teams to arrange for the necessary time.

10. Keep top management informed. One of the reasons given to members to join part-time teams is that it's good for their careers. The team leader should report periodically on the team's progress to the senior executives. In these reports make special mention of achievements of members who contributed maximally to the work of the team.

Completing the Assignment

Although many cross-functional teams are permanent and work on ongoing matters, most cross-functional teams are created to work on a specific project. When the project is completed, the team is dissolved.

Let's look at how the Sweet Sixteen Cosmetics Company used a temporary cross-functional team to plan and implement the introduction of a new product line.

Sweet Sixteen, a manufacturer of cosmetics designed for teenagers and young women, planned to introduce a fragrance line.

As Sweet Sixteen had never made perfumes, Diane, the CEO, opted to subcontract the manufacture and bottling to a specialist in that field. The purchasing department was designated as liaison with the manufacturer. A team was appointed to prepare the introduction to the market; it consisted of representatives of marketing, sales, distribution, and purchasing. Members were detached from their regular work for the duration of the assignment.

Deadlines and Time Frames

Karen, the product manager for the new line, was appointed team leader. At the first meeting, goals were established and assignments were made. They had eight months to develop the program and get the product into the stores.

At the meeting, the team broke the project into basic assignments, divided the work according to the backgrounds of the members, and agreed to meet in two weeks with a tentative timetable for each phase.

Karen's main job at this point was to ensure that the time frames were realistic and coordinated. For example, the sales reps couldn't start selling until samples were available, prices established, and advertising copy prepared. The distribution people had to have firm dates from purchasing as to when the subcontractor would deliver the product. Marketing had to coordinate corporate advertising, and cooperative advertising with retailers, public relations, and sales.

Measure Progress

Once the schedules were approved and deadlines established, Karen set up a control sheet to measure progress. She chose to use a Gannt chart, in which completion of work could be measured against projected time.

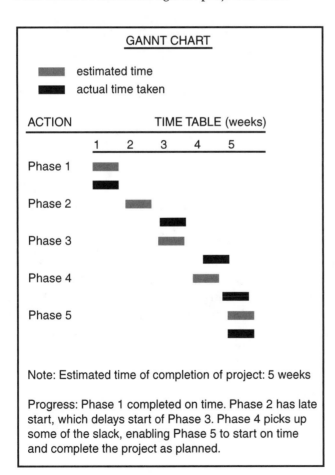

If any phase of any of the assignments fell behind, extra effort was put in to catch up.

Establish Criteria

Time alone is not the only measure of the progress of a project. Criteria should be established for every phase of the team's work.

As noted several times in this book, such criteria should be developed by the team members themselves, not superimposed on them by an outside authority.

FYI

W. Edwards Deming, the guru of the Total Quality Management concept, commented that "80 percent of American managers cannot answer with any confidence these seemingly simple questions: 'What is my job? What in it really counts? How well am I doing?'"

In the Sweet Sixteen project, Karen and her team set standards for each phase. Some examples follow:

➤ The sales segment of the project will have been completed when kits containing sample bottles, descriptive literature, price lists, and co-op advertising offers were satisfactorily completed. Time frames were established for each phase.

➤ The marketing segment of the project will have been completed when an estimated sales report by region has been compiled; advertising copy written, approved, and space purchased in magazines; endorsements by "teen idols" contracted; and a co-op advertising program for retailers prepared for the sales reps.

➤ The distribution segment of the project will have been completed when a delivery schedule from the manufacturer to our distribution center has been finalized, arrangements made for shipping and transportation to wholesale warehouses and major retail distribution centers, and time schedules solidified so customers will have merchandise available for sale at the time the advertising campaign is launched.

By developing criteria that can be measured and integrated with appropriate time schedules, the team can keep control over its activities and make corrections when called for.

"We did it! What now?"

As in any project snags and unexpected developments occur. But by factoring these probabilities into the time schedule, the project was completed on schedule.

Once the project was completed, the team was dissolved. But not before a celebration. The CEO took the entire team to an elegant restaurant for a gourmet meal. She complimented the team for its excellent work in getting the new product on the market on schedule, and told members that initial sales to retailers were going well, indicating enthusiastic acceptance of the new line. She presented each member with a sample bottle of the fragrance and a bonus check for his or her superb work.

Team Builder

When a project is completed, a full report detailing the steps taken, the problems faced and how they were overcome, and the results, should be completed, to be used as a guide to future teams created to deal with similar projects.

But that was not the end of the project. Karen wrote a full report describing in detail the steps that were taken to move the project forward. This was important, because it could serve as a model for introducing new products in the future.

Another advantage of cross-functional teams is that they enable companies to break down the artificial barriers that separate the different departments in the organization. Members serving on these teams get to know colleagues from other teams or departments and, once the project is completed and the team disbanded, these friendships carry over into their normal activities, facilitating communication between these former teammates and engendering cooperation among departments.

The Least You Need to Know

➤ Cross-functional teams work on assignments in which the expertise of members of diverse departments is needed.

➤ In creating a temporary cross-functional team, make sure each member knows the capabilities of the other members and feels free to call on them for help when needed.

➤ Cross-functional teams are sometimes established on a permanent basis. They are not usually full-time assignments, but additions to the members' regular work.

➤ The person who forms a new cross-functional team should be thoroughly familiar with its objectives and should learn a good deal about prospective members.

➤ In a cross-functional team, it's logical to assign those aspects of the work which are in a member's special area of expertise to that member.

➤ One barrier to successful cross-functional teamwork is that members tend to look upon themselves as representatives of their department or discipline, instead of as team members.

➤ To overcome barriers to team success, members must first become aware of their own negative behavior patterns and take steps to learn and use different approaches to team activity.

➤ Emphasize the need for all members to think in terms of the team's mission and objectives—not those of their previous or current full-time team goals— when working on this team's projects.

➤ When a project is completed, a full report should be completed to be used as a guide to future teams created to deal with similar projects.

Chapter 26

When Team Members Are in Remote Locations

In this ever-expanding economy, companies are spreading out all over the world. Local companies are acquired by national organizations, and they in turn expand into global companies.

As the companies expand, so do the teams. It's no longer unusual for team members to work in diverse locations. Some members may work in a branch across town; others in a city across the country, or even in another country.

In addition, many companies allow employees to work from their homes part or all of the time. The challenge to team leaders is to keep their teams coordinated and effective under these circumstances.

Dealing with Members Located at Other Sites

When team members are scattered over many sites, it's much more difficult for the team leader to ensure the team's success.

Here are some of the problems team leaders face when their members are scattered around the globe:

FYI

A good example of a spread-out team is the team that edited my previous book, *The Complete Idiot's Guide to Managing People.* I was in Long Island, New York, the editor-in-chief was in New York City, the development editor was in Indianapolis, the technical editor was in Houston, and the copy editor did her work in a tent in the Shenandoah Mountains in Virginia. All connected via the Internet.

➤ Coordinating the team when members are not nearby.

➤ Getting to know team members when personal contact is limited.

➤ Ensuring that work gets done when your team members are scattered in several locations.

➤ Motivating your team, solving problems, resolving conflicts, and carrying out all the functions of your job from a distance.

Now let's look at some of the ways spread-out teams operate and how team leaders can deal with the problems listed above.

Telecommuting

Over the past few years there has been a significant increase in the number of people working out of their homes. Some teams have members who do most of their work at home; even more have members who work at home part of the time. This has been made possible by the use of *telecommuting.*

Companies have discovered that it's often advantageous to let employees telecommute: It frees up office space for other people. It enables a company to use the services of experienced workers who may not be able to come to the office regularly. These workers include parents with young children, people who can't leave their homes because they care for elderly or ill relatives, and people with a temporary or permanent disability.

The computer and modem have enabled companies to communicate in real time with anyone at another location who also has a computer. Documents, drawings, and statistical tables can be transmitted electronically to one person or to dozens of people simultaneously.

Not every type of job is suitable for telecommuting. Many jobs require constant interaction with others on the job or the use of expensive or complex equipment that cannot be provided for home use. However, with a little imagination, jobs that seem to be limited to the office often can be redesigned so that they can be done at home.

Tips for Members Who Choose to Telecommute

Managers and consultants who have worked with companies that use telecommuters suggest that the key to success for both telecommuters and companies is a well-designed plan for orienting and training all people who are either hired as telecommuters or have transferred to that type of work. This plan should be followed by ongoing interaction between the leader and the telecommuter.

Team Terms

The process of **telecommuting** uses technology to enable people to perform their work at home or at a location remote from the central office by receiving assignments and submitting completed work through a computer equipped with a modem.

Set up your own rules to handle the special problems of working at home. Many people who are accustomed to the routine of an office find that they flounder when they have to work without direct supervision. If you are working from your home, here are some suggestions:

➤ **Set specific hours that you plan to work, and stick to them.** Although some telecommuters are paid on an hourly basis and must keep time logs, most work in salaried jobs in which their work is measured not by hours worked but by their achievement of key results areas.

Some jobs require telecommuters to be available at the telephone or at the computer during normal business hours; in others, the specific hours worked aren't important as long as the work is done and the team leader knows when the employee can be contacted.

➤ **Set up working hours when children are in school or napping.** If you have children who aren't in school, arrange working hours for times when you're less likely to be disturbed or when another adult is available to take care of them.

➤ **Set priorities so that you're always aware of deadlines and progress on each assignment.** Keep your to-do list current at all times. List new assignments and deadlines, check off work completed, keep a record of what data or materials you need from other team members, and what they need from you.

➤ **Keep the team leader aware of your progress** on each assignment and alert to problems as soon as they arise.

Don't be afraid to ask for help when you need it.

Heads Up!

Make sure that prospective tele-commuters are fully aware of the negative as well as the positive aspects of working at home. Have them try it for a trial period before agreeing to a permanent arrangement.

Keeping Remote Members in the Loop

No matter where the team member is located, he or she is still a part of the team and must never be forgotten by the team leader or associates at the base facility. Keeping in touch on a regular basis is not limited to passing work back and forth. Remote team members must be fully integrated into team activities.

Team leaders can learn much about this from managers who have experience in working with colleagues in other locations. For example, sales managers manage their sales staffs in locations far removed from the home office; dispatchers manage truck drivers who are continually on the road; and chain-store operators manage stores in hundreds of locations. Study the way these people manage their employees.

Emulate Joseph, the sales manager for a large housewares company. He manages 20 sales areas in the United States and Canada, each employing from 10 to 15 sales representatives and support crews. He attributes his success in keeping the sales staff motivated and productive to five principles:

1. **All area managers and their staff members are treated as full members of the sales team, not as second-class citizens.** They're continually informed about all the same things that employees in the home office are told. The company shows them previews of advertising campaigns, sales brochures, and other materials before the materials are released and encourages their input.

   No matter where team members are located, they're kept informed of team and departmental goings-on. Joseph believes that a major factor in building team spirit is the day-to-day chitchat among team members about their interests and activities. Because employees miss out on this type of conversation when they work in different locations, the company sends to every salesperson a weekly chatty newsletter that includes tidbits about what's going on in its employees' lives.

2. **The team leader takes a personal interest in each team member.** Joseph telephones each of the area managers at least once a week just to chat about how things are going. If a sales rep does something special, he personally makes a congratulatory call. On an employee's birthday, he sends a card or an e-mail message, and on special occasions, such as weddings, births, or special anniversaries, he sends flowers or a snack basket to the team member's home.

3. **Meetings are held periodically so that members from various locations can regularly meet face to face.** To supplement the annual convention that all

company salespeople attend, quarterly regional meetings are held. Sales reps at the meetings can meet reps from other areas in a more intimate environment than the convention provides. It gives them an opportunity to exchange ideas, get to know their colleagues as real people, and build up the team's esprit de corps.

4. **Sharing of ideas among members in all facilities is expedited.** The exchange of ideas isn't limited to meetings. Sales reps and area managers are encouraged to communicate with each other by phone, fax, and e-mail. They share with each other their experiences, sales approaches, and advice about handling problems.

5. **The team leader maintains personal contact with all members.** Joseph plans his regular office schedule so that he can go out in the field with sales reps, hold motivational meetings, and discuss special problems. He makes occasional unannounced visits, just to say "hello" and let them know that he's personally interested in them.

Team Builder

When telecommuting is instituted, higher level executives are often more concerned that members aren't at desks in the office than in what is being accomplished by the team. One way to alleviate this is to keep the manager to whom the team reports aware of the team's activities and accomplishments on an ongoing basis.

These principles can be helpful not only with salespeople, but with all team members who work in remote locations.

Making Telecommuting Work

As part of my research in preparing this book, I asked several team leaders who work with telecommuters the secrets of their success.

Following are some of the responses:

➤ "I keep the telecommuters informed of all team activities, even those in which they're not directly involved."

➤ "I invite them to come to the office for business meetings, training programs, and company or department social events."

Heads Up!

Don't overlook your telecommuters. They are as much a part of the team as people who work side by side in the office. Treat them accordingly.

➤ "As all our home-working members live within commuting distance of the office, I encourage them to participate in such extracurricular activities as bowling leagues, softball teams, and family picnics."

➤ "Our company puts all home-workers on the distribution list for all the same materials they would receive if they were in-house employees."

➤ "I require that they visit the office regularly—not just for discussion of their own work but also for in-person discussions about team activities and to give them an opportunity to interact with other team members."

➤ "I make it a point to be easily accessible by telephone. I return voice mail or other messages promptly. I encourage other members to phone telecommuters periodically just to show a personal interest and to give them the opportunity to exchange ideas about overall activities—not just specific work assignments."

➤ "Our members are connected through an intranet program that enables us to have instant messages sent by any team member to any or all others. As our telecommuters are at their monitors most of the time, it's less time consuming than telephoning."

➤ "We have a birthday party at one meeting each month for all members who have a birthday that month. E-mail greetings are also sent on the actual birthday."

Working at Home Isn't for Everyone

Be aware of the many potential problems of working at home. One home-based computer programmer complained that her friends and neighbors barged in for friendly chats or to ask her to accept deliveries, be available for service people, and even watch their children. She had to make clear to them that she was an at-home worker, not a lady of leisure. Being assertive cost her some "friends," but it was essential.

Another at-home worker soon found that the freedom of working at home, setting his own time schedule, and avoiding rush hour traffic didn't make up for the social life of the workplace. He missed the interaction of daily contact with colleagues, the gossip around the water cooler, and even the daily parrying with his boss. He chose to return to the office.

Betty was thrilled when her request to work at home was agreed to. She was a well-disciplined, self-sufficient person and she knew that even with two toddlers at home, she could accomplish a great deal. And she did.

Two years later, when her team leader moved up to a higher management position, Betty wasn't even considered for the promotion. When she complained, she was told that the job required being in the home office all of the time and as a telecommuter, she couldn't do it.

Betty agreed that being the team leader would mean giving up working at home, but her gripe was that she wasn't even given the opportunity to make the choice. She learned one of the hard lessons of being a telecommuter.

FYI

"The more enterprises come to rely on people working together without actually working *together*—that is on people using the new technologies of information—the more important it will become to make sure that they are fully informed."

—Peter F. Drucker, management consultant and author

Although there are some leadership jobs that can be done by telecommuting, most cannot. Career-oriented people should keep this in mind when opting for working at home. People who work at home one or two days a week are more likely to be considered for promotion than those who work exclusively at home.

The Virtual Team

The latest trend in team building is the creation of the *virtual team*. Team members may be scattered all over the world, may never (or rarely) see each other, and communicate primarily by computer-based techniques. As newer, faster, and more powerful processors and software become available, virtual teams may become a major part of global organizations.

Sometimes these teams are permanent groups that work together for years. Other teams are cross-functional groups brought together to deal with a specific situation.

They are connected by all the devices that currently exist in the workplace: telephones, fax machines, e-mail, and video-conferencing. To these have been added even more sophisticated communication tools, such as *group ware*—project management software that electronically links members and allows them instantly to trade and manipulate project information.

Why Virtual Teams?

As companies get larger and expand into areas far removed from the home office—often into different countries—employees are scattered around the world. Using virtual teams enables work to be accomplished throughout the organization no matter where the members are located. This brings both opportunities and problems in team leadership.

Team Terms

Virtual teams are teams whose members are located in many sites, and interact by means of electronic communications. **Group ware** is project management software that electronically links members and allows them to instantly trade and manipulate project information.

Some of the advantages of using virtual teams are

➤ Members of virtual teams can be drawn from many locations, bringing together members who might not ordinarily be available to work on the same team. Members can be located anyplace that can be reached by telephone or wireless communication.

➤ Virtual teams allow companies to tap into resources anywhere in the world to accomplish their goals. For example, a specially trained chemical engineer was needed to deal with an urgent problem. Through telephone, fax, and e-mail, the team leader was able to get the necessary information from a team member in Belgium without having to pay the high cost of bringing him to the Cleveland facility.

➤ Virtual teams allow organizations to hire and retain the best qualified people, no matter where they are located. An executive recruiting firm recently demonstrated this. A Silicon Valley software designer retained them to locate a top level electronics engineer. An offer was made to a man who was currently employed in Atlanta. He rejected the offer because his wife was a vice president of an Atlanta bank and they considered both careers equally important. By arranging for him to be part of a virtual team, he could remain in Atlanta and be able to contribute his expertise to the company.

➤ Virtual teams can be created rapidly to meet specific needs. To prepare a bid for a large contract, a construction firm created a virtual team located in four states and two countries to investigate and analyze the problems and put together the proposal. This worked because there were members located in strategic places who could work rapidly and at little cost to obtain what was required.

➤ Virtual teams are equipped to use the best software to deal with their assignments. Because the computer is an essential part of their roles, they are likely to be familiar with a variety of software products that have been designed for team collaboration.

➤ Virtual teams enable companies to get projects completed as quickly as possible in order to get new products into the global market.

➤ Virtual teams are cost effective. The cost of getting that combination of expertise together in person, even for a short meeting, is often excessive.

It's Not All So Easy

Despite all the advantages, virtual teams don't always run smoothly. After all, they are made up of people—and like people in any team, they may have problems working together.

One of the toughest problems faced in forming and using virtual teams is how to get members to work together compatibly and productively when face-to-face contact is limited and communication is primarily by electronic means.

Companies have dealt with this in a variety of ways.

Intensive orientation at home office. When a virtual team is formed, the members are brought to a central location—usually, the home office—for depth discussions of the team's mission and to give them the opportunity to get to know each other. While most of these programs are of relatively short duration—one or two weeks—some companies require the members to work as a standard team at the home office for several months before returning to their respective locations and functioning as a virtual team.

Heads Up!

Never ignore the human factor. Virtual team members are people, not robots. Consider their personalities and individualities in dealing with them, just as if they were actually working side by side in the same room.

Orientation via teleconferencing. Most managers agree that when members know each other, they'll work together more effectively than if they are just screen names and telephone voices. Bringing them to the home office is expensive, and in the case of ad-hoc teams that will only work together for one short-term project, it's an unreasonable expense. The solution is teleconferencing, sometimes called video-conferencing. It certainly is not perfect, but members get a chance to see what their associates look like and observe body language. A valuable part of a teleconferenced orientation is that it gives the members time to chat with their new associates and learn something about their backgrounds, personal lives, and interests.

Team meetings. As noted earlier in this book, team meetings are essential to team activities. Members meet to set goals, establish standards, discuss problems, and share ideas. Team meetings are just as important in the virtual team. These meetings can be conducted on a remote basis using telephone conferences, video-conferencing, or even online with group ware.

If the members of the virtual team are located relatively close together, in-person meetings can be scheduled on a regular basis. There is something about face-to-face meetings that cannot be duplicated electronically. Ideas flow faster; reactions are quicker, and often more cogent. Decisions can be made more readily. In addition, such meetings enable members to keep that personal touch with their colleagues.

Team Builder

If it is at all possible, new members should start the job at the home office. This will give them a clear concept of the goals of the company and the team. It will also give the team leader the opportunity to learn a good deal about the new member—not only his or her job capabilities, but those very important personal characteristics every leader should know about.

Visits to other locations. It's important for the team leader to visit every location at which a member works from time to time. How often depends on the nature of the work, the needs of the member(s) at that location, and the costs involved. Leaders certainly should get to know a lot more about the members of their teams than can be gleaned from telephone or electronic contact.

But visits need not be limited to team leaders. If a member is dealing with a problem where a personal meeting with a colleague at another site is desirable, let him visit that site. More important, invite members from other locations to come to the home office any time such a visit will expedite the work.

After Daimler and Chrysler merged a few years ago, teams working on related problems in each company were coordinated. For example, a team of purchasing agents from Stuttgart came to Detroit to work with their counterparts. A few months later the Detroit team visited them in Germany. Members of both groups felt closer to their new teammates, which resulted in a far more effective collaboration after the visits.

Share information with the whole team. When the entire team works in one place, ideas and information flow naturally from one to another. These exchanges are not limited to regular or formal meetings. Decisions are made by members while chatting around the water cooler or in the break room. The team leader meets a member in the hallway or on the parking lot and discusses a problem. These informal moments are lost in the virtual team.

This is exacerbated when a portion of the team is at the home office and the balance is scattered. It's normal for the team leader to have a closer relationship with the members who work at adjacent desks than with those in other cities or countries. This leads to an insider/outsider atmosphere. The members away from the office feel left out, particularly when they get information and news later than the insiders, or worse, don't get it at all.

Toby, a long-time team leader, was recently assigned to lead a virtual team. She told me that she had to change her entire management style. "I managed by walking around. I was accustomed to having frequent informal chats with members about their work, their progress, their problems. With more than half of my members in different locations, this became awkward. To overcome it, I scheduled daily telephone chats with each of my outside members, weekly conference calls with the entire team, and I visited each team member every few months. To ensure that all pertinent information is spread to the entire team, I record it in a shared database, so that any member can refer to it whenever needed."

Integrating new members into the team. Any time a new member joins a team, that person must be carefully prepared to work with the other members. Suggestions as to integrating a new member into a team were discussed in Chapter 23. In addition to these suggestions, newly appointed members of virtual teams need special orientation.

Training and orientation should take place at the home office before the new member reports to the location where she will work. Team leaders should arrange for other members at that location to fill her in on the local situation and assist in making her fully productive. However, some team members will work alone, often out of their homes. As there will be nobody there to help her, the trainee should spend more time at the home office. Once she starts her work at home, the team leader must spend more time on the telephone guiding her through the complexities of the job.

Resolving Conflicts Among Members

When members work in close proximity, the team leader resolves conflicts by bringing them together to discuss their disagreement (see Chapter 11). When members are in different locations, this becomes more difficult.

Here's how some leaders deal with this:

1. Put it in writing. If the disagreement concerns differing approaches to working on a problem, have the opposing members e-mail their arguments to the leader with copies to the other members.

2. After each party has had a chance to read each other's arguments, arrange a conference call among the members and the team leader to discuss the case. Follow the suggestions made about resolving conflicts in Chapter 11.

3. Attempt to reach a mutually acceptable resolution. If this fails, the leader must make the decision and impose it on all parties.

4. If the problem is the inability of the members to work together, and telephone chats don't help, the team leader should invite the parties to the home office or have all meet at a central location to try to resolve it in person.

Cultural Differences

In this growing global economy, more American companies are expanding into other countries, and many foreign companies are acquiring American firms or opening offices here.

One obvious problem that arises when virtual teams are created across national boundaries is the language problem. As most of the communication will be in English, all members from all countries must be fluent in English. Fortunately, most educated people on other continents do speak English, though their degrees of fluency vary.

Heads Up!

Although most American firms use English in communicating with teams in all countries, if you're a team leader, learn to speak the native language of your overseas team members. You'll develop a closer rapport and win their trust more easily.

In communicating with associates in other countries, avoid American colloquialisms that may be confusing to non-Americans. Often, we're not aware that words, phrases, and expressions we've used all of our lives are not understood—or worse, have entirely different meanings to our listeners.

For example, most non-Americans have no idea what you mean when you say, "Just give me a ballpark figure," or, "We'll have to play this by ear," or the thousands of other Americanisms we constantly use. Listen to yourself and ask, "If I were not an American, would I understand this?"

It's not only language that differs from one culture to another, but the way business is conducted. In some countries, they take two or more hours for lunch, but may work later into the evening. In some cultures, it's customary for employees to get four or five weeks of vacation. In every country there are holidays or religious feast days that are observed, which of course usually differ from American holidays. To work collaboratively with members of teams in other lands, you must be aware of these customs and be prepared to abide by them.

In planning work, keep in mind the customs and culture of the country to avoid unexpected lost time due to local holidays or religious observances.

Develop Team Norms

Protocols should be developed on how work will be assigned, what standards will be met, and how work will be measured against those standards. Guidelines should be agreed upon on the use of e-mail, voice mail, and other communication techniques. For example, one company set the following communications protocol for its virtual teams:

1. All urgent e-mail must be answered within four hours; all other e-mail within 24 hours.

2. In leaving a message on voice mail, briefly state the information desired, not just your name and number.

3. Unless it is an emergency, schedule all conference calls or video-conferencing at least one day in advance. The member originating the call will be responsible for notifying other members and make any other arrangements needed.

4. Team members will check the database once a day to check the progress of their projects and pick up any new information that has been posted.

5. Progress reports will be e-mailed or faxed to team leader no later than specified in the assignment. Any deviation must be approved by the team leader.

6. Any documents or reports that are too lengthy or bulky for electronic communication should be sent by express or priority mail depending on when they are required.

FYI

Although there are no current statistics on the use of virtual teams, some of the major companies that use virtual teams extensively are General Electric, Motorola, Hewlett-Packard, Intel, Bank of Boston, and Steelcase.

One of the main reasons virtual teams or other spread-out teams run into trouble is they become careless in their communications with their associates. The team leader should follow up to ensure that these standards are maintained.

The Least You Need to Know

➤ It's no longer unusual for team members to work in diverse locations—in a branch across town, another city, or another country.

➤ The computer and modem have enabled companies to communicate in real time with anyone at another location who also has a computer.

➤ Keeping in touch on a regular basis is not limited to passing work back and forth. Members must be fully integrated into team activities.

➤ Keep members who work in remote locations informed of what's going on in the home office and in other regions.

➤ Telecommuters should be made aware of the negative aspects of working at home or away from the office.

➤ How to get members to work together compatibly and productively without face-to-face contact is one of the greatest challenges of virtual teams.

Publications with Articles on Team Management

Managers, team leaders, and others who deal with people problems must keep up with what's going on. The best way to be on the cutting edge of change is to read regularly several of the magazines and newsletters that cover these matters.

Most every industry and profession has periodicals devoted to its field—and most of them have occasional articles on supervision and interpersonal relations. This is one excellent source of information.

Here is a list of some of the better general publications that either specialize in or have significant coverage of the practice of managing people.

Across the Board
The Conference Board
845 Third Ave.
New York, NY 10022
212-339-0345
Fax: 212-980-7014
www.conference-board.org

Business Week
1221 Ave. of the Americas
New York, NY 10020
800-635-1200
Fax: 609-426-5434
www.businessweek.com

Forbes
60 Fifth Ave.
New York, NY 10011
800-888-9896
Fax: 212-206-5118
www.forbes.com

Fortune
Time-Life Building
Rockefeller Center
New York, NY 10020
800-621-8000
Fax: 212-522-7682
www.fortune.com

Harvard Business Review
60 Harvard Way
Boston, MA 02163
800-274-3214
Fax: 617-475-9933
www.hbsp.harvard.edu

HR Magazine
Society for Human Resources Management
1800 Duke St.
Alexandria, VA 22314
703-548-3440
Fax: 703-836-0367
www.shrm.org

INC
477 Madison Ave.
New York, NY 10022
212-326-2600
Fax: 212-321-2615
www.inc.com

Management Review
American Management Association
Box 319
Saranac Lake, NY 12983-0319
800-262-9699
Fax: 518-891-3653
www.amanet.org

Manager's Edge
Briefings Publishing Co.
1101 King St.
Alexandria, VA 22314
703-548-3800
Fax: 703-684-2136
www.briefings.com

Nations Business
711 Third Ave.
New York, NY 10017
212-692-2215
editor@nbmag.com

Team Management Briefings
Briefings Publishing Co.
1101 King St.
Alexandria, VA 22314
703-548-3800
Fax: 703-684-2136
www.briefings.com

Training
50 South 9th St.
Minneapolis, MN 55402
612-333-0471
Fax: 612-333-6526
www.trainingsupersite.com

Training and Development
American Society for Training and Development
1640 King St.
Alexandria, VA 22314
703-683-8100
Fax: 703-683-9203
www.astd.org

Workforce
245 Fischer Ave.
Costa Mesa, CA 92626
714-751-1883
Fax: 714-751-4106
www.workforce.com

Working Woman
135 West 50 St.
New York, NY 10020
800-234-9765
Fax: 212-445-6186
wwmagazine@aol.com

Associations Dealing with Team Management and Human Resources

Professional societies are excellent sources of information on the areas in which they specialize. Membership in one or more can give you access to the latest developments in the field, the experience of other members in dealing with problems similar to yours, opportunities at meetings and conventions to meet your counterparts in other organizations, and often, resource material from their library or archives.

Here is a list of associations that may be of value to you:

American Association of Industrial Management (AAIM)
293 Bridge St.
Springfield, MA 01103
413-737-8766
Fax: 413-737-9724

An association of managers of manufacturing organizations. Provides publications and special reports.

American Management Association (AMA)
1601 Broadway
New York, NY 10019
212-586-8100
Fax: 212-903-8168
www.amanet.org

Membership is by company. Provides seminars, publications, library facilities on all aspects of management.

American Psychological Association (APA)
750 First St.
Washington, DC 20002
202-336-5500
Fax: 202-336-5708
www.apa.org

Provides literature and information on problems dealt with by psychologists. For matters related to leadership, management, and employee relations, ask for industrial psychology information.

American Society for Training & Development (ASTD)
1640 King St.
Alexandria, VA 22313
703-683-8100
Fax: 703-683-8103
www.astd.org

Dedicated to professionalism in training and development of personnel. Local chapters throughout United States. Annual national convention. Publications include magazine, special reports, and books.

Association for Quality and Participation
801B West 8th St.
Cincinnati, OH 45203
800-733-3310
Fax 513-381-0070
www.aqp.com

Dedicated to participative programs primarily, but not exclusively, related to quality management.

Employee Assistance Society of North America (EASNA)
PO Box 634
New Hope, PA 18938
215-891-9538
Fax: 215-891-9538
e-mail: 72722.465@compuserve.com

Source to locate individuals and organizations that provide various types of employee assistance programs.

International Foundation of Employee Benefit Plans (IFEBP)
18700 West Bluemound Rd.
Bloomfield, WI 53008
414-786-7100
Fax: 414-786-8670
pr@ifebp.org

Excellent source of information on employee benefits. Accredits benefits specialists.

National Association of Personnel Services (NAPS)
3133 Mt. Vernon Ave.
Alexandria, VA 22305
703-684-0180
Fax: 703-684-0071
naps@dc.infi.net

Source of information about private employment agencies.

National Association of Temporary and Staffing Services (NATSS)
119 S. St. Asaph St.
Alexandria, VA 22314
703-549-6287
Fax: 703-549-4808
natss@natss.com

Source of information on providers of temporary personnel.

Society for Advancement of Management (SAM)
630 Ocean Dr.
Corpus Christi, TX 78412
540-342-5563
Fax: 512-994-2725

Provides publications and conferences on various aspects of management.

Society for Human Resources Management (SHRM)
1800 Duke St.
Alexandria, VA 22314
703-548-3440
Fax: 703-836-0367
shrm@shrm.org

Membership is human resources specialists in all types of companies and organizations. Provides publications, special reports, books. Local chapters throughout United States conduct monthly meetings. National convention annually.

Women in Management
30 North Michigan Ave.
Chicago, IL 60602
312-263-3636
Fax: 312-372-8738

Dedicated to special problems of women in management positions.

Glossary of Team Terms

active listener   One who not only pays close attention to what the other party says, but asks questions, makes comments, and reacts verbally and nonverbally to what is said.

agenda   A list of things to be done at a meeting. Effective meeting leaders carefully prepare the agenda and control the meeting to assure the agenda is complied with.

amber light   Signifies *caution*; amber light situations develop slowly and—if caught in time by an alert leader—can be neutralized. The red light indicates *danger*. The leader may have to take drastic action to resolve the problem.

arbitration   Both parties present their side of a problem and an arbitrator decides what should be done. In mediation, both parties present their side of a problem and the mediator works with them to reach a mutually satisfactory solution.

assessment center   A variation of the panel interview in which, in addition to the interview, the candidates are given a series of exercises and the panel observes them in action.

associates   See *team members*.

behavioral expectations   Define how team members are to go about working together and relate to things like communicating, problem solving, providing timely support and resources, and resolving disagreements.

bona fide occupational qualification (BFOQ)   A specific qualification that limits a job to only men or only women. The only undisputed BFOQs are a wet nurse (for a woman) and a sperm donor (for a man).

brainstorming   A technique for generating ideas in which participants are encouraged to voice any idea, no matter how "dumb" or useless it may be. By allowing participants to think freely and express ideas without fear of criticism, they can stretch their minds and make suggestions that may seem worthless but that may trigger an idea that has value in the mind of another participant.

C-teams   Top management teams. They are called C-Teams because they are composed of the CEO (chief executive officer), COO (chief operating officer), CFO (chief financial officer), CIO (chief information officer), CMO (chief marketing officer), and others whose acronymic titles begin with *C*.

cadet corps   A select group of men and women chosen (usually right from college) to undergo intensive training in management.

channels   The path information takes through the organization. To get information, you go to your boss who goes to the other department's supervisor, who goes to the person with the information, gets it, and conveys it back to you through the same channels. By the time you get the information it may have been distorted by a variety of interpretations.

collaboration   The act of working together by sharing information, ideas, and actions.

collaborative evaluation   A team member evaluates his or her own performance, and the team leader also evaluates it. The final report results from a collaborative discussion between the team leader and the team member.

collegiality   The working together of two or more people as colleagues, each considered equal to the other.

comfort zone   The place in which we feel most at ease when doing a physical or mental exercise. Our muscles, nerves, brain, and senses are conditioned to being used this way and resist change from it.

communication   Takes place when persons or groups exchange information, ideas, and concepts.

consensus   Does not mean unanimous agreement. Consensus results when, after the expression of the problem by the team, compromises are made. Everybody may not agree on every detail, but members believe it to be a sound decision that they willingly support.

constructive discontent   When one makes a practice of studying a job and asking, "Can it be performed with less effort?" "Can it be done at lower cost?" "Can it be improved in any way?" he is practicing constructive discontent.

control points   Places in a project at which you stop, examine the work that has been completed, and, if errors have been made, correct them.

coordination   Synchronizing the activities of the team for smooth flow of its actions toward the ultimate goal.

counseling   A means of helping troubled associates overcome barriers to good performance. By careful listening, open discussion, and sound advice, a counselor helps identify problems, clarify misunderstandings, and plan solutions.

cross-functional teams   Sometimes called multidepartmental teams, they work on assignments in which the expertise of members of diverse departments is needed. For example, they may be composed of representatives of finance, marketing, engineering, and human resources.

cross-training   Training team members to perform the jobs of other people on the team so that members are capable of performing other than their own aspect of the job.

delegation   There is a difference between just assigning tasks and delegation. When you *delegate,* you not only assign work, but give the associate full responsibility to carry out the project.

distress, or bad stress   The chronic state of anxiety caused by unremitting pressures of job, personal, or societal problems.

downsizing   Involves the reduction in the workforce of an organization by eliminating or reducing the number of employees in various job categories.

employee assistance program (EAP)   A company-sponsored counseling service. The counselors aren't company employees, but instead are outside experts retained to help employees deal with personal, family, and financial problems.

empowerment   Means sharing your power with the people over whom you have power. Team members are given the authority to make decisions that previously were reserved for managers.

Equal Employment Opportunity Commission (EEOC)   The federal agency that administers most of the civil rights laws. It issues regulations, investigates complaints, and takes action to enforce the laws.

ESOP (employee stock option plan)   A means of rewarding employees by giving them rights to purchase company stock at a price lower than the market value.

exempt employees   Persons engaged in management, administration, and professional work, and others who use "independent judgment" in their work. Exempt employees can be required to work overtime with no extra compensation.

exit interviews   See *separation interviews.*

Goals and objectives   These are interchangeable terms that describe the purpose, or long-term results, toward which an organization or individual's endeavors are directed.

going rate   What companies are paying people with similar backgrounds in the industry or the community. It has also been defined as what you have to pay employees to keep them from going.

good writing   The process of taking words and phrases we already know and making them convey our message successfully.

grievance   A formal complaint, usually based on the violation of a union contract or formal company policy.

gripe   An informal complaint (see *grievance*).

group ware   Project management software that electronically links members and allows them to instantly trade and manipulate project information.

halo effect   If you greatly admire somebody, you put a figurative halo over his or her head and are inclined to accept whatever he or she says (see *pitchfork effect*).

hidden agenda   Describes the secret personal goals of a member who works to the detriment of the team's coherence.

internal customers   Persons or units in the organization to whom a team provides materials, information, or services.

internal suppliers   Persons or units in the organization that provide the team with materials, information, or services. A team will be a customer in some aspects of its work and a supplier in others.

interview   The first part, *inter,* means between. The second part, *view,* means a look. An interview is a look at a situation (in this case a job) between two people. It's not a one-way interrogation.

intranets   Internal Web sites only accessible by people associated within the organization.

job descriptions   Detail the duties, functions, and responsibilities of jobs and indicate the standards on which performance will be measured.

job enrichment   Involves redesigning jobs to provide diversity and challenge and to make them less boring.

job fairs   Are like trade shows. Instead of displaying company products or services to customers, participating companies present information about jobs and careers in the organization to prospective employees.

job specifications   The qualifications a person should have in order to perform a job.

job-instruction training (JIT)   A systematic approach to training people to perform tasks, involves four steps: preparation, presentation, performance, and postwork.

key results area (KRA)   Is an aspect of a job on which employees must concentrate time and attention to ensure that they achieve the goals for that job.

knowledge workers   Employees who invent products, innovate changes, develop systems, create concepts, plan projects, and keep their organizations ahead of the pack.

leadership   The art of guiding people in a manner that commands their respect, trust, confidence, and wholehearted cooperation.

MO   Method, or mode, of operation—the method or patterns of behavior that a person habitually follows in performing work.

mentors   Team members assigned to act as counselor, trainer, and "big brother" or "big sister" to another member.

micromanaging   Supervising every phase of an assignment. That means the leader looks over the team member's shoulder to check that every *i* is dotted and every *t* crossed. This stifles creativity and prevents team members from working at their full potential.

mission statement   More than just an indicator of the company's objectives. It is their credo, their reason for existence, the philosophy upon which they conduct their business.

motivators   Factors that stimulate people to perform beyond expectations (see Satisfiers).

multidepartmental teams   See *cross-functional teams.*

nonexempt employees   All employees not categorized by law to be exempt (see Exempt Employees). They must be paid at the rate of time and a half for all work done in excess of 40 hours in a week.

objectives   See *goals.*

orientation programs   Programs designed to give new employees information, to answer their questions about the company and the team, and to acquaint them with their teammates.

ownership   The feeling of being a full partner in the development and implementation of a project and of being committed to its successful achievement.

panel interviews   A group of interviewers (often the entire team) sit down with the applicant and collectively conduct the interview.

peer evaluation   Every member of a team is rated by each of the other members. The evaluations may be discussed in private conversations between the team leader and the member or with the entire team.

peer pressure   When team members exert their combined efforts to influence associates who are not meeting expectations.

performance standards   Define the results that are expected from a person performing a job. For performance standards to be meaningful, all persons doing that job should know and accept these standards. Team participation in the establishment of performance standards is one way to ensure this understanding.

perks (short for perquisites)   Goods or services given to an employee in addition to regular salary and benefits as an incentive to attract and retain personnel.

pitchfork effect (the symbol of the devil)   The opposite of the halo effect. If you fervently dislike a person you'll discount anything they say (see *halo effect*).

progressive discipline   A systematic approach to correcting rule infractions. A typical program has six steps, beginning with an informal warning. If the warning doesn't succeed, the following steps are taken, in order: disciplinary interview, written warning, probation, suspension, and termination (if necessary).

project managers   Team leaders assigned to head up specific projects, such as the design and manufacture of an electronic system or the development and marketing of a new product.

protected classes   Although discrimination against any ethnic, racial, or religious group is prohibited, because of the long history of discrimination against certain groups, the EEOC has designated certain groups as protected classes. They are: African Americans, Hispanics, Asian and Pacific Islanders, Native Americans, women, and the disabled.

recorder   The meeting recorder is not an electronic taping device. He or she is a team member who keeps the minutes of a meeting.

rightsizing   See *downsizing*.

satisfiers   Factors people must have from the job in order to produce at least minimum work (see *motivators*).

self-directed teams   Teams in which there are no formal or permanent leaders. Members may work collaboratively on projects or, if appropriate, select an associate to lead a specific project. All members can serve as temporary leaders when and if needed.

separation interviews or exit interviews   Give organizations insight into the real reasons people quit their jobs.

soft skills   The skills needed to work effectively with other people. They include communications, interpersonal relations, leadership, and personal development.

SPAM   The computer equivalent of junk mail. Sometimes it's tough to identify SPAM by its source or subject, but with a little experience, most can be picked out and deleted.

standard operating procedures (SOPs)   Sometimes called "the company bible"; they include detailed descriptions of practices and procedures followed by the organization.

stock options   Rights that enable recipients to purchase company stock at a fixed rate no matter what the market value may be. The incentive: If the market value increases, the recipient can exercise the right and make an immediate profit on the sale.

synergy   Two or more people working together so that the individual contributions of each, when combined, enhance the results. The whole is greater than the sum of its parts.

team   A group of people who collaborate and interact to reach a common goal.

team leader   The coordinator and facilitator of the work of team members.

team members or associates   Make up the staff of the team.

"teamability"   The ability of a person to work as a collaborative member of a team.

telecommuting   Uses technology to enable people to perform their work at home or at a location remote from the central office by receiving assignments and submitting completed work through a computer equipped with a modem.

teleconferencing   Using computer and video techniques to enable interactive meetings participated in by people in several locations.

virtual teams   Teams whose members are located at many sites and interact by means of electronic communications.

Index